The HIDING PLACES

Also by Katherine Webb

The English Girl
The Night Falling
The Misbegotten
A Half Forgotten Song
The Unseen
The Legacy

The HIDING PLACES

KATHERINE WEBB

First published in Great Britain in 2017 by Orion Books,
an imprint of The Orion Publishing Group Ltd
Carmelite House, 50 Victoria Embankment
London EC4Y 0DZ

An Hachette UK Company

1 3 5 7 9 10 8 6 4 2

A CIP catalogue record for this book is
available from the British Library.

ISBN (Hardback) 978 1 4091 4856 2
ISBN (Export Trade Paperback) 978 1 4091 4857 9

Typeset at The Spartan Press Ltd,
Lymington, Hants

Printed and bound in Great Britain by Clays Ltd,
St Ives plc

www.orionbooks.co.uk

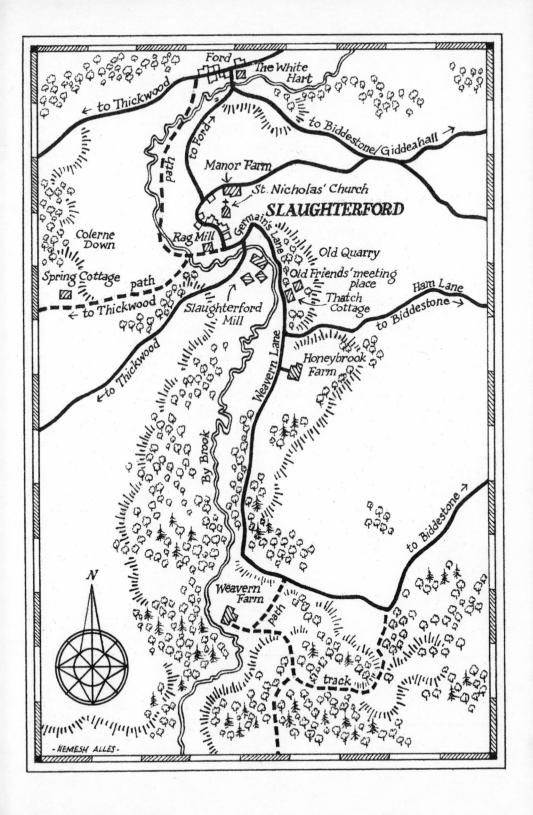

← to Thickwood

Ford

The White Hart

to Ford

path

to Biddestone/Giddeahall →

Manor Farm

St. Nicholas' Church

SLAUGHTERFORD

Colerne Down

Rag Mill

Germain's Lane

Old Quarry

Old Friends' meeting place

Spring Cottage

path

Thatch Cottage

Ham Lane

← to Thickwood

to Biddestone →

Slaughterford Mill

Weavern Lane

to Thickwood

By Brook

Honeybrook Farm

to Biddestone →

N

Weavern Farm

path

track

- HEMESH ALLES -

Firstly

On the day of the killing the sky above Slaughterford dropped down – almost to the treetops – and it poured with rain. Lavish, drenching summer rain, the first in weeks. The villagers all claimed, on having woken to such weather, to have known that something was very much amiss. They were superstitious people, prone to seeing signs and portents everywhere, and to suspecting the worst of every one. Sid Hancock, out at Honeybrook Farm, swore he saw the By Brook run red. Heads were nodded, ruefully, though the murder hadn't happened near enough to the riverbank for blood to have reached the water. Woolly Tom, who kept a flock of sheep on a small-holding up on the ridge, said he'd known a death was coming ever since one of his ewes had birthed a two-headed lamb back in the spring. He'd been carrying a desiccated rabbit's foot everywhere with him since then, in case the shadow tried to fall on him. Death was common enough, in Slaughterford. But not this kind of death.

What troubled people most was the sheer *blamelessness* of the victim. Nobody could think of a single bad thing to say of them, or recall a single cruel or shameful thing they'd done. There was a *wrongness* about it that shook them. Grave illness could happen at any time, as could a fatal accident. Only the year before, six-year-old Ann Gibbs had climbed over the cock-up stones designed to prevent exactly that, and had fallen into the well at the top of the lane to Ford. She'd drowned because her brother had told her the fairy folk lived inside. Fits, flu and seizures took their annual tithe of loved ones, but if your time was up you could hardly argue with that. Tragedy and ill-luck abounded, but for one of their own to be cut down with such savagery, for no reason at all . . . It simply wasn't natural. They were people of the land, and struggled with anything that wasn't natural. They channelled the shock of the murder into the rocks beneath their feet, just like lightning rods. And they all wondered whether one such act of violence could help but lead to another.

I

Three Girls

The morning before it all began, Pudding paused by the little window at the top of the stairs and saw her mother outside on the lawn. Louise Cartwright was near the back wall, looking out over the drenched tussocks of the paddock that sloped away down the valley, and fiddling with something in her hands that Pudding couldn't see. It was early, the sun not yet clear of the horizon; the sky had an immaculate, pale clarity, and it looked like being another hot day. Pudding felt the little thump of dread she was coming to know so well. She waited for a while, but when her mother didn't turn or move, she carried on down the stairs, more slowly now. A gentle snore came from the darkness of her parents' room, where her father was still asleep. In earlier days he'd been the first to rise every morning. In earlier days he'd have fed the stove and put the kettle on, and been shaved and buttoned into his waistcoat before Pudding and Donald stumbled down to the kitchen, rubbing the sleep from their eyes. Now Pudding usually had to go in and wake him, feeling guilty every time she did. His sleep was like a stupor.

The kitchen at Spring Cottage was more chaotic than it had used to be – the bowls on the shelves were no longer stacked in exact order of size; the hop garland looked dusty; crumbs in the cracks and splashes of grease made the smell of stale cooking hang about. Donald was waiting at the kitchen table. Not reading, or mending anything, or jotting a list. Just sitting, waiting. He'd stay like that all day if nobody roused him up and sent him on his way. Pudding squeezed his shoulder as she passed behind him, and saw him swim up from the unfathomable depths inside himself to smile at her. She loved to see that smile – it was one of the things about him that hadn't changed at all. She kept a tally in her head: things about Donald that were just the same; things about him that had changed forever. It was the *forever* part she struggled with. She kept expecting him to shake it off, get up from the table with his old abruptness, quick with energy, and say something like, *Don't you want some toast with your jam, Pudding?* They'd spent the first two years after he'd come home watching, waiting to see what would return to him. A few things did, in the first year: his love of music; his love of Aoife Moore; his fascination with machinery; his appetite – though he sometimes struggled to swallow, and ended up coughing. But during the past year, nothing else had come back. His dark hair was just the same – soft, shiny, unruly. So very lovely. And that ironical curve to his mouth, though irony was one of the things he'd lost.

'Morning, Donny,' said Pudding. 'I'll just see what Mum's up to, then we'll have some breakfast, shall we?' She patted his shoulder, and was already by the back door by the time he managed to reply.

'Good morning, Puddy.' He sounded so normal, so like her big brother, that Pudding had to take a deep breath, right down into her gut, to stay steady.

She pulled the door to behind her, then looked up for Louise with that stubborn optimism she couldn't suppress. She hoped her mother would have moved, hoped she'd only been picking parsley for the scrambled eggs, hoped she'd been on her way back from the privy and had stopped to watch hares boxing in the field. But her mother hadn't moved, so Pudding distracted herself by noticing other things instead. That her breeches were getting too small again already, the waistband dragging down at the back so that her braces dig into her shoulders; that one of her socks was already sagging, bunching infuriatingly in the toe of her shoe; that her shirt was pinching under her arms because her chest seemed to get bigger every day, however much she willed it not to. It felt like her clothes were at war with her – delivering a constant, unnecessary commentary on her unwelcome expansion, upwards and outwards. The air was glassy-cool, fresh and green. Louise's footsteps through the dew showed up dark green against the silver. Pudding stepped into them exactly, shortening her stride.

'Mum?' she said. She'd planned to say something jovial, to brush off the oddness of the scene, but it wouldn't come. Louise turned her head sharply, startled. For a moment, there was no recognition in her face. That blank look, tinged with trepidation, was becoming the thing Pudding feared most. She found she couldn't quite breathe. But then Louise smiled, and her smile was only slightly vague, slightly hollow.

'Pudding! There you are, love. I've been looking for you,' she said, and in her eyes was that struggle to catch up, to guess at the truth of her statement. There was nothing in her hands, Pudding saw. The constant fiddling had been with the bottom button of her yellow cardigan. She always started at the bottom, but she'd got no further with doing them up that morning.

'Have you, Mum?' said Pudding, forcing her clenched throat to swallow.

'Yes. Where have you been?'

'Nowhere, just up in my room. I can't have heard you calling. Come on.' Pudding rushed on, before this fiction had time to bewilder her mother. 'Let's go in and get the kettle on, shall we? Make a nice pot of tea?'

'Yes. That's what we need.' Louise sighed slightly as she turned to walk back beside her daughter. They obliterated their original footsteps; the dew flicked up and soaked through Pudding's socks around her ankles. Still, she felt an irresistible surge of cheeriness as a phalanx of swifts shot across the sky above them, screeching out their joy, and the Manor Farm dairy herd, on the other side of the valley, lowed as they were let out from milking.

'Did you see hares in the field, Mum?' she asked, recklessly.

'What? When?' said Louise, and Pudding rushed to retract the question.

'Oh, nothing. Never mind.' She took her mother's arm and squeezed it, and Louise patted her hand.

Dandelions were crowding the back step, and the ash pail needed emptying; the blackcurrants were going over, unpicked except by blackbirds, which then left purple droppings on the path and down the windows. But when they got back into the kitchen Pudding's father, Dr Cartwright, was there, stoking up the stove, and the kettle was hissing on the hot plate, and he'd combed his hair and dressed, even if he hadn't shaved yet and his eyes were still a little sleepy.

'Two roses, fresh with dew from the garden,' he greeted them.

'Morning, Dad. Did you have a good sleep?' Pudding put the butter dish on the table; rattled open a drawer for knives; fetched yesterday's loaf from the crock.

'Far too good! You should have woken me sooner.' The doctor rubbed his wife's upper arms, smiling down at her. He pushed some of her unbrushed hair back from her forehead, and kissed her there, and Pudding looked away, embarrassed, happy.

'Toast, Donny?' said Louise. She'd done up her cardigan, Pudding noticed – every button in the right hole.

'Yes please, Mum,' said Donald. And they moved around each other as breakfast was assembled, perhaps not quite as they always had, but in a version of old habit that felt blissfully familiar. Her family strayed in the night, Pudding thought. They scattered like thistle seeds, carried here and there by currents she couldn't feel, and didn't understand. But she understood that it was up to her to gather them together again in the morning. As she sliced the bread she sang a snatch of 'Morning Has Broken' in her worst possible singing voice, to make them smile.

✎ ✎

When Irene heard the rattle of Keith Glover's bicycle her heart gave a lurch, walloping into her ribs, and she was careful not to look up or twitch – so careful not to react at all, in fact, that she wondered whether her extreme stillness would give her away instead. She felt as though her guilt were written all over her face in bright red letters for Nancy to read; Nancy with her eagle eyes and her disbelief in everything Irene said and did worn quite openly. She was sitting opposite Irene at the breakfast table, putting the merest scraping of butter on her toast and frowning at any overly large pieces of peel in the marmalade. The sun glanced as brightly from her silver hair, combed back into its usual bun, as it did from the rosewood tabletop. She was small, slim, hard as iron, and sat with her tiny feet crossed at the ankle. She flapped the page of the newspaper to straighten it, read for a moment and then grunted in derision at something. Irene had already stopped expecting her to elucidate, but Alistair glanced up, expectantly. He glanced up every time, with half a smile on his face, ready and waiting. His optimism appeared fathomless, and Irene marvelled at it. It made his eyes sparkle above the soft pouches in which they sat, and made him look younger than his middle years – younger than Irene's twenty-four even, though she was almost fifteen years his junior. She felt she'd aged a decade in the six weeks she'd been in Slaughterford.

Boot heels sounded on the yard; the brass flap on the letter box squeaked. Irene stared at her fingers on the handle of her coffee cup, and forced them not to tremble. The diamond in her engagement ring and the yellow gold of her wedding band stared back at her. As usual, after the guilt came the anger – at herself, at Fin, at blameless Alistair. A rush of bright, hot anger at the situation she was in, and at those who had put her there – herself most of all. She rejected her new role completely, even as she played it as best she could. The anger burnt out as quickly as it flared, and despair came hard on its heels. Despair like a pit she could drown in, without something to save her, something to cling to. The lifebuoy of a word, a sign, a token. Some proof that, even if her misery couldn't end, she was not, at least, alone in it. What she would do if she actually saw Fin's writing on an envelope, she had no idea. She wouldn't be able to keep still then – she'd probably fly to pieces. Her stomach writhed, tying itself in knots. She remained perfectly still.

'Well, it looks like being another beautiful day,' said Alistair, suddenly. Irene glanced at him, startled, and found him smiling at her. She tried to make her own face respond and couldn't tell if it moved or not.

'Yes,' she said. Flick, flick, flick went Nancy's eyes – from Alistair to Irene, back to Alistair.

'What are your plans, darling?' Alistair asked Irene. He put his hand over hers on the table, and her coffee cup rattled as her stiff fingers fell away from it.

'Oh, I . . . I hadn't thought.' Irene heard Florence coming along the hall to the breakfast room – her light, apologetic tread on the boards. The girl had the beady eyes and pointed nose of a mouse, which matched her personality well. Irene's heart escaped her control, and went bounding up into her throat.

Florence knocked softly, came in with the letters on a tray and put them on the table by Alistair's elbow, bobbing awkwardly before she went again. Alistair flicked through them – four envelopes. Irene couldn't breathe. Then he picked them up, straightened them, and slipped them into his jacket pocket as he got to his feet.

'Well, enjoy the day, anyway, both of you. I'll be back for lunch – if it's as fine as yesterday, we should have it out on the terrace.' He pushed his chair away tidily and smiled at Irene again. His smiles seemed in endless supply, like his optimism, when Irene felt like she'd run out of both. His whole face was geared for it – that softness to his eyes, and the upward curve of his lips and cheeks. Without his smile, his face looked bereft. 'You might visit Mrs Cartwright, and see how she is.'

'Mrs Cartwright?'

'Yes – the doctor's wife. You know. Pudding and Donald's mother.'

'Yes, of course.' Irene knew she should be learning all these names, and matching them to faces – the wheelwright, the smith, the vicar's wife, the woman who ran the shop and her son who brought the post. She knew that in a village as small as Slaughterford it was unforgivable not to know. She seemed to have done much that was unforgivable of late, but, just then, she couldn't face paying a call to the doctor's wife – a complete stranger and an invalid, she vaguely remembered being told. She hadn't the first clue what she should say to her. But then Alistair left, and Irene was alone with Nancy again. The long day yawned ahead of her, a void to be filled. She looked up at her husband's aunt, knowing that Nancy would be watching her, judging her openly without Alistair to moderate her. Sure enough, there was the knowing look, the arched brows, the mocking half-smile. Nancy seemed a particularly cruel part of Irene's penance. She was in her seventies but lean and well-preserved; the lines on her face were thin, faint, refined. When Alistair had told Irene his aunt lived with him at Manor Farm she'd imagined a separate cottage and a pleasant old bat filling her time arranging flowers for the church, and holding charity luncheons. A separate wing of the house at least. Not this constant sharp edge, everywhere Irene went, waiting to cut her. When she remarked on it – on her – to Alistair, he'd looked hurt.

'My mother died the day I was born, Irene. Nancy has raised me as her own – she's the closest thing to a mother I have. I don't know how my father would have coped, if she hadn't been here with him. Well, he wouldn't have.'

Irene took hold of her coffee cup again, though she had no intention of drinking the contents. It was stone cold, and filmy on top. Eventually Nancy folded the newspaper away and stood.

'Really, Irene, my dear, you must eat something,' she said, offhandedly. 'It may be all the rage in London to look at death's door, but you'll stand out like a sore thumb down here. Anyone would think you weren't happy – unthinkable for a new bride, of course.' Nancy kept her pinned for a moment longer, but Irene knew that she wasn't expected to reply. Unthinkable, unforgivable. All these new words for Irene to describe herself, and for others to describe her. 'You're a Hadleigh now, young lady. And Hadleighs set the standard around here,' said Nancy, as she turned to go. Only when she'd shut the door behind her did Irene let her chin drop, and her hands fall lifelessly into her lap. The silence in the breakfast room rang.

❧ ❧

Kingfisher, wagtail, great tit, bunting. Clemmie kept a list in her head that almost became a chant as she walked, keeping rhythm with her steps and her breath puffing in and out as she climbed. *Kingfisher, wagtail, great tit, bunting*. The early sun was a glorious flare in her eyes, and sweat prickled under her hair – her mad pale curls, so like her mother's, which defied any attempt at order. She was climbing the narrow path that cut between the field hedges from Weavern Farm to the lane that led down to Slaughterford. The path was tolerable then, early in the morning. By the afternoon it trapped the sun, and hummed with gnats and horseflies, so she came back along the river's edge instead – the longer way, and winding, but cooler. The hedges were full of dog roses now, laden with flowers and baby birds. Her father's cattle tore up the grass to either side of them; she could hear them, and smell their sweet green stink. *Kingfisher, wagtail, great tit, bunting*. The bottles of milk and rounds of cheese in the baskets yoked across her shoulders clanked as they swung. The yoke was almost too wide for the path; cow parsley flicked her arms, and foxgloves, nodding with bees, and wild clematis.

Her parents no longer bothered urging Clemmie to come straight back from her errands; she got back when she got back, sooner or later, depending on how long she spent with Alistair Hadleigh, or watching the river, or caught suspended in a daydream. She usually tried to hurry – she knew there was always work to be done. But even if she set off fast she tended to slow down by the water, or in the woods. Sometimes she saw things that stopped her, and absorbed her, and she didn't even realise it – didn't even realise time had passed until she noticed where the sun was in the sky, or the way her sisters rolled their eyes when she finally did get home, greeting her with varying degrees of resentment, depending on the hour, saying, *Here's our pretty ninny*, if she hadn't been needed, or *Look what the cat dragged in*, if she had. But Clemmie would wander. She had to wander. So they set her to delivering the milk to the mill canteen, though they knew they might not see her for hours. Like the other, larger, dairy herds in the area, Manor Farm, which also owned the mill, sold its milk by the gallon to the butter and condensed milk factories, which left the local deliveries to the smaller Weavern herd.

'At least she gets that one errand run,' her father said, ruefully. He set off in the cart at dawn, twice weekly, to take the bulk of their milk, cheese, butter and eggs to Chippenham market.

Flies circled in the shade of Germain's Lane, despite the early hour; the air hung heavy with the garlicky stink of the ramsons gone over and the fox-musk foliage of wood anemones. The white dust lane ran down the wooded northwest slope of the hill that Clemmie had just climbed, out of the sunken pocket of land that cradled Weavern Farm, bypassing several large loops of the By Brook river. Clemmie tipped back her head to watch the torn fragments of sky, painfully blue, beyond the branches. A dark shape circled there; she added buzzard to the morning's list, and then squirrel, as one leapt between trees overhead – an agile flash of bright red fur. Beech and oak and elm; a thick new canopy that had caused the spring flowers to die back. Only honeysuckle remained, scaling a young elm and blooming among the high branches. When she walked on, imprinted scraps of the bright sky stayed in her eyes and half-blinded her.

Clemmie had walked this route, and carried this aching yoke across her shoulders, more times than she could count, but when Slaughterford Mill appeared at the bottom of the slope, it always made her stop to look. An array of buildings and sheds, hunkered on the river; the tall, steaming chimney; the thrum of noise from the paper-making machine, thudding down into the ground and then up through her feet. As she crossed the little footbridge over the river she heard the roar of the overshot waterwheel, hidden in its pit below ground. The sudden smell of metal and steam and grease, of men and brick and labour, so unlike anything else in the world. And there was a new reason, too, that the mill made her senses prickle. The boy. She might walk around a corner and catch sight of him, and knew her thoughts would both scatter and narrow in, onto him, to the exclusion of everything else. She couldn't forget what he'd done, and wanted to see him exactly as much as she did not, so, in confusion, she stopped to listen to the wheel for a moment, tipping her forehead against the wall to feel its constant beat, and the crash of the water, vibrating into her skull. She was still there when the foreman happened to pass, and roused her.

'Up you get, lass, and take that milk out of the sun.' He smiled kindly beneath his thick moustaches, which were redder than the rest of his hair, and bushy like a fox's tail. Clemmie trusted this man. He never came too close, nor tried to touch her.

She did as he said, walking on into the mill yard, but it troubled her, this looking out. This watching; this hoping to find. She had never done it before; she liked to simply see, not to look. Only a few women worked at the mill, in the canteen and in the bag room, a long, low building close to the water's edge. It was immaculate inside, but freezing in winter – swept elm floorboards and polished walnut benches, not a drop of machine oil or ink anywhere to spoil the finished paper as it was stitched and glued into strong bags for sugar, flour, suet. In summer it smelled deliciously of beeswax, cotton and wood, but Clemmie wasn't really allowed inside – not with her filthy feet and her muddy hem. A couple of the female workers were on their way to clock in as she passed, and one waved to her – dark-haired Delilah Cooper, who was in Clemmie's memories of long hours spent at the dame school in Slaughterford, when they were barely old enough to walk. Watched for a fee by an old woman with a sour face, in her cottage; kept out from underfoot during the working day and eventually taught the bare basics of the alphabet, some songs and prayers. Delilah's face conjured up the smell of ten small children, kept all day in one room; of watery porridge and smuts and the cold stone floor. The other woman eyed her flatly, suspiciously, but Clemmie didn't mind. She liked the scrape and clatter of the women's pattens on the yard, and the clonk as they kicked them off at the door, carrying on in their boots and shoes. She shut her eyes to listen.

'Not right in the head, that one,' said the scowling woman.

Clemmie took the milk to the canteen, then went across to the old farmhouse, a substantial stone house around which the mill had grown up and taken over like unchallenged nettles. Few now remembered Chapps Farm before the mill, and the farmhouse, in which Clemmie's great-aunt Susan had been born – suddenly one morning, on a straw mat in front of the range – now housed the mill's offices, where the foreman and his clerk had their desks, and Alistair Hadleigh too, from Manor Farm, who owned it all. He was a kind man; Clemmie liked his face, which was always ready to smile, and the way he nodded and spoke to the men when he inspected their work. As though he respected them, even though, to Clemmie, his wealth made him seem another order of being altogether. The clean glow of his skin fascinated her; he seemed to breathe different air. Sometimes she carried on walking, through the yard and out the other side. That morning, she went up the old farmhouse's stairs and knocked at the door to Alistair's office. He looked up from his desk, his forehead laddered with worry lines.

'Ah, Clemmie. You've caught me quite unawares. Had we arranged for a lesson?' he said, in a vaguely distracted manner. Clemmie turned to go. 'No, no – do come in. Fifteen minutes won't make or break a thing today.' He got up to shut the door behind her. She caught a whiff of his hair oil, and the very masculine scent that hung about his jacket. No one else in Slaughterford had hands as clean as his. The surface of his enormous desk was hidden beneath piles and piles of paper – some samples that the mill had made, some finer than that, and typed upon. Clemmie couldn't have read the words even had she been inclined to try. She went to her usual place by the window and turned her back to the glass. She liked to stand in silhouette, knowing that her face was partly obscured. 'Now,' said Alistair, perching on the edge of the desk. 'Have you been practising?' Unabashed, Clemmie hitched one shoulder to tell him that she had not. Alistair didn't turn a hair. 'Well, never mind. Shall we start with the breathing exercises I showed you?'

The lesson did not go well. Clemmie swayed her weight from foot to foot, and wished she hadn't bothered. The time was not right; she couldn't concentrate, and tired easily. Looking defeated, Alistair patted her shoulder as she left. 'Never mind,' he said. 'We shall get there in due course, Clemmie. I'm certain of it.' Nancy Hadleigh was climbing the stairs as Clemmie went down. Instinctively, Clemmie turned her body away slightly, clamping her arms to her sides, and avoided her gaze. Nancy was difficult, and hard. Nancy had a stare like iron nails, and only ever spoke past Clemmie, never to her.

'Really, Alistair, what do you hope to achieve?' said Nancy, at the office door.

'There's no earthly reason why that girl shouldn't talk,' said Alistair, quietly. 'She only needs to be taught.'

'I don't understand why you must take it upon yourself to be the one to do so.'

'Because nobody else cares to, Nancy.'

'Well, you must realise that speech is not all people say you're teaching her, shut away in your office together. It's hardly wise, to make yourself the subject of such rumours. Least of all now.'

'Really, Nancy. I'm sure nobody thinks any such thing.'

'I doubt your hothouse flower would approve, if she knew.'

'You make it sound like something seedy, Nancy, when it's nothing of the sort.'

'Well, I just hope you're not giving the girl ideas, that's all.' Their voices faded as the door closed, and Clemmie carried on down the stairs, unconcerned.

She went over to the shop to collect any letters for Weavern Farm – there were generally precious few. The shopkeeper gave her something small – sweets or cheese or an apple – for saving her son the long walk out to Weavern to deliver them, and that day Clemmie chewed a toffee as she carried on her way. But the boy. The boy. His name was Eli, and his family were bad – the Tanners. The worst on God's green Earth, her father, William Matlock, had once said, as he forbade any of his girls to fool about with any of their boys. They'd had a Tanner in to help cut the hay one year. He'd made several attempts to corner Clemmie's sister, Josie, who'd been twelve at the time, and in the end left her with a cut lip; and when he was told to go he'd gone with two of their hens. Now William's face curdled dangerously at any mention of a Tanner. But Clemmie couldn't help thinking about the thing she'd seen the boy do – the thing he'd done for her. She couldn't help but picture his face, so at odds with itself that she hadn't quite worked it out yet – her instincts, normally good enough at guiding her, went blind and were no help. There'd been blood beneath his fingernails, and deep scratches on his hands. He'd smelt of beer and sweat, of something hard and mineral, but, underneath that, of something better. He'd told her his name – defiantly, as if she'd challenged him: *I'm Eli*. And then not another word. The silence had been painfully loud.

But he was nowhere around; if he was working at the mill that day then he was already inside. Sometimes he worked at Rag Mill, the smaller mill, just a little way upriver, which pulped rags for the paper mill. Clemmie remembered seeing him leading the shaggy pony that pulled the cart of sloppy stuff between the two. Tugging at its bridle as it twisted its head in protest, his face screwed up in anger. So much anger in him – so at odds with what he'd done for her. She gazed towards Rag Mill, but had no call to go further upriver. The malty smell of Little & Sons brewery – one of her favourites – drifted down to her, but she left the mill yard troubled. She would go back along the western side of the river, through the trees. There was no path but she knew the way. She felt watched as she went; she was used to the feeling and knew it at once: the weight of eyes. This time, though, she looked around and tried to see who it was – tried to see if it was the boy. *Eli.*

2

The Doll

Pudding did her best to look smart. The new Mrs Hadleigh was – finally – coming to the stables to see the horse Mr Hadleigh had bought for her, in the hope that she would take to riding. Irene Hadleigh had been at Manor Farm for almost six weeks already, as spring had swelled into summer, and the fact that few in the village had seen or met her was causing mutterings. The most sympathetic rumour was that she was an invalid of some kind. There'd been enough of a hoo-hah already, when they'd married up in London after a whirlwind courtship, rather than in St Nicholas' church, squat and solitary in a field in the centre of the village. When the old Mr Hadleigh had been married, the whole village had been invited to a fête in the orchard at Manor Farm, with beer, bunting and apple bobbing. Not that Pudding had been alive to see it, but she'd heard it talked about; and recently she'd overheard Mrs Glover, who ran the tiny shop, complaining to Dolores Pole about the lack of a celebration. Before she'd even arrived and apparently shunned them, the villagers had felt cheated by the new Mrs Hadleigh. Pudding liked the idea of this sudden wedding though – she imagined a passion too urgent to be borne, the need to possess and be possessed, and the thought gave her a hungry feeling. She yearned to yearn for somebody, and to be yearned for; a puzzle of feelings she couldn't yet decipher. Such passion must surely have left traces on Irene Hadleigh. Some kind of glow from within, perhaps. And since Pudding had only caught brief glimpses of her – sitting out on the back terrace with her face down; or blurry, gazing from a window of the house – Irene Hadleigh had become a kind of distant, glorious, near-mythical figure. At the thought of actually meeting her Pudding's heart galloped absurdly.

Manor Farm had five loose boxes and a larger stable they called the cob house – where the two-seated gig and the cob pony who pulled it lived – arranged around a small yard to the west of the farmhouse. It was all built of the same golden limestone as the rest of Slaughterford, quarried out of the hillside above the mill in some earlier century. This yard was where the riding horses were kept, and it was Pudding's domain. The farm's three pairs of working horses – six mighty shires, all feathered feet and muscle – were kept together in skillings behind the top barn, and looked after by a short, wiry man called Hilarius. He wore the same long canvas overalls every day, come rain or shine; nobody knew his age but he was ancient, and had been at the farm since he was a child – far longer than anyone else. His parents had come from some-where in Europe, originally; his eyes watched the world from within a network of creases, and he didn't say an awful lot. In summer he slept on a straw mattress on a mezzanine in the cavernous great barn; in winter he moved into the loft above the cob house. It was his job to get the working pairs harnessed by seven o'clock every morning, ready for the carters to take out; and to rub them down, feed them and turn them out when they returned from ploughing or sowing or whatever at the end of the day. With nods and gestures and demonstrations, Hilarius had taught Pudding a lot of what she knew about stable work, and the rest she'd taught herself from a book called *Sound Horse Management*, which she'd got from the library in Chippenham.

Hay was fetched from the rickyard, up the hill, where it was stacked and thatched on staddle stones to keep it dry. One of the farm's many small sheds had been put aside as a tack room and fitted out with a pot-bellied stove, to prevent the leather blooming, on which Pudding could boil a kettle to make tea. There was an ancient stone water trough outside which doubled as a handy mounting block. Pudding kept the tack room as spotless as the yard – so spotless that the laundress had joked, one day, that the sparrows would have no scraps to build their nests. After that she'd taken to scattering a few wisps of old hay onto the muck heap each morning. Just during nesting season. At least there was plenty of mud around the field gates for the swallows and martins – they'd arrived a few weeks before and set about patching up their nests in the eaves of the stables, and were so sweet Pudding didn't even mind it when they dropped their mess in her hair. Pudding's charges were five: Mr Hadleigh's towering brown hunter, Baron; Tufty, the pony he'd had as a child, now implausibly saggy and ancient; Nancy Hadleigh's hack, Bally Girl – though Nancy rode less and less frequently, with her hip; Dundee, the cob that pulled the Stanhope gig when someone wanted to go into town; and now Robin, the gelding for Mrs Hadleigh. He was only just bigger than a pony and as mild as anything, but not heavy or a plod. Even his colouring was gentle – honey brown. Irene Hadleigh couldn't fail to like him.

Pudding brought him out onto the yard just before eleven and gave him one final polish. She nudged him to straighten him up when he slouched, tipping a back hoof, wanting to show him in his best light. He was a reflection of her work, after all, and Pudding wanted more than anything to be the best girl groom possible. Well, not more than *anything*. She thought of Donny, and her mother too; and of the mystery of yearning. But otherwise, it was what she wanted most. Her father still wanted her to go on to secretarial college, or perhaps even university, as Donny had planned to, once upon a time. Donny was meant to have been an engineer – he had a natural talent for it, and understood machinery of all kinds – but the Great War had changed all that. Dr Cartwright called this summer a *trial run* at being a groom, but, at fifteen years old, Pudding knew exactly what she wanted. She was going to excel. She was going to make herself indispensable to the Hadleighs, and she was going to stay in Slaughterford with her family. For a minute or two she wondered who on earth she would marry, there in Slaughterford, but then the clip on one of her braces popped open as she bent down to pick up Robin's foot, and she blushed even though there was nobody to see it, and reminded herself that marriage was the least of her concerns. Then she heard footsteps and voices from the house, and, flustered, refastened the clip and brushed the horsehair from her sleeves as best she could.

Manor Farm was the most northerly house of Slaughterford, on the steep lane that headed off to Ford, the next village north along the By Brook. From the farm there was a wide, sweeping view of the rolling valley, almost impossibly green with summer, with the church on one side, the mills down on the water, and the cottages in between. The valley was too steep for crops – it was all woods and grazing, and the far fields were dotted with sheep and bronze cattle. The riverbanks to the south were so thick with trees that the water was only visible down by the bridge, where three lanes met – Germain's, which joined Ham Lane to Biddestone; the lane to Ford in the north, and the lane towards Thickwood in the west. All the lanes were narrow and made of crushed limestone, and anyone travelling along them caused a cloud of white dust. The weather had been hot and sunny but it had been raining at night, so that the field gates and water troughs sat in churned mud. The air was slightly damp, the By Brook ran swiftly, and there were insects everywhere. With this glorious backdrop

Nancy and Irene Hadleigh walked across to the yard from the house. For an idiotic moment, Pudding felt she ought to stand to attention, and clean forgot what to say. Luckily, just as the women arrived alongside him, Robin broke wind quite loudly, and she couldn't help but laugh.

Irene Hadleigh recoiled, and kept her distance, watching Robin as though she half expected him to lunge at her, all teeth and fury. It gave Pudding the chance to have a good look at her. She was medium height and whip-thin, with the kind of elfin delicacy that Pudding longed for. Her dark hair was cut into a glossy bob across her ears; her eyes were similarly dark, with smudges underneath them, stark in her pale face. And there was something so immobile about her face, something so frozen, that Pudding couldn't imagine her laughing. She was like a china doll, and quite unreadable. She was dressed in immaculate riding clothes – white breeches, a tweed jacket and a stock – and Pudding racked her brains in panic, having no recollection that Robin should have been tacked up for riding.

'Well, that's a charming welcome,' said Nancy, stepping forwards. She wore her usual shirt and slacks, tidy but just slightly faded; her old, creased boots; a silk scarf over her hair, knotted under her chin.

'It's all the summer grass after the rain, Miss H,' Pudding blurted out.

'I'm well aware of that, Pudding.' Nancy slapped Robin hard on his neck, and ran practised eyes over him. 'Nice enough creature. Not too big. Nothing to alarm – a bit fat, mind you.' With this she gave Pudding a stern look. 'What do you say, Irene?'

'Well,' said Irene, starting slightly. Her voice was subdued. She clenched her hands together. 'He seems fine.' There was a pause while Nancy skewered Irene with one of her smiles, which Pudding knew well, so she stepped forward and held out her own hand.

'It's a pleasure to meet you, Mrs Hadleigh. Mr H mentioned that you haven't done very much riding before, but I've been out on Robin a few times now, and he really is as gentle as a lamb. He didn't even spook when the charabanc passed us in the lane on Monday, and heaven knows it makes enough smoke and racket. You'll be as safe as houses on him, I promise you.' She shook Irene's hand perhaps too vigorously, and faced down her nerves, even though Irene's eyes were as glassy and blank as ink spots. For a moment Pudding baulked, and felt a pang of puzzled sorrow that lovely, sunny Mr Hadleigh should have wed such a cold creature. But then it dawned on her that Irene simply looked fagged. Utterly exhausted.

'Well,' said Irene, pausing to clear her throat. 'In fact, I've never even sat on a horse. I've never quite seen the point, when I've two good legs of my own.'

'Yes, and a car to drive you everywhere,' said Nancy. 'Come the winter, not many things with wheels are any use around here.'

'Oh, and riding is so much fun! And such a wonderful way to see the world,' said Pudding.

'The world?' Irene echoed, with a trace of something bitter in her tone.

'Yes. Well . . . that is, this corner of it, anyway,' Pudding amended. 'Shall I saddle him up for you? I could walk you out on the lead rein, if you like, just to get a feel for it? Or even just around the paddock.'

'Now?' said Irene, alarmed.

'Yes, why not hop up? Only way to find out if you like it. Alistair would be thrilled to hear you'd given it a go,' said Nancy, brightly, and Irene looked horrified.

'I just thought . . . since you'd dressed for riding . . .'

Pudding trailed off. Two spots of colour had appeared on Irene Hadleigh's cheeks. She looked as though she'd like nothing better than to turn tail and flee. 'But you needn't, of course,' Pudding added.

'Nonsense. No time like the present. How are you ever going to hunt at Alistair's side if you won't even get on?'

'I just . . . hadn't thought to . . .' Irene floundered, and Nancy stared at her meanly, and didn't help at all, so Pudding came to her rescue again.

'Well, why don't I ride him in the paddock for a bit, so you can see his paces?' She saw Irene's shoulders drop in relief, and with a small noise of derision Nancy went over to feed Bally Girl a carrot from her pocket.

So Pudding rode Robin in some large circles, loops and figure-eights; in walk, trot and canter. She even popped over a few small jumps, and was enjoying herself so much and concentrating so hard on showing him off that she didn't notice at which point Nancy and Irene stopped watching and left – Nancy across the field to the churchyard, and her brother's grave, and Irene presumably back to the house. Puffed out and sweaty, Pudding let Robin walk on a loose rein back to the yard. The horse was puffing too, and Pudding worried that if she got any bigger, she'd be too heavy to ride him. She spent the next hour scouring off the last of Tufty's winter coat with a curry comb – clouds and clouds of greasy, greyish hair; something for the swallows to line their nests with – and tried not to be disappointed by this first meeting with Irene Hadleigh. She'd been tentatively looking forward to having someone a bit closer to her own age to ride out with, even if she was a Londoner and very upper. Or at least to hearing a bit about London life – the constant parties and balls and bohemian salons and jazz dancing of which she imagined London life to consist. But Irene Hadleigh, though she'd married one of the nicest and best men for fifty miles in any direction, had looked as though she'd rather have been anywhere else than at Manor Farm. A china doll who longed to be back in her box.

At one o'clock, Pudding went to fetch Donny to go home for lunch. Her brother worked at Manor Farm as well, helping the head gardener Jeremiah Welch, whom everyone knew as Jem. He'd been the gardener at Manor Farm for forty years; his body was a strip of bone and sinew, stronger than tree roots and just as brown, and he kept ferrets – there was usually one about his person somewhere, and if there wasn't then their particular smell remained.

'Hello, Jem, are you well?' Pudding called to him, waving.

'Lass,' Jem replied, his Wiltshire drawl stretching out the word. 'Your Don's hoeing the rose beds.'

'Right you are.' The rose garden was behind high brick walls, sheltered and hot. The perfume of the flowers was as rich as their mad profusion of colour. Donny was in the far corner, with his shirtsleeves rolled up and a brown apron over the top. Pudding was always surprised by the breadth of his shoulders, the solidity of him through the hips and waist that told of his strength. A man's strength. She still half expected to see the lanky boy he'd been when he'd gone off to enlist. He'd been tall enough, and his brows heavy enough, for his lie of being eighteen to pass, but he'd been only sixteen. Pudding remembered being on fire with admiration for him that day, and could hardly bear to think of it now. She hadn't had a clue what going to war meant. Donny was sweating, and though he held the hoe ready to work, he was standing stock-still. It happened sometimes – if something made him pause, he might remain paused until somebody came along to restart him. Pudding made sure she'd stepped into his line of sight before she touched his arm to rouse him, but he still flinched. 'It's just me, Donny,' she said, and he smiled, reaching out to pinch her chin between his thumb and forefinger. The sun threw the scar on his head into relief – Pudding could hardly look at it. A flat depression the size of her palm, on the right side of his head, mostly under his hair but coming onto his forehead too, surrounded by knotty scar tissue. 'Time for lunch,' she said. Donny straightened up, bringing the hoe to his side.

'Right you are,' he agreed.

'Looks like you've been working hard this morning.' Pudding looked around at the neat beds and the fresh, weed-free soil Donny had worked between the rose bushes. Then she looked down at the bushes nearest to them, and said 'Oh!' before she could stop herself.

The two rose bushes at Donny's feet were in shreds. Mature bushes, two and a half feet high, one white, one pale yellow – the colours Nancy Hadleigh liked for her brother's grave. Their petals, leaves and green stems had been chopped to pieces by the hoe. Pudding stirred the sad confetti with her toe. 'Oh, Donny, what happened here?' she said quietly, immediately trying to think of a way to conceal the damage. It would be impossible, of course. She felt a tremor go through her brother and looked up at him, fearfully. 'It's all right,' she said, but it wasn't. Donny's face had clouded with rage – that anger with himself that was so terribly destructive for having nowhere to go; no object other than his own intangible frailty. His mouth worked, his skin flushed carmine, and he shook. His hands on the shaft of the hoe were white with the strain of gripping it, and Pudding had to ignore the urge to step back, out of its range. Donny would never hurt her. She knew that so deep down it was written on her bones. But sometimes, since Donny had come home, he stopped being Donny, exactly, and got lost inside himself. Pudding stepped closer, so that he had to see her, and rubbed her hand on his forearm. 'Well, Donny, they'll grow back, won't they?' she said. She could feel the tension in him, like the vibrations in the ground near the beating house of the mill; like the way she could feel when a horse was about to bolt – that shuddering of pent-up energy that had to go *somewhere*. She could almost smell it. 'What do you fancy for lunch?' she said, refusing to show the least concern.

She kept on talking to him, and after a while his breathing slowed and the tension left him, and he shut his eyes, covering them with one muddy hand, squeezing tears into the lashes. 'Come on, then, or we'll miss out,' she said, and he let himself be led away. She would see Jem and Alistair Hadleigh about it after lunch, when she was sure that Donny was calm again. Jem would chew his lip and set about tidying the plants in silence; Mr Hadleigh would smile that sad, sympathetic smile he used when these things happened, and say something like, *Well now, there's no point crying over spilt milk*, and Pudding would struggle to keep herself together. Even Nancy Hadleigh was kind when it came to Donny – although Pudding had long suspected that Alistair's aunt was kinder underneath all the bristle than she liked to let on. Pudding had once seen her wring the neck of a duck the fox had got hold of – it had been left with big, bloody holes in its breast, one eye gone and a wing twisted, hanging limply behind it. Nancy had despatched it quickly and flung it onto the bonfire heap, wiping her hands on a rag, saying, *No point trying to nurse it*, but Pudding had seen the way her eyes gleamed, and the sad set of her mouth.

They walked down into the village, across the bridge at Rag Mill and up the steep footpath through the field that led home. The field was still called Bloody Meadow by the villagers, after the legend that King Alfred had defeated the Danes in battle there, centuries before, making the river run red with the blood of fallen warriors. They said that was how Slaughterford got its name. Donny had told Pudding the story over and over when she was little, before the war – re-enacting long, fictional accounts of the battle, blow by hideous blow, complete with sound effects and swoops of his hazel sword. She'd loved the excitement of it, the imagined glory and wonder of such an ancient time. Magic and thanes and treasure. It was on the tip of her tongue to ask Donny for the story again, or to tell it to him; to bring back that time. But battles weren't as alluring any more, and heroic death meant something now – it meant fear and pain and broken lives. Too many other boys had left Slaughterford for the war, from its precious population of eighty-one, including two Tanners, a Matlock, two Smiths and three Hancocks. Only Donny had come back. Alistair Hadleigh too, of course – but he hadn't been a boy, or a Tommy. Instead, as they climbed and started to puff, Pudding told her brother about Irene Hadleigh, and how she hadn't wanted to ride. She wasn't sure Donny was listening until he stopped walking, frowning, and said:

'You never could understand a person not wanting to ride, could you, Pud?' He spoke slowly, concentrating hard, and Pudding grinned.

'No, Donny. I never could.'

Spring Cottage was named after the rill of freshwater that bubbled up from the ground in front of it, trickling through a swathe of luminously green duck weed into a stone trough, and then down pipes to give Slaughterford its supply of drinking water. The house was Georgian, not particularly large but handsomely square and symmetrical, with sash windows and a big brass knocker on the front door. Inside, everything was wonderfully normal – Louise had made pea soup from the garden, and gave them a half-proud, half-annoyed list of the chores she and Ruth, their daily, had got through that morning: new paper and pink disinfectant powder in the privy, all the beds changed, the blackcurrants picked and jellied – and Dr Cartwright came bustling in late, as he always did, apologising profusely. Their house was up too steep a hill for his consultations to be held there, so he rented a room in the schoolmaster's house in Biddestone, and cycled to and fro. Pudding surreptitiously checked her mother for signs of mishap. That was how she and her father termed what was happening to Louise. *Mishaps.* It was a terrible misnomer neither one of them could bring themselves to drop. But her mother looked fine, if a little tired. Her blond hair was fading as grey invaded it; there were deeper lines around her eyes and mouth than a woman of forty-eight should have, but most of those had appeared the morning Donny went off, seven years previously. It wasn't a beautiful face, but it was wide and appealing. She was soft and rounded and perfect for hugging. The first sign of mishap was when she began to look around the room with the beginnings of a frown, as though she couldn't remember why she'd come in, or – worse – which room she was in. Pudding was always watching for it. She never again wanted to be as unprepared, as frightened, as the time she'd come down for breakfast and found her mother standing at the stove with an egg, still in its shell, smoking in a dry pan. Louise had turned to her and smiled politely, and said, *Oh, excuse me, young miss – perhaps you might help me? I'm rather worried I've come to the wrong address.*

Pudding remembered their kitchen table from her earliest memories – gouging ancient crumbs from its seams with her thumbnail when she was bored of practising the alphabet; the cutlery drawer that jammed; the slight stickiness to the wood that no amount of scrubbing could get rid of. There was a dining room as well, with a far nicer, polished, table, but they used it less and less. The kitchen table was like the enamel pans on their hooks above the stove, and her mother's yellow apron, and the brown teapot with the glued-together lid – anchors; things Pudding could rely upon. Ruth, who refused to give her age as anything but *somewhere in the middle*, sat down to lunch with them and gave the doctor the usual report of her large family's ailments. Pudding's father did his best to advise.

'And my Teresa's acne never gets any better,' said Ruth, as they dipped their spoons into the pea soup. 'Poor thing's got a face like wormy meat. How's she supposed to find a husband, looking like that?' She appealed to the doctor as if there was something he could have been doing to help her daughter, yet wasn't. Louise put down her spoon in protest; Donny slurped away, unconcerned. The doctor nodded kindly.

'A girl of Teresa's sunny disposition should have no trouble there, Ruth. These things are often simply grown out of. But she mustn't pick at them, and damage the skin.'

'Hilarius put a tincture of witch hazel and ash on Tufty's infected bot bite last month,' said Pudding. 'It was miraculous. The boil was as big as a walnut, and really smelly, but it dried out in three days flat.'

'Oh, good grief, Pudding, *not* at the table,' said Louise.

'Sorry, Mum.'

'Witch hazel, you say?' said Ruth.

Pudding wondered whether to mention the rose bushes. The last time something like that had happened, Donny had got into trouble soon afterwards. His frustration seemed to build gradually, as though the daily fight to get back to himself wore him out, and weighed him down, until it grew too much to bear. The incident at the White Hart in Ford the year before had been the worst. Patches of sticky blood on the dark stone flags, and a broken tooth; the police sergeant fetched out from Chippenham when Pete Dempsey, the local constable, couldn't hold Donny by himself. But it hadn't been Donny's fault — none of it was Donny's fault. He'd seen Aoife Moore earlier that afternoon. Aoife with her black hair and green eyes, and the dimple in her chin, who he was supposed to marry. They'd been sweethearts since they were twelve, and got engaged before he went away, but when he got back she managed ten minutes with him, and the crater in his skull, and the way he struggled to speak and eat, and ran away crying. She got engaged to a carrier's brawny son the following month. Then Donny saw her buying black and white bull's eyes for her little sister – five for a farthing – from the widow who sold sweets through her front window in Ford. Aoife had struggled to reach through the window, what with her pregnant belly so huge. And then the man she'd married was in the pub, with some others, and had goaded Donny. Pudding hadn't been there, of course, but she was sure Donny *must* have been goaded. But the rose bushes were just a slip-up. Just a loss of concentration – his arms still working the hoe though his mind and gaze had drifted off. Pudding decided not to say anything about it.

Her father stopped her as she went upstairs to bed that night.

'A good day today, Pudding?' he asked, softly. Upstairs, Louise was putting Donny to bed. In some ways he'd become an oversized child, needing prompting through the bedtime rituals. *Brush your teeth, Donny. Into your pyjamas, now.* Their footsteps made the floorboards squeak. Pudding didn't like to think what might happen if her mother ever didn't recognise Donny, or forgot what had happened to him. The idea of their confusion clashing, and frightening them both, was sickening. Dr Cartwright was a gentle, smallish man – shorter than both of his offspring – with a neat face and grey whiskers. Behind round spectacles, his eyes were sad. When Donny had absconded to join up he'd gone into his consulting room in Biddestone and hadn't come out, or admitted anyone, for the rest of the day. When he'd finally returned home he'd hugged his daughter tightly, and his eyes had been pink, and he'd said, in a tight voice, *The boy'd never forgive me if I sent a telegram with his real age, would he?* And Pudding, still star-struck by her brother, had said, *He's going to be a hero, Daddy.* The exchange still haunted her. She was sure it haunted the doctor too. The hope in his voice, when he asked Pudding about their day, was painful to hear.

'Yes, Dad,' she said. 'A good day.'

At night, Pudding read. She still had books of pony stories she was far too old for, as comforting as slipping under the blankets and finding the warm spot where the hot water bottle had been. Or she read the tuppenny story papers – love stories and lurid accounts of true crimes. Ruth sometimes passed on well-thumbed copies of *Weldon's Ladies' Journal* and *Woman's Weekly* for her to read as well.

'Since your own mother's in no state to teach you,' she'd said the first time she'd brought one over, pursing her lips afterwards and colouring up. Pudding did like to read about clothes and hosiery and lipstick, and what she should be knitting, or doing to her skin to make it bloom (in fact, her skin was perfect), but at the same time she felt that none of it was really relevant to her. It was interesting, but like reading the romances or the murder stories – not something that would ever happen in real life. She had bobbed her hair the year before, though, in imitation of the cover star of one of the magazines, and much to her mother's upset. But it hadn't hung in a straight, glossy line like Irene Hadleigh's, with razor edges and a halo of reflected light. Pudding's hair was thick and bushy, so it'd stuck out from the sides of her head in a triangle, and made her look even wider. Appalled, she'd let it grow back, and in any case it spent most of its life in a hairnet, held back with clips or crushed into the shape of a riding hat and sweaty at the edges.

That night, though, she picked up *Murder Most Foul – true*

stories of dark deeds in Wiltshire; a book she'd found in a junk shop in Marshfield. It contained fifteen stories of horrible things that had happened in the county throughout its history, two of them in Slaughterford itself, most fascinatingly, albeit years and years ago: 'The Maid of the Mill', the murder of a local girl; and 'The Snow Child', which told the terribly sad story of a family of tinkers (*beautiful as exotic animals are, and similarly devoid of morals*, the book said) who had perished from the cold one bitter winter night, having been refused shelter by everyone in the village. Only a little boy had survived, and was found lying half-buried by snow, between his dead parents who'd huddled around him and his sister, trying to keep them warm. Pudding normally couldn't read it without shivering in sympathy, and being grateful for her warm bed, but she couldn't seem to concentrate on it that night. She read to the end anyway, then put the book down and wondered, for a moment, how different life might be if one were slim, and beautiful, and married to Alistair Hadleigh.

When she was little her mother had marked her bedside candle with her thumbnail, and once the flame had burnt down to that point Pudding would know it was time to blow it out and go to sleep. Now it was up to her when she twisted the knob on her gas lamp to extinguish it, and she was usually the last one awake in the house. She liked to be. Her father worked so hard, and worried so much, he was exhausted. And Donny and her mother needed to be watched over, so watch over them she would. Sometimes, on windy nights, she felt like crying. Which was stupid, she told herself, when there was nothing to cry about, really. She had her home, and her parents, not like the little boy in 'The Snow Child'. And what about the Tanners and the Smiths, whose sons and brothers hadn't come back from the war at all? What about Maisie Cooper, whose mother had been kicked in the head when her pony was stung by a bee, and had lain unconscious ever since? Maisie had to be back from college for the holidays by now, but she hadn't come up to see Pudding. Of course, Pudding had far less free time now she was working, and she understood why some of her other friends stayed away – not everybody knew how to talk to Donny any more, or to Louise, and it made them nervous. But she'd thought Maisie, out of everybody, wouldn't have minded as much. Pudding refused to cry, not when it was only the wind, making her feel like the last human being on earth.

≪ ≫

In the circle of light cast by the bronze lamp on the desk, Irene's hand cramped over the paper. She'd been gripping the pen too hard, as though she might have been able to squeeze words out of it. *Dear Fin*, she'd written. *I don't think I can carry on much longer without a word from you. Just a single bloody word*. After that, her hand had stalled. She'd meant to write with a lighter tone. Something more conversational, as though they might manage to pretend a friendship. She'd meant to write something dry about Nancy's ever watchful presence, or about the absurdity of life in Slaughterford – what kind of name was *Pudding*, anyway? – or that there only seemed to be four different surnames to go around, or that when Alistair had told her about Manor Farm, she'd heard the 'Manor' part louder than the 'Farm' part, when the reverse was closer to reality. But those words wouldn't come. They'd have been false, anyway. Irene shut her eyes and he was there at once. A quiet, diffident presence behind Serena, who was anything but serene. Not overly tall, not overly handsome, but with something warm and deeply compelling about him, so much so that once they'd exchanged a word and a glance, weeks after meeting, Irene had felt both – glance and word – travel right through her like a wave rolling ashore, and hadn't afterwards been able to want anything but him. Serena had towed him here and there behind her, by his hand, like a child. He'd been so silent, so overshadowed by her for the first few weeks Irene knew them that she hadn't heard his Scottish accent, or realised that Fin was short for Finlay, a name she'd never heard before.

Serena was a different kettle of fish. All bright, all spark-ling, all smiles and loud laughter. Irene had first met her at a costume party, dressed as a peacock – sequins and paste jewels twinkling everywhere, iridescent feathers wafting as she moved, blue and green, turquoise and silver. From then on Irene always saw her that way – even when Serena was wearing brown wool, she dazzled. It took a long time to see that it was armour, in fact, to hide what was going on inside her. Serena had bowled Irene over. She bowled everyone over. She didn't so much make friends as assume that everyone she met was already her friend – and they usually turned out to be, sooner or later. It seemed impossible to resist Serena; so impossible that, later, when Irene asked Fin why he'd married her and he hadn't been able to explain it, she'd understood at once. She remembered clearly the first time she hadn't been able to eat in Serena's presence. Just as she couldn't in her mother's presence. It had been in a restaurant in Piccadilly, over a lunch one Tuesday. Sole Veronique. A group of seven or eight of them, some Irene knew, some she did not. Fin sitting opposite her at the far end of the table. She'd caught his eye by mistake and looked away quickly. *Irene has a secret pash, you know*, Serena had announced, smiling with her eyes ferocious, drawing attention to Irene when she knew Irene would hate it. *Look at her blush – isn't it adorable? Tell us who it is or we'll make it up!* When the food had arrived Irene's hands had refused to touch the cutlery, and her mouth had refused to open; just like it did when her mother was watching.

She blinked and took a deep breath, looking down at the scant, wretched words of her letter and hating herself anew. The gas lamp hissed and she thought of all the things she missed about London – not just Fin, or the motor taxicabs Nancy had mentioned earlier. Electric lighting, for one thing, and indoor lavatories; the theatre, and the flicks; music that didn't involve a squeeze box, washboard or fiddle. The comforting, anonymous throng of busy people; the ease with which new clothes – new camouflage – could be got. The sense, stepping out of the front door, that an infinite variety of things to do, places to be and people to see lay within easy reach. In Wiltshire, there was nothing beyond the front door but mud and animals. The only motor vehicle she'd seen attempting the steep, stony lanes was the lumbering chara-banc bus that brought mill workers in the morning, and took villagers off to Chippenham and Corsham. The only thing that both places had in common was the unnatural dearth of young men, and the blank eyes of those who had made it back from the trenches. Carefully, Irene tore away the page with her short letter on it, and was about to screw it up when she heard Alistair's step outside the door. She quickly slid the page beneath the blotter and arranged her hands in her lap as he came in. He smiled and crossed to her, kissing her cheek.

'How are you now, darling?' he asked, solicitously. 'You gave us quite a scare.'

'Rather better, thank you. It was really nothing – that sauce was just a little rich for me.' A cream and sherry sauce, laced with walnut oil. It had coated the inside of her mouth and throat, and she'd felt her cheeks water in protest as her head began to cloud.

'Yes. Well . . .' Alistair trailed off, looking awkward. 'Irene,

I can't help thinking . . . I can't help wondering whether, if you ate a little more, perhaps your system would be more used to . . .' He fell silent again.

'I'm simply . . . not hungry, a lot of the time. That's all,' said Irene. She tried to say it lightly, but it sounded as phoney as it was – her empty stomach clawed at her from morning to night. Yet the thought of food closed her throat. Alistair crouched down by her chair, and took her hands. Guiltily, she noticed the ink on her fingers. Alistair had long hands, pianist's hands, with very neat fingernails. Not like Fin's, all bitten down in frustration. Her new husband was undeniably handsome; tall and slim, his hair a muted gold, his eyes half green, half brown. And that way his face was always either smiling or about to be.

'But you're so thin, Irene.' He shook his head slightly. 'I'll call Dr Cartwright in the morning, and get him to take a look at you. Just to be on the safe side.'

'There's really no need. I'm perfectly all right. Really,' said Irene.

'Are you, though? You promised to always tell me the truth, remember? That's all I ask.'

Alistair looked up at her in a beseeching way, full of the love she felt so unworthy of. How could she possibly keep that promise? She reached out and ran a hand over his hair and down the side of his face, feeling the beginnings of stubble on his jaw. Alistair shut his eyes and turned his face into her touch, kissing her palm, and Irene froze, caught between duty, gratitude, and the urge to flee. Alistair caught her hand tightly and pressed kisses along the inside of her arm, where bluish veins showed beneath the skin. He took a long breath, and shut his eyes, and Irene fought not to pull away.

'Alistair, I—' she said. He laid his face along her arm for a moment, then stood up, letting it go, smiling a strained smile.

'No. I quite understand, what with you under the weather, you poor thing,' he said, and relief swooped through her. 'Could you stomach a little Bovril, do you think? Just a small cup?'

'I think that might be just the ticket, thank you.' She breathed more easily as Alistair reached the door, but then he paused, and turned. He looked at the blank paper in front of her, and her pen discarded to one side, and the ink on her fingers. He opened his mouth but it took a moment longer for the words to come.

'I . . . I do understand how difficult this must be for you, Irene. People are quick to lay blame but . . . I personally think *he* treated *you* abominably. I don't expect you to forget it all right away. I don't.' He swallowed, and met her eye with a wounded gaze. 'I only ask that you try.' He shut the door and left her alone again, in the circle of light by the desk, surrounded by the darkness.

In the morning Irene was woken, as she was every morning, by the racket of the heavy horses' feet on the yard, the incomprehensible banter of the strappers and carters as the teams went out to work, the mooing of the dairy herd, the geese honking with a sound like metal hinges, and the collie dogs barking to be fed. She felt surrounded by baying animals of all kinds. After breakfast, she went down to what was going to be her writing room and hovered outside the door, not announcing her presence at once. It was a small room, half dug into the rising ground on the north-east side of the house, where there was little natural light and the flagstones were so cold, even then in summer, that they felt damp – and possibly were. The walls were painted a faint pink – no panelling, no cornicing, no ceiling rose. The plainest of rooms. The two ancient metal casements were crooked, and the curtains were simple, chequered affairs. The fireplace had been boarded up with a wooden frieze showing an arrangement of flowers and fruit. Overall, the room felt like one that nobody had used in a very long time, and Irene had been drawn to it immediately. In every other part of the house she felt that she was trying to make space for herself in somebody else's life, somebody else's house – and that *somebody* was Nancy.

'I still don't see why she need do anything so drastic,' said Nancy, looking on disapprovingly as Verney Blunt, the village builder, and his lad carried in their ladders and sheets and metal boxes of tools. Verney tipped his hat in a bid to get her to move out of his way, as he struggled to find room for everything, but Nancy ignored him. 'And why this room, of all of them? She might as well set up camp in the cellar.'

'I loved this room when I was a boy,' said Alistair, standing by the window with his hands behind his back.

'No you didn't, you goose. You only loved escaping from it. What boy loves his schoolroom?'

'All right, but I did love it in some ways. Especially when I had Mr Peters. He used to bring me toffee, you know.'

'I do know. You'd come out with it all over your chin.'

'Well, Irene likes this room, so as far as I'm concerned she can have it. It's quiet, and cosy. Quite suitable for a writing room.'

'Cosy? Tosh. She'll go blind in here – there's no light. And she'll change her mind come winter – that chimney has never done anything but let the wind howl down. Why do you think it was blocked up in the first place?'

'I know. But look, Aunt Nancy, she needs a room to make her own – no small thing when everything else in this house has been here for centuries. She's chosen this one, so let's just say no more about it, shall we? It's not as though it's being used for anything else.'

'But new furniture? New fabrics? New everything?'

'Why not? It's about time at least one corner of this old place was brought up to date. I hope she might take on some of the other rooms, in due course. She has quite the eye for it, you know.'

'Does she indeed. Well.' Nancy sighed. 'You're as soft as my dear departed brother was before you, Alistair.'

'We can afford to be soft with you to watch over us,' Alistair told her, smiling.

Irene put her shoulders back and lifted her chin before she entered the room, and refused to let any hint of an apology suffuse her face or voice.

'I'm really very grateful,' she said.

'There you are, darling,' said Alistair. 'Mr Blunt here is ready for your instructions.'

'Mornin', Mrs Hadleigh,' said Verney, grudgingly. He was stout, red-faced, white-haired.

'Hello,' said Irene. The younger of the workmen, who only looked about fifteen, eyed her curiously, and Irene wondered what account of her was making it out into the wider realm of Slaughterford. The lad had dark, unwashed hair and a thin face, almost ferrety. His eyes were guarded, his whole body poised to flinch.

'You're one of the Tanner clan, aren't you?' Nancy said to him. The boy nodded, ducking his head.

'Get on, then, and fetch the rest of the gear,' said Verney brusquely, sending the boy scuttling from the room.

'Is the silver quite safe, Mr Blunt?' said Nancy. Verney Blunt swelled his chest, but looked a little uneasy.

'I reckon so, Miss Hadleigh. He's a good lad, not as bad as some of them. And I'll be keeping my eye on him, you've my word on that.'

'What is he – a Noah? An Abraham? A Jonah?'

'A Joseph, madam.'

'One of Slaughterford's little jokes,' Nancy said to Irene. 'That the least godly family in the whole county should decide to opt strictly for biblical names for their offspring.'

'Oh? But they don't attend church?' said Irene.

'Some of them do. When they aren't too drunk to stand.' Nancy shrugged. 'Well, I shall leave you to your artistic endeavours in here. I must see Lake about the new fencing in Upper Break.' She strode from the room with her hands thrust hard into the pockets of her jacket.

In her absence Alistair smiled, and pulled Irene into a quick embrace before the workmen's footsteps approached along the hall again.

'Who is Lake, and what is an Upper Break?' said Irene.

'You met John Lake – remember? The farm manager. Huge chap.'

'Yes, of course.' Irene remembered the man's towering height, and bullish shoulders all but blocking out the sky, but she couldn't recall his face; she remembered the bass growl of his voice, but not what he had said. She found the Wiltshire accent of the villagers all but unintelligible, and in the first few weeks after their wedding she'd been more of a shell than a whole person. She dreaded meeting again the few of Alistair's acquaintances she'd been introduced to, since she'd forgotten their names at once.

'And Upper Break is the high field – the one that goes over the hill towards Biddestone, where the ewes are at the moment. Good pasture, rocky as anything but it drains well.'

'Nancy's rather indispensable around here, isn't she?'

'I suppose so. Well, not indispensable, but very involved. The farm and Slaughterford are her life.'

'The farm, Slaughterford, and you.'

'Yes, I suppose so. Especially since we lost my father.'

'She must have had suitors, in her day? I've seen her deb portrait. She was very beautiful.' The portrait hung in the study, opposite those of Alistair's parents – Nancy's brother and sister-in-law. There were early photographs as well, ghostly and pale, including one of Nancy with long dark hair, piled up high, cheekbones like a cat and flawless skin. Something cool and angry in her eyes.

'There were. But the one she really wanted got away, and it seems as though that was that for Aunt Nancy. That was before I was born, of course, and she's rather prickly when you ask her about it.'

'You do surprise me.'

'Do you feel up to coming down to the mill later today? Then I can show you what I get up to all day long.'

'I was always given to understand that most men don't want their wives to know what they get up to all day long,' said Irene.

'Well, I am not most men, and you are not most wives. This is your home now, as it's been my family's home for generations. My dearest wish is for you to come to know and love it as I do, and be happy here. I know it will take a bit of time to adjust, but you'll see . . . There's a good life to be had here.' He took her hand and gave it a squeeze, and Irene saw how badly he wanted her to see it, and how she had become a feeble thing, an invalid, who needed to 'feel up to' things.

'All right, then. I'll come to the mill with you after lunch.'

Irene hadn't known what to expect of the mill, but a place of such size and complexity certainly hadn't been it. With the rest of the village so sedate and bucolic, she'd half pictured most industry being done by hand. Instead, the place was powered by steam and electricity, and the din and smother of it all was shocking. She drew curious glances from the workers as Alistair led her from building to building, but when she met their eyes they jumped and went back to work with extra vigour, as though she were some sort of visiting dignitary. Which, perhaps, she was. She was introduced to the foreman, George Turner, and to his second in command, the paper-maker. Alistair talked her through the process as they went into the vast machine room – how scrap paper and old rags were cooked down, pounded into pulp and then pumped onto the Fourdrinier machine. This behemoth was near enough a hundred feet long, and six feet wide. The stuff – as the pulp was called – went onto an endless mesh that drew out the water before it rolled onto felts and proceeded, at a steady walking pace, through a succession of huge, steam-heated cylinders to dry it out. It ended up on a vast reel at the end, as finished paper. Irene nodded a lot, and tried not to sweat too visibly in the clinging heat.

Light poured into the machine room through tall metal-framed windows; the floor was awash, the air was a ruckus and the walls and every surface were spattered with paper pulp. Irene was happy to leave it for the smaller rooms where the paper was cut and stacked, and the bag room where women, whose scrutiny was more calculating, were sewing and gluing. Plain metal lanterns hung down from the ceilings, and there were large time clocks on all the walls, where the workers punched their cards in and out at the change in shift. These reminded Irene of the station clock at King's Cross, and one of the worst days of her life, just a few months before. She struggled to keep listening, and keep smiling. Alistair took her hand and squeezed it.

'Come along outside, darling,' he said. 'A breath of fresh air is what's needed.'

'Yes,' said Irene. 'But thank you very much for explaining it all to me.'

'What do you make of it all?' he asked, as they returned to the sunny yard and walked slowly towards the old farmhouse that served for office space.

'It's very impressive. Far ... bigger than I'd imagined.' Alistair looked dissatisfied with this answer, so Irene sought about for more to say. 'So much machinery and noise and ... and steam. It looks like hard work for the men. And it must be dangerous – I mean, it must all take careful management.'

'In fact, Mr Turner keeps it running almost as smoothly as the Fourdrinier itself, as a rule. He's jolly good; been here for years, like a lot of the more senior men. As for dangerous – not as much as you might think. There's only been one serious accident, but that was years ago, before I was born.'

'What happened?'

'It was just along at Rag Mill. The villagers used to roast apples and potatoes in the coals beneath the boiler. By pure ill-luck, some of them were fetching theirs out when the boiler exploded. It's a very rare occurrence, and the man in charge was fired at once for not having replaced a faulty valve.'

'And people were hurt?'

'Three were killed, in fact, including a young boy, only ten years old. He was blown clean across the river, by all accounts. A terrible tragedy. I can assure you that I take the safety of my workers very seriously.'

'How awful,' said Irene.

'Yes, but other than that – and one robbery, also years ago, when an office boy was hit over the head – we've never had any trouble. Now, what shall I show you next?'

'Oh, I don't know,' said Irene, struggling to muster the enthusiasm Alistair seemed to need. 'You choose.' He looked down at her for a moment – he was a good head taller – then smiled.

'I know,' he said. 'My office, and a cup of tea.'

Irene looked in on Verney and the Tanner boy when she got back to the farm, but there wasn't much to see in the old schoolroom except mess, and she felt awkward, as if checking up on them, so she left them to their work. The walls would be bright white; there'd be a translucent marble surround for the fire; curtains sent down from Liberty; a red lacquered table by Eileen Gray; a gold chair by Jean Dunand; the turquoise and grey silk Persian rug she'd inherited from her grandmother; her black Underwood typewriter and a stack of immaculate bond paper. Things the likes of which Manor Farm had never seen before. She would make herself a corner of her old life to retreat to, when the reality of the new one became unbearable. Maybe then she would be able to start writing again, and have that solace as well. Her newspaper column – just society gossip, really, even if she'd tried to make it more than that – had ceased, of course, with her departure from London, and the manner of it. The novel she'd begun – a romance – had stalled at four chapters. Whenever she tried to write now, she was faced with a blank page, a blank mind, and feelings of profound futility. She drifted through the rooms of the farmhouse, making Florence the maid and Clara Gosling, the housekeeper, dodge about her as they tried to work, always polite but radiating impatience. The main body of the house was long and narrow, with low ceilings and bulging plaster. The rooms followed each other along a corridor in steady succession. Sunlight flooded through the windows, onto the comfortable carpets and furniture, all of which were from some previous century. Elm floorboards creaked beneath her feet; the turgid air parted for her then swirled to stillness again.

Irene went into the study, a deeply masculine room of dark oak and leather books, and stood for a while in front of the portrait of Alistair's parents. Alistair looked a lot like his father – after whom he'd been named – and very little like his mother. Tabitha Hadleigh had been short and serious; her eyes fractionally too close together, her mouth fractionally too small. In their wedding portrait she was swathed in a very Victorian dress involving mounds of ruffles, lace and ribbons, yet still managed to look sombre. Irene wondered how she would have felt if she'd lived to see her son grow up, and seen how little of her there was in him. Alistair was no memorial to her whatsoever. In a photograph of him as a boy of about seven, his arms wrapped around a wire-haired terrier, the features he would have as a man were visible, if unformed, and the warm light in his eyes was already there. Alistair senior must have been chipper, she thought – or young Alistair must have had a kindly nanny; surely no child raised solely by Nancy could look so happy.

From a south-facing window she watched the wind ripple the long grass between the apple and pear trees in the orchard. Down the hill to the south-west sat the church of St Nicholas, its graveyard aglow with buttercups. Beyond that rose the smoke and steam of the mill, seething on the riverbank like some vast creature. She saw the girl groom, Pudding Cartwright, sweeping the yard with vigour. None of the girl's clothes seemed to fit her – she always looked as though she might be about to burst out of them. But then, that had been the overall impression she'd given Irene – of being about to burst out. With words or enthusiasm, or energy; or perhaps something else. There'd been something eager about her that was almost desperate. Now she was sweeping the yard as though, if she swept it well enough, good things would happen. Pausing to catch her breath, Pudding turned her face to the sky, to the sun and the breeze, and closed her eyes, and Irene wished she herself knew how to be outdoors. Here, in the countryside, surrounded by endless fields and grass and trees and water and mud and animals. It was all alien to her, but unless she could find a way to love it, Manor Farm would close its walls around her, forever, and she didn't think she would survive that. There was a knock at the front door, and the sound of Nancy greeting a female caller and taking her into the back sitting room, which was unofficially Nancy's, for tea. Irene was not asked to join them. She dithered a while in the corridor outside, wondering if she should knock and introduce herself, but then she heard Nancy say:

'The girl's quite useless. Honestly, I don't know what my nephew was thinking, in marrying her. He's always had a soft spot for birds with broken wings, but as far as I can tell, this one hasn't even *got* any wings.' So she left them to it.

Sometime later Florence came to find Irene, leaning on the door handle in the way that Nancy always berated her for, as though, at sixteen, her body was exhausted.

'Beg pardon, ma'am, only that Verney Blunt asks for 'ee, down in the schoolroom,' she said. 'Reckons he's found something.' Her accent made the last word sound like *ʒome-urr*, and *down* had two syllables: *dow-wun*.

'Thank you, Florence.' She felt the girl watching her as she left the room ahead of her. They all watched her, Irene realised. Perhaps they, too, were wondering how on earth she'd got there, and why. She tried not to be nervous of talking to the workmen by herself, and when that failed she tried not to let it show. 'What is it, Mr Blunt?' she said, as she came into the room, surprised by how frigid she sounded. The old furniture had been removed; the floor was covered in dust sheets; the ceiling gleamed whitely, wetly, and the frieze that had covered the fireplace was off. On the hearth, on another sheet, was a slew of soot, fragments of mortar, and the broken remains of birds' nests. Verney Blunt and the Tanner boy stood to either side of this pile, their faces tense and their bodies braced. They looked up as though startled.

'Excuse me, Mrs Hadleigh, but it's *that*,' said Verney. He pointed at the mess from the chimney as though a live snake lay there. Irene's pulse picked up.

'What?' She followed his pointing finger with her eyes.

'*That*, missus! The votive!' said the boy.

Puzzled, Irene stared down at the pile. Then she saw it. Blackened, dishevelled, incongruous amidst the dreck, was a doll. However it had once looked, it now looked hideous – whatever had been used to give it a face had shrivelled beyond recognition; its wired limbs were all twisted and broken. But it was still recognisably a doll; it had a bonnet and a rough dress of blue fabric, held together with big, neat stitches, and someone had also stitched a simple daisy motif on its front. Irene crouched down and reached for it.

'Don't *touch* it, yer daft cow!' said the Tanner boy, urgently, and Irene's cheeks blazed.

'Joseph, watch your lip!' said Verney. 'Sorry, Mrs Hadleigh, but he might be right about not touching it.'

'Why on earth not? It's just somebody's old doll,' said Irene.

'It may be, but when dolls is put up chimneys ... well, round here, that can be witchery, ma'am,' said Verney.

'Witchery? You're not serious?'

'I'm proper serious, ma'am.' Man and boy went back to staring at the doll, as though daring it to move or hex them in some way. Irene decided that they were pulling her leg. Mocking her. That this would become a funny story, told in the pub at her expense. She swallowed.

'Well, I don't believe in witchcraft, so I suppose I'm safe.' She reached for the doll and picked it up, ignoring a frustrated hiss from the boy.

'That's gone and done it,' he muttered, darkly.

'It's filthy, Mrs Hadleigh. You'll spoil yer nice things,' Verney grumbled.

Irene turned the doll over gently in her hands, feeling bits of twig and soot come away onto her fingers. It was only about eight inches tall, and its little head, which once might have been canvas wrapped around some kind of fruit, had been painted with a rudimentary face – blobs for eyes and nose; a rough, uneven smile. Beneath its dress, its body felt like lumpy rags. It looked like a doll home-made for a child out of whatever could be found, and though Irene wanted to find it charming there was something about it that was not. Perhaps it was only the men, still watching her intently, waiting for whatever would happen next, but Irene began to feel uneasy. She stared into the doll's smudged face and noticed a slip in time – the moment stretching out too long, and the silence in the room ringing in her ears with a high bell tone. She felt something shift, though she couldn't tell if it was within her or without; she felt that she had passed a mark of some kind, and that things must change thereafter. Troubled, she curled her hands carefully, protectively, around the grotesque little doll.

3
Nature's Child

Sometimes, Clemmie's sisters turned on her. She had three: Mary and Josie, who were older, and Liz, who was younger by a year. They'd had a brother too: Walter. But he was five years dead and they rarely spoke of him – the gap at the table where he should have been was enough of a reminder of the hole he'd left in all of them. None of them needed reminding of the way he'd died. Blown to pieces; barely enough left to bury. His room stayed empty, when the girls could have spread out into it. Instead, they remained in their loft room, like pigeons, sharing two vast old beds with their monthly cycles perfectly synchronised and their moods like a single tide of ebb and flow. But sometimes the others reached a point of saturation with Clemmie being the most beautiful, the most strange and often forgiven, the most talked about. Even Josie, with whom Clemmie had always had a special connection. Past that point they couldn't stand it any longer – they lost their individuality, like water droplets merging, and became a single entity of sibling rivalry that turned hard eyes on its mute sister. How long this would take to pass varied a great deal.

When it happened on Friday morning Clemmie was wise to it at once: Liz's glower, putting a crease between her dark brows; the way Mary snatched the hairbrush away when Clemmie reached for it; the way Josie rolled her eyes and ignored her when she signed good morning. It hurt, every time, but Clemmie knew she had no choice but to weather it; no choice but to wait for it to break. At breakfast, Mary put salt in Clemmie's tea instead of sugar, and handed her the cup with a smirk. Liz and Josie refused to 'hear' any of her requests for things to be passed – the gestures she used that the whole family knew. Then Liz grabbed Clemmie's favourite black kitten from her lap and dropped it out of the kitchen window, leaving it squeaking in fright on the yard. At this, Clemmie slapped her palm on the table top in distress, which made their father look up sharply.

'Was there a beetle, Clem?' Mary asked, innocently.

'You wenches pack it in,' said William Matlock. He was grizzled, weatherworn, his skin like creased bronze leather around a salt and pepper thatch of beard. His wife, the girls' mother, Rose, drifted from stove to table, bringing fried eggs and bread soaked in dripping, and slices of ham and cheese. There was grease in the whiskers on William's chin. Once, he'd been hard on the outside and soft on the inside – Clemmie remembered his rough hands under her arms, lifting her onto his shoulders when she was very small. But since Walter's death he seemed to have gone hard all the way through, and his teenaged daughters seemed to plague him like gnats around his head.

The kitchen table was scrubbed, bleached by years of sun and wear; every wall and low beam of the room was hung with tools and pots and utensils, some related to cooking, some to farming – sieves, drenching funnels, coils of wire, scythe blades, shears, rasps and branding irons. Some things were so rusted and ancient they'd been forgotten about, and colonised by spiders. The door was so often left open in the warm weather that a robin had nested in the top of an old jar of nails, and the hens wandered in and out, hopeful of scraps. The room faced south-west – the whole farm faced south-west – and was still shaded. By noon, sunlight would burnish every surface. Clemmie's hands smelled of milk, muck and coal tar soap – all of the girls' hands did, after morning milking.

They cornered her as she hunted for eggs in the small barn, where the hens nested in the hay and fouled it up with feathers and droppings. Mary and Josie wrestled her down and held her, and she fought them pointlessly for a while, her face pounding with blood and injustice. She knew nothing truly bad would happen, but still felt traces of unease and remembered fear — the man at the edge of the woods on the way to Ford, a year ago, holding her wrists in one hand as he groped her with the other, saying, *You want it, don't you, girl? Tell me I'm wrong.* She wondered if her sisters realised that they reminded her of this, as they gritted their teeth with the effort, and let their fingers bruise her arms. She kicked for a while but they stayed out of range, and when she fell still, Liz, with her cute pug nose and bow lips, knelt beside her with an egg in her hand.

'If you don't want this in your hair, you've only to say,' she said. She'd have to wash it out in a bucket of water; go through the painful process of teasing the knots out of her wet hair all over again, fall far behind with her chores, risk the back of William's hand.

'I think she wants it,' said Mary.

'You've only to say, Clem, if you don't,' Josie urged her.

'Perhaps she's tired of being so pretty,' said Mary.

'Perhaps she's tired of being so strange.'

'Or perhaps she loves it. Perhaps she loves being nature's child.' This was a term their teacher had used, during the few brief years they'd gone to school in Biddestone, as she'd petted Clemmie's pale frizz of hair and not scolded her silence or lack of attention.

'If she's *nature's* child then she can't be our sister, can she?' said Liz.

The egg slapped into her scalp with a wet crunch. Clemmie screwed her eyes tight shut as the gluey liquid rolled down towards them. She was aware of making a sound in her throat, a strangled sound which, in anyone else's mouth, would have come out as words; as *get off me.*

'Oh dear, what a mess,' said Liz, finding a glob of chicken shit on a wisp of hay and adding it to the egg. This done, the three girls went still, and silent. For a while the only sound in the barn was of their rapid breathing, and, from high in the haystack, the fussing of a worried hen. Then they let her go and stood back as she struggled to her feet. The four of them glared at one another and Clemmie felt the shift, as they watched her shake and the mess drip down her forehead – the subtle shift from triumph and spite to sheepish defiance, and the inevitable onset of contrition. Josie broke first, as she always did. She held out her hand to Clemmie, rolling her eyes and blowing a lock of mouse-brown hair off her forehead.

'Well, come on. I'll help you wash it out.' And, as always, Clemmie's anger disappeared in an instant. Feelings were like that with her – they flashed and fired, and then were gone again. Traces of the hurt stayed in her memory, but she forgave without hesitation.

'Well, you do ask for it sometimes, Clem!' Mary called after her, still angry, but mostly with herself by then. Later on they would be kind to her, to make it up; Mary would plait her hair before bed so it wouldn't knot; Josie would whisper secrets to her in the darkness, and make her laugh; Liz would leave her alone.

One of Clemmie's first memories was of being held in her mother's lap in front of the inglenook at Weavern Farm, in the capering light of a fire, listening to her soft humming, and then her saying, close to Clemmie's ear so no one else could hear:

'You cried when you were a baby, you know, my Clem.' Rose had wrapped strong arms around her, squeezing her sleepy body. 'The day you slithered out you set up a wail they heard in the mill, above the paper machine. So I know you've a voice in there, whatever folk say. And you'll use it when you're good and ready.' Clemmie remembered wanting to answer her, and the utter relief of not having to. She guessed, looking back, that she'd been around three or four years old, and that her lack of speech was becoming impossible to ignore. She remembered trying to talk, and something happening to the words between her mind and her mouth – a disconnection that made her impatient, then frantic, then panicky, and got worse the harder she fought. And the more she tried, the bigger the gap between her mind and her mouth got. It cleaved her tongue to the back of her teeth, and froze her lips, so that she ended up lowing like a cow, or making some other sub-human sound that made her schoolmates laugh but filled Rose's face with fear. And so she stopped. She didn't take to her letters at school – her mind was too ready to wander, and the teacher didn't try very hard with her. However carefully she copied out the alphabet the letters were often back to front; when put together into words they shifted and changed their shapes, *p* becoming *q*, *d* becoming *b*; and they jumped around, refusing to stay in order. Clemmie was mystified by how easily her classmates came to recognise patterns in them, when she could see none. So they sent her home at twelve, saying she was simple-minded, and left her with nothing but gestures to tell the world what she thought. What she wanted; what she didn't want. Clemmie didn't mind it, though. There was precious little she wanted, and the world seemed precious unconcerned to know her thoughts. From the age of five, when she had stopped trying to talk, until now, rising eighteen, Clemmie hadn't been troubled by any of it. But she was troubled now.

Once her hair was clean, and she'd listened to Josie prattle on about Clarence Fripp, an apprentice to the stonemason who was courting her with a kind of bawdy sweetness – all winks and laughs and suggestive remarks with his mates around him; all shyness and posies when he came to walk with her to church on Sundays – Clemmie finished her work as quickly as she could. A bucket full of eggs boxed for market; a shift at pressing Monday's washing; the cheeses turned; the butter pats scoured and a portion of the twenty pounds of butter, summer-yellow instead of winter-pale, that they would churn each week done. A hapless old hen who'd stopped laying needed to be drawn, plucked and jointed for stewing, and wringing its neck was the only thing Clemmie wouldn't do. She'd done it once, years before, and felt such a barb of sorrow as the inconsequential life ended in her hands that she'd burst into tears, and refused to do it ever since. It had been before Walter died, so her father had chucked her chin wryly, and called her a mollycoddle, and Mary had elbowed her aside declaring that she wasn't scared.

The work was never done, of course; there was always more. Mending, scrubbing, sweeping, shovelling; putting away, getting out. Walking the cows from one pasture to another, through air ripe with their flatulence; watering the vegetables in the kitchen garden and hoeing out the weeds; kneading bread dough; skimming curds from whey and bagging up fresh cheese to drain. And since there was always *something* to be done, Clemmie slipped away. The farm work was a constant stream that had flowed without pause through every one of her days, and to wait for a break in it would be like waiting for the sun not to rise. Breaks had to be made, else it was a long wait for the Sunday school summer outing; the harvest home; the Slaughterford revel.

She got up before dawn and slipped away into the half-light, as she had often times before, when the course of the By Brook was shown by the white ghost of mist hovering over the water. She took the hump-backed bridge across the river to the south of the farm, and then the path up onto the ridge. From the top of the hill she could look down at Weavern Farm: the squat farmhouse three storeys high, its top floor nestling into the mansard roof. The yard was surrounded on three sides by stone barns and stables and skillings, and opened south onto pasture dotted with cow pats. Behind the house were the vegetable patch and privy, and then the land rose steeply up to Weavern Lane. Her sisters and her mother often complained about how cut off they were – how they only ever heard news from the villages second- or third-hand, at church or via their neighbours at Honeybrook Farm; or when William had been to the pub – and that was rare enough. But Clemmie loved it. She wasn't interested in what other people did, generally; she liked the fact that there were no passers-by at Weavern – few callers, few intruders.

She'd all but stepped on the boy, at the edge of the steep woods near the Friends' chapel, opposite the mill. She'd had her eyes on the sky; he'd been hunkered down behind a thicket of birch saplings, with a young rabbit – just a kit really – kicking in his hand. He'd had two more rabbits, tied by their feet to a length of twine, slung over his shoulder. An intake of breath and they'd both frozen, eyes locked. Clemmie had recognised him as a Tanner from his cornflower eyes and long face – his cheekbones making hard, slanting lines beneath his skin – and she'd got ready to run. They were thieves and thugs, the Tanners. Everybody knew. They were drunks and cheats, and murderers, and there were more of them, connected by blood ties as tangled as a bramble thicket, than anyone but the Tanners themselves really knew. The chapel wasn't far from Thatch Cottage, where twelve members of one branch of the family lived, so Clemmie guessed he'd come from there. One of his uncles had beaten his wife to death, two years before, for no other reason than drink. The beatings were commonplace, but that time he'd delivered one too many blows when he should have left off. Gin had dethroned his mind, he said in court, but it wasn't much of a defence and they'd hanged him for it, not that he'd seemed to mind, by all accounts. Another one – a woman – was hanged for killing her baby with a draught of opium. She'd mixed it herself, from the pale pink poppies that grew along the top and shivered in the morning breezes. She said she'd only meant to keep it sleeping while she got on with her work.

Clemmie had looked down at the little rabbit. Kicking away in terror, every bit of its strength in every futile movement, ears flat to its neck. One of the rabbits hanging over the boy's shoulder had had a bubble of blood gleaming at its mouth, and a deep wound around its neck, but the little one had only been caught by the foot, so the snare hadn't killed it. The boy's fist around its neck had been filthy and thin, all tendons and smears, and something about it brought on a deafening roar of feeling in Clemmie – as though it were *her* hand about to crush the quickness of life from the animal. She'd seen enough animals go to their deaths and felt nothing much about it as long as she hadn't done the killing, but suddenly she'd felt the rabbit's manic heartbeat beneath its fur, and its unthinking terror; the briefness of its life and needlessness of its death – the butcher certainly wouldn't pay the usual sixpence for such a small one. Nothing on it to eat. She'd felt her eyes fill up and her mouth gape in horror, and hadn't been able to run even though he was a Tanner and she should have got away. But the boy had frowned slightly, never breaking off his gaze, and when the long moment had passed he'd lowered the rabbit to the ground and let it go. It had darted off into the undergrowth, leaving a dark pearl of blood behind on a burdock leaf. Then the boy had stood up, and she'd seen from his height and the bony width of his shoulders that he wasn't really a boy, but almost a man.

'I'm Eli,' he'd said. And when, a moment later, she'd found her feet and hurried away, she'd felt her own name poised behind her teeth. *I'm Clemmie.* She'd turned to look back before the trees hid him and he'd been in just the same spot, still watching.

That had been a week ago, and she hadn't seen him since. But she'd been looking, and the more she didn't see him, the more important it became that she should. As yet, she had no idea why this should be, but she had never worried much about the whys in life. She could picture his hand around the rabbit kitten so clearly – a starving, damaged hand. In an abstract way, she wondered if her need to see him again would be explained in the doing so. She walked a long route on high ground, going wide of the river and the mill's long tail race, coming down past Spring Cottage and crossing the river north of Rag Mill. This was far smaller than Slaughterford Mill: three slope-roofed buildings with whitewashed walls, housing a big iron boiler to cook down old hessian rope, twine and grain sacks, and a small waterwheel to run the beaters that would pummel them for days, reducing them to the pulpy half-stuff that could then be turned into brown paper packaging. Clemmie liked to watch the spoked hammers turning in the tanks, and the beater man resting a cane on the drive shaft and putting it to his head, to feel from the vibrations when the half-stuff was ready.

From Rag Mill she went on to the big mill, and walked from building to building, always staying outside, always peeping from a place of shelter. Trying to find him. Her stomach dropped oddly when she saw a tall, thin figure at the bottom of the big winch, fastening a bale of old paper scraps to be hoisted up to the sorting floor. But when she blinked, and looked again, it wasn't him. She peered into the bag room, and the canteen, and the machine spares sheds, and even spent a while watching the privies. There was no way to see into the machine room or beating house without going inside, and getting sent out with a flea in her ear. Frustrated, she slunk around the back of the old farmhouse and hunkered down in a spot beneath a window where she could see the workers coming into the yard. She picked daisies and threaded them into a garland, as the day got older and brighter, and heard Alistair Hadleigh come into the office to have his morning meeting with the foreman. They spoke of things that didn't interest her, but when Alistair Hadleigh's voice began to sound anxious, she paid more attention.

'But what about Douglas and Sons? Have they still not placed their usual order?'

'Not yet, sir. I wrote to them again last week, but they've yet to reply.'

'It'll be a close-run thing.' Mr Hadleigh sighed. There was a long pause. 'I'll find a way, never worry.'

'I don't doubt it, sir. This mill has run without pause for centuries. Run on a while longer, it surely shall.'

'Well spoken. Let's hope you're right.'

After that, they spoke more of customers and orders, of the problem of dye leaching into the By Brook downstream, and the poor quality of the last lot of rags from Bristol, and Clemmie stopped listening. As the sun began to burn her scalp through her hair, she got up and went back the way she'd come, towards Rag Mill. On the hill behind it, the brewery breathed out its ripe, yeasty smell, and alongside it was a long open storage shed, jammed to the rafters with rag scraps tied into bales, ready for pulping. As Clemmie headed for the trees beyond it all, she saw him at last. Tall, raw, angry. He came striding out of the mill and lit a cigarette, then held it between his teeth as he hauled out a bale and wrestled it into a handcart.

Clemmie took a step forward, then stopped. Eli Tanner turned the handcart and wheeled it back into the mill, cursing through his teeth as it stuck in the hard ruts left after winter. He was lanky and angular; his nose was crooked, and looked like it had been broken more than once. She thought of the boy's father, called Isaac but known simply as Tanner – patriarch of the lot who lived at Thatch Cottage.

He was a brute of a man, everyone knew. You didn't cross him, and even then it didn't make you safe. People edged back from him like sheep from a dog they didn't know. He sometimes worked as a strapper on one or other of the farms; sometimes in the mill, doing unskilled work – sorting scrap paper or rags, scrubbing out the stuff tanks between runs, stoking the boilers. He worked wherever he could get work, and until he was dismissed for fighting, or stealing, or drinking. Once for passing out drunk and letting the steam generator go out – something that ought never happen. Mrs Hancock at Honeybrook Farm swore that the last time he'd gone to church the water in the font had boiled. They said his wife had given birth to twins over the winter and he'd drowned the littlest like a rat in a barrel, because they had too many mouths as it was. Only it couldn't be proven because no one had attended the birth, or seen both babies, so Clemmie had no idea how the story got about. When she'd asked her mother – raised eyebrows, the tilt of her head that signalled a query – Rose had pursed her lips and said, *There's no smoke without fire.* Clemmie couldn't imagine what it must have been like to live beneath the cosh of such a man. Her own father could change the mood at Weavern Farm with a mere look or a word, and he never did anything worse than put the back of his hand across their faces now and then.

When Eli came back for another rag bale, he saw her. Clemmie twisted on the spot, uncertain of herself. Uncertain of him. With a glance back over his shoulder, Eli came across to her. He opened his mouth to speak but then didn't, and scowled instead. He looked so angry, and she wondered why. She would have been afraid of that anger if it hadn't been for the rabbit, and the conflict she saw in his every move and gesture – the suspicion, the doubt; of her, of himself. She wondered if his anger were somehow a means to survive.

'Hello,' he said at last, looking down at his bare feet, then up at her through the roughly cut ends of his fringe. He stank of the soda solution the rags cooked in. She raised her fingers to say hello back, and thought she saw disappointment in his face. As though he'd half hoped the stories weren't true, and she wasn't mute. She smiled a quick apology and saw him blush, and then how angry that made him. 'You're Clemmie Matlock. From down Weavern,' he said, curtly, and she nodded. 'I seen you before. Bringing the milk. And out walking, in the woods and that. I like it out there too. I like being out on me own.' He stood askance, his weight in his toes, his arms loose at his sides. She got the feeling that if she made too sudden a move he might run. Or lash out. His hands were as restless as his gaze; always moving. In the pause where she should have spoken the boiler roared inside the mill, and steam plumed from the chimney, and the beaters thudded and rumbled. A blackbird in the trees behind them sang as loudly as it could; bees hummed in the ivy and the sun streamed down, gold and green. Clemmie wished she could say, *Why did you let that rabbit go for me?*

'Eli, where's that bale?' came a shout from inside. Eli flinched, then glowered again. Clemmie wanted to put her hand on his arm, to still him. As soon as the thought occurred to her, it took over – sending its roots down into her bones. More than *anything*, she wanted to touch him, and still him. He looked back at her and shrugged one shoulder, shifting his weight.

'I'd say you're the loveliest thing I ever saw, Clemmie Matlock,' he said, and even then he sounded angry. As though she'd taken the advantage, or insulted him. 'I've got to get back to it. Maybe I'll see you again though. Out walking.' He pinched a fleck of tobacco from his lip and flicked it away, and then his hand hesitated in the air between the two of them, not dropping back to his side, not reaching for her. The tips of his fingers were stained, the nails all broken away, and they shook slightly. Almost too slightly to see, but Clemmie saw. 'Maybe I'll walk along this way when shift's over,' he said awkwardly, his cheeks burning. 'Towards Ford; about sundown.' Before he turned to go, Clemmie smiled again.

❧　☙

Alistair Hadleigh came to find Pudding one morning a little later in the week, and she felt a familiar little flood of happiness at seeing him approach. He had a diffident way of walking that she loved – he never just came striding up, even though he owned the place, and was usually busy. Instead he joined his hands behind his back and moved with a measured step, looking around as though taking in some magnificent garden, not the muck heap or the pig skillings, or Jem Welch's baby leeks in their parade-day rows. She supposed it had to do with knowing that he owned it all, in fact – that whatever was happening, it would wait for him. Pudding's father always seemed to be in a hurry – except when he was with his patients. Dr Cartwright galloped between house calls, bag swinging; he galloped to his consulting room in Biddestone – pedalling frantically, puffing as he pushed his bike up Germain's Lane. Only once he was actually face to face with a patient was he calm and soothing – even if he hadn't quite caught his breath.

Pudding had been stropping the cob, Dundee: whacking a

folded cloth into his meaty parts, over and over, to promote circulation, muscle tone, and, as witnessed by the great clouds around them, beat some of the scurf out of his coat. It was probably unnecessary, given the amount of work the sturdy pony did, up and down the hills between Slaughterford and Chippenham, but it was what old Hilarius had taught Pudding to do, so it was what she did. She was pink, rather sweaty, and her nose was running, but there wasn't much she could do about that. Alistair smiled as he reached her. That was something else she liked about him. The sun was bright in his fair hair, and on the shoulders of his tweed jacket. He gave Dundee a hearty pat on his neck.

'Good morning, Pudding. Looks like you've your work cut out for you there,' he said.

'Rather. It's not very different to beating out a carpet, if truth be told,' she said.

'Indeed. Poor Dundee. A rather ignominious comparison.' Alistair rubbed the cob's neck for a while longer, and Pudding recognised his slight hesitation. Whenever he had something to say about Donny, he showed this gentle reluctance to do so.

'Donny was most upset, and very sorry about the roses, Mr Hadleigh. Really, he was,' Pudding rushed in, to help him.

'Of course he was. And, really, it's not important.' Alistair looked at her frankly. 'My wife doesn't seem to care for the gardens overly much. Chances are the bushes will have quite recovered by the time she goes out to see them. And Nancy only cuts them for my father's grave each week. She doesn't really like them for themselves, if that makes sense.' He sounded so sad that Pudding searched desperately for something cheering to say.

'Well, perhaps it's only roses Mrs Hadleigh doesn't care for? My aunt can't stand the things – they make her eyes stream. They were so bloody and swollen when I saw her last year, she looked diseased.' Pudding stopped, sensing she'd gone too far with this description.

'Yes? Poor woman,' Alistair murmured. 'Well, perhaps that's it. In any case, they'll all have gone over in another week to two, so Donny really needn't worry about... what happened, and neither should you.'

'Thank you, Mr Hadleigh. It's... jolly good of you to be so understanding.'

'As I've said, your brother will have work here as long as he wants it,' said Alistair, gently. 'I know something of what he went through, over there. In the war. I went through some of it myself... That he returned to you at all is miracle enough. One cannot expect... wholeness. One cannot expect there to be no changes in a man who has witnessed such things.'

'Thank goodness *you* came back whole, at least, Mr Hadleigh,' said Pudding, and then regretted it at once. Alistair's expression turned pained, and he didn't reply. 'I mean, where would Slaughterford have been if you hadn't? With the farm and the mill, and everything,' she carried on. 'That is to say—' But she couldn't think what to add, so she lapsed into a silence she wished she'd found sooner.

Dundee sighed the exaggerated sigh of a bored horse warming its rump in the morning sun. Sparrows hopped along the gutter of the cob house, chattering and scavenging for barley; the mills rumbled in the valley and something set the geese in the rickyard off into outraged honking.

'That'll be Keith with the letters,' said Pudding, pointlessly.

'I wondered if I might ask you a favour, Pudding,' said Alistair, at almost the same time. He looked sheepish, and Pudding blushed on his behalf, busying herself with the exact fold of her strop cloth to cover it.

'Of course, Mr Hadleigh. I'd be happy to help.'

'Irene – that is, Mrs Hadleigh – has found something rather

odd in the chimney of the old schoolroom. A doll, it appears to be. Which is odd, because there wasn't a little girl here for a hundred years until Aunt Nancy, and she's quite adamant that it isn't hers. Anyway. Verney Blunt and the Tanner lad think it might be some kind of votive.'

'A votive, I see,' said Pudding. 'What's a votive?'

'Well, something placed in the chimney as a kind of . . . offering, I suppose. A charm, or a spell.'

'Like the children's shoes you find in old thatch?'

'Exactly like that. Only the Tanner boy is saying she should take it to show his grandmother – apparently, she's some kind of expert on these things, and will be able to tell if it was left for good or evil, and can take steps against any . . . ill effects that may come from removing it.'

The glance Alistair gave her was steeped in embarrassment, and Pudding couldn't decide whether to pretend credence of such things when she had none, or to scoff when perhaps it would insult Mrs Hadleigh if she did.

'Well. I have heard that Ma Tanner's the person to see, about all kinds of things. You know that when people are ill and can't afford to call my father, they go to her instead – she mixes up all kind of things from herbs.' Pudding was careful not to betray her opinion of this in her tone, but her father had described the state of Teresa Hancock after she'd taken one of Ma Tanner's white bryony draughts to get rid of an unexpected baby. No more than fourteen, writhing like a snake on her sheets with her insides doing their very best to be on the outside. Her little boy, Micky, was now a sturdy toddler, spoiled rotten by everyone despite being born of shame and all that.

'Well, I'm quite sure it's all bunk. The witchery, I mean,' said Alistair.

'Oh, yes. Probably.'

'Only . . . my wife has rather taken to the idea. Not of it being witchcraft, per se, but of going to see Mrs Tanner and asking her. The boy – Joseph – has her quite convinced. Of course, she doesn't know . . .' He gave Pudding another careful glance. 'She doesn't really know about the Tanners. Their troublesome reputation. And I have rather been carping on at her to get out and meet some of the neighbours, you see. Nancy refuses point-blank to be involved in any way, which only seems to make Irene more determined . . . Well, I was wondering, Pudding, whether you'd mind awfully going down with her? To the Tanners, I mean? I'm sure it won't be a lengthy visit. Safety in numbers, you understand; and they do know your face, at least.'

'Of course I will! I'd be happy to,' said Pudding. Alistair looked relieved, and she swelled inside.

She would, of course, have agreed to whatever he'd asked, even if it had been to roll in a muddy puddle, or spend the rest of the day hopping on one foot, or change her name to . . . Well, in fact she couldn't really think of a worse name than Pudding, so changing it would have been a blessing. Her loyalty and obedience towards her employer were partly down to the way he was with Donny, and partly to do with the fact that he was constant – he'd been at Manor Farm since before she was born, like some benevolent overlord – which, of course, he was; at least to the men who worked in the mill. He was a steadying presence, and a reliable smile, and he was fairness and moderation when a lot of other people seemed to be shifting, and unsteady, and unpredictable. Even the people she loved best in the world.

'Thank you, Pudding. I'm most grateful,' he said, interrupting her thoughts. 'I'll be going into Chippenham this afternoon, to talk to the bank, so if you could have Dundee hitched up by two, I'd be much obliged.'

'Of course, Mr Hadleigh.'

'Then perhaps you and Mrs Hadleigh could go visiting, after lunch?' He turned to go. 'Ah, yes, Pudding, I meant to ask after your parents . . . Are they well?'

'Oh,' said Pudding. The words *perfectly well* died on her lips. She found it impossible to lie to Alistair Hadleigh, and most especially impossible when he would know the lie at once. At Easter, he'd greeted Louise Cartwright outside church, as he greeted everyone – holding out his hand, saying her name. Pudding's mother had backed away abruptly, shaking her head in panic, not recognising him, or the situation, or what was expected of her. She'd worn an expression of complete perplexity throughout the service, as though the vicar had delivered it in Latin, and hadn't sung any of the hymns. Everyone had seen; everyone knew. Things amiss. 'Muddling through,' she said instead, trying to sound easy. She couldn't bear the pity in Alistair's eyes – it seemed to melt all her strength away, and as though he realised it, he backed away at once.

'Splendid,' he said, nodding. 'Jolly good. Well, Pudding, back to work for both of us. And . . . should you need anything . . .'

'Thank you, Mr Hadleigh. In fact, I could rather do with a new head for the yard broom,' she said, knowing that this was not at all what he'd meant.

When Pudding was about five years old, back before the war, the Hadleighs had invited Biddestone Sunday School, which most of the Slaughterford children attended, to have its summer picnic in the great barn at Manor Farm. It had become clear that a spell of wet, dreary weather that had been slouching over Wiltshire for a fortnight wasn't going to shift. The children, young and old, had been generally downhearted to begin with, since the picnic usually involved a long ride in a horse-drawn bus, with wooden benches down the sides and a canvas roof, either to the station for a trip to the seaside, or to some high hill miles away, with a view they didn't know, to have their games and sandwiches in the waving grass of a meadow. Blind Man's Buff and Thread the Needle; I Sent a Letter to my Love and Twos and Threes. Now they just had a short walk up the road to a muddy farmyard they all knew anyway, where the geese hissed and ran at them, and the collie dogs nipped at their calves, trying to herd them. And it wasn't even lambing season.

The cowslip posies in their best straw hats got damp and bedraggled on the way. Admittedly, few of them had ever been inside the great barn, but the general consensus was that a barn was more or less a barn. But the Hadleighs, particularly Alistair, had done their best to make it magical. Bunting and paper lanterns, and the trestle tables used for the church fête covered with checked cloths, and cream from that morning's milking for the scones, and – a thrill beyond everyone's ken – ice cream from the farm's own kitchen, rich and flecked with strawberries. Disconsolate foot scuffing had turned to excited fidgeting. The great barn was ancient, from some earlier time when Slaughterford and its mills were granted to the monastery at Farleigh Hungerford by a king with the deeply un-kingly name of Stephen, and a tithe was collected there from every farm and mill. The roof soared, its hammer beams twisted with age; it had wood-mullioned windows eaten away by beetles, and crumbling stone walls that nevertheless gave the impression of being immortal, indestructible. There was at least a century's worth of farm junk built up at one end, which had been pushed back as far as possible and strewn with more bunting. Doves roosted in its dusty entanglements, cooing and flapping at the intrusion of twenty-three children, in various states of cleanliness, driven wild by more sugar than they usually had to eat in a month.

In spite of being the doctor's daughter, and therefore higher up than the farm and mill children, Pudding was always the butt of jokes because she was so round and so plain. She'd felt the disappointment of not getting out of Slaughterford particularly keenly, and consoled herself by touring the tables, licking every last smear of ice cream from the bowls and picking the last crumbs from the plates. She was well-liked, since she was cheerful and eager to please, and had no trouble making friends – even with the little Tanner girl, Zillah, who was so skinny that her arms at the shoulder weren't as thick as Pudding's wrists, and who had been known to kick and bite with very little provocation. One of the farm boys from Ford, Pete Dempsey, was chubby too, but instead of being Pudding's ally he was usually the first to start the teasing – perhaps to be sure none of it came his way.

When Miss Wharton announced Pig-in-the-Middle, and asked who would be the first pig, everyone laughed and pointed at Pudding. When Nancy Hadleigh called them to attention and demanded to know who had been into the back kitchen and taken half a loaf of bread from the crock, everyone laughed and pointed at Pudding, even though it was far more likely to be Zillah Tanner (and it was – the loaf dropped out from under her skirt as they trooped from the barn at the end of the afternoon). And when they began the treasure hunt and Pudding got stuck between the broken slats of an old manger, nobody helped her, but stood laughing instead as she struggled and bruised herself, and tears drenched her scarlet face. They stood and they laughed until Alistair Hadleigh appeared, forced the slats wider so Pudding could wriggle free, then picked her up and set her on her feet – not without effort – and brushed the dirt and chaff from her dress.

'There, now. All pretty again,' he said, even though there was snot running down her chin, and her hair had come out of its ribbons. 'Shame on you, children,' he said to the others, who shuffled crossly. 'You must learn to be kinder to one another – especially today, when you've all been having such a lovely time.'

Her classmates' eyes went wide as they absorbed this reprimand. Alistair Hadleigh was the most important man in the village. Alistair Hadleigh was clean and handsome and rich. Alistair Hadleigh employed, one way or another, near enough every one of their fathers. Alistair Hadleigh had picked Pudding up and tidied her dress and called her pretty, and she loved him without question from then on. The other children spent the rest of the day being as conspicuously nice to Pudding as they could, even though by then Mr Hadleigh was nowhere around. The spell didn't last, and they soon went back to laughing at her, but it didn't matter. Pudding's heart was his.

She was brought out of this reverie by going into the tack room and finding Hilarius inside, sitting on a stool by the stove in spite of the heat, with an open book in his hands. He never normally came to the tack room, since the work harnesses were all kept in the great barn, and she wondered if he'd run out of leather soap or clean cloths, or needed to borrow the hole punch. Then she saw that the book he'd been reading was her copy of *Murder Most Foul*, which she'd brought with her to read on her tea break. Pudding was ashamed to admit to herself, just then, that she hadn't supposed Hilarius knew how to read.

'Oh! Hello, Hilarius. You made me jump,' she said. The old man nodded and stood up. He frowned, but he didn't look annoyed – more puzzled by something, or troubled. 'Is everything all right?'

'Ar,' said Hilarius, distractedly. His accent was unique to him; an odd mixture of Wiltshire and something else – something foreign, left over from the land of his birth. Pudding had asked, once, where he was from, but he'd let his eyes rebuke her, and had changed the subject in a way that had made her feel very rude, so she hadn't asked again. He closed the book and turned it over in his hands, frowning down at it, his face as cracked as oak bark.

'What is it, Hilarius?'

''Ee shouldn't read such things,' he said, putting the book down on the stool behind him. It was an odd thing to do; Pudding had expected him to hand it back to her. He stood there, between her and the book, and folded his arms as if guarding her from it. 'Bad things'll come to bide in 'ee.'

'Oh, you mean it'll give me nightmares? Yes, my mum says the same thing whenever I read the dreadfuls. But don't worry, it doesn't seem to happen to me,' said Pudding, brightly, to reassure him. She smiled but old Hilarius kept his frown. He looked past her, down at the floor, and there was a long pause that Pudding wasn't sure she should break.

''Ee shouldn't read the likes o' it, girl,' said Hilarius, then nodded as though he'd said his piece, and went out. Feeling a bit guilty about it, even though there was no reason at all for him to be upset, Pudding tucked the book away out of sight, and tried to remember why she'd gone into the tack room in the first place.

❧ ☙

Irene had wrapped the fragile, dirty doll in an old scarf, and was being as careful as she could not to break it. Truthfully, her interest in it might well have waned as soon as it had sparked in spite of the vehemence with which Nancy had scoffed, and the look of genuine consternation on Joseph Tanner's face, if it hadn't been for her own odd intuition about it. The feeling wouldn't let her drop it – it nagged at the back of her mind like the tiny glimpse of a memory from earliest childhood; amorphous and tantalising. She couldn't put her finger on what it was, and didn't know what she wanted to know about the doll, only that she wanted to know *something*. 'Our Ma'll see it right,' Joseph Tanner told her, quietly, when Nancy was out of earshot. As if determined to offer her help he was sure she was going to need, despite the impropriety of it. It had felt like the kind of offer that would only be made once, and then never again. There was something compelling about that, and about Joseph Tanner, with his nervous energy and his dark, dirty hair.

Nancy gave one last opinion on the mission as Irene came downstairs after lunch, dressed for her outing in her least city-like clothes – a beige skirt and a long ecru jacket, and her sturdiest leather shoes. Nancy was wearing breeches and a linen shirt; buttoned in, creaseless. She swept her gaze over Irene's outfit before she spoke.

'I feel I ought to warn you, since my nephew is too soft to speak ill of anybody,' she said, 'the Tanners are a bad lot. Thieves and murderers, for the most part – including the women. You've managed to select the one set of people it most ill-behoves you to become acquainted with.' She raised her eyebrows in that way she had, and Irene tried to see the least bit of good humour in her face. Nancy with her straight jaw and her diamond-hard eyes.

'Well, I'm sure they won't murder me just for knocking at their door. And I do have an invitation,' she said, trying to sound unconcerned. Nancy replied with a quiet scoff.

'They just might, you know,' she said. Still no humour. Irene's resentment flared.

'Well, Pudding Cartwright will protect me. Or, if needs be, I can use her as a barricade,' she said, and regretted it at once. Nancy's gaze hardened even further.

'That girl works hard, tells the truth, and carries her entire family. You'd do well to emulate her, Irene, rather than mock her.' She turned on her heel and left the room before Irene could retract the remark. It was not the kind of thing she would ever say, normally. Heat bloomed across her face and neck, and as she stared at Nancy's retreating back she realised that she had no idea who she was any more. It was the loneliest feeling.

Pudding Cartwright talked a lot, as she stomped alongside Irene. *Stomped* was the best word Irene could find for the way the girl moved – it was a kind of economical, ground-covering, wide-set stride; entirely unfeminine, and not unlike the horses she so doted on. She wore long rubber boots caked in mud, and didn't bother to step around puddles or piles of manure in the lane, so that she frequently drew ahead and had to turn and wait as Irene caught up.

'Has Mr Hadleigh told you how the village got its name?' she asked, as Irene walked gingerly down the steepest section of lane from the farm. She wasn't used to the feel of dust and pebbles beneath her shoes; wasn't used to slopes that hadn't been fashioned into steps. The day was warm but overcast, the air humid and thick with smells – Irene couldn't remember London ever smelling so much, even when the tide was out. It smelled . . . alive, and not necessarily in a good way. It was like being breathed on by some huge animal.

'Something about Vikings, wasn't it?' she said, distractedly.

'That's right. Shall I tell you?' said Pudding, proceeding to do so without waiting for Irene to answer, and obviously enjoying the gorier bits of the battle story. Irene stopped listening. She was trying to think about Fin, trying to remember exact words he had said and the exact way he had said them, trying to see his face without Serena's appearing to obliterate him – her eyes with their slight slant, her teeth glittering, and hidden things flickering inside her like flames.

'And then the river ran red with the blood from so many horrendous wounds and dead men,' said Pudding, and Irene failed to think of an appropriate response. 'Of course,' the girl went on, 'some people also say that *sleight* means water meadow in some ancient language, and that's the origin of Slaughterford. But I like the river-of-blood story better, don't you? I do admire your hair, you know, Mrs Hadleigh. I tried mine cropped like that last year but it looked frightful. Everybody said so. But yours looks simply perfect.'

'Thank you,' said Irene.

'You know – it might be an idea to pop into Mrs Glover's here and get something to give the Tanners,' said Pudding, halting beside some steep steps that led up the bank to a crooked stone cottage.

'Get them something?' Irene echoed, confused. She looked at the cottage and saw the downstairs window thrown wide open, and a hand-painted sign propped outside, reading *Groceries*. This was what passed for shopping in Slaughterford. Pudding thumped up the steps and stuck her head through the window.

'Shop!' she called, loudly, then turned back to Irene again. 'Yes – doesn't matter what, really. They have little enough of most things. Some soap, perhaps?'

'Wouldn't that be a little tactless?'

'Would it? Oh, yes – I see what you mean. Not soap then. Some tea, and barley sugars for the littlest ones. Or biscuits? Mind you, Trish Tanner makes the best lardy cake you've ever tasted. She sells it at Biddestone fête sometimes; we might get a slice if we're lucky. Mrs Glover had some lovely boxes of

Huntley and Palmer's last week, though, with Jackie Coogan on the tin. Dad took us all to the cinema in Chippenham last month, to see *The Kid*. Have you seen it? I expect so – I expect you went to the pictures all the time in London, didn't you, Mrs Hadleigh? You must miss it terribly.'

'I do,' said Irene. It was finally something she could say with feeling.

'But you gave it all up for Mr Hadleigh,' said Pudding, with a kind of wistfulness. 'It's all terribly romantic. That he swept you off your feet like that.'

'Yes, I suppose so,' said Irene, sensing Pudding's disappointment when she didn't elaborate.

In fact, her courtship with Alistair had been far more a case of him picking her up and setting her back on her feet, rather than sweeping her off them. It had begun the first and only horrible time her parents had induced her to go out with them after it had all happened, after everybody knew. They decided to put on a front, to feign unconcern until unconcern could be achieved. Irene remembered the looks and the laughs, the muttered remarks, the invisible circle around their table that nobody was willing to cross. She remembered mottled colour on her mother's rigid cheeks, and the flush of alcohol across her father's; not enough air and time grinding to a halt, and then Alistair appearing, crossing the line and asking Irene to dance. The horror of it all had been so loud inside her head that she was up and in his arms before she knew what had happened, or whether she had spoken. His hold around her offered some protection but she'd still felt naked. Her steps had been stiff and clumsy.

'Just keep dancing, dear girl,' Alistair had said, as a ripple of laughter chased them across the floor. 'Forget them. People are quick to enjoy the misfortunes of others; it doesn't make them right.'

75

'Please,' she'd whispered back, wretchedly. 'Please, can't I just leave?'

'Yes. Perhaps you shouldn't have come out so soon, but you must finish this dance first. Don't let them beat you.' If it hadn't been for his hands, his arms, holding her, she'd have fled and caused another scene.

He walked them out after that, and came to call on her the next day. This had been back in March, and there'd been sunshine on the window with a promise of spring at last. It had made him seem bright as he'd crossed the room to her, like he'd brought the light with him, and Irene had turned her face to the glass because it was too much. She wanted Fin. She wanted to be somewhere else – anywhere else – with him. She wanted to understand. Those were the only things she wanted. Alistair had sat down across from her, with his trousers riding up over his ankles and his gloves in his hand, and she'd felt his optimism, his care and his regard, as he glowed there, in the corner of her eye. She wanted none of it – rejected it outright, and ignored him when he asked how she was. Surely he would see, when he looked again, how worthless she was. How lost. And then his pointless visit would come to a merciful end.

'I learnt a lot of things during the war, Irene,' he said, after a pause. 'Most of them of no use whatsoever. But there's one thing I can't unlearn, even if I wanted to, and it's that life is very short, and very precious, and if we can't find a way to be happy in the one brief span we're allowed, then there really isn't a lot of point to any of it.' He paused again and Irene finally turned to look at him. He smiled slightly, kindly, and she knew he lived in a different world to the one she did. 'So I've a proposition for you, and I don't want you to think about it too much. We get so tangled up in knots, we humans, trying to think everything through, trying to guess at outcomes we can't possibly know. So please just listen. I adore you. Marry me.'

Irene thought she'd heard him wrong, but then an odd noise burst out of her mouth, which might have been the mangled beginnings of a laugh – at him, at herself, at the mad words he'd just spoken. She stared at him for a while, from what felt like many miles away, and decided there and then not to inflict herself on this absurd, kindly lunatic, who clearly had no idea what he was saying. When she shook her head he smiled again, sadly, and looked down at his hands.

'No,' she said. It was all she could find to say. Alistair stood to leave.

'You need to get away from here. You need to start again. You need rest, and someone to care for you.'

'No, I don't.'

'Only until you're feeling better. Only until . . . the shock has passed. Because none of it matters, Irene. None of it really *matters* – don't you see? What people say, and what they think. I've seen it so many times . . . The absurdity of it all. Most people don't have the first idea how fragile it all is. How fragile *they* are. The only thing is to be kind, and to love, before it's all over. Marry me, and I'll show you.'

'No,' Irene murmured, exhausted by him, deadened to it all. 'I did love. I do love. But I don't love you.' She saw him wince a little, and swallow.

'I know you don't. But perhaps – for now at least – it might suffice that I love you. That I want to help you.'

'If you want to help me,' she said, turning her face away again, 'then leave me be.'

The Tanners lived in the only thatched cottage remaining in Slaughterford; the others had been stone-tiled as the straw had rotted off, or in some cases covered with tin. It was entirely unadorned; a rectangular box of a place, none too large. As close as it was to the mill, the rumble of machinery was constant. The thatch looked dark and mouldy, even now in summer; the cobbled path that ran around the base of the walls was furred with moss, and the yard was an obstacle course of junk – boxes and crates, broken wheels and tools, rolls of wire, piles of stone and tiles. Three small children were playing on a simple rope swing hanging from an elm tree behind the house, and as she and Pudding walked up to the front door Irene felt eyes following them. She looked around and saw a boy of about six, peering out at them from the makeshift den of a tea crate, his eyes glossy in the shadows. Irene repositioned the basket in which she carried the doll, and felt uneasy. She had no idea what she was going to say, and hoped that Pudding would fill in the gaps. It seemed entirely likely that she would.

'I've never been inside this house before. I think it might be the only one in the village I haven't been into, in fact, at one time or another,' said Pudding, excitedly, as though this was what passed for an adventure in Slaughterford.

'But I thought you knew them? And they knew you?' said Irene.

'Well, sort of.' Pudding led the way to the door and knocked without the least hesitation. Irene thought back over what Nancy had told her, and felt her unease grow. Pudding lowered her voice. 'Mostly from all the many stories one hears. Everyone knows everyone here, but the Tanners aren't the overly sociable sort. Most people steer well clear of them. They ought to know who I am, at least. Oh, hello,' she greeted the thin, grubby girl who opened the door. 'I'm Pudding Cartwright, the doctor's daughter, and I've brought Mrs Hadleigh here to see Ma. Joseph invited us, so hopefully she's expecting us. And we've brought you some biscuits.' Without a word, the thin girl, who was perhaps only thirteen or so, stepped back to admit them. Irene's heart began to pound.

Inside, the cottage seemed bigger than it looked from outside. It was split into two rooms, the first leading to the second; from the first, steep stairs led to the upper floor, and in the second a large iron range was running at full chat, so that the heat was suffocating. The girl led them through to this second room, where a smell unlike anything Irene had met before was rising with the steam from a huge crock pot on the stove. In one corner, an ancient man watched from a truckle bed, with a thin blanket pulled up around him. Irene risked only the briefest glance at him – a fleeting impression of sunken cheeks and eyes, wisps of grimy white beard, hands of a size and strength that even age couldn't wither, and the emanation of a powerful hostility, incongruous given his obvious frailty. At least eight other people were arranged around the room – three barefooted children sat on the floor in watchful silence; two older teenaged girls were at a butcher's block, skinning rabbits and adding the iron smell of blood to the air. An older woman was sitting near the bedridden grandfather, mending a shirt, and the person Irene took to be Ma Tanner was seated in regal solitude in a carver chair nearest to the stove, her skin waxy and flushed. Pudding and Irene approached uncertainly, and under the scrutiny of so many eyes, Pudding turned pink.

Little light penetrated, since the windows were hung with thick felt that was obviously awkward to tie back; and what light there was was greenish from the algae on the glass. It could have been any hour of the day in there, any season, and Irene wished more than anything to go back in time and undo the stupid decision to come. Even Pudding had gone quiet, and was looking around the room with a slightly frantic smile, her hands continually fussing and smoothing her clothes. Irene took a deep breath and stepped in front of her chaperone. She hated her own fear of people, and where it had led her; it was running though her every fibre just then, but she rejected it.

'I'm Irene Dal— Hadleigh,' she said, stumbling slightly over her maiden name, Dalby. She carried on quickly, but the old woman in her carver chair noticed the mistake. 'How do you do?'

'Well enough,' said Ma Tanner, in a voice far more melodious than Irene had been expecting, and not in the least bit eldritch.

'I've come to show you a thing that was found in one of the chimneys at the farm. Your boy Joseph thought it might be significant.'

'Yes, he said you'd be along. New bride, aren't you? Not yet truly wed, are you? Not wed with your heart,' said Ma, peering up at Irene in a relentless way that wasn't unkind. Irene stared back at her, at a loss. Behind her, she felt Pudding shift her weight, and could practically feel the girl's curiosity burning through the back of her jacket. The old woman grunted, and smiled. 'Not like the doctor's lass, there.'

'Who, me?' said Pudding, in an overeager way. Ma Tanner's smile got wider.

'Perhaps you'd like to see what was found?' said Irene, hearing how cold she sounded.

'Yes, your ladyship,' said Ma Tanner, with a chuckle. One of the teenaged girls with the bloody hands scowled at Irene, but the old woman shifted up straighter in her chair, her hands gripping the arms in obvious interest. Her outfit was an amalgamation of garments from several prior generations, patched in and repaired; layers of rough cotton, lace and linen beneath a green woollen shawl. How she hadn't expired from the heat, Irene couldn't guess; a trickle of sweat was twisting down her own spine, and she longed to take her jacket off. But she stepped closer to the glowing range and took out the doll, unwrapping it carefully.

More bits of dirt and thread dropped off the doll as the old woman turned it over in her hands. She brushed them off her lap and peered at it, screwing up her eyes so that her face followed, crumpling like paper in a fire. For a while, the only sound in the room was the scrape and slither of the rabbit carcasses, and the rattle of air behind the old man's ribs. The attention of everybody in the room was fixed upon the old woman and the doll in the ratty blue dress. The fire in the range seethed; the pot bubbled; one of the children had a perpetual sniff. Pudding, who looked mesmerised, stepped forwards next to Irene to see better. Nobody spoke, and the moment dragged on. The old woman sucked her lower lip. The smell in the room made it hard to breathe; Irene took shallow sips of the air until she began to feel dizzy.

'Pinned up the chimney, or just tucked behind the baffle?' said the old woman eventually, so suddenly that they all jumped.

'I don't know. By the time I saw it, it was on the floor in a mess of soot,' said Irene.

'Hm. Probably just hidden up behind the baffle then.'

'Does it matter?'

'It might.' Ma Tanner went back to her silent contemplation, and the rest of them went back to waiting, and Irene's impatience to leave grew and grew. She fought to stifle it.

When the front door banged open again they all jerked – all except Ma Tanner. Three men came into the room, and Irene felt Pudding trying to be smaller. Two were just lads, perhaps not yet twenty, but the other, Irene guessed, was Tanner himself, the master of the house. He was tall, not thickset but broad at the shoulder, with a kind of lean, knotted strength to his frame. His face was a mass of suspicious frown lines, and there was something sour about the set of his mouth. His nose and cheeks were mapped with the broken red veins of a heavy drinker, and his hair had plenty of grey through the dark. The lads flanking him were thin and restless, their eyes watchful and angry; one had a split lip surrounded by livid purple bruising.

'Who's this, Trish?' Tanner demanded, nodding at Irene but addressing the middle-aged woman at her mending.

'The new Mrs Hadleigh, down from Manor Farm,' said the woman, in a voice entirely without tone.

'Is it now?' he said, his expression turning even uglier – suffusing with something like contempt. Irene felt the weight of it and refused to buckle. She lifted her chin, but couldn't quite bring herself to say 'How do you do' into the face of such open hostility. 'And what does the new Mrs Hadleigh want with us?'

'Peace, man, she's come to see me,' said Ma Tanner, and the man was stilled, though he didn't seem to like it. Then he caught sight of the doll the old woman was holding, and his face changed at once.

He crossed to the old woman and reached for it as though he would take it from her, then seemed to change his mind. He began to turn away but only made it halfway before something stopped him. He couldn't take his eyes from the dirty, broken doll. Ma Tanner squinted up at him, speculatively.

'Where in hell did that come from?' Tanner asked. His voice was a growl, but it shook.

'Up at the farm,' said Ma, always watching him, never blinking. 'Hidden away a good long while. In a chimney.' Pudding and Irene exchanged a glance of bafflement at the scene.

'*Garn!*' a voice said suddenly, and, startled, Irene turned to find the old man glaring at her from under his blanket. She blushed, embarrassed both by his sudden rousing and because she didn't understand him. He raised a thick, trembling finger and pointed it squarely at her. 'Garn, and get!' he said, and this time she understood. She was being told to leave. Pudding pulled at Irene's sleeve.

'Should we go?' said Irene, to Ma Tanner, but the old woman was still staring at her son, and he was still staring at the doll from the chimney. A moment later Tanner broke off his study to glare at them with such ferocity that they both took a step backwards.

'Peace, man,' said the old woman again, but she handed the doll back to Irene. 'You'd best be on your way with this, Mrs Hadleigh. Pudding. Take it and go.'

'But . . . what is it? What does it mean?' said Irene, bewildered.

'It's no votive, no spell, so don't worry about that. As to what it means . . .' She looked up at her son again, who was standing stock-still, staring into the shadows in the corner of the room as though stupefied. Ma settled back into her chair and said, without expression: 'It means change is coming.'

4

Touched

Alistair's best friend, Charles McKinley, lived with his sister Cora and their elderly father, Gerry, in Biddestone Hall, a sprawling Tudor house of gables and mullions and creaking doors. It sat back from the village green in Biddestone, behind gates and a high stone wall. The front door was lit by a pair of torches as Alistair and Irene climbed down from the Stanhope, and two of the McKinley footmen appeared to take the horse and usher them inside. It felt odd to be in evening dress. Irene's shoes pinched across her toes in that way she remembered so well. She hadn't worn her fox stole since London; hadn't worn her debutante diamonds since London. Since her wedding day, in fact, when she'd presented herself to Alistair with the numb, guilty sense that she'd sold him something broken; something faulty, that wouldn't work. The trouble was, she knew that Alistair had known it already. And he'd wanted her anyway.

'Don't be nervous, Irene,' he told her softly, as the door of Biddestone Hall swung open. He kissed the back of her hand. 'They're jolly nice, and they're going to love you.' An immaculate butler admitted them, but a woman of perhaps thirty appeared behind him at once, giving the immediate impression of huge eyes and a huge smile, with perhaps slightly too much tooth and gum. Her chestnut hair was close-cropped, with a wave; she had a long neck and long arms, and the overall effect was instantly appealing.

'There you are, Alistair!' She gave him a hug on the doorstep.

'How are you, Cora? You look ravishing,' said Alistair.

'Oh, you know – simply *melting* in the heat. Thank heavens for the pool. And you must be Irene.' Her handshake was hearty. 'I just *know* we're going to be the best of friends,' she said, with such bulletproof conviction that Irene immediately wondered who she meant to convince. Cora was a war widow, Alistair had told her; she'd married a childhood sweetheart called Bertram, only for him to be shot dead on more or less the same day he'd arrived in Belgium. Since then, she hadn't found anybody eligible to marry amongst the ranks that stumbled back from the war. But within half an hour of seeing how she beamed at Alistair, and glowed whenever he looked at her, and laughed his way, Irene had an idea about where Cora might have put her stock.

The inside of Biddestone Hall was as imposing as the outside – all Turkmen carpets, gleaming silver, mirrors and liveried servants. Gerry, into his eighties, was a quiet, dignified sort of man, clearly quite deaf, and Charles was as vivacious as his sister; a handsome man, if running a little to fat. They ate an enormous dinner, served at one end of a vastly long dining room table.

'The next time you come we'll invite more people,' said Cora, leaning towards Irene. 'But this time, we wanted you all to ourselves, didn't we, Charlie?' Irene smiled, but couldn't think of a reply. She wondered whether Alistair had told them she was shy, or unwell, or otherwise feeble, and felt small. She dropped her eyes to her salmon mousse and kept them there for a while. But Cora was undeterred. 'Tell me everything about London – I do so miss it, between seasons! Not that it isn't divine down here in Wiltshire, and nobody in their right mind would want to be in town in this weather. But one does feel so out of it, after a while. Have you met the St Iveses yet? Johnny and Maria? Alistair! What *have* you been doing, closeting her away like this? Their house near Malmesbury is *the* place to be when it's this hot. We're going for a Friday to Monday next week.'

'Cora, take a breath, old thing, and let Irene fit a word in,' said Charles, laughing.

'Oh – am I talking too much? I do do that, it's true,' said Cora, not in the least abashed.

Irene was perfectly happy to let them talk and, like Gerry, contribute little. There was little she could contribute, since they'd clearly been primed not to question her about her London life, or her swift departure from it, and she didn't know any of the people or places they wanted to talk about. Gerry met her eye over dessert and gave her a benign, tolerant smile, as Cora dissolved into laughter at the shared memory of a Christmas party when they'd all been in their teens, and Charles had drunk too much rum punch, and they had to hide him behind the curtains until he was less of a giveaway. After the meal the men went off together to smoke and play poker.

'Not that it's worth it, with Alistair. I can never get your husband to bet more than a shilling, Irene,' said Charles.

'He's exaggerating,' said Alistair. 'Will you be all right?' he said to her, quietly. Irene had little choice but to nod.

'Of course she will,' said Cora, taking Irene's arm and giving Alistair a knowing look. When the men had gone she toned it down a little, draped herself languidly over a sofa and lit a cigarette. 'Good,' she said. 'Now we can get to know each other properly.'

'Yes,' said Irene, more stiffly than she'd intended. Cora took a deep breath of smoke and blew it out through painted lips.

'So tell me, how are you getting along with Aunt Nancy?' There was a definite glint in her eye, but Irene couldn't tell, yet, if it were directed at Nancy or at herself.

'Nancy is . . .' she began, thinking carefully. 'I don't think Nancy has warmed to me terribly much, yet.'

Cora tipped back her head and laughed delightedly.

'I should think that's the understatement of the century!' she said. 'Gosh, I do feel for you, really. I'm sure Alistair would have been married five times over by now if it wasn't for Aunt Nancy. I know of at least one girl she chased off.'

'She's like a mother to him, I suppose. And rather picky.'

'She's a demon! And don't pretend otherwise,' said Cora, frowning at Irene's reticence. 'Why else would it take a sweetie like Alistair so long to find a wife? We were all *terrified* of Nancy as children – I still am a bit, I don't mind admitting. And as for her being like his mother,' she tipped her head to one side, and cocked an eyebrow, 'you don't know how right you are.'

'How do you mean?'

'Well.' Cora shook her head and reached for her brandy. 'Far be it from me to spread scurrilous rumours. But perhaps I will, just this once.' She chuckled. 'You know Alistair's father was Nancy's twin brother? They were inseparable as children, by all accounts – nothing unusual there. But I've heard it remarked upon that perhaps Nancy remained a trifle *too* devoted to her brother, as they got older. She only let him get married because it was that or lose the estate, since he'd all but gambled the whole lot away, and Tabitha Hadleigh brought her whopping inheritance with her from America – her parents owned half the goldmines in California. And when Tabitha died Nancy came back in a flash, and devoted her whole life to taking care of her brother and her new nephew. Almost more like a wife than a sister.'

'You can't mean to say . . .' Irene trailed off, aghast. Cora waved a hand through the cloud of smoke around her head.

'Oh, nothing *biblical*, I'm sure. But more than one new

acquaintance mistook them for husband and wife until it was pointed out that they were brother and sister. And since old Alistair died, your Alistair has been the sole focus of all of her energies.' Irene didn't miss the slightly strained way in which Cora said 'your Alistair'. 'So I'm not at all surprised that she hasn't taken to you.' Irene wondered how much of what had gone on in London the McKinleys knew, and whether Cora knew that her disgrace formed part of Nancy's distaste for her.

'I don't think she ever will,' she said, heavily.

'No,' said Cora, not without sympathy. 'I fear you've your work cut out for you there.' She swilled her brandy around in its huge glass. 'But if any man were worth putting up with her for, it's Alistair, isn't it?' She leapt up before Irene could reply. 'Come on. Why should the boys have all the fun? Do you fancy a swim?'

'I . . . I haven't a costume.'

'Me neither. Don't worry, it's dark as pitch out there. Come on, it'll be a hoot!'

In the end, Cora swam and Irene perched on the side of a steamer chair, smoking, watching moths batter themselves against the lamps and the way the profusion of stars turned the night sky mauve. The air filled with the smell of swimming pool water on still-warm stone. It was a dream of a night, too benign and beautiful for words, but Irene noticed the way it failed to move her, and felt a kind of creeping despair that she would never feel anything properly, ever again. She'd expected Alistair to be half-cut by the end of the evening, but he seemed quite sober. He put his jacket around her shoulders on the way home, and his arm around that, and held the reins easily in one hand.

'Was it all right?' he said. 'Did you like them?'

'I think it would be impossible for anybody not to like them,' she said, and he smiled.

'I'm glad.'

'How did you do at poker?'

'Oh, not very well. I never do, that's why I refuse to bet real money. I really only play to keep Charles company. It's one way in which I'd prefer not to follow in my father's footsteps,' he said, and Irene remembered Cora's remark about the estate being almost gambled away.

'He liked cards too much?'

'He did. Not that I ever saw it – one of Nancy's looks was enough to keep him in line when I was a boy, as I recall it. But I've heard she wasn't always able to rein him in when they were younger.' They drove on in silence for a while; the Stanhope's lamps only lit a few feet in front of them, and a barn owl swooped overhead on silent wings.

'I think Cora carries a torch for you,' said Irene, in the cover of darkness.

'Perhaps,' said Alistair, uncomfortably. 'She's a lovely girl. But my heart belonged to you the moment I saw you, Irene.' He pulled her closer, and kissed her hair.

When Alistair made love to her, Irene noticed all sorts of things. The well-worn softness of the sheets, and the slight itch in her eyes of dust from feather pillows that could have done with replacing. The odd creaks and knocks of the house as it cooled down with the night outside, the shadows cast by the sinuous beams that wriggled across the ceiling, and the rasp of Alistair's cheek against her own. The way his face seemed to blur as he was carried away by sensation, and emotion; the way her mind did the precise opposite – calling everything into sharp, unforgiving focus. She wished she could stop feeling as though she were betraying Fin, each and every time; and she wished she could stop hoping, in the exact same moment, that he would feel that betrayal wherever he was, and be wounded by it. In his bed, she supposed; Serena sleeping beside him. Or perhaps not sleeping at all. She knew deep down that it was only herself she was hurting with such thoughts, and she knew that, to the rest of the world, that would seem entirely just. She didn't mind Alistair's touch. He didn't repel her – he was wonderful in his own way. She liked the smell of him, and the width of his hips, and the rhythm of his movements. Her body ignored her, treacherously, and responded to him. She wondered if, were she whole, she wouldn't come to feel for him what she should, and fall in love. She wondered if she could ever do that again. If she had any love left.

Afterwards, Alistair got up for a glass of water, climbing back into his pyjama trousers. He was boyish, with his flushed cheeks and tousled hair. Made light by happiness. His limbs were long and smooth; neither muscled nor soft, but lean, economical.

'Is there anything you need, my darling?' he said, lying down beside her and propping himself up on one elbow, and she shook her head, though there were many things. She could hardly bear his efforts to please and the guilt they made her feel. 'Oh, I meant to say – I hear we're not about to be struck down by voodoo,' he said, lying back, letting his hand rest on her midriff. His smile put gentle creases around his eyes, and smoothed out his brow.

'What?'

'The doll you found. Pudding told me Ma Tanner confirmed it: no witchcraft.'

'Oh, yes, that's right. No witchcraft.'

'Well, that's a relief.' He smiled. 'I'm afraid I can't think of any other way to establish who it belonged to, or what it was doing there.'

'It really doesn't matter,' said Irene, truthfully. She'd been tempted to throw the doll away once they'd escaped from the Tanners, but that weird sense of significance had persisted, and in the end she'd rewrapped it and put it away in a drawer. The whole expedition annoyed her now – pointlessly putting herself in such an uncomfortable situation. Shouted at by a bedridden old man in front of a herd of unshod children. The thought made her hot with shame, and she had to keep re-minding herself that it hadn't been Nancy's idea, but her own. One more way in which she'd managed to do the wrong thing. 'I've forgotten all about it already,' she said.

'Well, anyway, I'm happy you went out and met some of the villagers. Even if it was old Mrs Tanner and her nefarious brood.'

'There did seem to be a lot of them.'

'Who did you meet?'

'Well, "meet" is perhaps an overstatement. Ma, of course, a lot of children and some older girls, and a woman called Trish, who looked past fifty. And an old grandpa. Then after a while Tanner himself came home, with two older lads – but he didn't make a point of introducing himself or them, so I didn't get their names.'

'Well, Trish is Tanner's wife. The older lads were probably their two eldest sons, Jacob and . . . Elias? Elijah? I forget.'

'It doesn't matter. I don't think I'd have gone at all if it hadn't been for your aunt Nancy, telling me so many times I shouldn't. And I don't think I'd have knocked at the door if it hadn't been for Pudding. She's quite fearless, isn't she?'

'About a lot of things, yes. I suppose it comes from so long being teased by her companions. I imagine she's had to develop a thick skin.'

'What on earth possessed her parents to call her Pudding? Surely she can't have been *born* fat?'

'Goodness, that's not her real name. Just a nickname from early days that has hung on ever since. Rather a pity for her. No, her real name is . . .' Alistair frowned. 'Do you know, I've quite forgotten it? It's something very grown-up – perhaps that's why it never took. Does it begin with an L? It's no good – you'll just have to ask her.'

'It doesn't matter.'

Irene realised then how many times she'd said *It doesn't matter* since moving out of London. She glanced at the clock as Alistair turned out the lamp; it was a little after midnight. The witching hour – she hadn't called it that since she'd been a child. As soon as she'd turned seventeen, most of her witching hours had been spent out, at the Embassy Club or some other night spot; with her parents and then with friends – groups made up of young marrieds, young hopefuls, her cousins and a schoolfriend or two. Crammed elbow to elbow at tables that encroached onto the dance floor in the middle of the huge room; snatching a course of dinner and washing it down with gin and tonic before getting up to foxtrot again, to visit another table, to watch and be watched while the band played up on their balcony, all but lost in the haze of smoke. Talking, shouting to be heard above the din; dancing and laughing with that mad energy, that frantic need for joy, that swept through England after the Great War. Unemployment wasn't an issue for the members and guests at the Embassy, but the shortage of young men was. It gave the single women an edge of desperation, of constant questing, and made the remaining young men feel hunted – which some of them relished. It made some young women, the shyer ones, too terrified to even talk to a man, since it would be immediately assumed that she wanted to marry him.

Irene had been one of this latter group. She was shy to begin with, anyway. Added to that her parents' continual mania that she be married to the first young man in whom she took an interest, and she determined to show an interest in none of them. Irene's mother, who approached fashion as a matter of life or death, decided that her lack of confidence stemmed from not being thin enough for the dresses coming across from Paris, and put her on so strict a diet that Irene passed her days in a daze of dizziness and detachment, weak with hunger. Her mother watched her so sternly whenever she did eat that Irene soon found she couldn't at all, in her presence. Many nights, she felt she didn't have the resources left to make any effort at overcoming her shyness. The very last softness disappeared from her body, leaving a boyish shape with knobbly knees and arms like pipe cleaners, and a bloodless face in which her mascaraed eyes bloomed like black flowers. She took up smoking; it helped her not to think about food. When she didn't have the energy to dance, she simply sat; when she didn't have the energy to talk, she stayed silent, watching the room with the dispassion that was all she could muster, hoping that nobody would attempt to engage her. And they did try – because she looked the part, and because of who her parents were, and because they mistook her fatigue and fear for a glamorous kind of *ennui*. So she sat there, night after night, draped in silk and strings of beads, smoking through a tortoiseshell cigarette holder and wondering how and when it would all end. But that was life, and that was what passed for enjoyment, and to be anywhere else – to be at home – felt like stepping off and leaving the whole world to turn without her. Like dying.

The first time Serena and Fin came to the Embassy was on Irene's invitation, in 1920, after they'd met at the costume party – Serena as a peacock; Serena just as vivid without her feathers. Irene had no idea what Serena saw in her as a friend. Whether it was her connections, or the way the Paris fashions hung perfectly on her starving body; or whether she, too, mistook exhaustion for a fashionable disdain that she envied. Or perhaps Irene was a blank canvas onto which Serena might paint colourful images of herself. She towed Fin around behind her, always holding his hand, taking him from group to group, table to table: a husband, a rarity, as a dress accessory. And then he touched Irene's arm for the first time, sitting side by side on an upholstered bench, late in the evening, well after midnight. The witching hour. Beached together to one side of the shifting sea of people – the maelstrom of the dance floor, the high-tide line of tables all strewn with the detritus of a five-course meal and too much to drink. Irene hadn't had a thought in her head that she knew about, other than that it was entirely comfortable to have him there, with the sleeve of his jacket just brushing her bare shoulder, giving her gooseflesh. Not really noticing him, as people generally seemed to not really notice him. She remembered a vague sense of there being safety in numbers; of it being unlikely that she would be approached while he was there. She noticed the discomfort of the sequins on her dress more, cutting into the skin on the undersides of her arms. Did he speak before he touched her? It seemed likely, and she just hadn't heard him. His touch was to get her attention.

She couldn't pick the single thread of it out of the tangle of what came next. It seemed, in her memory, that his touch had roused her from a nightmare. Pulled her out of a cage she'd built for her own protection. Four fingers on her forearm, and through the quagmire of champagne and stress she'd felt easier. A little unlocking inside. She couldn't even remember exactly what he said. Was it, *You mustn't mind Serena, when she says things like that?* Or was it, *Will you dance with me one evening, Irene?* Or was it, *I wish I knew what you thought about all this?* It didn't matter. Of course it didn't matter. She lay there next to Alistair as his breathing deepened towards sleep, and remembered that he'd been there that night too. Alistair Hadleigh, up from the country for a visit with some other old Etonians; old – almost forty – but still handsome. She remembered being introduced to him, then seeing him at a few parties – one might even have been at his apartment in Mayfair – and driving about in his brand new Alvis. A tall man with straight fair hair, kind eyes and a slightly weak chin. She'd danced with him, she thought, if not that first night Fin touched her then another, soon afterwards. She remembered thinking that his laughter lines made him, conversely, look a little sad. But Fin's touch on her arm. The feeling of being woken, and shown the way out, was far stronger than the unreal sense of danger that came with it. That was easy to ignore.

Eli Tanner wanted to touch her, of that much Clemmie was certain. She wondered why he didn't. It seemed entirely obvious to her that he loved her, and she thought it must be obvious to him that she loved him – that she was on fire for the love of him. The kind of love that came into being a full-formed thing, living and breathing, strong, and needing no more explanation than the sun or the wind. They met most days – walking through the water meadows beside the river up towards Ford, or down towards Box, as far as Widdenham Mill, which had made paper until ten years earlier but now sat still and empty. Water rushed busily over its weir, unaware of its redundancy. The summer grass was lush; the cows stood over their ankles in mud at the By Brook's edge, pulling up greedy mouthfuls of it, swatting endlessly at the flies on their flanks. Eli and Clemmie always stopped short of civilisation; they kept to the quiet curves of the bank, and the shade of trees, and the hidden paths tucked between the high, ancient banks at field edges, where the bluebells were dying back. Climbing through squeeze-belly stiles and gaps in the hedgerows, they made sure they weren't seen. This was agreed mutually, in silence. Clemmie didn't know if Eli's father's objection would be to her specifically, or only to Eli not working. Eli taking time for himself, out from under his father's heavy hand. She knew her own family's objections would be to Eli, and his Tanner blood. And perhaps to the very idea of her having a suitor – she didn't know, since it hadn't happened before, despite her pretty face. Because she didn't speak; because they thought her touched.

Touched. Simple. Nature's child. All it meant was that Clemmie had been set aside and talked over all her life, and was not expected to have thoughts or plans of her own. She was expected to always stay exactly where she was. Perhaps it was this that made her appreciate all the other living things around, which many people didn't. The birds and the vermin and the livestock – they were also speechless, also very much alive. Like them, she preferred to go her own way, unnoticed; like them, she was largely left to do so. Exempted from the expectations other people had for one another; occasionally approached by men and boys, but never considered for a wife. Never considered as a mother to somebody's children. So Clemmie hadn't considered herself that way, and had never needed to challenge this assumption that she was flawed.

The touching should have been simple; she couldn't understand Eli's hesitance. When he waited too long, Clemmie took his hands in hers, meshed their fingers together, pushed his palm against her stomach or her thigh or chest. If he wanted to touch, then she wanted him to. There was no explanation for this other than an innate trust, a feeling of complete safety and understanding. His whole body shook, and his breathing got quicker, and his eyes seemed to catch alight. The taste of him in her mouth was heaven. She didn't seem to have enough skin on her whole body to press against his. She wanted to say his name. She wanted it so much she even practised at home, when nobody was around – using the exercises Mr Hadleigh had taught her, breaking the word into pieces, letting her mouth get used to each one before moving on to the next. Like learning the steps of a dance. She practised behind the barn, or in the dairy when everyone else was outside – tucked away amidst the churns and scrubbing brushes, the pails and pans and the wooden box of salt. The stress of it was incredible. Just a few minutes left her panting, damp with sweat, heart pounding like she'd been running. The first sound was all right. She could do it, the E. But switching from E to L made everything lock, and her brain jar against the stone wall of her tongue. It had been so long since she'd tried to speak, without Mr Hadleigh to help trick herself, that she'd forgotten the horror of it, and after fifteen minutes or so she stopped, spent. One day, she tipped her head back against the dairy wall to rest and said the one part of his name that she could, drawing out the sound:

'Eeeeeee . . .' A soft footstep made her gasp, and there was Josie in the doorway, a bundle of clean smocks in her arms, wide-eyed at hearing her sister make a sound.

'Go on, Clem. Go on, you almost had it,' she said, but Clemmie shook her head, scattering tears of frustration from her eyelashes.

Once she had the knack of it, if she ever had the knack of it, she would whisper it into his ear, with the animal smell of his unwashed hair in her nostrils and the impossible softness of the skin at his hairline. *Eli*, she would whisper, and feel the shock of it run through his body like a delicious kick. The sun catching in his eyes brought out the blue; flashes of bright colour like the kingfishers that arrowed away along the water's surface. He was so gentle with her she couldn't believe anything bad about him, even though she still saw the anger in him sometimes, when they were first reunited. Anger that soon ran out of him and left him almost dazed, as though the relief of being free of it made him drunk. He shut his eyes and concentrated when she put her hands through his hair, on the back of his neck, on his face. Like he was memorising how it felt to be touched in that way – with kindness.

'We should marry, Clemmie,' he whispered, as she lay back, as she reached for him. A bed of grass and curtains of fox-gloves, cow parsley and figwort; the sound of the river nearby, and the rattle of a big green dragonfly darting back and forth, spying on them. 'We should marry first.' But he shut his eyes as he said it, rapturous, and his shoulders blocked out the sun above her, and she closed his mouth with kisses. If she could have spoken, she'd have said, *Why wait?*

On Sunday afternoon, after a deeply tedious morning service during which the vicar had droned on about constancy in the face of adversity, Dr Cartwright and Donny went fishing, and Pudding and her mother went along simply to sit on a blanket in the sunshine and eat the picnic they'd made – cheese and tomato sandwiches, small pork pies made by Ruth the day before – greasy in the heat but delicious – apples and short-bread fingers. They spread their blanket on the flat meadow upriver towards Ford, in the shade of a gnarled hawthorn, where the water was wide and deep, and moved with smooth insistence down towards the mills. The current tugged at bright green weeds along the riverbed. Pudding and Donny had swum in the same spot every summer as children; Pudding might have quite liked to swim that day, but having to appear in a bathing suit when anybody could walk past had robbed the fun from it. As he unpacked his rods and tackle, Dr Cartwright pointed.

'Look, there! Donny, look – the fattest trout I ever saw, just waiting for us. The cheeky blighter – I swear I saw him wink,' he said, just as he would have when his offspring were much younger.

'Did you, Dad?' said Donny, after a while. It took him a lot longer than it used to to get himself set up, but his first cast was smooth, effortless, and sent the fly arcing out across the water to land softly, silently on the surface. Donny's muscles remembered some of the things that his brain had forgotten, the doctor had explained to Pudding.

'That's my boy,' he said. 'All in the elbow, just like that.' And then the doctor had to look away, so that the brim of his boater hid his face. Donny could fish for hours without getting bored, squinting at the shining water from underneath his cap – for even longer now than before he went off to the war. And just like then, he didn't seem at all bothered about actually catching a fish.

Louise Cartwright sat with her legs tucked neatly to one side, and tapped Pudding's arm to correct her when she sat cross-legged.

'You're not a little girl any more, Puddy,' she said. 'Try a smidgen more form.'

'Sorry, Mum,' said Pudding, too pleased to be noticed and spoken to by her mother to mind being corrected. The four of them, just then, were perfect. No hint of anything amiss. If Pudding concentrated, she could pretend that nothing was. The sun flamed down at them, so that the grass seemed to steam; swallows swooped, a pair of swans sailed by, and a robin watched them from the hawthorn, waiting for crumbs. Pudding picked a blade of grass, clamped it between her thumbs and whistled with it. Donny drew in his line and cast again, and the doctor fiddled with a tiny carp he'd hooked, ready to throw it back. Pudding watched a two-spot ladybird climb the whole length of a red campion stalk and then stop at the top, and her mind drifted back to a day before the war – a day of similar chalk sky and languid heat – when they'd caught the early train from Chippenham down to the coast at Swanage. Pudding had only been six; already sturdy and round enough to have the nickname that would never leave her. It had been the year before the war broke out; Donny had been a strapping fifteen; all long limbs and burgeoning strength. Pudding remembered his skin in the sunshine, so different from her own – darker, and freckle-free; deepening in colour the second his shirt was off. He'd caught the eye of many a young lady on the beach that day, and along the quayside where they'd gone to tea; but he'd already fallen in love with Aoife Moore by then and had hardly noticed.

Pudding watched the easy way her brother cast his line, and remembered his hands around her ribs, sliding up to her armpits, tight with the effort of lifting her. But lift her he had, again and again, lobbing her as high as he could into the waves while she shrieked and laughed so hard she got water up her nose and they had to stop. She remembered him kneeling on the sand in front of her while she coughed and spluttered and her eyes streamed, grinning, saying, *You're not supposed to drink the sea, silly Pud; you're supposed to swim in it.* The sun gave his hair a deep mahogany glow; the beginnings of whiskers just shadowed his jaw. She stayed in the sea for hours – her puppy fat kept her warm. She heard her mother calling her in, but pretended not to. Her father wore the same straw boater to keep the sun off his pate; her mother wore her blue dress with the sailor collar, and never went further into the sea than her ankles. The day had seemed endless and joyful; like the summer, like life. Try as she might, Pudding could no longer feel quite the same way, in spite of the beauty of the day, and her mother's lucidity, and Donny's calm contentment, and a picnic. The careless feeling of being a child had slipped beyond her reach. She felt herself at a point of fine balance between happiness and fear.

'Can't we eat the picnic yet?' she said to her mother, to stave off sombre thoughts. She knew what the answer would be, and longed to hear the familiar words, spoken in her familiar voice.

'Certainly not! Good gracious, Pudding, it's not yet one.'

'Well now, I think you've a bite, my boy,' said the doctor. 'Donny? Did you hear me?'

For something to say, Pudding began to tell her mother about Irene Hadleigh, and their trip to see Ma Tanner at Thatch Cottage. Pudding had hoped that it might have marked the start of a thaw in Irene Hadleigh, of her coming out and talking to Pudding a bit more, and riding, but it didn't seem to be happening. Pudding had been alight with curiosity after Ma Tanner said that change was coming. She was desperate to know what Ma had meant, and how she could tell, and what kind of change. But when she'd said all that on the walk back up to the farm, Irene hadn't shown the least interest. Something else the old woman had said was plaguing Pudding. She'd said that Irene wasn't married *in her heart*. Pudding wondered if that could possibly be true. It seemed inconceivable to her that anyone – least of all his new wife – might not love Alistair, given the chance to. But then, Irene did seem a bit of a *cold fish*, as Ruth might have said. However many times she told herself that it was none of her business, Pudding couldn't seem to leave the thought alone. She'd been quite happy when Alistair got married – happy to think he'd found someone to cherish him as they ought. The thought that he'd married someone who didn't cherish him was just deeply *wrong*, in a way she couldn't quite put her finger on. She'd also hoped, in some abstract way, that Alistair being married, and bringing a new resident to Slaughterford, might jolt the world from the rails it seemed to be on, and alter its course, because she didn't like the way it had been going. The growing certainty that Donny was as recovered from the war as he was ever going to be. The inescapable fact that her mother only ever got a little worse, never a little better.

On Monday morning Pudding hacked out on Robin, the horse meant for Irene Hadleigh, and took a hilly route to work some weight off him. But as the lane climbed and Robin began to puff, she felt a bit guilty – he didn't have a lot of bone, and, really, she was probably too heavy for him. Her lower legs dangled down, clear of his flanks. She sat as well as she could, as though that might somehow mitigate her inexorable growth. She'd had to ask Nancy to buy some wider stirrup irons for the ladies' saddles, since by now her feet were far closer to man-sized. Not like Nancy's tiny, neat feet, which even looked delicate in boots. She knew for a fact that by the autumn, when the hunting season began, she wouldn't be able to fasten her one decent jacket over her chest any more.

When she got back to Manor Farm, Pudding saw Irene Hadleigh at one of the upstairs windows and gave her a wave, but Irene didn't seem to see her. For some reason that, and thoughts of her hunting jacket being too small, ruined Pudding's fragile good mood, and when the farrier's lad turned up, asking where she was since he'd been expecting Dundee and Baron down at the forge, it took her by surprise. She would never normally forget such a thing, and had to run to bring the horses in from the field and wash the mud off their feet. Baron was outraged and refused to be caught, swinging his hindquarters at Pudding and laying back his ears, until she almost wept with frustration, and Hilarius had to come across to help her.

'What ails thee, girl?' he asked her, squinting shrewdly at her red face and harried expression.

'Oh, nothing! Nothing,' she said.

'Can't lie to the beasts,' he replied, with a shrug. 'They smell the truth on you.' The old man caught Baron without mishap, murmuring incomprehensible things in the language he'd learnt as a child – he always did this so softly that Pudding never heard it clearly enough to have a guess at where he might have been born – then handed her the lead rope without another word.

'Wench must be in love,' said the farrier, aptly named Smith, as Pudding finally towed the horses into his rickety shed. He gave her a lopsided flash of his brown teeth with the perfectly round notch where the shaft of his pipe sat. He had hands thick with scars, and a limp where he'd been kicked once; he only ever called Pudding wench, but she didn't mind. She smiled vaguely, feeling too distracted to blush.

'Are you, then?' said Ben, Smith's apprentice, who was only a year older than Pudding and as awkward with his new body as she was. His face was a series of misshapen features, on the move, not yet settled where they finally would; he had spots on his cheeks and watched the world sullenly through a messy fringe of hair, but he had a way with horses that Smith called 'the touch' – any animal he handled immediately fell calm, and was at least grudgingly cooperative as its feet smoked beneath the hot metal shoes.

'Am I what?' said Pudding.

'In love?' The question had an accusatory note, as though love were an act of gross stupidity.

'Hardly,' said Pudding, airily, assuming she was being teased about Alistair Hadleigh. 'Who on earth is there to fall in love with around here?' At this Ben flushed crimson and glowered, and turned away to top the forge embers with a shovelful of slack. Smith observed the exchange and grinned again.

'Reckon the wench ain't the only one,' he said, but Pudding wasn't really listening.

At the end of the day she went to collect Donny to walk home, but he was nowhere in the grounds of Manor Farm, so she made her way down into the valley, and along to the mill. The sky had clotted by then, and the air felt thundery. Tiny black beetles appeared from nowhere to dot Pudding's clothes and skin, and the river's surface teemed with gnats. Donny loved the mill, and all its machinery and steam and smoke and racket. He'd understood the workings of it, apparently inherently, from the age of about ten, when to Pudding it had always been a mysterious, alarming catastrophe of a place. Not somewhere she belonged at all. She only liked the bag room, where the women stitched and glued with an air of quiet industry, and everything was spotless. On bad days she saw the mill as a cancerous blot on the beauty of the By Brook, and wished it didn't even exist. Such intrusive modern industry was wrong in such a timeless place, and it seemed to grow all the while. Like the massive brick building and towering chimney Alistair had built just two years earlier, to house the new steam boilers and generator; a 1920 date-stone set proudly into the wall. Pudding could hardly guess what the building and all the new equipment it housed must have cost, and it stuck out like a sore thumb. But then, she couldn't mind it too much, because it was Alistair's. And because the mill employed men from villages all around, when many of them would be impoverished otherwise, their families along with them. Without the mill, Slaughterford wouldn't be Slaughterford.

The beater man gave her a nod and a wave as she passed the doors to his domain. With the Fourdrinier machine and the beaters running full tilt, and the agitators in the stuff tanks turning, and the water turbines thundering, it was easier to gesture than to talk. Most of the workers were used to Donny and Pudding, and knew that their occasional presence was to be expected and tolerated. Still, Pudding knew that the men had work to do, and that it wasn't a safe place to be, and she made it her business to extract Donny as swiftly as she could when he paid one of his visits. The engineer pointed at the new generator house, and Pudding waved to thank him. She found Donny in front of the huge Belliss and Morcom steam engine, which – somehow – made electricity for the whole mill. It was still shiny in spite of all the soot and smoke in the air, rearing fourteen feet above the tan and white tiled floor. Donny was standing with his arms loose at his sides and the machine looming over him like some great black animal. To Pudding's eyes it was all pipes, belts and cylinders, and pressure dials with trembling red needles. She wondered if Donny still understood how it all worked, or if, like her, he simply saw metal and mess now. She didn't know which would be worse – she hated to think that he stood there in full knowledge of his new, flawed existence. There was sweat on his brow, but whether it was from the heat or some internal struggle, she couldn't tell.

Then, with a jolt, Pudding noticed Tanner. He was behind them, tucked into a corner near the coal heap, asleep with his cap pulled down low over his face and a brown bottle nestled tenderly in his arms like a baby. She caught her breath, filled with dread at the thought of him waking up and finding them there, as witnesses. His clothes were all sooty and dark; smuts had settled into the creases of his face so that he looked like an old, old man. He'd been let go more than once before, she knew, for just the same thing. Drinking on the job – or drinking and being incapable of the job. Or, once, drinking and throwing a junior beater into the mill race during a row over an imaginary insult that had nearly ended with the other man drowned. Somehow, Alistair always managed to give him another chance, but the last time, six months earlier, Pudding had overheard Nancy and Alistair arguing about it in the mill office when she'd passed on the way to find Donny.

'No more, Alistair. The man is a liability,' Nancy had said, at her most adamant, which was when she usually went unchallenged.

'Nobody else will employ him, Nancy.'

'And there's a good reason for that.'

'What of his family? All those youngsters?'

'Enough youngsters to send out to work, and cover his lost earnings. Of all the inbred peasants we're forced to employ, he really does take the biscuit – he will be the death of himself, or somebody else. Or of the mill.'

Alistair's subsequent silence had been telling, but perhaps he'd spoken to Tanner because the man's presence in Slaughterford had been relatively unobtrusive for many months, and Mrs Glover'd had it from Trish Tanner – his wife, who rarely spoke a word and trudged through life with the air of a woman who'd abandoned hopes and dreams at a young age – that he'd given up the drink altogether. He'd come back to work at the mill again, and now he was passed out drunk in the coal heap. One of his sons, one of those Pudding and Irene had seen at Thatch Cottage, was shovelling coal into the two boilers. He gave her a black glare when he saw her looking, and Pudding jerked her eyes away. Whether the man was found out or not, it wouldn't be her who reported on him; it could hardly be her business, when she wasn't even supposed to be there. She roused Donny with a hand on his arm.

'Time to go home now, Donny.' The steam hissed, the boilers roared. The gentle summer day outside was lost and forgotten in that building, with its alien machinery and high metal rafters, and suddenly Pudding longed to escape from it. She tugged at Donny's arm but, in spite of her size, there was no way she could move him until he wanted to move. He looked down at her in that underwater way of his.

'I used to know all this,' he said. 'Didn't I?' Pudding's heart sank.

'You did, Donny. Yes, you did.'

'It's like I still know it, Pud. Only . . . I can't remember what I know.'

'Never mind, Donny,' she said, trying not to show her dismay. 'You've other work now, haven't you? In the gardens.' He nodded, turning back to the steam engine. His brow creased with thought – with the effort of thought.

'Yes,' he said. 'But I used to know all this.' Pudding didn't know what to say. The Tanner boy watched them, suspiciously, resentfully; he was filthy from the coal and the sweat, and Pudding could see his exhaustion at that late hour of the day – a judder in his muscles with each dig of the shovel.

When she finally managed to coax Donny out, the evening had mellowed, and the western sky had a bruised, yellow look. Pudding crossed her fingers behind her back and hoped there wouldn't be a thunder storm. The noise terrified Donny, and left him wild-eyed and piteous, unable to escape from himself or the fear. Last time, Pudding and her father had played records for hours to drown out the weather, but Donny had flailed and crashed about, attempting to barricade himself into his room by heaving the furniture about, and when Pudding had looked into his eyes it had seemed as though her brother were no longer in there at all. She didn't like to remember it.

'I dreamt I was back in the mud in France, Pud,' Donny had said, quietly, the morning after. 'Stuck there near the lads on the washing lines, and the smell they had. And I couldn't get away; I couldn't.' They walked up the hill to Spring Cottage in silence, since every time Pudding thought of something to say, a glance at her brother's closed-off face silenced her. Buzzards wheeled above, with their high, lonely cries; rabbits scattered into the bank, and glossy black bumblebees milked the clover. Change was definitely coming, Pudding thought then. She could feel it gathering, drawing in its breath. She was just no longer at all sure that it would be for the better.

☙ ☞

However early Irene got up in the morning – and she had been getting up earlier each day, with the noise of the farm and the sun streaming through the crack in the curtains – Nancy was up and dressed before her. Irene wondered if she needed sleep at all, or merely carried on throughout the night, being impenetrable and efficient and entirely correct. Now, only a single place remained at the breakfast table, for Irene; Alistair's and Nancy's had been used already and cleared away. On the sideboard, the mushrooms and kidneys had gone cold, and the house already had the left-behind air of a place abandoned by busy people. Irene was completely unprepared for the letter that had been left for her, beside her place setting. She knew the handwriting at once, and her face flooded with blood, knowing that Alistair and Nancy must have seen it already, and known exactly who it was from. She stood staring at it for a long time, listening for anyone approaching, wondering whether to open it there, as she ached to do, or to take it somewhere private. Somewhere she could revel in it – her writing room, perhaps, where the paint wasn't quite dry. She could hide herself away and let his words – his voice – wrap themselves around her. When she picked it up, her hands juddered uncontrollably. There could be nothing in the letter that would change what had happened, nothing that could undo the fact that she was married to Alistair Hadleigh, and living in a different universe to the one she knew. Nothing that could undo the fact that Fin was still married to Serena. Yet seeing his handwriting felt like being given air. She held it to her face and inhaled, hoping for a trace of him.

Nancy came in so quietly it was as though she'd simply materialised. She was dressed for going into Chippenham, in a calf-length skirt and matching jacket; her heels had hardly made a sound on the rug. She stood with one hand on her hip and a revolted expression on her face, and Irene felt like a child caught picking her nose. Or worse. Nancy's judgement weighed more than a millstone, and Irene took a breath.

'May I not have a letter from a friend without being casti-gated? Must I *always* be castigated?' she said, not caring that her voice shook. Nancy cocked an eyebrow.

'We weren't born yesterday, you know, my dear. If it were simply a letter from a friend, believe me, nobody would castigate you. But then, from what I gather, you have few enough friends left. I've always taken it as a good measure of a person – how far back in time they can trace their friendships. It implies a constancy of character, wouldn't you say?'

'It must be nice to be unimpeachable in that regard, Nancy.'

'Yes. It is.' Nancy sounded amused at this, in her hard way, which only made Irene feel more wretched. More angry.

'Perhaps it's easier to achieve when one feels nothing whatsoever, for anyone. What gives you the right to . . . to treat me with such *disdain*, Nancy?' said Irene, forcing out the words in little more than a whisper, terrified, knowing that they could never be unsaid. Nancy pursed her lips for a minute and studied her, as if she were having the same inward battle. There was no trace of doubt in her voice, though, when she did speak.

'Because as far as I am concerned, Irene, you entirely

deserve it.' In the pause, the mantelpiece clock ticked, and a horse kicked at its stable door outside. 'My nephew is one of the best men you'll ever meet. One of the best men anyone will ever meet. Goodness only knows how he turned out as kind and loving as he did, having been raised by me, but he did. Goodness only knows how he came through the war without it ruining him, but he did. And he deserves a far better wife than a chit of a girl, starving herself for fashion, who's only married him to dodge a scandal of her own creation, and hasn't the slightest idea how to behave.'

Shocked into silence, Irene stood rooted to the spot with Fin's letter in her hands. Something flickered in Nancy's eyes, and it might have been the acknowledgement of how far she had gone – a seed which might have germinated into repentance, in another person. But Nancy was too stony ground for that.

'I see,' said Irene, too shaken to say anything else.

'We Hadleighs set the standard, as I told you before. This family's good name is sacrosanct, and I'm damned if I'll let you make a laughing stock of us. Had Alistair's mother been alive, you'd still be under house arrest in London, you know. Tabitha was very Catholic, and you'd have been quite beyond the pale. She might have been a papist delusionist, whom I never much liked, but we saw eye to eye on certain things. Why do you think Alistair married you in such a hurry?'

'Because he . . . loves me.'

'Perhaps he does, silly boy. But he also knew I'd have put a stop to it, if I could. I'd got him out of an inappropriate engagement before, and I'd have got him out of this one, too. I have always done what needs to be done around here, even when others may not see it, to begin with. It would certainly have been better for this family if I'd had a say in your . . . union. But, here you are.' She sighed slightly, through her nostrils. 'But this isn't a game, you know, Irene. You're married to Alistair now, so I suggest you get on with it.' Her eyes flicked to the letter. 'I simply won't have you embarrassing my nephew. Besides, only an idiot would cling to . . . flotsam, when a ruddy great lifeboat was sailing right by.'

The front door thumped shut behind Nancy, and Irene sank into a chair at the table. It took a long time for her pulse to slow. She wondered how on earth she was supposed to go on living under the same roof as Nancy; how she was supposed to cope with the woman reiterating every bad thing she thought about herself on a daily basis. Clenched in her hand, the envelope of Fin's letter had grown damp. Irene opened it, reeling with the mad hope that whatever he'd written, it could somehow save her. It could make her feel again the perfect rightness of being with him – a rightness that had flooded out and encompassed the whole world around her. *Dear Irene,* he'd written, *I hope this letter finds you well. We are both quite well, and will be leaving London soon to spend the remainder of the summer in France, with Serena's parents, so I thought I would take this opportunity to write. Serena had wanted to do so herself, but I persuaded her to let me. It just won't do, you see, Irene. Your continuing to write to me. It bothers Serena terribly, when everyone is trying so hard to carry on with life as it ought to be lived. It makes the servants smirk, and you know how she can't bear that. And you are a married woman yourself now, after all. I can't imagine your husband welcomes the knowledge that you and I continue to correspond, if, that is, he is aware of it. I hate to write a letter such as this, but thought it for the best, in the long run. Your letters pain me more than I can say, and must stop. I wish you all the best, Irene. Kind Regards, F. S. Campbell.*

Irene stayed at the table for a long time. At some point, she became aware that the remainders of breakfast had been cleared away, though she hadn't noticed it happening. The buttery sunshine outside seemed, like everything else, to deride her. For the first time in weeks, she wished her mother were there; but even though she had come to Irene and Alistair's wedding, her mother hadn't forgiven her yet either. More judgement. More castigation. She sat, without moving, and felt as though she were drowning – cold waters of despair closing over her head. It was the feeling of all her hopes dying; the snuffing of that last final spark inside, the one that had whispered, treacherously, that love would somehow save her. If it were a good thing, she couldn't believe it just then. Outside the window, Pudding Cartwright rode past on Robin, the horse that had been meant for Irene. The girl looked too big on him, and the horse looked put upon, and the absurdity of it was as bitter as everything else. Irene wondered where the lifeboat was, that Nancy had mentioned. She wondered if she were simply blind to it, or incapable of reaching it, because the drowning feeling continued, unabated, however long she sat there, and she didn't think she could be expected to carry on that way. She could not carry on that way.

Towards lunchtime, Alistair came to find her in her writing room. She had little memory of making her way there, but when he appeared at her shoulder and roused her she found herself in front of her typewriter, with a clean sheet of paper loaded and Fin's letter open on the desk beside her, for anyone to see. She didn't know if she'd planned to write anything, and when she realised that Alistair would see the letter her heart gave a jolt, but it was too late to hide it. She couldn't even look at him.

'Irene . . .' he said eventually, quietly.

'I'm sorry,' she said.

'Were you going to write back to him?' His voice was unsteady.

'No. I wasn't,' she said, truthfully.

'To whom, then?'

'No. No, I was just . . .' She looked up at him, numb, guilty. 'I honestly don't know what I was going to do.' For a while, neither of them spoke. The air in the old schoolroom was cool and clammy; in spite of all her expensive new furnishings, the prevailing smell was of mildewed books, old wood, forgotten things. The sounds beyond the walls – of animals, labour, life – seemed to come from very far away. Alistair pulled up a chair and perched beside her, taking her hand. His expression was heavy, weary and sad, and suddenly the thought of being the cause of that, the thought of him giving up on her, made Irene feel even more wretched.

'I know you're lonely, Irene. I know . . . I know you're unhappy here. I just wish . . .' He shook his head, opened her hand and dropped his forehead into her palm. 'I just wish I could help.'

'You are! You do . . . Alistair, You do. I just . . . I don't feel I belong here.'

'I know. And we won't always have to stay here in Wiltshire, we can go up to London. It just might be better not to until . . . the dust has settled.' He sighed. 'I thought I could make you happy. I thought coming here would make you happy.'

'No, Alistair – please don't say that. Please. I can't bear it. I'll get better, I know I will. It will get better. I'll . . . try harder.'

'No, you're right, I ought not to say that. And you mustn't *try*, Irene. Nobody can try to feel anything – we either feel, or we don't feel. We must both be patient, that's all.'

'Yes,' said Irene, trying, nevertheless, to feel hopeful. Alistair smiled.

'You could . . . invite a friend down to stay. Or your mother . . .' He trailed off, having never got along with Irene's parents. 'Or anybody, really. Anyone you like. If it'd make you feel more at home.'

'Perhaps I will,' said Irene, not wanting to say that she had written to all her friends, repeatedly, and to her cousins, and had asked them all to come to stay, or to have her stay with them. She'd had few replies, but those she'd had had been full of apologies that people were far too occupied with their summer plans already.

'Or Cora — why not invite her around, or take a trip into town together?'

'Town?'

'Yes, Chippenham. It's not exactly the West End, I'll grant you.' He smiled again. 'But it has coffee shops, a cinema, shops. People who might have travelled beyond the bounds of Wiltshire now and then... It would be a change of scene, I suppose.'

Alistair stood, and pulled Irene up by her hands. She looked up into his face, and her relief at seeing that the heaviness had vanished from it surprised her. Her shoulders dropped, and she felt a little of the tightness behind her ribs ease.

'Why do you love me, Alistair? Why did you want to marry me?' she asked.

'Why?' He shook his head. 'I really don't think love needs a *why*. Some things simply are. I saw you, and I watched you dance and smoke... always with that lost, embattled look in your eye, and I knew that you were kind, and bright, and different... and it simply happened. It came into being. And I am so, so happy that it did.' He touched her face, smoothing back a lock of her hair.

'But how can you be? How, Alistair?'

'Because I get to see you every day. And every time I see you, I feel better.'

'Better about what?'

'Better about everything.'

'Oh, Alistair . . . I just feel so . . .' Irene hung her head and felt her eyes fill with tears, stinging and hot. 'I just feel so . . . *stupid*. And so pointless.'

'Well, you're neither. Irene . . . I know that just now you don't believe you'll ever feel right again, but you will. I promise you. One day, you will have forgotten him – it might take time, and it won't happen all at once, but gradually your thoughts of him will lessen, and the pain will fade along with them. I can promise you this, because I have also been forced by . . . circumstances . . . to separate from somebody. It was a long time ago now, but I also felt, for a while, as though the world had come to an end. But it hadn't, Irene. It hadn't. And now I have you, and I'm so, so glad.' He held her for a long time while she cried like a child; she couldn't seem to stop, and she wondered how long the tears had been building up. Thinking back, she realised she hadn't cried once since the storm had broken over her. She'd been numb, she'd been angry; desperate and in terrible pain. But she hadn't cried once. Alistair simply stood, and rested his face against the top of her head, and waited it out with perfect patience.

❧ ☙

On a day so sweltering hot that the cows could hardly be bothered to graze, and the horseflies were legion, and biting, and Rose Matlock had turned puce halfway through mangling the sheets and gone for a lie down, Clemmie and her sisters swam. Just in front of the farm was a lazy curve in the By Brook; the water slowed as it swung round it, and had carved out a pool about five feet deep in places. It was bone-achingly cold, but, once the shock of it had passed, blissful. They filled the air with their voices as they plunged in – squeals and laughter and, from Mary, some salty curses. Clemmie took a deep breath and dived straight in, shivering at the cold touch of it on her scalp, which the sun had scorched through her pale hair. They swam in their underwear, which clung to their chests and hips; their hair smoothed to their necks, their skin gleamed. The vicar, walking past with his laced-up gaiters, alpine boots and thumb stick, and sweating profusely, gave them a peculiar, strained sort of smile, and muttered something awkward about naiads in a crystal stream before hurrying on his way. Liz stared after him a moment too long.

'You're not serious?' said Mary.

'What?' said Liz, colouring.

'Liz has a passion for the vicar!'

'I do not! You shut your mouth!' said Liz, lunging at Mary, who waded away, laughing.

'It'd be no fun at all, Lizzie!' she called over her shoulder. 'He'd have to say so many prayers before and after he laid you down, you'd nod off!'

'I wish Clarence would lay me down,' said Josie, wistfully. 'When he holds my hand, I swear, it sends me into shivers all over.'

'Don't let Father hear you talking like that or he'll tan the hide off you,' said Liz, obviously grateful for the change of focus.

'I'm not daft,' said Josie.

'Are you sure?' Mary grinned at her, and Josie put out her tongue. 'You wouldn't catch me letting on who's caught *my* eye. After what happened with Tom, I'm dead set on being quieter than Clemmie about it.'

The three girls turned idle gazes to their mute sister, and found her smiling. She couldn't help it. Eli Tanner was never far from her mind, and their talk had brought him right to the fore – all the shuddering delight of him moving inside her, and the taste of him, and the way he looked at her and melted into her touch. She was saturated with him, but only ever wanted more. There was no way she could not smile, even when she sensed a single thought coalesce in her three sisters, and felt a tingle of danger. Liz, Josie and Mary paddled closer to her, dripping water from their chins, watching her with their expressions changing from teasing to consideration, to incredulity.

'Clemmie Matlock!' Mary exclaimed. 'Have you got a sweetheart?'

'She can't have . . . she's touched,' said Liz, outraged, always jealous.

'Boys don't care what comes out of your mouth, only what goes in,' said Mary.

'Have you, Clem?' said Josie. 'Tell us!' They came closer, circling her; a moving wall of sunlit ripples on skin. 'Tell us who.'

'How's she going to do that, you dunce?' said Mary. 'For all those lessons the squire has given her, she's still not once uttered a proper word.'

'Well then, nod us yes, Clemmie – is there someone?'

She could have shaken her head. She thought about doing it, but for some reason she *wanted* to tell them, she wanted to share it – she wanted to shout it out. It felt too big to keep inside, and for once she wanted to be on equal footing with her sisters, not different to them, not behind in some way. Happiness made her giddy, and gave the illusion of safety when she wasn't safe, and neither was Eli. But there was no way her sisters could know or guess who it was, and no way they could make her tell them. The sun burned down on their skin, and the water soothed, and the world was as benign a place as she could imagine, just then. She nodded. Josie gasped, her fingers flying to her mouth, her eyes lighting up with excitement; Mary's face was incredulous, Liz's too.

'Oh, that's so wonderful, Clemmie! Is he handsome?' said Josie.

'Wonderful? Are you mad?' said Mary. 'Someone must have taken advantage of her! Who is it, Clem?'

'Leave her alone – why shouldn't she love someone?' said Josie.

'We'll have to tell Father,' said Liz. Her fingers were splayed in the water, near the surface, as though to keep her balanced. As though to catch Clemmie if she tried to escape. Panic flooded through Clemmie; she shook her head, her mouth dropping open in fear.

'Don't you dare!' Josie flared. 'Don't you dare tell, or I'll tell him you tried to coax the vicar out into the woods – I swear I will!'

'You wouldn't *dare*!' Liz gasped. Clemmie whined in her throat and grasped at Mary's hands, silently pleading: *Don't tell, don't tell!*

'Is he married, Clem?' Mary asked. Clemmie shook her head vehemently. 'And he's your own age, thereabouts, not some dirty old man?' She nodded just as hard. Mary thought for a moment longer. 'We won't tell on you, Clem. And if you say a word,' Mary rounded on Liz, 'we'll make you wish you'd never.'

However many times she told herself that it was fine, and that her sisters would keep their word, Clemmie felt uneasy. She wished she'd shaken her head, but it was too late. It was out there now, and couldn't be got back. That moment of wanting to share – to boast, really – and now her precious secret was only half a secret. She made her way through the woods opposite the mill, towards Thatch Cottage, stopping now and then to listen, to look behind her. She wasn't being followed, by her sisters or by anybody else, but the nagging feeling remained. A shadow of unease. The sun was sinking as the afternoon aged, but the heat was still stifling; the air between the trees was sluggish and overripe. There was sweat in her hair and between her thighs; she could smell the river water on her skin – dank now, vegetal. Clemmie climbed up onto the ridge, panting, sliding on loose soil; she waited a while then slithered back down again, watching for him, waiting for him. A bluish shade gathered beneath the trees. She sat down on a gravestone at the Friends' chapel, with a view of Thatch Cottage's roof, to empty the stones from her shoes. She was restless, impatient for him to appear. Then there was a loud crash from the cottage, and the sound of Tanner shouting, his voice so huge and full of rage. Clemmie's heart flung itself against her ribs.

She knew who was responsible for Eli's nose being so crooked, and for the split lip he'd had recently, when he'd stayed out too late with her and returned home after dark – they'd fallen asleep beneath the wizened roots of a fallen tree, tangled up together. She was suddenly afraid that he was in trouble because she'd revealed their love, before remembering that there was no way her sisters could have guessed who, or told anyone. Frightened for him, outraged for him, her blood raced in her veins. She dodged nearer, keeping close to the trunks of trees, the cover of bushes, then a pile of broken stones, and then the Tanners' privy, which stank and buzzed with flies. The cottage's windows were open, so the voices inside were clear.

'I'll have his bloody guts!' This was Tanner – bitter, hard, furred with drink.

'Christ, but he gave you enough chances, Dad!' A boy's uneven voice, newly broken; not Eli's. There was the sound of a blow and a woman's cry, and the scrape of shoved furniture.

'Don't hit the boy! It's none of his fault!' A woman – Eli's mother, Clemmie guessed. There was more shouting, more thumping. 'Stop it! Lay off!' the woman said again.

'You're all of you naught but wasted space! I should have drowned you each as she whelped you!'

'And what does that make you, Dad? Passed out drunk on the job again, where any bugger could see you?'

'You come here, you little shit! You're no son of mine.' The front door banged wide and a thin boy ran out, arms pumping, head down, dodging the detritus in the yard. Tanner followed but lost his footing and sprawled to the ground. He stayed down a while, ribs heaving like bellows, until his wife came to his side, looking too weary to be frightened. Tanner let her help him up then pushed her away, staggering back inside.

Clemmie still hadn't heard Eli speak, but if he wasn't inside and he hadn't come to find her then she didn't know where he could be. There was no more shouting for a while, no more crashing. Clemmie sidled closer, watching every footstep, so careful not to make a sound that her head began to thump. She crouched down below the back window. The smell of stewed carrots and bone stock drifted out to her; a baby cried for a moment and was quickly hushed; there was the sound of a plate being put down on a table.

'Here. Eat something,' said Mrs Tanner. For a long time after that, nobody said anything. There were at least ten or twelve Tanners living there; many of them little. Clemmie found their silence unnatural, ominous. She wished she had the courage to peer in at the window, just to see if Eli were there, but she didn't dare. 'What'll you do, then?' said Mrs Tanner, at last. Tanner grunted.

'I'll have his bloody guts.'

'Alistair Hadleigh's always been good to us,' she said, cautiously.

'He was itching for an excuse to get shot of me this time. Rich folk are all the same. They're all slippery bastards; holier than the likes of us, they think.'

'Perhaps he'd have you back again, given a bit of time . . .'

'I'll not work for that grinning idiot again.'

'But . . . the money, Isaac. We can't do without it.'

'I'll get money.' Another long silence followed his words.

'What do you mean?'

'He's got more than he needs, especially now, with all the wages due to be paid. Reckon it's time I paid him a visit.'

'You can't mean to rob him . . .' Her voice was hushed, frightened now. 'It'd be madness, right here in the village! We'll be hounded out, Isaac—'

'Shut your mouth, woman. I weren't planning on leaving a calling card. Me and Eli and John'll do it, just like always. Haven't been caught yet, have we? We'll take care of him, and your bloody money. Nobody calls me what he did today and gets away with it. Ain't that right, boy?'

'When do you want to do it, Dad?' Clemmie went cold. He sounded frightened, he didn't sound himself. But it was Eli who had spoken.

5

The Change

Pudding tried not to notice the way Irene Hadleigh's hands shook as she gripped the leather strap around Robin's neck. Her face was pale, her jaw clamped shut. Pudding wondered whether to say something specific about there being no need to worry, or whether that'd only make Irene feel worse. Like when people pointed out that she was blushing – as if she might be unaware of the hot blood thumping in her cheeks – which always made her blush harder.

'That's right. Now, he's not going to move until we're ready for him to, I promise; I've got hold of him.'

'You're sure?' said Irene.

'Perfectly sure. Now, left foot into the stirrup, right leg over the back and you're on. That's the way.' Pudding had never taught anyone to ride before. She felt proud, knowledgeable, and under a terrible weight of responsibility. Now that Irene had finally decided to try, Pudding supposed it would be her fault if she didn't take to it. 'Comfortable?' she asked, having adjusted the length of the stirrups.

'Not remotely,' said Irene. Pudding glanced up with a smile, thinking she was joking, but Irene's fixed expression made her change her mind.

'Oh. Well, er . . .' she said. 'It does take a little bit of getting used to.' Except that Pudding remembered first sitting on a horse – a pony, in fact – and her reaction had been instantaneous joy and excitement. She busied herself for a while, showing Irene how to hold the reins and where to have her legs and feet. 'But for now, just hold onto the neck strap if you feel wobbly, and we'll go for a bit of a walk. All right? Ready?' Irene took a short breath, re-clamped her lips, and nodded.

She sat stiffly, swaying awkwardly with every step Robin took, as Pudding led them across to the flattish paddock where she normally schooled the horses. She wasn't sure how to continue the lesson. It didn't seem fair to start drilling Irene about keeping her heels down or her thumbs to the top – *you're holding teacups, not pushing a pram* – as her own instructor had done – not when Irene seemed to be concentrating so hard on simply staying sat, and not giving in to panic. They made a few sedate loops of the paddock, until Pudding couldn't stand the silence any longer. 'What made you decide to give riding a go, Mrs Hadleigh?' she said, smiling up at her. Irene flicked her eyes at Pudding for the briefest second, as though keeping them fixed on the horizon were essential to success.

'Oh. It was high time, I suppose,' she said, tonelessly. 'Or rather, Nancy and my husband thought it was high time.'

'Well, you do have a super horse to learn on. I learnt on a pony so fat I could barely straddle him. We should count ourselves lucky we're allowed to ride astride at all, though. A lot of ladies Miss H's age still think it's obscene. And a lot of chaps.'

'In London, most ladies still take the side saddle.' Irene's tone left Pudding none the wiser as to whether she approved of that or not.

'Really? Well, astride is infinitely better, and easier.' Pudding wondered, once she'd said this, about her own authoritative tone. 'That is, I think it is,' she amended, but Irene didn't seem to have a strong opinion about it.

They went on in silence for a while. Irene was so quiet that Pudding glanced back now and then, half expecting her to have toppled off some way back and be sitting among the daisies. The saddle creaked; Robin chewed his bit thoughtfully; from further down the hill came a loud curse and the delighted squealing of a pig. Irene cleared her throat carefully.

'Have your family always lived in Slaughterford?' she asked.

'Oh yes. It's the best place, really.' Pudding thought about that for a moment. 'Well, I like it anyway. But I should like to see London, one day. I truly would.'

'You've never been? Why not?' Irene sounded surprised.

'Oh. Well. We just . . . live here.' Pudding's mother had always said they would take a trip up to London when Pudding was old enough to appreciate it. Pudding felt that that time had definitely come, but now, of course, her mother might not enjoy it as once she might. And Donny certainly wouldn't like all the noise and people.

'But . . . you must have been away before? Away from Slaughterford, I mean?' Irene sounded vaguely appalled.

'Oh, yes! Of course.' In fact she hadn't gone anywhere in ages – not since Donny had come home from the war, in fact. 'We used to go to the seaside all the time, when we were little. Three or four times, every summer. And I've an aunt in Porlock – we go to visit her quite often.'

'Oh,' said Irene, and Pudding guessed that it sounded very parochial indeed to her. She felt caught between defending her small corner of England and naming all the many places she would love to visit. 'Well, I've been planning to pay a call to your mother. I . . . ought to have done so sooner,' Irene added. 'So perhaps I could mention it to her – that a visit to London is a very good thing for a young person. If you'd like me to, that is? I'd be very subtle.'

'Well . . .' said Pudding, her heart sinking. Clearly, nobody had explained the nature of Louise Cartwright's illness to Irene. She hunted around for the right words to do it, but soon gave up. 'That's very kind of you, Mrs Hadleigh,' she mumbled instead, and to change the subject completely, pointed at one of the rounded hills on the horizon. 'That's Cold Tump. It's probably an old barrow – did you know that when a place is called "cold"-something around here, it means it's haunted? Or rather, that whoever named it thought it was haunted. Which usually means it was named by some Celt or Saxon settler who was superstitious about the prehistorical bits and bobs left behind – burial mounds and things. Old bones in old tombs. There's a Cold Harbour Farm on the way to Chippenham, and people still say it's haunted.' She went on to describe the spectral procession of dead warriors, all with spears, helmets and ghastly empty eye sockets, who'd been seen marching past the farm on frigid, moonlit nights. She kept on with the story, even though she wasn't sure if Irene Hadleigh were even listening, or wanted to know about it all, because when she stopped talking the silence seemed to rebuke her. It was something like guilt that made her rattle on – guilt to have said nothing about her mother's illness; nothing about how Donny's injury had made trips away even rarer; and guilt to have implied, even to herself, that she might wish for things to be otherwise.

Irene walked stiffly back towards the house after her lesson, feeling relieved it was over until she reminded herself that riding just once was not going to wash. She would have to do it again, and again, and try to master it and enjoy it. She fought against the sinking feeling that gave her, and paused in the yard to pull off her gloves, a finger at a time. There was movement from one of the farmhouse windows, and Irene hoped Nancy had been watching, and had seen her on the horse. Just then, the old groom, Hilarius, came out of the great barn, and since

Irene's first impulse was to turn away, go indoors and pretend not to have seen him, she made herself square up and introduce herself. She hoped that Nancy were *still* watching.

'Hello,' she said, holding out her hand for Hilarius to shake. 'I'm Irene Hadleigh.' The old man paused in his progress, and peered down at his filthy palm before apparently deciding not to take Irene's. She let her hand drop, feeling foolish, and hoped Nancy had stopped watching.

'Ar,' said Hilarius. Irene couldn't guess his age. He was bald on top, with straggles of grey hair around his collar; she couldn't tell the colour of his eyes – they were merely a glint through narrow gaps in his eyelids. She noticed that his eyelashes, though they were few, were still jet black.

'You ... look after the work horses, is that right?' she tried, floundering. Her mouth had gone dry and she didn't feel right. Something fluttery and strange was inside her head, making it hard to think, or focus her eyes. She blinked rapidly, and every time she did a shadow seemed to coalesce around the old man, receding when she tried to see clearly. The sun was high in the sky, and her own shadow was stunted, close to her feet. But the old man somehow seemed to cast a huge shadow. Far bigger than himself, and fathomless. He watched her with that distant glitter of his eyes, and Irene found herself backing away.

'Ar, that's right,' he said, but Irene hardly heard him.

'I'm sorry,' she murmured, powerfully unwilling to look him in the eye, or to be near him. The fluttering inside was getting worse, and she felt cold. He seemed to radiate cold. 'Won't you please excuse me,' she whispered.

Inside, Irene sat down on the horribly uncomfortable chair that lived in the hallway, and had been designed to be looked at but not sat in. She took a deep breath, and swallowed.

'Everything all right?' said Nancy, coolly, as she came along from her sitting room.

'Yes. Quite all right. Thank you.' Irene rose, smoothing her gloves between her fingers.

'Jolly good. Excuse me.' Nancy went past, and up the stairs.

'Is that my good lady wife?' Alistair called, from the kitchen.

'Alistair! You're home,' said Irene, relieved to find she wasn't alone with Nancy.

'A bit early for lunch, I know, but I couldn't wait to hear how you'd got on. Well?'

'Oh, I don't know – you'd have to ask Pudding. I didn't fall off, anyway.'

'Well, that's a start.' Alistair laughed. 'But how did you like it?'

'Well enough, I think . . . I wasn't sure what to expect. Pudding's talkative, isn't she?' she said, to head off any questions about when she would next ride.

'Oh, yes.'

'And rather ghoulish. She always seems to want to tell me some hideous story about a battle or a ghost or something.' At this, Alistair chuckled again.

'Yes, she always did like the more blood-curdling stories. I once caught her and a companion – little Maisie Cooper, I think it was – under a hedge, dissecting a rat. They'd each brought a paring knife from home to do the job. They can't have been more than eight or nine years old.'

'That's hideous!'

'Thoroughly. They told me it was *anatomy*, in fact, and insisted that the rat had been run over by a wagon full of beans, so it was quite humane.' He smiled at Irene's disgusted expression. She thought about Hilarius, and when she did the fluttering returned, albeit in a weaker way. She'd decided against saying anything when the words came anyway, unbidden.

'I just met Hilarius, the horse groom.'

'Oh yes? Solid as a rock, that old chap. People have never taken to him, in the village; they can be so spooked and peculiar at the idea of a foreigner, at times. But he's a good sort.'

'Yes, of course,' said Irene, not in the least bit surprised to hear that the man was not well liked.

She'd written to Cora McKinley, since Alistair had been so keen that she write to *somebody*, and Irene found herself wanting to try harder for him. Besides, doing all these things that scared her was proving a good way to distract her from Fin's last letter and what it had said. She very much still needed to be distracted from that. Her letter to Cora had been rather vague, suggesting that they might go into Chippenham or Bath together one day, and the morning after her riding lesson, Keith Glover brought Cora's reply. Her handwriting was a series of exuberant swoops in black ink. *We must! Or – even better – how do you fancy the coast? My cousin Amelia has a little villa – well, perhaps I'd better call it a hovel, to manage your expectations – in the hills near Lyme Regis. I'd been thinking about descending upon her, with it so terminally hot. You must come with me! There's simply nothing like sea bathing for whipping up the spirits. Write back immediately and say you'll come. Just us girls.* Alistair looked delighted when she showed him.

'Good old Cora,' he said. 'You'll have a lot of fun, I'm sure.'

'You think I ought to go?'

'Well, yes.' He looked surprised. 'If you'd like to, that is. I'd miss you, but if you promised to come back again before very long...' He smiled, pleased, and gave her a kiss. Irene attempted to stifle her reluctance to go. Cora had been easy enough company – garrulous enough to make up for Irene's lack of conversation. But she wasn't sure if she could pretend to be all right in front of Cousin Amelia; she wasn't sure how they would take her, how it would go. She imagined hearing whispered conversations, and stifled laughter behind her back. It caused her a flood of nerves, but she went to her writing room and took out a note card, and penned her acceptance of the invitation. Her mother had often instructed her, growing up, to feign the proper feeling, the proper form, until the proper feeling arrived. Or simply to keep on feigning if it didn't.

Every time Irene did one of these new things – went for a ride, introduced herself to somebody, exchanged a civil word with Nancy – Alistair seemed happy. Happy that she was trying, that she seemed to feel better, that she was making herself at home, at last. And Irene had started to find that making Alistair happy made her feel a little better too. She wavered, frequently. Twenty times a day she told herself that she couldn't do it – she couldn't accept that Manor Farm, and her marriage to Alistair, were her life from now on. They were her present reality, and they were the only future she had, and she had no idea how she would ever be reconciled to that. Twenty times a day she felt despair lapping, dangerously, around her ankles – a rising tide that would drown her if she let it. If she stood still, and watched it rise. So, twenty times a day she tried to take a step towards higher ground, even though it wasn't always obvious where that might be. But Alistair – and the ease with which she could please him – seemed a reliable stepping stone. The following morning, when Irene announced that she was going to visit Louise Cartwright, the doctor's wife, she let Alistair's warm smile of approval be her reward in advance. It also prevented her from backing out.

'Bravo, Irene,' he said. 'She always did love Clara's raspberry lemonade – you might take her a bottle from the pantry.'

Following Alistair's careful directions, Irene went on foot, which was the best way until she was confident enough to ride on her own. The lane up to Spring Cottage was too steep for the gig; the only way to reach it by road was by making a huge loop through Ford. The sun beat down and Irene walked incredibly slowly, ostensibly so that she wouldn't arrive sweating like a shire horse but mainly because, now she was out and on her own, she was horribly nervous. She tried to think of at least five safe topics of conversation she could rely upon if it all dried up: the weather, of course; Pudding teaching her to ride; how very busy the doctor must be; the best places to shop in Chippenham. Try as she might, she couldn't think of a fifth, and was terrified that she'd mention Pudding's brother Donald. She'd tried to talk to him about flowers for the house a few days before, and his terrible scars had been such a shock that she'd recoiled before she could stop herself. When she'd realised that the young man was simple she'd retreated, loathing her own inadequacy. What could one possibly say to a mother about a son who'd been so damaged by the war? Irene prayed that Louise wouldn't want to talk about it.

However, once the Cartwrights' hatchet-faced housekeeper had led Irene to where Mrs Cartwright was sitting, limp, in a garden chair, it became abundantly clear that she wouldn't want to talk about Donald. Or about anything else. When none of her overtures met with any response she could understand, Irene sat in terrified silence, entirely wrong-footed. Her heart hammered and her mind, though it churned and sped, drew a complete blank as to how she should proceed. In the end Mrs Cartwright sat forward, shaking her head, and said:

'But who *are* you, young lady? I don't understand why you refuse to tell me.' Irene repeated her name but Mrs Cartwright simply shook her head again, looking lost.

'Not a good day,' said the housekeeper, as she ushered Irene out. 'Try back another time, why don't you? Good of you to call. I'll tell the doctor, he'll be sorry to have missed you.'

But Irene walked a few yards down the hill, until she was safely out of sight of Spring Cottage, and burst into tears. The despair swilled around her feet. She felt shocked, exhausted; the tremulous relief of having survived a situation far out of her depth. And then she thought about Pudding, coping with her mother being so confused as well as her brother being so altered, and forced herself to stop crying. It wasn't herself she ought to be pitying. Cringing, she remembered offering to nudge Pudding's mother towards taking her up to London.

By the time she got back to Manor Farm, Irene was angry. She was angry with herself for being so useless, and not knowing what to say; for being frightened by the unfamiliar, and for adding to Mrs Cartwright's puzzlement and obvious unease. But she was angry with the others too. She might have coped – or at least coped better – if somebody had let on to her that Mrs Cartwright's illness wasn't physical. Alistair might have told her. Clara, the housekeeper, might have told her. Nancy certainly might have – she'd merely smiled thinly as Irene had announced her plan to visit. Perhaps there *had* been a glimmer of amusement, or malice, in her eyes. Quite possibly, now that Irene came to think about it. Still shaky, she went in search of Nancy, not sure what she would say but thinking of something along the lines of it possibly being easier, in future, for her to maintain the *Hadleigh standard* if Nancy didn't set out to deliberately sabotage her, and make her look a fool. Nancy would doubtless find it highly amusing, but she resolved to say it anyway. She went through to the back sitting room, where Nancy had her desk and books, but Nancy wasn't there. The room was incredibly hot and stuffy. Puzzled, Irene looked at the hearth, where the remains of a fire was burning low. She sat down in the fireside chair, took the poker and stabbed at the ashes. Why Nancy had thought she needed to light a fire on such a fine day was a mystery. There were shreds of paper in the ashes, and traces of something blue – a colour that tugged at Irene with its familiarity for a second.

She stirred the glowing embers about and stared into them, searching for something she would recognise, waiting to understand why she didn't feel she could simply walk away and forget about it. She had that same distracting feeling of something being wrong, or perhaps merely familiar, as when she'd first handled the doll in the old schoolroom – a discordance that was almost like a déjà vu. The sense that there was something to notice, but she wasn't quite able to see it. Staring hard, she remembered the day her cousin Gilbert had died, and how her greatest shock, when she'd been given the news, had come from realising that she was not surprised. She had known. She'd been to visit him the day before, with her parents. She'd been twelve, Gilbert seventeen. Blond-haired and lithe, and so full of himself Irene hadn't liked him much at all. She'd played tennis with him on the lawn outside her aunt and uncle's imposing house in Richmond – a wildly one-sided match, since Gilbert wouldn't hold back his shots or his serve just because his opponent was so much younger and smaller – and when they'd shaken hands across the net after his inevitable victory, Irene had scowled up at him and seen something flicker in his eyes. A shadow of something passing, like a shred of cloud across the sun; and from the way his nostrils suddenly flared, whatever it was had made Gilbert take a breath. Irene hadn't thought of anything specific happening, at all – she'd only known that it was significant. That something important was going to happen.

When Gilbert died the next day, from what the doctors eventually decided was a catastrophic and hitherto concealed defect of the heart, Irene had felt peculiar. And not surprised. She'd said nothing about it to anyone, and it was only as she got older, and was able to think about it more, that she wondered.

She wondered if sometimes a hindquarter of her mind took more from the things her eyes saw and her ears heard than the main part of her brain was aware of. She wondered whether that hindquarter sometimes jumped up and down and waved its hands, metaphorically speaking, and did its best to be heard, to no avail. So she sat a while longer, sweating, in Nancy's overheated room and tried to put her finger on what it was she'd noticed without realising it. Then again, there was always the possibility that Gilbert had been a complete fluke, and the feelings she sometimes got were the self-aggrandising delusions of a child. After all, nothing whatsoever had come of finding the old doll. Feeling cross and exhausted, Irene gave the ashes a final stir. She got up and tried to open a window to let in some air, but couldn't get it to budge.

In the kitchen, Clara and Florence the maid were shelling peas.

'Excuse me,' said Irene, distractedly. 'There's a terrible fug in Nancy's room and I can't find the key to open the window.' Clara blinked at her, then exchanged a glance with Florence, who shrugged.

'A fug, Mrs Hadleigh? What kind o' fug might that be?' said Clara.

'The kind that makes it hard to breathe. Why on earth did she want a fire lit, on a day like this?'

'A fire, Mrs Hadleigh?' Clara frowned. 'There's no fires lit; not been for weeks.'

'Well, I'm quite sure I didn't imagine it, Mrs Gosling.'

'Miss Hadleigh never would take it upon herself to light the fires. They weren't even laid up ready. And certainly no one's been to ask us to do it. I don't believe Miss Hadleigh has even been back since lunch.' Clara glanced at Florence, who shook her head.

'Well, I can assure you there is a fire going in her sitting room, and if neither you nor she lit it, then who on earth did?' said Irene, exasperatedly.

'Well,' said Clara, giving Florence a look that might have been meant to imply that Irene had gone peculiar. 'I'm sure I don't know, Mrs Hadleigh.'

'Never mind.' Irene sighed. 'Is there a key to the window?'

'Ar. 'Ee bides zomewur hind o' the shutter,' said Florence. Irene stared at her. 'Cassn't thee follow I?' said the maid, incredulously.

'It'll be hanging on a nail behind the shutter, ma'am; same as with all the windows,' Clara translated, speaking slowly, as if to a child.

At the end of the day, Irene told Alistair about her difficult visit to Louise Cartwright, and he looked pained.

'But I did tell you, darling. I explained that she suffers a degradation of the mind, right back in the beginning,' he said.

'Oh.' It was quite possible. Irene had almost no memory of her first weeks in Slaughterford, back in early May. Alistair took a sip of his gin. They were out on the terrace, which was alight with late sunshine beneath a vast span of clear sky.

'I . . . spoke to you about Donny as well. Do you recall? That he was injured in the war and is . . . well, somewhat slower, these days.'

'Yes, I remember,' Irene lied.

'Have you met him properly yet? Donny, I mean?'

'Sort of. I . . . went out to ask about flowers, but I didn't get much of a response.' She sensed what was coming next, and was about to say that she wasn't up to it, but just then Nancy came out onto the terrace and gave her a measuring look.

'Yes, you're better off speaking to Jem about anything you'd like brought in from the gardens. Would you like to meet Donny again now?' said Alistair. 'He's just over in the potting sheds, though I expect he'll be heading home for supper soon.'

'Yes, all right,' said Irene. Happily, with Alistair at her side, the conversation with Donald went far better than the one with his mother had gone. The scars of his wound were still terrible, and at first Irene didn't know where to look, until she realised that Donny himself wouldn't notice anyway. He seemed sweet; there was something soft and almost childlike in his slow responses, and the careful way he moved and spoke. Alistair seemed delighted that it had gone so well, and Irene felt again that delighting Alistair might in fact be a worthwhile way to spend her time. She decided, as they returned to the aperitifs on the terrace, that the day hadn't been a complete bust after all.

In the evening, she and Alistair played cribbage while Handel's *Water Music* played on the wireless, and Nancy read a book on the sofa, her legs crossed at her elegant ankles. Irene won three times in a row.

'You have me quite licked, darling,' said Alistair. 'Excuse me while I nip out to greet the prince.' By this he meant visit the privy, which, whilst it could only be reached by going outside, did at least flush – with such a roaring, gurgling thunder of water that it had been nicknamed the Royal George, after the ocean liner. As soon as he left the room, Irene felt Nancy's presence grow. Sure enough, she heard the book close, and the creak of the sofa as she rose.

'I owe you an apology, Irene,' she said, coming to stand beside the card table. Irene was struck dumb. 'I ought to have explained to you about Mrs Cartwright's condition. It was unkind of me not to – to the pair of you.'

'Well,' said Irene, fingering the green baize of the table. Nancy grunted.

'It seems to me that, as much as anything, you're frightened of people.' There was mild exasperation in her tone as she said this. 'You'll grow out of it, I'm sure. But there we go. I ought to have said. It can't have been an easy visit for you.' With that she went back to the sofa and her book, and Irene steeled herself to continue the conversation.

'Nancy, did you light the fire in your sitting room today?' she said. Nancy peered at her across the top of her book.

'I beg your pardon?'

'I looked for you in your sitting room earlier, and found the fire lit. It was dreadfully hot in there. Clara and Florence both say they never lit it. I was just . . . wondering, I suppose.'

'Well, why on earth would they? Why would anyone, on such a glorious day?' said Nancy, looking back at her book, and Irene still hadn't decided whether or how to go on by the time Alistair returned. 'What did you want me for, anyway?' Nancy asked.

'Sorry?' said Alistair.

'Irene was just saying that she came to look for me, earlier.'

'Oh, nothing. It doesn't matter,' said Irene, relieved beyond words that she hadn't found Nancy and tried to tell her off over Louise Cartwright, when this apology had been in the offing.

'Shall we go up, darling? I don't think I can take another pasting at cards tonight.' Alistair smiled and held out his hand, which Irene took gratefully.

It had been so long since a day had dawned dark and wet that when Irene woke the following morning, she thought it was still night-time. Alistair was gone, and she hadn't been aware of him getting up; she was becoming accustomed to sleeping beside him, and to the small sounds and movements as he rose and disappeared into his dressing room, as softly as he could. She turned over and looked at the clock, and even though it was late in the morning, she settled her cheek back into the pillow for the last peaceful half an hour before she would have to rise and face another day. To her surprise, she found that the thought of the day ahead wasn't so very bad at all. Her stomach growled hotly for some food; she put out her hand to feel if any warmth remained between the sheets on Alistair's side of the bed, and wished she'd seen him before he'd gone out for the day. She'd started to look forward to his smile, and the way he cared for her in spite of it all – when it felt like nobody else did. She lay a while and thought about that, wondering why her first impulse was to resist it. Something her mother had shouted at her – during one of the many rows once she and Fin had been discovered – came back to her then. *Why do you actively seek to destroy yourself, Irene? You always have. Ever since you were five years old and took scissors to your own hair.* Neither at that time, nor at any time since, had Irene been able to explain that it was because she had never felt good enough. But she didn't want to resist Alistair. There and then she decided not to, and shut her eyes to pledge it to herself.

She got up and peered out at the rain – a steady downpour that draped a curtain across the valley, muting the trees and fields to grey. It washed the smoke and steam from the mill chimneys before it could rise, and the sound of it hitting the window drowned out the thud of the machinery. It was like waking up in a wholly different place. Irene dressed, ate some of the dried-out scrambled eggs in the breakfast room and sat down with the paper, and it was a while before she began to feel as though something might be amiss. The quiet was too quiet; the house felt as though it were holding its breath. For no reason she could trace, the skin prickled restlessly at the back of Irene's neck. She got up and went to the window again, and was still staring out when Nancy came in and stood beside her. Irene braced herself, but Nancy was looking down at the mill and seemed lost in thoughts other than Irene's failings that morning.

'Good morning, Nancy,' said Irene.

'Good morning. Did you see Alistair before he went off?'

'No, not this morning.'

'Me neither. Odd.'

'Is it?'

'He hates rainy days. Always has, even when he was a boy. I used to have to chivvy him up, and now he's a man he still uses it as an excuse to lie about in bed.'

'I can't imagine that, somehow.'

'No, well.' Nancy shrugged.

'Will the river flood?'

'If it keeps this up much longer, it just might,' said Nancy. It was the closest they'd yet come to an easy, civil conversation, and Irene was pleased, even if it was about the weather.

'You can't even see the smoke from the chimneys, or hear the Fou ... the paper-making machine,' she added, and Nancy frowned.

'The Fourdrinier. No,' she said. 'You can't. And that *is* unusual.'

They stood side by side for a while longer, and Irene searched for something else to say – something pertinent – but had come up with nothing by the time Nancy turned to leave again. She paused by the door, and seemed to weigh something up. 'I'm going down to stick my nose in,' she said. 'Are you coming?' She fixed Irene with an accusatory look, as though daring her to decline, or perhaps to accept. Irene nodded.

'Yes, all right,' she said. 'Only ... I haven't a raincoat.'

'Not to worry. I've an oilskin mackintosh that will fit you, since there isn't a shred of flesh on you.'

'I've had some eggs this morning,' said Irene, and then loathed herself for trying so blatantly to please.

'Well, good. Let down your hair and have some lunch later as well, why don't you? Come along. You'll want a hat as well.' Nancy strode off along the corridor towards the back kitchen where coats and boots and walking sticks waited in their ranks, and Irene went along in her wake, with the anxious sense of having found a point of balance that might very easily be lost again.

A torrent of muddy water poured down the lane outside the farm, towards the village; fast and deep enough to roll small stones along with it. Pudding was newly back from a hack on Baron, Alistair's hunter, and looked as wet and bedraggled as a drenched cat. Water dripped from the peak of her cap, but she hallooed them as they passed.

'Dismal day for a walk!' she called. Steam rose from the horse's flanks.

'Don't be ridiculous, girl,' said Nancy. 'We're off to the mill. I think the machines have stopped.'

'Not really?' said Pudding, looking aghast, and Irene wondered how bad it could really be, since presumably the machines could simply be started up again at some point.

'Seems so, but I'm not sure. Do get that horse in and thatched, Pudding.' They carried on into the village, where they didn't see a soul. The beaters of Rag Mill were audible, and ragged pennants of steam rose from the brewery in spite of the rain, and Nancy's face darkened.

'Is it so very bad, if the machines stop?' Irene asked, tentatively. Nancy grunted.

'Not life and death, no. But it usually means the boilers have been allowed to go out, and it takes an awful lot of fuel and effort to get them back up again. It ought not to happen at all, and if it has I shall very much want to know why.'

The mill was eerily still. Outside the bag room, two women were standing idle, holding a coat over their heads as an umbrella. They stared at Nancy and Irene with wide, fearful eyes, and though Nancy drew breath to interrogate them, the words died on her lips. Most of the rest of the mill workers appeared to be gathered around the huge sliding doors to the new boiler house. The rain had soaked their shoulders darkly; they stood hunched, hands in pockets, staring across the yard at the old farmhouse. A few more men clustered at the door to the offices. Standing in the rain as though they'd been prevented from going inside. 'What in hell's name is going on here? Why is nobody at work?' said Nancy, as she strode over to the farmhouse door. Irene hastened after her, the rain pattering loudly on her hat. One of the men put out his arms to block their path, and Irene recognised him as the paper-maker she'd been introduced to. The look he gave her was so grave that Irene's throat went dry.

'Best not to go in, Miss Hadleigh, Mrs Hadleigh,' he said, sombrely. 'Best not to.'

'Get out of the way, man,' said Nancy.

'Miss Hadleigh—' Nancy pushed past the man and, with Irene on her heels, walked into the dry warmth of the offices. And there she stopped.

For a few moments, Irene could make no sense of what she was seeing. Something was heaped on the floor near the old inglenook; spilt dark liquid had puddled there, lustrous as oil, and more men were standing in the way, so that the thing could only be glimpsed through their legs. There was an odd smell, metallic but fresher than the hot, greased metal of the steam engine and boilers. A butcher's shop smell that made the hair stand up along Irene's arms, and her stomach start to turn. Nancy rushed forwards, fell to her knees, then froze. Irene took two steps after her, but her legs felt numb and watery, and she no longer trusted them to carry her. She stopped, and stared. In the weird hush of a roomful of people not talking, Nancy started up an awful keening. It sent a shiver right through Irene, but she couldn't react. She had no idea how to react, as her eyes registered what they were seeing.

It was Alistair, lying on the floor, and the dark, lustrous stuff was his blood. His neck was a ruin of deep, ugly wounds, and one had cut into his right cheek as well – there was a grey-white flash of bone, a ghastly flap of skin, hanging loose. He was sprawled on his back with his arms flung out and his legs at odd, uncomfortable angles. His eyes were open, gazing up at the metal lamp above his head as though mesmerised by it. It seemed, to Irene, far too gentle an expression for him to wear, when he had been subjected to such violence. But then, that was Alistair, she supposed. Had been Alistair. She swallowed. There was no chance that the broken thing on the floor was a living person any more. Irene felt a hand on her shoulder, but couldn't turn her head.

'He was found this way soon after the first shift started, Mrs Hadleigh,' a man told her, softly. 'We've sent Kenny – the office boy – to Biddestone to fetch the police constable, and they're sending to Chippenham for more men, too, in case he gives us any trouble. They oughtn't to be much longer.'

'Why weren't we told?' Irene whispered. She pictured herself feeling Alistair's side of the bed for warmth; sitting at the table, eating scrambled eggs. 'Why weren't we told right away?'

'Nobody wanted to be the one to . . .' The man trailed off. 'There didn't seem to be anything to be gained by it,' he said, heavily.

'But I should have been told,' she said, her voice shrinking. She felt as though she were shrinking. Nancy was still weeping, kneeling beside her nephew, and Irene knew she ought to go over and try to comfort her. But it was a ridiculous idea. Nancy couldn't possibly be comforted in the face of such a loss, and the sight of her bent and broken on the floor was almost as bad, almost as unnatural, as the gentle expression on Alistair's face.

Then they all just stood, for a while. Nancy cried, and Irene didn't blink, and one of the men coughed, and the rain hammered down outside, trickling musically along the guttering. The implausibility of it all robbed Irene of the slightest idea of what to do, and from the way the men fidgeted and glanced at one another, they were all similarly stupefied.

'Someone ought take the women away,' one of the men muttered, but nobody moved to. The idea of making – or even suggesting – Nancy do something was alien to them all. Irene was steeling herself to be the one to try, and had even managed a step forwards, with her heart hammering so loudly she could hardly hear above it, when she was barrelled from behind by the wet, breathless form of Pudding Cartwright.

'Here you all are. See! Keith came up to the farm to tell us, but I knew it couldn't be . . .' she said, but halted abruptly when she saw. Irene turned to her, and saw her face contort into an expression of such utter agony and disbelief that Irene felt it in her own bones. With a small cry, Pudding seemed to deflate, and she sobbed unashamedly, like a child, with her chin on her chest and her shoulders heaving. Behind her, Jem Welch the gardener appeared, and old Hilarius the groom – servants who'd known Alistair since he was a baby. Their lined faces were heavy and afraid, and neither one of them spoke. The smell of it all wormed its way inexorably into Irene's nose – wet bodies and blood and horse and earth and hair. A cacophony that her mind reeled from. Black blotches crowded in at the sides of her vision, and she staggered to one side, reaching out for balance.

'That's quite enough, now,' said George Turner, the foreman, finally taking charge. 'You men – take these three ladies back up to the farmhouse, and get Mrs Gosling to make them sweet tea. It's a terrible shock, and none of them ought to have seen him this way. I'm sure the police constable will be up to call on them very shortly. And Pudding ought not see her brother carted away in irons.'

Pudding's head came up in an instant. Her face was blotchy and red.

'What? What did you say?' she gasped. George pressed his lips together until his moustache all but hid his mouth.

'Best you get on home, Pudding. Or up to the farm with Mrs Hadleigh here. We've sent for your father but he's attending a difficult birth in Yatton.'

'Yes . . . a doctor. My father could help . . .' said Pudding, hopefully. Then she looked at the blood and the wounds again, and that hope vanished. 'But what did you say about Donny?'

'Now, Pudding—'

'Is he hurt too? Tell me!'

'Girl's going to find out sooner or later,' said another man, gruffly.

'Speak up, man,' Jem told George, curtly.

'It seems that . . . Donald was the one to attack Mr Hadleigh.'

'No.' Pudding shook her head. 'He wasn't.'

'He was found in the machine room with bloodied hands, and shirt, and . . . holding a shovel, also bloody. One of the coal shovels, it seems. He was just standing there, and still is, and he'll not speak a word in his own defence.' George's reluctance to give this news was evident. Jem Welch's face went through outrage and disbelief to a kind of resigned sadness, but Pudding shook her head madly.

'But that's just what he does — he likes to watch the machines! That's just what he does. It doesn't mean a thing! You can't *possibly* believe he would hurt Mr Hadleigh?'

'Perhaps he didn't intend to . . . inflict such injuries as he did, but nevertheless—'

'He didn't do it,' said Pudding. 'I know he didn't. I'll ask him and he'll tell you!'

At that point the sound of an engine came into the yard – the police superintendent from Chippenham, with the Biddestone constable beside him and two other young officers, in a steaming, spluttering car with mud splashed all up its sides. A wave of palpable relief went through the men in the room, and they began to file out like some kind of sombre welcoming committee. Nancy hadn't moved from Alistair's side; Pudding was still gabbling, struggling to breathe through her tears – Hilarius had hold of her arm and was trying to lead her outside. The superintendent came in, wiping rain from his spectacles, and began at once to order them away from the corpse, out into the rain. On sudden impulse, Irene struggled forwards through the moving wall of shoulders and chests. She knelt down close to Alistair's head, and was careful to look at his eyes, which were going dry and losing their shine, rather than at his terrible wounds. They drew her gaze with a hideous, irresistible fascination. There was blood in his fair hair, matting it. His mouth was soft, lips slightly parted; Irene's skin still had the memory of their touch from the night before. It was all so impossible – what she was seeing, what had happened – that it felt like a terrible, terrible ruse. She reached for one of his hands, wanting to hold it, tightly, as though he might still feel it, but it was cold and oddly hard, and didn't feel right at all. She dropped it and recoiled, losing her balance, and when she put her hand down to steady herself it smeared the pool of his blood, and that was cold too. The room receded behind the deafening crash of her heart, and the black blotches crowded in again. Then she felt hands grasping at her arms, lifting her up.

*

Pudding and her mother sat at the kitchen table with their tea gone cold. Outside, the rain had cleared and the sky had turned an ugly, incandescent white as the sun set about burning through the cloud. Pudding wondered how it could dare to. How it could show such disrespect. Louise's eyes were red and puffy; Pudding was sure her own were worse, but she was at least grateful that when she'd told her mother what had happened, Louise had understood – Pudding hadn't had to explain it three different ways, when she could scarcely believe it herself. It felt like a nightmare she should wake up from at any moment. She prayed that she would. They'd only let her see Donny for a second before they'd taken him away. She wished more than anything that her father had been there – he would have made them wait; he would have made them see sense. Somehow. Donny had gone as quietly as a lamb, climbing obediently into the car and not seeming to mind when nobody answered his question about the type of engine it had. Pudding had told them that they didn't need to put handcuffs on him, but they hadn't bothered to answer her either. The rain had begun to wash the blood from Donny's hands but it still daubed the front of his shirt, and was smeared up his sleeves. Alistair's blood. It had made Pudding's throat close up in horror.

'Donny – you didn't hurt Mr Hadleigh, did you? Tell them,' she'd said.

He'd given her a faraway look, and said: 'I tried to get him to safety, Puddy. Just like I tried with poor Catsford.'

'But it wasn't you that hurt him.'

'I found him there. I found him.'

'There! You heard that! It wasn't him!' she'd said to the superintendent, who was very tall and thin, with black hair, a pale face and a steady, unsettlingly gaze. He'd asked who

Catsford was – another young Tommy, Donny's new best friend, who'd died in France, Donny had written home to tell them, draped on the barbed wire like dirty laundry – and then told Pudding to move out of the way. He wouldn't have treated her father in such an offhanded manner, and if she'd had room to feel it, she would have been furious. She reached across the table and took her mother's hand again, and gave it a squeeze.

'It'll be all right, Mum,' she said, for perhaps the tenth or eleventh time. She knew it was mostly for herself that she said it, and wished she could believe it. 'Dad will make them see sense. And they'll find out who really killed Mr Hadleigh, and they'll...' She had to stop, and swallow a fresh storm of tears. Mr Hadleigh, dead. Alistair, murdered. Gone. The pain of each reminder was terrible. She sat there, shuddering, utterly helpless.

When Dr Cartwright got home he looked bedraggled and exhausted. His hair was messy and damp, as were his clothes. His face had a grey heaviness to it that Pudding had only seen once before – when he'd got back from visiting Donny in the convalescent hospital where he'd spent the first two months after returning from the front. She leapt up and took his coat and hat and bag, and put the kettle on to boil again, as the doctor sat down wearily and took Louise's hands.

'Well, well,' he said, softly. 'A day we won't soon forget, however much we might wish to.'

'Where's our Donny?' said Louise. 'Is he not back with you?' Dr Cartwright glanced up at Pudding, but she could only shake her head.

'I'm sure he'll be back soon, my dear,' he said, quite calmly, though his knuckles, as he held his wife's hands, were white. For a long time, they didn't speak. Pudding passed her father a cup of tea. Warm, damp air drifted in from outside as the sun finally broke through, and the birds began to sing. It was mid afternoon, Pudding supposed, but that didn't seem to mean anything any more – neither did what day it was, or what month, or what year. She felt it ought to be night. It ought always be night from then on.

'Well, I'd best get the supper on, I suppose,' said Louise, rising and brushing her skirt. 'I've got some pork loin, and there are finally enough broad beans to make a meal.' She paused, frowning in thought. 'Does Donny like broad beans? It's quite gone out of my head.'

'Yes, he loves them,' said Pudding, dully.

'Of course he does.' Louise smiled. 'What a thing for a mother to forget!' She hummed as she put on her apron, and stood at the sink to wash her hands. Pudding sat down opposite her father.

'What have they done with Donny, Dad? Where is he? Can he come home?'

'He's in the holding cells at the police station in Chippenham, Puddy – he can't come home just yet. They've given him something to eat, and dry clothes. I asked for his others to bring back and wash but they . . . said that they'll be kept as evidence.'

'Evidence? You mean . . . they still think it was him? Didn't you tell them it wasn't?'

'Of course I did. Of course I tried.' Dr Cartwright sighed, and rubbed his chin. 'But they still think it was him – and we must try to be patient with them. They don't know our Donny; they can only go on the evidence as they perceive it. They say he was holding the very shovel that was used to kill Mr Hadleigh, and nobody else was seen at the mill who could have done it.'

'But he just *found* Mr Hadleigh like that – he told me! He said he tried to help him, and that must be how he got blood on himself. And . . . and he was probably just taking the shovel back to where it belonged, in the boiler house – you know what he's like about odd things like that, and—'

'Hush now, Pudding; you don't need to convince me!' The doctor took Pudding's hand and tried to pat it but she gripped it so hard he winced.

'But we have to make them *see*. We have to make them realise he would never do such a thing.'

'And we will. We will.' But with a sinking feeling, Pudding realised how tired her father sounded already; how defeated.

'You look exhausted, Dad. You need to rest. How did the birth go? The one that kept you from coming to the mill?'

'Not well. The child was lost,' said the doctor. 'A dark day indeed.' He took a sip of his tea, carefully, because his hand was shaking.

Pudding was so beset by the urge to be up and doing – something, *anything* – that it was soon impossible to bear it another second. It felt as though something were creeping up behind her; she didn't know what it was, but it was frightening, and she was sure she didn't want to let it catch her. Everything was wrong, and Pudding's first impulse had always been to put things right.

'I'm going down to the mill to talk to whoever it was first found Donny. And whoever it was first found . . . poor Mr Hadleigh,' she said, pulling on her boots.

'Pudding, you can't. The mill's closed off. The police are still talking to the workers,' said her father. She paused with one boot on and the other in her hands, and her eyes filled with tears again.

'Poor Mr Hadleigh,' she said, quietly. 'Who on earth can have wanted to hurt him? I don't understand.'

'Neither do I, my dear. Neither do I.'

'What's happened to Mr Hadleigh?' said Louise, from the stove. Her voice was high, and anxious.

'Remember I told you, Mum? He's been killed.' Pudding fought to keep her voice steady.

'Pudding,' said the doctor, in a warning tone.

'But we can hardly go about pretending that he hasn't!' she cried.

'Oh, how *dreadful*!' said Louise. 'Was it an accident of some kind? How simply dreadful!' Unable to bear another second of it, Pudding wrestled her foot into her other boot and went out into the glare of the sun. The spring tinkled its crystalline water into the stone trough, as pretty as anything, and Pudding felt as though a huge crack had opened up right through the middle of the world. She stood on the track and wept, and through the burn of tears saw a figure, coming slowly up the hill. It was Hilarius, his gaunt features as unreadable as ever.

'Horses want seeing to,' he said, curtly, when he reached her. He squinted into the sun, his eyes all but invisible. A watchful glitter, hard as diamonds. Pudding gaped at him for a moment.

'But . . . Mr Hadleigh is *dead*!' she said, anguished. 'And . . . and they've taken my brother away!' Hilarius considered her for a while, then nodded.

''Tis bad enough,' he said. 'Knew young Alistair afore he were born, I did, and he went a long way towards lifting the dark off that house. But those beasts don't know aught about it. Waiting on 'ee for their well-being, they be.'

'Well, I can't come now . . . I can't! I need to . . .' Pudding tried to think what it was she needed to do. 'Can't you just see to them, Hilarius?'

'Not my job, girl. It's 'ee thar kicking at doors for.' He stared at her a moment longer, then nodded and turned to make his way back down the hill, awkward on his bandy legs.

Pudding watched after him a while, rubbing her face where the salt made it itch. Then she followed behind him, and went to work.

❧ ☙

In the sultry nights that week, Clemmie couldn't sleep. She fidgeted and turned and kicked off the sheets, until Josie sighed and Liz threatened to strangle her if she woke her one more time. Clemmie slid out of the bed and knelt down by the open window, low beneath the eaves. Their room trapped the heat of the day and exhaled it at night, and the air outside was only a little cooler. Bats wheeled and twisted along the river and across the yard, feasting on moths; a tawny owl called across the valley, and was answered by another. The river's soft rush was constant; the sky was blue-black, and a crescent moon turned everything else to grey. Clemmie didn't know what to do. The police constables from Biddestone and Chippenham had been lingering at the mill for days, eyeing everyone with such suspicion and gravity that Clemmie, with her guilty heart, fled from them as soon as she saw them. She could feel their scrutiny like a physical touch, and felt utterly transparent. On one of her visits she'd tried to take the milk into the canteen as usual, and been turned back. She'd overheard one of the women who usually worked in the bag room complaining at having been asked to clean the blood off the office floor.

'Can't be my job, can it?' she'd muttered, with a sickly, buttoned-up look on her face. 'How can it be my job to do it?' On another occasion, Clemmie had overheard someone talking about Isaac Tanner.

'Got an alibi, so they say, but hasn't he ever? They're a bad lot, all them Tanners, and I said as much to that copper when he asked me.' Her heart had got into her throat then, and all but choked her.

She hadn't seen Eli since it had happened; she didn't know what she would do when she did. She was torn in two, knowing what he had done, even if his father had made him, but loving him so completely. She'd been to Thatch Cottage and lingered for a while, half hoping he would come out and half hoping he wouldn't. Then, beneath the window, she heard one of Eli's brother's say, shakily: 'Why'd he have to hit him so hard? I don't see why . . . I don't see why he had to go at him so hard.' Clemmie didn't know who the boy was speaking to, and she didn't hear the reply, if there was one. She'd shut her eyes, feeling cold, hot, and full of fear. She prayed that the words had been spoken about Isaac, and not about Eli. But Isaac had infected all the Tanner boys with his anger, and his violence. She had seen it.

Her thoughts, as she knelt by the window, were in constant, kaleidoscopic shift. She had overheard their plan; she hadn't known how brutal it would be, how serious, but she had known something bad was coming. She could not have spoken of it to anyone, and she didn't know if she would have done so even if speech had come easy to her. She didn't think she could ever say anything to bring trouble down on Eli. But she felt culpable; she felt a liar of some kind. She hadn't even let on to Eli that she knew of their plan, or tried to discourage him from taking part – she'd let him kiss it away, and carry her out of herself with his touch. But she also knew she could not have stopped him – not if his father was set on it. She'd felt Eli's anger, worse than ever, and seen the cage he lived in, and had felt only love, only desperation on his behalf. But now there was blood to be scrubbed from the mill office floor, and nothing would be the same again, and the weight of what she knew would not go away. She would do nothing to betray him, yet she could not do nothing. She gripped big handfuls of her hair, yanking at it till it hurt, trying to force the thoughts to come clearer, and make sense. Her skin was as softly clammy as the night air, and her breath felt too hot in her mouth. There was no peace to be had, and as if in agreement a vixen shrieked, down by the river's edge, a harsh sound echoing against Weavern's walls, and in Clemmie's ears.

By morning she was dull with fatigue. She seemed to be tired all the time lately as it was – nagged by a lassitude that dragged at her steps and made everything seem like harder work than it should have been. There were purple shadows under her eyes.

'Buck up, my Clem,' said her mother, Rose, as Clemmie stood staring at a jug of yesterday's milk, gone sour because she'd forgotten to scald it before bed. 'What's got into you?'

'Got other things on her mind, I reckon,' said Liz, and Mary shot her a dark look that wiped the smirk off her face. They all glanced at their father to see if he'd noticed anything, but he hadn't. He hunched over his plate of food, ate with a mechanical rhythm, and paid them no attention. The look on Rose's face as she watched her husband was sad, exasperated, and a little lost. Clemmie lingered around the farm that morning, unsure whether to go to the mill again, or to look for Eli. Still unsure what she would do if she found him. She helped Rose put the rhubarb through the mangle, to squeeze out the juice for wine. They did it in the shade to one side of the house, turning the ground sticky and pink with juice, the air impossibly sweet. They covered the crushed stalks with sugar and packed them into earthenware jars to macerate out the last of the juice they would ferment.

'*Is* anything amiss, Clemmie?' Rose asked her, as they finished the job. 'You needn't be frightened – I won't be angry with you, my girl, whatever it is.' Clemmie held her eye for a moment before shaking her head. For once, she was glad to have no voice with which to have to try to explain.

It had taken a few days for work to resume at the mill, but farms were different. Animals couldn't wait, and neither could crops. Farms were living things, systems that had to carry on breathing or die. Everywhere, as she walked along the high ridge to the east of Slaughterford, Clemmie saw teams of horses, with their glossy mahogany coats and their leather collars black with grease, turning the first cut of hay, or pulling great carts loaded with timber, or beans, or women and children being taken out to walk the fields and pull the weeds and wild oats from the wheat. She usually liked the clank of the box bells on the horses' harnesses, and the hair flying around their feet, and the stink of their sweat as she pressed to the hedge to let them pass by. But now she couldn't enjoy anything, because of what had happened, and what she knew about it. Knotted thoughts, and fear, and missing Eli like air. Driven by those three things, Clemmie found herself in the yard of Manor Farm. The cob pony looked out over its stable door at her, the chickens peered side to side at her, and swallows arrowed above her head. Mrs Kent, a widow, was doing the laundry in big vats beneath the half-portico at the front of the house. She gave Clemmie a little wave then stood with her hands on her hips, taking the chance to straighten her back. When Clemmie neither gestured nor approached, she went back to work with a sigh, stirring the sheets with a wooden paddle. Clemmie stared at the farm's front door, the date stone above it and the iron knocker, hanging there, waiting.

But what could she do, if she could neither speak, nor write? She'd always relied upon people asking the right questions – and they couldn't possibly know the ones she needed them to ask now. She wished she could see Alistair. She wished she'd seen him in time. He might somehow have been able to coax the words from her, in the quiet seclusion of his office – he had come closer than anyone at showing her how to master it. She could have warned him of Tanner's plan to steal from him, at the mill, which had gone so horribly awry. Guilt came over her in a wave, and galvanised her to act. But Alistair wasn't there, and Nancy Hadleigh was another thing altogether. And then there was the chance that Eli would be arrested because of her. In an agony of indecision, she paced back and forth by the yard gate. She could not ignore what she knew, but could do nothing about it either. She ground her teeth together and moaned in her throat, and then, out of the blue, as if to surprise herself, she tried to say, *I know about what has happened*. The *I* was fine, but by the *n* of *know* her mind had caught up, and the rest of the word gathered behind her teeth and stuck there, an immovable thing she could neither swallow nor spit out, blocking everything. Her heart raced and she felt her face reddening with the effort, and she balled her hands into fists, and when she finally gave up it was with a cry of pure frustration.

'What in heaven's name's up with 'ee, hen?' called Mrs Kent, but at the same time the farm door opened and Nancy Hadleigh came striding out.

She moved with such angry purpose that Clemmie took an involuntary step backwards. Nancy was slight but her body was hard and her will was like thorns all around her that you ran into at your peril.

'What do you want?' she said, barking out the words. Clemmie flinched and dithered, shifting from her left foot to her right and back again. She saw Nancy's red eyes and pale face, her mottled skin and bitten lips; saw then that she was in anguish. The strain of it was making her wiry form thrum. 'Oh, what is it? What do you *want*?' Nancy cried. 'Alistair told me that there's no reason why you can't talk, so go on. Talk!' But Clemmie couldn't. Nancy's eyes narrowed, her face went tight. 'Perhaps I can guess what you want, in fact. Perhaps I can.' Her voice dropped as she said this, and Clemmie waited, hope kindling. 'Is it not enough to haunt the mill, and have your . . . *lessons* – is it decent to come and bother us here as well? Is it?' she demanded. Clemmie shook her head, confused. 'Go away. Alistair isn't here. Don't you understand that, you stupid girl? He's gone, and it's too late. You can't have him!' Tears choked off these final words, closing Nancy's throat so that she had to wait and catch her breath. Clemmie watched her cautiously, waiting for whatever would come next. The misunderstanding was so huge that she couldn't bring herself to go, and let it remain. She shook her head, but Nancy was dabbing at her eyes and didn't see, and then she threw up her arms and shooed Clemmie back, pushing her when she resisted. 'Go on, why don't you? Go!' she said, not looking up, her face shining wet. Defeated and afraid, Clemmie hurried away.

In the afternoon, William Matlock put the back of his hand across his mute daughter's face, after she lost control of the herd between fields and they jogged off happily, raiding the hedgerows along Weavern Lane towards Honeybrook Farm. Hedgerows still full of wild garlic that would taint their milk for at least a day, maybe two. Clemmie tried without success to get ahead of them and turn them, and they were only turned back by lucky chance, when Honeybrook's dogs barked and sent them into a panic of blown breath and clattering hooves.

'Will!' Rose exclaimed, as the blow landed, then said nothing more as her husband strode out into the yard and Clemmie stood with her hand pressed to her throbbing face. It was a good blow and she could taste blood where her lip had split a little. 'He don't mean it, Clem, you know how he is,' her mother said, dabbing at the blood with a wet cloth. Clemmie nodded, not even minding. Her lip had soon swollen up and felt odd – huge, numb and sore at the same time. She batted her mother's hands away, then went around the kitchen searching until she found an old chitty for cattle drench and the stub of a pencil, then sat down at the table and tapped the paper urgently with one finger. Rose frowned slightly. 'You want to write something down? You've something to tell me?' she said. Clemmie nodded emphatically. 'But... we've tried you with learning your letters before, love, and not managed it,' she said, gently. Clemmie jabbed the paper even harder, tears in her eyes. 'All right, all right; don't get in a lather. We'll find a way.'

Rose sat down beside her, and began, laboriously, to write out the alphabet, as she had done a hundred times before; sounding out each letter as she wrote it. She glanced at Clemmie, to see if she would echo the sounds, but Clemmie wasn't going to start trying to talk – it would only confuse things, and make it harder. She stared hard at the shapes her mother drew, and tried to learn them, tried to keep all their lines and curves in order in her mind, but her eyes seemed to dodge away from them, without her bidding, and when she looked again she could not recall which one she had been looking at, and they all seemed subtly different. She pointed to the sky outside, and then gestured for her mother to write it down. The three letters Rose chose were not at all what Clemmie had expected. She got up and pointed to other things around the room – the door, a pan, a dish, a spoon, a knife. *Niffe*, Rose wrote, obediently, carefully.

Try as she might, Clemmie couldn't spot a pattern between the sounds and the symbols. She dropped her chin, ground the heels of her hands into her eyes in exasperation. 'Oh, don't cry, my Clem! Whatever it is, it can't be as bad as all that, can it?' said Rose. 'Are you in trouble? Are you in any danger? Or one of your sisters?' she asked, and Clemmie shook her head. 'Well then, whatever it is will work itself out, I'm sure of it. Only don't get yourself in such a stew over it, it won't help.' Rose held her at arm's length and thought for a moment. 'Are you still upset over what happened at the mill? That's it, isn't it?' Cautiously, Clemmie nodded. 'I know it was terrible, but you're in no danger, I'm certain of it. I heard it today from Libby Hancock that the police have arrested someone, and they're sure they've got their man. He's locked away fast, so that's that. He's not at large no more; he can't hurt you.' Clemmie stared at her mother as this news sank in. 'I can get Josie to make the milk run instead, if you want? So you don't even need to go over to Slaughterford. There'll be no more of your lessons with Mr Hadleigh gone, in any case,' she said, but Clemmie shook her head to that.

In the evening, after supper, she sneaked away and went to Thatch Cottage. Hopes had bloomed like flowers inside her – the hope that Isaac Tanner was locked away for good, and Eli was free of him; free to be happy. The hope that she was free of her terrible dilemma. She made her way closer, tree to tree, and then to the back of the privy, trying to be cautious but too eager to know, too eager to have her hopes confirmed. She was just crossing the patch of ground between the privy and the wall of the cottage when the privy door banged open. Clemmie gasped and turned around as Isaac Tanner emerged, fastening his flies. She froze. He hadn't looked up or seen her yet, but it would be a matter of seconds. She had seconds. She knew she should run but couldn't decide which way; her feet faltered, pulled in all directions at once. Tanner looked up, and stopped; his face registered surprise, and then suspicion. He had such heavy brows, such a cruel mouth, such stony eyes. He moved like a fighter, always ready to react.

'Well? Who are you?' he said, flatly. 'What you doing back here? What do you want?' He didn't sound drunk, or angry – yet. Clemmie's breath whistled out of her and she couldn't seem to get more in. 'Well?' he said again, louder, harder. He started walking directly towards her, and with a stifled sound Clemmie darted away, towards the front of the cottage and the gate out to the lane. 'Oi!' Tanner shouted behind her, and now he sounded angry. 'I asked you a question, girl! You come back here and answer it!'

Clemmie ran until her heart was bursting and a stitch had stuck a knife into her left side. Then she walked, gasping, her fingers burrowing into the pain, trying to stifle it. When she had the breath for it, she cried for a while. Whoever the police had locked away, it wasn't Isaac Tanner. She didn't understand how they could have got it so wrong; she thought that surely they must know, surely there must be some evidence, pointing to Tanner's guilt. Clemmie found a safe place to sit – on the raised roots of a massive elm by Cold Tump, high above the village – and thought. If Isaac Tanner had not been arrested for the crime, then she could only suppose that either John or Eli Tanner had. All her hopes were replaced by fear; a dry-mouthed, queasy kind of fear. *They've got their man*, her mother had said. So just one of them, not both. She hated the idea of Eli hurting anybody; hated the thought of that anger boiling out of him as violence. She knew it was not who he really was – it was something that had been done to him. And whoever the police had taken, that person might hang. Eli might be hanged. Clemmie put her face into her hands and moaned, wordlessly. She longed for the power of speech. She longed to be able to walk up to the police and say that, however it was Tanner had managed to escape suspicion, he was the architect of it all. *He* was the source of all the pain. However he had managed to escape the blame. Clemmie thought about that. She wondered if her Eli could possibly have done such a terrible thing. Beaten a man down like that. The thought brought more tears, more sickness.

Later, she went to a place on the river where she and Eli had once lain down together. She tried to find the exact spot – tried to see the grass still crushed – but the summer growth was too vigorous for that. With her knees drawn up and her chin resting on them, she sat and watched gnats dipping and careering over the water, and realised that without Eli she was lonely for the first time in her life. Horribly so. It had only been days since she'd seen him but it felt like weeks. If he was taken away from her, if he was hanged, she didn't know how she would carry on living. She shut her eyes to the gloaming and wished for Eli to find her there – wished for it so hard that it came true.

When she heard his footsteps, swishing through the long grass, she got to her feet with her heart speeding, weak with relief. She knew the rhythm of his walk exactly, she didn't need to open her eyes to know it was him but she was hungry for the sight of him. Tall, angular, hunched; he had shadows under his eyes and his clothes were dirty and creased. He looked exhausted but restlessly alert. He radiated his hostility for the world, so much so that as he reached for Clemmie she almost flinched. However she longed for him, she still knew he'd been a part of it, and she still didn't know who had struck the blows. But the police didn't have him; the police weren't blaming him. She realised there and then that nothing else mattered. Whoever had been arrested, whoever might hang, it was not Eli. She reached out her arms to him. A moment before he kissed her, Eli noticed her split lip, and she noticed that some of the shadows and smudges on his face were bruises. He turned her chin to the last light in the western sky. His mouth was slightly open; eyes harried.

'Who hit you, Clem?' he said, his voice so hard the words seemed to take shape in the air between them. She shook her head minutely to say it didn't matter. 'Who? Your father?' he pressed, and she stayed still. 'I'll knock his bloody head off,' Eli whispered, and Clemmie shook her head, urgently. His hand on her jaw tightened painfully, and she whimpered. At once, he softened; his fingers loosened but stayed on her skin, resting gently. 'Sorry, sorry,' he whispered. She put up her own hands and felt the knots at the corners of his jaw, shifting as he ground his teeth together. 'What gives them the right?' he said. 'What in bloody hell gives them the right?'

Eli let go of her and stepped away, putting his hands over his face for a moment, pacing here and there. There was no stillness inside him. He stifled a loud cry, and Clemmie murmured her anxiety. 'God, I hate him,' he said, the words muffled through his hands. She tipped her head at him, tried to take his hands. *Who?* she asked, without a word. 'I hate him so much. Isaac. My *father* . . . I want to kill him. I'd happily kill him, Clem!' There was something wild in his eyes as he said it, and she believed him. His pain and anger broke the quiet night apart, and suddenly Clemmie saw that part of him was broken, and might never be mended. She might never be able to mend it. She couldn't help but start to cry. She wasn't afraid, just awash with sadness – drowning in sadness – that the world had done such a thing to him. 'The things he does; the things he makes *us* do . . .' Eli was just talking now – not to her, not to anyone, just talking because he had to. He shook his head wildly. 'Perhaps I will kill him. He wouldn't expect that, would he? Won't make much difference to me now, but it might to the others . . .' Clemmie watched him and wept, filled with ill-defined longing. Perhaps it was the longing to take his pain from him. In the silence her stifled sobs were loud, and so was Eli's breathing, and the nervous cough of a moorhen they'd woken, and the gentle push of the breeze in a willow tree. There was no way she could reject him; no way she could turn away from him – he had filled her heart to brimming.

But when he finally looked up at her again, and then walked towards her, quickly, decisively, she took a step backwards. She couldn't help it. She'd been pushed and shouted at by Nancy Hadleigh; she had been hit by her father, chased away by Isaac Tanner. She'd been tormented by her own thoughts, and by the terrible stain of violence at the mill; she was weak and bewildered from lack of sleep, and desperate. He had perhaps only meant to kiss her, or gather her into his arms, but when she took a step backwards Eli froze. The disbelieving shock on his face was terrible to her. 'Are you frightened of me, now, Clemmie?' he said quietly. She shook her head and stepped towards him, and put out her hands, but he held her back. 'Why would you be scared of me? When I've never made any move to hurt you – me, who loves the very bones of you?' He grabbed her wrists, gave her a shake. 'I haven't slept with a roof over me head in three nights, Clem, did you know that?' Clemmie took a huge breath. She shut her eyes to concentrate, and tried, as Mr Hadleigh had taught her, to think of the parts of the word as stepping stones – not reaching for the next one too soon, but going steadily, one at a time.

'Eee . . . l . . .' she managed, before stopping to recover.

'What? What do you know, Clem?' he said, not recognising the beginnings of his own name. But with his breath hot on her face, and the grip of his hands on her wrists, and the anger burning in him like a fire, she could not concentrate, or be calm. She could only weep. 'Why would you be frightened?' he said again. 'Look at me, Clem.' She did, and could no longer tell if he were cross with her, or hurt, or confused. His eyes were strange to her. 'Why would you be frightened? What do you know?' And what she wished for then, as she saw his anger ignite, right before her eyes, was that she could simply open her head, and her heart, and let him see inside. But she couldn't.

Irene got up when she heard the farmhouse door thud shut. She'd been lying on the bed upstairs, hiding from Nancy. After the rain the woods and fields had exploded with renewed growth when the sun returned, a frenzy you could almost see happening, and which seemed menacing to Irene – as though the human world might soon be smothered by swathes of foliage and writhing roots. And then she couldn't help but think of those roots going down into Alistair after his burial the following day, which would be nine days since his death. His eye sockets, and the soft gap between his knuckles; his ears and nose and mouth; all the cavities not protected by bone. Her stomach swooped in protest at this, but she couldn't keep the thoughts away. To Irene, the worst travesty of Alistair's death was not that he was now absent, but that his body would be violated in such a way. It was the only tangible way she could comprehend his death – she could not miss him, yet, could not mourn him properly, honestly. Not the way Nancy could, and was. The gulf between the two of them seemed unbridgeable now; perhaps, eventually, Alistair would have bridged it. Irene felt adrift again, she felt homeless. Even though she hadn't had a chance to fall in love with Alistair, he had become a place of safety. In vulnerable moments deep in the night, between islands of fitful sleep, the feel of his dead hand appeared, like a ghost, in her own hand, and she sometimes sat bolt upright with a gasp, and ran her fingers through her hair, certain that it would be matted, stiff with blood.

Clara and Florence responded to the shocking death of their master by working with a kind of silent expectation that only served to keep the house on edge. They watched Nancy and Irene constantly, as if seeking validation, or expecting some extraordinary instruction or announcement. Perhaps they, like Irene, questioned the point of doing any of the things they had done before. There was no point cooking meals for a household that wouldn't eat. There was no point cleaning rooms that nobody cared about, or was using. Their aimlessness was too much for Nancy, who was like a raw nerve – impossible to touch. She snapped at them frequently, when she wasn't so closed off that she didn't even see them. She veered from businesslike stoicism, as impenetrable as stone, to an excess of emotion so alien to those who knew her that it sent them scattering like hens. She'd sent Pudding away more than once, damp and red-faced, when she'd tried to come inside and talk. Jem Welch had caused an explosion by asking if he should cut white roses or red for Alistair's wreath. The old man had gone away as steadily as he'd come, but his face had shown his distress, and Irene gathered it was as much down to Donald Cartwright being arrested as it was to Alistair being dead. Nobody was talking about Alistair's killer much; people seemed in the uneasy position of wanting to condemn the sin but not the sinner – that it had been Donald, it seemed, was as big a tragedy as that it had happened at all. He'd been damaged fighting for king and country, after all; nobody was in any doubt that the Donald who went off to war would never have done such a thing. Irene peered out of the window at the top of the stairs on her way down and saw a figure in poor clothing walking away across the field towards the church with a crabbed, uncertain gait – head down, arms clasped around herself, pursued by a mad mess of pale, frizzy hair.

Nancy was in the hallway, going through the letters and cards that had come that morning. She was crisply dressed, with a black cotton cardigan buttoned over her shirt; her pose would have been entirely normal had it not been for the tears on her cheeks and her hollowed-out eyes.

'Did somebody come to call?' said Irene.

'No. It was just that odd creature from Weavern, hovering

around, as she's always done,' said Nancy, curtly. 'I sent her on her way. Not the full ticket, that one.'

'Oh. And how are you this morning, Nancy?' Irene hadn't once tried to hug the older woman; hadn't once tried to take her hands. She'd been watching, as closely as she could, for any sign whatsoever that Nancy would welcome the gesture. Even at the inquest, which had opened the day after Alistair's death and returned a verdict of unlawful killing almost immediately, Nancy's hands had remained in her lap, fingers laced. Now she looked up at Irene with an expression so flatly hostile that Irene's mouth went dry.

'This morning? It's half past three in the afternoon, Irene. Most of the day is over, and as usual you have contributed nothing to it whatsoever. As to how I am, I . . .' Here her rancour failed her, and for a moment she looked so lost it was painful to see. She glanced down at the white envelopes in her hands, some of which were edged in black. 'So very Victorian, some of our acquaintances,' she murmured. 'Most of these condolences are addressed to you. I suggest you get on and answer some of them before they pile up too much. You have such a lovely new writing room, after all, as well as all these others.' She thrust the envelopes at Irene and moved away.

'All which others? Nancy, wait,' said Irene. 'Please. Look, I . . . I know we've not seen eye to eye over much since I got here. I know you don't think I deserved Alistair. I don't know if it matters now, but I really didn't think I deserved him either. I know I didn't. He offered to rescue me from a horrible situation, but perhaps I wouldn't have married him, even so, if my mother hadn't made it my only option. And I know I didn't . . . love him the way you did. But I just wanted to say . . . I just wanted to say . . .' She realised only then that she didn't know what she wanted to say.

'What?' said Nancy, with a wintry smile. 'That you share

my pain? That we are united in our grief? That we are *in this together*?'

'No. No, not that. I'm sorry. Perhaps that's it — I'm sorry you've lost him, and . . . however hard this might be for you to believe, I'm sorry *I've* lost him, too. I just . . . I just don't know what to do next.'

'Don't you?' Nancy stopped smiling. She slipped her hands into her pockets and lifted her chin. 'I should rather think the world is your oyster now, Irene.'

Irene did as she was told and took the cards into her writing room, slitting each one open with a knife and trying to place the names of the senders. Some she knew, most she did not; none at all were from any of her own friends or family. She smoked until the air was hazy, and answered each one as best she could, noticing the un-summery chill in the air and the draught from the chimney that Nancy had foreseen. She stared at the hearth, with its new marble surround, and thought again of the strange broken doll that had been found there. She thought, with a shiver, of Ma Tanner's pronouncement of change, and the odd feeling of prescience she'd had herself. She felt as though she'd been at Manor Farm for years, decades — like her unhappiness had trapped time, and slowed it down. And then she realised, with a jolt, that she was free to leave now. There was nothing to keep her there — that was what Nancy had meant about the world being her oyster. The desire to be gone was a sudden, irresistible craving, even if it came with an ill-defined taint of failure. She could go back to London; she could go home, as soon as the funeral was out of the way. No doubt the residents of Slaughterford would denounce her for abandoning the home Alistair had intended for her, but she could hardly start caring about what the residents of Slaughterford thought of her now. There was no good opinion to risk losing. Finally, one of the cards she opened was from her parents, who'd probably read about the murder in the papers. Irene quickly wrote a reply, asking to come home to them in London as soon as possible after the funeral. She wrote so fast that she smudged the ink, which her father would hate, sealed the envelope and got up to walk it down to the post box in the shop wall herself, not caring if it was decent or not for her to be out and about; not caring if the scarf she draped around her neck was emerald, rather than black.

Superintendent Blackman, from the Chippenham branch of the police, had his hand raised to the knocker just as Irene dragged the front door open. Tucked away in the old schoolroom, she hadn't heard the rattle and growl of the car, pulling into the yard. Constable Dempsey from Ford, a fresh-faced young man with clear green eyes, stood at Blackman's shoulder. Startled, caught off guard, Irene's first instinct was to smile. Just as she had always been taught to. But the superintendent's face was so firmly chiselled into an expression of respectful gravity that he could do nothing to alter it; Constable Dempsey smiled before he could help it, but then fell serious again. Irene blushed and took a step backwards, dropping her eyes. Her levity, her green scarf, her ridiculous smile. As Nancy had once said, she really had no idea how to behave.

'Mrs Hadleigh,' said Blackman. 'My continued condolences at this tragic time for you, and your household.'

'Yes. Thank you,' said Irene.

'Have I called at a bad time? I've come to keep you – and Miss Hadleigh – appraised of the progress of our investigation.'

'Oh? I'd understood there wasn't to be much of one,' said Irene, and straight away wished she hadn't. The two policemen stood in silence until she stepped back to admit them. 'Won't you please come in? I'll ask Clara for some tea.'

She took them into the drawing room at the far end of the house, where there was too much floral fabric – swathes of curtain and pelmet, cushions, rugs and upholstered footstools. The air smelled of dust, dog, and the rankness of the vase of flowers in the swept-out fireplace, where the water had gone murky. The two police officers looked ill at ease in their setting, clasping their hats in their hands, and Irene remembered that Nancy had taken them into the front kitchen before, and seated them at the long pine table. 'Please do sit down, gentlemen. I'll go and find Nancy,' she said, awkwardly, but then heard Nancy's smart footsteps coming along the corridor anyway.

'Why on earth have you come in here?' she said, from the doorway. 'Hardly fitting. Shall we up sticks?' The young constable got to his feet.

'Well, since we've already settled, perhaps we might remain?' said Irene, with a flutter of defiance, and the constable glanced at Nancy before sitting down again.

'Hardly matters, I suppose,' said Nancy, going to stand by the window with her back to them. Superintendent Blackman cleared his throat.

'As you know, ladies, the jury at the inquest into the death of Alistair Hadleigh returned a verdict of unlawful killing, for which Donald Cartwright has now been formally charged. He will soon be moved from Chippenham to Devizes prison to await his appearance before magistrates, where he will, I have no doubt, be committed for trial at the next assizes, in six weeks' time.' The superintendent paused as Florence came cringing into the room with the tea tray. Irene found her hands shaking as she poured. The policeman's words returned her to the inquest, and the horror of listening to the doctor – Dr Holbrook of Chippenham – describe the post-mortem examination he had carried out on Alistair, and the violence of his wounds: a blunt trauma wound to the back of the head, significant but not having caused the skull to fracture; five deep lacerations to the neck, severing the major blood vessels there; a further laceration to the face, most likely caused by the same instrument – consistent with the weapon being a heavy shovel, used first flat, and then with its edge to hack at the neck. The attack was hurried, passionate, and carried out by an assailant of significant physical strength. The cause of death was loss of blood. Now, as when she had heard the words spoken, Irene had to swallow down a hot rush of nausea that swept through her. The exact feel of the cold, slippery blood, sliding beneath the heel of her hand, returned with horrible clarity.

Blackman watched her carefully, and with more sympathy now, as she handed him a rattling cup and saucer. 'Are you well enough for me to go on, Mrs Hadleigh?' he asked gently, at which Nancy snorted, then waved a hand for him to continue when he looked across at her. 'Young Cartwright claims innocence, in the vaguest terms, but the evidence against him is as clear-cut as any I have encountered before. Such grievous injuries could only have been inflicted by a man of some strength, and in an outburst of rage, to which, many will testify, the young man is prone. The case is as open and shut as any I've known.'

'He was such a gentle lad before the war damaged him,' said Nancy, shaking her head. 'And very bright. He'd been planning on going up to Oxford to read engineering.'

'I didn't know that,' said Irene, thinking of Donald's slow movements, and the faraway look in his eyes. As though the air were thicker for him, as thick as water, and he was forced to swim rather than walk.

'Anyone would have told you, if you'd asked.' Nancy shrugged. 'He destroyed some rose bushes, recently. Hacked them to pieces with a hoe. For no reason – just one of his lapses. I don't know if Alistair spoke to him about it, or perhaps rebuked him. Perhaps Donald felt aggrieved.'

'Perhaps. It is most tragic,' said Blackman, perfunctorily. 'But the fact remains that the young man has now proven himself a danger to others. The judge may be lenient, given the circumstances of his ... alteration, but then again – as with a mad dog – perhaps it would be wisest and kindest all around to ...' He was interrupted by a gasp from the doorway, and there was Pudding Cartwright, face stricken, mouth open in shock.

'Good grief, Pudding!' Nancy cried. 'You can't just come wandering *in*, child!'

'How can you let him say such things about Donny?' said Pudding. 'You're talking about hanging him, aren't you? Aren't you?' she demanded of the superintendent, who had the grace to look uncomfortable.

'Now, Miss Cartwright, it—'

'My brother is *not* a mad dog! Or a murderer! Tell them, Miss H – he would never have hurt Mr Hadleigh! He just wouldn't! There's been a terrible mistake – this is all a terrible mistake. Donny has always been as gentle as a lamb, and—'

'But that's not entirely true, is it, Miss Cartwright?' said Blackman. 'Constable Dempsey here was called out to an incident only last year, in which your brother attacked another young man—'

'He didn't *attack* him! He just ... it was just ... he was provoked!'

'Indeed. An altercation over a young lady, as I understand it.'

'Aoife Moore. Donny was supposed to marry her, but after the war ... They were goading him about it. It wasn't his fault.'

'Young miss, I'm afraid that violence is always the fault of the one who perpetrates it, whatever duress they might be under.'

'But what possible reason could Donny have to hurt Mr Hadleigh? I'll tell you – none at all! He always loved Alistair! And Alistair was always so kind to him . . . to everyone . . .' Huge tears brimmed along Pudding's eyelashes. Constable Dempsey got to his feet, drew out his handkerchief and offered it to her clumsily.

'Here you go, Pud— Miss Cartwright,' he said, but she looked at the handkerchief as if she didn't know what it was for.

Horrified by the scene, Irene folded her arms tightly and perched on the edge of her chair. She was so ashamed that Pudding, the girl groom, was visibly more upset about Alistair's death than she was herself that she could hardly stand to witness it. She stared down at the faded rug and imagined herself far away, in London, with the reassuring drone of traffic and a throng of anonymous faces in which she might hide. No longer on display, no longer watched all the time, no longer always wrong. At that exact moment she realised she hadn't had any word from Fin, when he must by then have heard about Alistair's death.

'This is ridiculous.' Nancy's hard voice interrupted her thoughts. 'Pudding, do stop that din, child. I know how desperate it all is, I really do, but you must brace yourself up. Wailing won't help.'

'But, Miss Hadleigh, I can't bear it! I can't! Donny would never have hurt Alistair; he had no reason to. Alistair wasn't at all cross about the roses . . . He's innocent – he told me so himself!' Pudding's voice was drenched in misery. Constable Dempsey hovered near her, uneasily, and seemed uncertain whether he ought to pat her shoulder or not.

'As far as anyone can tell me, Miss Cartwright, *nobody* had any cause to harm Mr Hadleigh. Which, I fear, only makes it all the more likely that the attack was carried out by someone beyond reason,' said Blackman. For a moment, Pudding simply stood, panting, the breath hitching in her chest.

'I saw Tanner passed out drunk at the mill! Just a couple of weeks back . . . I saw him. I'd gone in to fetch Donny out of the generator room. He was asleep in the coal heap with a bottle in his arms! I bet Alistair spoke to him about it. Maybe he even threatened to fire him from the mill – he'd been drunk so many times before! And everybody knows what he's like – he's a brute! He—'

'He has an alibi, Miss Cartwright. And I have checked up on it. You aren't the only one willing to point the finger at Mr Tanner, and—'

'An alibi from some member of his own family, I bet!'

'Indeed not. From Bob Walker, the landlord at the White Horse in Biddestone, who informs me that Mr Tanner was so drunk by closing time the night before the murder that Mr Walker felt obliged to carry him out to a storage shed at the rear of his premises and leave him to sleep it off, where Mr Tanner was still to be found when he was ejected at nine the following morning, by which time Mr Hadleigh had already been slain.'

'But . . . he might have come away, and gone back again, mightn't he?'

'It's highly unlikely, given the distance involved and the state of incapacitation he was reportedly in. And, let us not forget, there simply isn't a single shred of physical evidence that he was involved in any way.'

Pudding's chin sank to her chest for a moment, and she took a deep breath. Then she looked up, and her eyes landed on Irene, and they were lit with desperation.

'What about her?' she said, wildly. There was a pause, and Pudding raised her hand to point at Irene. 'What about Mrs Hadleigh? She didn't love Alistair! Anyone could see that – Ma Tanner said as much, right to her face! And ... and she inherits everything, doesn't she? Manor Farm and the mill and all of it – it's all hers now, isn't it? And she can do as she pleases!' The air in the drawing room seemed to curdle. Irene was stunned. A hindquarter of her brain was amazed that this matter of inheritance hadn't occurred to her sooner, and noted that the cause of much of Nancy's continued hostility, and her sideways remarks, were now a good deal clearer. The thought of what she had inherited settled onto her with the weight of a millstone. There could be no scot-free escape to London; she was far more tangled up in Slaughterford than she'd realised. But mills and farms could be sold, she reminded herself – or tenants found. Which left Nancy without the home she'd lived in all her life – evicted from the last place where she might surround herself with the ghosts of her family.

'But ... I don't *want* it!' said Irene, like a child.

'See?' said Pudding, her conviction seeming to grow. 'See? She doesn't even deny that she didn't love him!'

'Pudding, that's enough. Irene was here all that morning, as the servants can testify. And she's so thin she's practically feeble – there's no way she could have ... hurt Alistair in that way,' said Nancy.

'She might have sneaked out! She didn't love him, but she was stuck with him until death, otherwise, wasn't she?' Pudding was trembling all over, though Irene couldn't tell which particular emotion was shaking her. Superintendent Blackman got to his feet.

'Miss Cartwright, it doesn't do to go about flinging accusations at innocent people,' he said, severely.

'But . . . but that's exactly what you're doing to Donny!' she said.

'No, indeed it is not.'

'Of course it wasn't me! How could it have been? I could never do such a thing.' Irene sprang to her feet and found her voice.

'Mrs Hadleigh, nobody is accusing you of anything,' said Blackman.

'I am! I'm accusing her,' said Pudding. 'I knew there was something not right about her when I first met her. How could anybody not love Alistair? She probably planned this all along – she probably planned it when she married him.' This said, Pudding dissolved into uncontrollable sobs.

'Clara!' Nancy called sharply down the corridor, and the housekeeper, who'd clearly been loitering within earshot, appeared and led Pudding away. Constable Dempsey watched her go, his expression full of concern until he noticed his superior watching him.

Irene sat back down again, tingling, feeling naked; Nancy stood across from her with her arms folded, and the two policemen exchanged a glance.

'Perhaps that's enough for now,' said Blackman. 'We'll see ourselves out, Mrs Hadleigh, Miss Hadleigh. I'm sure we will meet again before long.' He nodded to each of them, politely enough, but Irene noticed that his eyes, as they settled on her, were different from before. A good deal of the sympathy had gone from them, and something harder had come in its place. Something questioning, and watchful, and a lot like suspicion. Irene thought of the way she'd smiled as she'd opened the door to them, and the emerald scarf around her neck, and went cold.

6

Allies

The holding cell at Chippenham police station was small and sparse, with a grubby stone floor gored here and there with deep scratches, and bars on the tiny window. An officer from the front desk led Pudding and Dr Cartwright through, though every line of his face read of disapproval. The brass buttons on his uniform gleamed, he smelled of boot polish and camphor, his breath of onions, and Pudding was glad her father had come with her. It seemed unlikely that she would have been admitted on her own. The officer made a big show of checking, through the hatch, that Donny wasn't waiting just inside the door to ambush him, before rattling his keys in the lock and steadily pulling back the bolts. Once Pudding and her father were inside, he locked the door behind them, and the sound of it gave Pudding a shudder. The foul smell of the slop bucket was strong. Donny was sitting on the edge of his narrow bed wearing the same shirt and trousers Dr Cartwright had taken him days before. They were well creased, and looked stale, and Pudding's first thought was that when Donny got home he'd need a damn good scrub in the tub. It was still beyond her comprehension that he might never get home. She refused to think it.

'Hello, Donny,' she said. She didn't want to sound tremulous, or grave, or too perky, so in fact she didn't know how to try to sound. Normal was out of the question. Her brother smiled fleetingly, and got up to come closer to her. He held her arm in his right hand, squeezing it gently.

'Hello, Pud, Dad,' he said, shaking his father's hand as he had always done. But this time Dr Cartwright pulled him into a quick, tight embrace, clapping a hand on his shoulder as he let him go. Donny didn't like to be hugged, though he had done, before the war. This time, however, he didn't pull away. 'Can we go home now?'

'Not yet, Donald. I'm afraid not. Soon, I hope,' said the doctor, and Pudding heard how he hated to lie. 'But it could be a goodly while yet. You've to go before a judge first.'

'And the judge will say I can come home?'

'We hope so, Donny. We do hope so.' Pudding saw the way her father's smile refused to kindle, repeatedly sparking but then dying on his lips. She saw the desperate sorrow in his eyes. Donny nodded slowly, and sat back down on the bed.

'I used to like Chippenham. But I don't like it here much,' he said.

'No,' said Dr Cartwright. 'I don't suppose you do, son.'

There was a long pause then, in which Donny merely sat, and Pudding and her father merely stood. Noises came from the street outside, and it seemed obscene to Pudding that life should just carry on as it always had – with farmers carting in their produce to sell, and livestock being driven to market, and travelling quacks and salesmen proclaiming their latest miracle cure or must-have gadget, and newspaper boys shouting the headlines, and children bickering over cigarette cards. Chippenham was carrying on as normal, as though nothing was wrong, when nothing was normal and nothing was right. With a sudden loud roar of machinery and clanging of bells, they heard the fire engine approach and fly past, on its way to some emergency, and instinctively she and Donny looked to the window. It had been one of their favourite things, before the war – seeing the big, shining pump engine go flying past, with the men and their ladders clinging to its sides, cheered on from the street, shouting at people to move out of the way. Back then it had been pulled by horses, now it was horseless, which Donny liked even better. But they couldn't see out of the tiny, high window, and so they turned away again. Pudding refused to start crying, so she went and sat down next to her brother, and took his hand.

'What's the food like, Donny?' she asked him. He shrugged one shoulder.

'It's not up to much, Puddy. Stew with too many carrots, most days. Not like Mum's cooking.'

'Well, we've brought you some bits and pieces to keep you going – a coffee cake, and some fruit.' Donny nodded absently, and Pudding wondered how much of his situation he really understood. The hope that where there was ignorance there was bliss was tenacious, but Pudding had been caught out, time and again, assuming that just because her brother didn't react, he didn't realise.

'I didn't hurt Mr Hadleigh, Pudding,' he said then.

'I know you didn't.'

'I've been thinking and thinking, and making sure I remember it right, and I do remember. I went over to the offices because the door was open and the rain was getting in. And I found him lying there. I don't . . . I don't remember exactly what came next. For a while I . . . got lost. I thought about Moggy Catsford, my friend in France. And then I was in the generator house, looking at the machines, and I must have picked the shovel up, I suppose, and then.' He stopped talking suddenly, as though he'd simply run out of words.

Pudding gave her father a significant glance, and couldn't understand the doubt in his eyes. It made her feel she needed to try harder, go faster, push further.

'Did you see anybody else in the offices, Donny? Did you see anybody . . . perhaps running away?' she said. Donny stayed quite still for a long moment, and then shook his head. 'Did you see Mrs Hadleigh?'

'Pudding, that's quite enough.'

'Mrs Hadleigh?' Donny's brow furrowed in confusion. 'No. Or if I did, I don't remember. They think I did it, don't they?'

'Oh, Donny. They do, at the moment – but I am going to change that.'

'Pudding—' Dr Cartwright shook his head, but added nothing else.

'Mr Hadleigh is always kind to us. He's kind to everybody. I should never want to harm him.'

'I know, Donny. And I am going to make sure they realise that. I am going to prove who it was that *did* hurt him, and then they'll let you come home. All right?' She squeezed his hand hard, until he looked at her, from that far-off place, and nodded.

'Right you are, Pud,' he said, and her heart swelled up to bursting.

'Now, son, they'll be taking you to Devizes jail soon, so you can see the magistrate there. I don't want you to worry about that. You just do as they ask you, and always tell the truth, and we'll come and see you there very soon, all right?'

'All right, Dad. Will Mum come next time?'

'Well, we'll just have to see about that. It might upset her, you see, and we wouldn't want that, would we?' Donny shook his head, and Pudding smiled at him as best she could. She stared into his eyes, searching, and recoiled when she saw, deep in the depths of them, a flicker of fear. She stood up quickly, because she couldn't bear it and didn't know what else to do.

'I shall find out the truth of it, Donny, and you'll be home with us soon. I promise,' she said, with her heart hammering and a feeling like she might overflow. The camphor and onions man came back then, rattling his keys again.

'Time's up, I'm afraid,' he said curtly. So they left Donny perched on the edge of the bed as he had been upon their arrival, and went back out into the heedless, sunny day.

'You must be very careful, Pudding, who you go about accusing. You will lose your job at the farm,' said Dr Cartwright. Pudding hadn't told him that she'd already named Mrs Hadleigh to the police. And right in front of Nancy. Her gut gave a spasm when she thought about it. 'But then,' her father went on, 'perhaps that wouldn't be such a terrible thing. Perhaps we ought to think about you continuing on in college somewhere. Somewhere away from all this.'

Pudding kept her silence as they walked back to the bus station, not stopping to eat or go shopping or to watch the busy street life – it had not been that kind of outing. She could feel her father's reprimand, his fear for her and for her brother, and part of her did indeed struggle to picture Irene Hadleigh – frail, tired, immovable Irene Hadleigh – picking up a shovel and attacking Alistair with it. It was hard enough to imagine her leaving the house to go down to the mill in the first place. But she had all but confessed to not loving her late husband, Pudding reassured herself, so she was clearly flawed in some significant way, and she was the only person with any kind of motive. Pudding took a deep breath, trying to marshal her thoughts when they threatened to scatter out of control. She would make it all come right, she swore to herself. She felt again the shudder as the cell door had locked behind them, and the terrible, unimaginable horror of Donny never coming out of there again. She would not allow herself to fail.

She didn't like to think about the immediate consequences of her accusation. With Hilarius's wisdom still fresh in her mind, she went to fetch in the Hadleigh horses in the afternoon, just as she normally would, and rode Baron, Robin and Bally Girl in succession, by the end of which her legs were tired and she was as grimed with sweat as the animals. She rubbed them down and mixed their feed, then stood in the blessed shade of the tack room, cleaning all the bridles, and all the while she cast furtive glances at the house, expecting to see Nancy or Irene Hadleigh coming across to tell her to leave, permanently. Each time a door opened or closed, her heart jerked. But neither woman appeared, and she was left to wonder whether they even knew she was there, still at work. Whether they assumed she had resigned, after her sensational performance. She sat a while to think whether or not she should announce her continued presence in some way, until she realised that they must know, since, clearly, no other provision had been made for the care of the horses. Then she was left with the simple realisation that they'd disregarded her words, her outburst. That nobody had taken it seriously. That nobody took *her* seriously. She went to muck out the cob house and found a swallow's nest that had dropped from the rafters and smashed against the cobbles. Three naked baby birds were dead amidst the wreckage, and their oversized yellow beaks were so tragically clownish, and Pudding felt so powerless, that she surrendered to tears for a short while.

At the end of the day she trudged up the hill towards home, watching the daisies disappear beneath her big, booted feet and not knowing whether to be happy or angry that they merely sprang back upright once she'd passed. She stopped, realising that she was angry, and was deliberately grinding one into the sod when movement in the woods to her left caught her eye. Startled, she looked hard into the dappled shadows and tangled undergrowth beneath the trees, and then relaxed when she saw a woman in rough, peasant clothes – a long skirt snagging on the brambles, a collarless blouse with the sleeves rolled up – with a familiar thatch of thistledown hair obscuring her face. Pudding didn't bother to call out to her – she knew from experience that she'd get no reply. But there was movement and the sound of a twig snapping underfoot from further down the hill as well, and when Pudding refocused her eyes she saw a man moving away in the opposite direction. She couldn't make him out clearly, but he was tall and angular, and moved with a kind of steady, resigned tread that spoke of hardship. A Tanner, perhaps. Pudding waited until they were both out of sight and earshot, and wondered about the secret, other world they lived in, so different to her own. A world of clandestine meetings in summery woods; a world where you were wanted, and your brother was not in jail, wrongly accused of the murder of one of your favourite people in the whole world. Her envy of them was like a sudden, sharp pang of hunger.

She was so surprised to see the police superintendent's car parked outside Spring Cottage – spoked wheels dusty, headlamps like wide, alarmed eyes – that she stopped and stared at it for a moment, trying to imagine what it meant. They were all at the kitchen table, stifled by an uncomfortable atmosphere, with cups of tea in front of them. Superintendent Blackman and Constable Dempsey, and her parents. Ruth, their daily, was at the stove with a pan full of acrid piccalilli, her ears and eyes practically on stalks. Louise Cartwright looked clear-eyed and harried – like a mother missing a son ought to look, though Pudding couldn't be pleased about that just then. The silence as she came into the room rang, and she blushed crimson at once, feeling as though she must have transgressed in some hideous way and not even been aware of it.

'Hello, Pudding,' said Constable Dempsey, and was silenced by a glance from his superior. Just then Pudding remembered a game of Assassin, played one Sunday afternoon when she was about eleven: a group of Ford and Slaughterford's youngsters, standing in a circle in silence, the assassin winking at people to 'kill' them, and everyone else trying to see them do it and denounce them before they themselves got killed. She'd looked across at Pete Dempsey and found him staring at her, and she'd stared right back, and they'd kept it up for a long time, each one waiting for the other to wink, until the look of constipated intensity on Pete's face had given her a fit of the giggles.

'Miss Cartwright, I wonder if you and I might have a further conversation about recent events,' said Blackman, without preamble, and it wasn't a question.

'Well. Yes,' said Pudding, dry-mouthed, wondering if it was in fact a crime to accuse somebody of another crime; wondering if the Hadleighs were going to prosecute her for it, and how on earth she would save Donny if she herself were in jail.

'Good,' said Blackman, getting to his feet. 'Is there some other room we might use?' He addressed the question to Pudding's father, who also got to his feet.

'Yes, of course. We'll go into the sitting room,' said the doctor, but the superintendent held up one hand.

'That's quite all right, Dr Cartwright. I am sure your daughter can guide me there. Perhaps you might remain with your wife for the time being.' He nodded to Pudding to lead on, and with an anxious glance at her father, and at Ruth behind him, she did just that.

Blackman closed the sitting room door behind them, and Pudding waited to be told to sit down, even though they were in *her* home. The policeman had such an impenetrable watchfulness about him that Pudding could hardly bear to be alone with him; though she had nothing to hide, he made her feel as though she most decidedly did. The reflection of light on his round spectacles made it hard to see his eyes clearly. His hair was darkly oiled, and his skin was smooth – in spite of his air of authority, Pudding wondered if he wasn't much older than Alistair had been.

'Now, Miss Cartwright—' he began.

'Oh, everyone calls me Pudding,' she said, trying to smile, trying to relax. He gave her a steady look, and she decided not to interrupt again. He spoke with the deliberate elocution of a man trying to lose a regional accent.

'Miss Cartwright, I understand that this whole business has been very upsetting to you. That it continues to be so. For a child such as yourself to have witnessed the terrible scene at the mill of last week is to be most deeply regretted. I understand that you were fond of Mr Hadleigh, and are very fond of your brother as well. I can imagine that to lose both of them in such a way is distressing.'

'I'm not a child, I'm almost sixteen, and I haven't lost Donny,' said Pudding, resolutely. 'Donny didn't kill Mr Hadleigh.'

'So you keep saying. Now, Miss Cartwright, I need you to listen very carefully to the questions I am about to ask you, and I need one other thing to be wholly clear: it is imperative that you answer them as truthfully as you possibly may. That means with facts that you are certain of, not with ideas that you wish to be true. Do I make myself clear?'

'Yes, Mr Blackman.'

'It's Superintendent Blackman. Now, Miss Cartwright. What can you tell me about the relationship between Mrs Hadleigh and your brother, Donald?'

'Their relationship? What do you mean?'

'Were they close? Were they perhaps . . . on friendly terms?'

'Well . . . no. I don't think so. I don't think Irene Hadleigh is on friendly terms with anybody here.'

'Yes. I've been told that she hasn't cared to involve herself with the village since her arrival. That she doesn't seem to care overly much for . . . making Slaughterford her home.'

'Well, that's certainly true.'

'So you never saw Irene Hadleigh and your brother to-gether?'

'What do you mean, together?'

'Talking together, for example. Or perhaps was Donald invited into the house? For tea?'

Pudding stared at the policeman in bewilderment. He stared right back, and didn't blink.

'No, of course he wasn't,' she said.

'You're quite sure of that?'

'She wouldn't invite anybody in, least of all Donny. I saw her talking to him once and she looked horrified – she looked like she was afraid of him. Which is stupid, just because he has a scar on his head, and—' Pudding cut herself off, beginning to see what Blackman was driving at.

'So you did see them talking together?'

'Just that one time, but it was out in the garden, and I think she was asking about some flowers for the house.'

'You overheard the conversation?'

'No, I just—'

'Stick to facts, please, Miss Cartwright.' Superintendent Blackman made a note of something in a small black jotter. 'Mr Hadleigh spent much of each day at the mill, or in town. Nancy Hadleigh is also out a good deal of the time, on farm business or on social calls. Which means that Irene Hadleigh has often been left alone in the house. Would your brother have told you if he'd had any other kind of contact with her? She's a very attractive woman, after all. And very fashionable. Did Donald ever tell you that he found her so? Did you ever see him, perhaps, watching Mrs Hadleigh? Do you think he would still notice . . . such a thing, since his injury?'

'No. I don't know,' said Pudding, dumbly. 'How could he watch her? She almost never comes out. He never said any such thing to me, and the only thing he likes to watch is the machines in the mill. He was going to be an engineer, before it happened – did you know that? He was so clever.'

'Yes, your mother told me as much. Now, are you quite sure you can tell me nothing whatsoever about a friendship between your brother and Mrs Irene Hadleigh?'

'Donny doesn't have any friends,' said Pudding, quietly. 'None but old Jem Welch. And Alistair Hadleigh. All the other people he used to know find it too hard now.'

'And you, of course,' said Blackman, staring at her again. 'A most loving and loyal sister.' He made it sound like a bad thing to be.

'A loving and loyal sister is not the same as a friend.'

'Indeed.' Blackman snapped his jotter shut and stood up.

'Wait – do you think Irene Hadleigh is involved, then? Please tell me – have you realised it wasn't Donny? Because I *know* it wasn't him!'

'However hard it may be, Miss Cartwright, I fear you've little choice but to begin to accept that your brother, though he may have been out of his mind at the time, did kill Alistair Hadleigh. All the evidence points to it. What is puzzling to me is the reason why. As you say, nobody has a bad word to say about Mr Hadleigh, and every man in the mill tells me that your brother only ever went into the machine rooms at the mill, never the offices.'

'Yes! You see? It can't have been—'

'I'm also told by those who have worked with Donald since his return from the war that he rarely takes anything upon himself. That he has little initiative, though he works hard and steadily at a job when somebody sets him to it.'

'That's right, yes. So you see—' But Pudding cut herself off again, as she began to see. 'You think Irene Hadleigh put him up to it?' Disbelief made her voice rise.

'She has inherited the estate in full, and she does seem

curiously unmoved by her husband's untimely death. And she is a beauty . . . I wonder if she might not have found out a way to persuade your brother to act on her behalf.' The policeman clamped his mouth shut and blinked rapidly three times, as though realising he'd said too much. 'But this is merely a theory voiced aloud, Miss Cartwright, as yet entirely uncorroborated and certainly not to be bandied about.'

'If . . . if it's true, would they let Donny go?' Pudding asked, her mind racing ahead.

'No, indeed. I fear not, Miss Cartwright. Whatever the reason he did it, the fact remains that he has murdered a man. There can be no doubt about that – Mrs Hadleigh's servants confirm she did not leave the house that morning, and in any case it is inconceivable that she would have the strength to inflict such wounds.'

'But . . . if it was all her idea? If she coerced him somehow . . . or tricked him?'

'I presume she would need to have his trust, or his . . . admiration, in order to achieve such an aim. And you have just finished telling me, Miss Cartwright, that there was no such close relationship between the two of them. I suspect this theory of mine will prove to hold no water whatsoever. I merely wanted to see if you could give it any credence, and you have answered me well enough.'

He opened the door and held out his arm to usher her back through it, and Pudding rose reluctantly. She didn't want to return to the kitchen, and let the moment pass. She felt that, somewhere in the conversation they had just had, there was a glimmer of hope for Donny, though she couldn't quite catch it. She was loath to leave in case she missed it altogether.

'My brother did not kill Alistair Hadleigh, Superintendent Blackman,' she said, weighting the words with every ounce of her conviction. 'And the worst part of it is that the person who *did* kill him is out there somewhere, right now, knowing that they are getting away with it. Knowing that *you* are letting them get away with it.' Blackman paused, letting his arm drop back to his side. Behind his glasses, his eyes were entirely impenetrable; his breathing was so soft and slow it was imperceptible, and beside him Pudding felt like a gasping, wobbling, helpless thing. But he was considering her words, she could tell. Eventually, he gave a minute shake of his head.

'One must always try to find the *why* in these things, Miss Cartwright,' he said. 'Who else has a reason to kill Mr Hadleigh? The answer is nobody. But your Donald, since his injury, does not seem to need much of a why at all.'

'You're wrong about that. And somebody did have a reason,' said Pudding, and saw interest light Blackman's steady eyes. 'The real killer had a reason,' she said, and the interest vanished. Blackman turned away from her, and she knew she had failed.

❧ ❧

Clemmie's sisters were so desperate to know the identity of her lover that when they saw the alphabet Rose had written down, they made Clemmie sit at the table and tried again to teach her to write. Clemmie had been apathetic towards the letters at school, but the fact that she now had cause to learn made no difference. The letters fought her, just like spoken words did, and she certainly wasn't going to let them coax a secret from her that she was more determined than ever to keep.

'What's this nonsense?' said William, coming in for his lunch and seeing them there, three girls huddled around the fourth. 'Haven't you lasses enough work to do?'

'We'll do it, Pa. Only it's wrong that Clem can't even write her own name,' said Mary.

'Or anyone else's name,' added Josie.

'She's no need of it,' said William, ruffling Clemmie's hair, sitting down heavily. They all stared at him. It had been a long time since he'd touched any of them in kindness, or with affection. He glowered at their scrutiny so Rose broke the silence hastily with sliced bread and ham, and pickled onions. But the girls were on Clemmie's side now – even Lizzie, who'd spotted a bite mark on her neck, and woven her mad hair into a loose braid on that side to hide it. Perhaps they hoped to encourage her confidence with such displays of loyalty, but she remained resolutely uncommunicative. In the night, disembodied whispers came through the darkness.

'Is it Bobby Silcox, Clem?' This was a slow-witted Biddestone boy who worked in the sawmill there, stacking cut planks, sweating all day long.

'Is it Jared Hinckley?' A thin young man with a wall eye, who appeared at Honeybrook Farm now and then, looking for work. Clemmie didn't know whether to be happy or sad that they never once thought to suggest a Tanner.

When they'd met at the river, for the first time after what had happened at the mill, Eli had asked enough of the right questions to work out that Clemmie had overheard the plan to rob Alistair Hadleigh.

'I didn't want to, Clem. I swear to you, I never would have, left to my own devices,' he'd said, and Clemmie had taken his face in her hands to show that she believed him. 'And then with what happened . . . I wanted more than anything for the coppers to take the old bastard in. Even if it meant taking me and John as well . . . I wanted them to finger Isaac for it. But you can't count on 'em for a bloody thing.' He'd had to pause and breathe, slowly, through his anger. In the fortnight since then, and since Eli had realised that Clemmie still wanted him, and wouldn't betray him, things had changed. His passion for her had crystallised into something deeper, and less childlike; something so intense it gave her a shiver along her spine when she saw it, and a seasick feeling, like the ground was tilting.

'No one's ever been as good to me as you have, Clem. No one's ever been as true,' he told her, with kisses so strong they bruised her lips, and left them puffy and red. 'You're an angel. You're *my* angel.' She couldn't tell if the shiver were a warning or a thrill, but it was addictive, utterly addictive. It made her feel like a different person to the one she was before – more awake somehow. More real. And she needed his salt-metal taste in her mouth like she needed to breathe; she craved the unexpected softness of his skin in places nobody else knew; she was fascinated by his eyes – older than the rest of him but blue and beautiful, when everything else about his face was ferocious.

And when the police did not return to hound the Tanners, when the investigation seemed closed, she began to wonder if she'd got it all wrong. If she'd misunderstood what she'd overheard at Thatch Cottage – if the robbery at the mill had been aborted, or had happened sooner than she knew, and had nothing to do with the violent attack. If the Tanners had had nothing to do with that, and news of their robbery had been lost in the sensation of the worse crime, or attributed to whoever had dealt the blows. She wished she could ask Eli, wished there was some way she could find out for sure. When she thought back to what she had heard, and what Tanner was like, and how Eli had been afterwards, it seemed obvious to her that it had gone just as she feared it had. But the notion that Eli had no part in it was tempting, and seductive, and as long as she didn't think about it too much, it remained a possibility. Sudden rushes of emotion assailed her all day long, bringing strange physical side effects – a dizziness, the feeling that she was receding from the world into some wrong-moving tunnel; tastes in her mouth that came from nowhere, stemmed from nothing, and made her either ravenous or nauseous; overwhelming surges of love for her family, accompanied by a wobbling weakness in her legs, which then quickly ebbed into a kind of simmering hostility she had never felt before, which somehow made her notice that her clothes were too tight, and cutting into her.

With Isaac Tanner safely away from home during the day, or safely at the pub in the evening, Eli began to take Clemmie home to meet his mother and younger siblings at Thatch Cottage. They were nervous; there was a watchful uneasiness about them all – except for his grandmother, who slept in a chair by the stove the whole time Clemmie was there. At first she thought they were unsure of her, or bothered by her silence. After a while she saw that they were scared for Eli. Frightened that he was there, where his father might catch him not working, might catch him bringing an outsider into their home. Mrs Tanner looked up sharply at any sound from outside – a pheasant coughing in alarm, a snapping twig, any sudden noise from the mill. She had long, bushy hair that stayed in a bun at the back of her head without the help of pins, and a weary, knowing look in her eye. But her smile was ready enough, though it was wry rather than warm. Whenever they were there she made sure that the windows stayed covered with the thick felts that the mill gave away when they got too worn for the paper-making machine. So for Clemmie the inside of Thatch Cottage was a place of shadows, with dark corners and watchful inhabitants moving in them, whatever the time of day. A place that had turned its back on the rest of the world. She could hardly bear it when it was still daylight outside. She fretted and fidgeted, feeling the walls close in around her. But once it was dark the cosiness drew her in, and the candlelit dimness seemed soft and cosseting, and Clemmie stopped feeling as though she had walked willingly into a den of thieves.

Clemmie knew that her family were poor – God knew there was never any money for anything – but compared to the Tanners she saw that her life was blessed in many ways. That at Weavern Farm they had eggs and milk and cheese and fresh vegetables, and clean air and space, and the reassurance and rhythm of constant work. Thatch Cottage was dank amidst the trees, and dirty for having too many people inside, trying to live, trying to breathe. The patch of ground they had outside was muddy and too shaded to grow anything; it stank of the privy and the pigsty, from which the sow gazed out, unhappily, through her white eyelashes. There was never enough food, and the food they had was unappetising, and monotonous. The children had coughs and snivels, even then, at midsummer. Two of the littlest had angry skin rashes, all red and scaly, which they scratched at constantly. Mrs Tanner cut their nails as short as she could and mixed up an ointment of tea leaves, comfrey root and pork dripping to rub on, though they grizzled as she did. The smallest child, a little boy called Jacob, took an instant shine to Clemmie and crawled into her lap whenever she was there, knotting his fingers into her hair and sucking his grubby thumb. The child, not yet two years old, smelled of earth and leaves, and Clemmie remembered the story she'd heard, that Tanner had drowned this baby's twin sister in the river at birth. Seeing the way their mother was with them, and the way she made do, Clemmie knew it was nothing but a vicious rumour. Eli brushed his little brother's cheek with his knuckles, his expression keen, tender.

'Takes after you, this one, Ma,' he said.

'For a change,' said his mother, with a smile. She looked at Clemmie. 'Every other boy I've had has been a copy of his dad – like they were struck from the same mould. But if you marry a strong man, perhaps you'd best expect it. I'd all about despaired of having a sweet one until my Jacob there came along.' Clemmie smiled, but Eli's face had closed off, and he went to the cupboard to look for something. 'If this first of yours is a boy, perhaps you'll have a sweet one too, young Clemmie,' Eli's mother said, quietly, so that he wouldn't hear. 'My Eli has always been soft underneath, even if he can't let himself show it. Drink this, child.' She handed Clemmie a steaming cup. 'Nettle tea. It'll stop you looking so swollen up and ripe. But your folks'll work it out sooner rather than later, as will Eli – best to just tell him.' Clemmie sipped obediently, and thought little of it.

Eli returned to the table with a cloth doll of a little boy: soft, stuffed arms and legs, with dark brown wool hair and blue eyes in needlepoint – just like a Tanner. It was wearing a yellow twill waistcoat and trousers, a white shirt and tiny black shoes, which Clemmie felt sure no Tanner child had ever worn. It was dirty, but not as dirty as it could have been – the pale cream fabric of its face had been grimed yellowish from the touch of human skin, but on the whole it looked as though it had been kept safe, for special use.

'The vicar's wife gave us this, when I was only knee-high,' said Eli. 'She brought us a load of stuff – clothes and shoes the church had collected, and other toys. Dad chucked it all out. He got into such a rage, saying we didn't need their charity, and how they thought they were so godly and above us. I only managed to save this by sitting on it.' He tucked the doll under Jacob's arm, and the toddler squeezed it tight to his ribs, his eyelids drooping with sleep. 'Why shouldn't the littl'uns have a doll?' Eli murmured. Clemmie wanted to ask how they'd kept it hidden from his father all that time, and it was as though Eli heard the question. 'We keep it in a flour pot. My dad never looks there – you can't eat flour right out the jar, after all.' He smiled briefly, and it caused Clemmie's heart to clench. She realised how few times she had seen him smile.

'The two of you need to think,' said Mrs Tanner, gently enough. 'When he finds you out – and he will find you out – he'll like as not turn you out from under this roof, Clemmie, and like as not you'd be glad of that. He's worse than ever of late, since what happened at the mill. I don't know what ails him.' Mrs Tanner shook her head. 'But something ain't right. He's full of nightmares and pain, and the only way he knows how to deal with that is with his fists. But I dare say your folks'll turn you out an'all. So. You need to think.'

Eli's smile vanished. One of his sisters worked at the stove, jamming in a poker, feeding in dry twigs. From upstairs came a loud thumping.

'Go on and see what your granddad wants,' Mrs Tanner told one of the children. 'Tell him supper won't be long.'

'We'll get gone,' said Eli, rising and holding out his hand to Clemmie. She took it, and got up, and nobody argued that they should stay longer, or eat supper. They slipped out into the night together, moving quietly, assuredly, west of Slaughterford through the mill's potato fields and up the hill, until there was no chance of being seen. Then they stopped and kissed, held each other tight, carried on walking again, until Eli stopped by the bridge to Weavern Farm, with the river's rush to hide any noise they might make. 'Go on in to your bed,' he told her, pushing her gently. Clemmie held his hands and wouldn't go. He would sleep rough to keep out from under Tanner's feet – a bed of long grass under a hedge somewhere. He'd wake before dawn, drenched with dew, chilled, restlessly exhausted. He was becoming a bird, a rabbit, a fox. Becoming wild. She wanted to stay with him, and be like him, and at the same time she wanted to take him inside with her, to a feather bed and the clinging safety of the loft room, and give him that life instead. 'Go on, Clemmie,' he insisted. 'We'll think of a plan, just like Mum said. But not tonight. I'll think of a plan, I promise.'

Clemmie woke with the sun. Her head was thumping and her body felt limp. Her sisters were stirring, and she forced herself to sit up. There were small twigs in her hair and mud under her fingernails. Josie, beside her, pinched her arm fondly as she got up.

'Scarecrow,' she said. Clemmie shut her eyes and swallowed. There was a lump in her throat that wouldn't go, and a taste of iron, or blood. She tried to ignore it for a moment, then lurched over the side of the bed to reach for the pot, but it was too late and she threw up all over the rag rug and Josie's feet. 'Oh, Clem!' Josie cried in horror.

'Oh, for pity's sake,' Mary grumbled.

'What did you eat, Clem?' said Josie.

'What *didn't* she eat?' said Lizzie, always at her worst first thing in the morning. 'No wonder she's getting so fat.' Shakily, Clemmie got to her feet and patted Josie's arm in apology. She wanted to go and get water and a cloth to clean up with but couldn't quite make her legs work. Mary was watching her intently, with her head on one side; thoughts marched across her face, and the quality of her silence was such that, gradually, the other three stopped and stared at her.

'No!' said Lizzie, her face falling into astonishment.

'What?' said Josie, frowning.

'Fewer rags to wash last month, weren't there?' said Mary.

'And she's been as moody as a mare. And eating like a pig,' Lizzie pointed out. Realisation dawned on Josie. Her hands flew to her mouth, and she turned wide eyes on Clemmie.

'Oh, no . . . oh, you're not, are you, Clemmie?'

'I reckon she is,' said Lizzie, excitedly.

'Well, we can't keep *that* a secret for you,' said Mary, her shoulders dropping wearily. 'You daft cow. Dad'll go spare.'

They fell into a heated debate about when to tell Rose,

and how their mother might react, and what was to be done, and how they could find out the man responsible and whether William would force them to marry, or kill him and then beat the baby right out of his daughter, and solve it that way. There was a kind of frenetic excitement to their words, their voices, their movements. Clemmie was buffeted to one side of the flow, and drifted over to the window. She pushed the thin drapes aside, sat down on the sill and took a deep lungful of the morning air. The chickens were muttering for release from the barn, the cock was warming up his disjointed crowing, and the cows were milling at the yard gate to be let in and milked. Clemmie put her hands flat on her stomach, and thought for a while, sending her mind inwards until she found what she was looking for – the unmistakable sense of new life. Chicks and goslings, kits, kids and piglets, and now herself. Clemmie and Eli. *Hello, piglet*, she said silently, and smiled. She let the early sun fall onto her at the open window, hoping that, however impossible it was, Eli would see. It seemed to her entirely right, and entirely as it should be. She felt certain that all would be well. The piglet would become a part of their plan, and all would be well.

The whole of Slaughterford turned out for Alistair Hadleigh's funeral. The mill was left to fall silent – the machines halting their endless turning, beating, stirring and drying, the hiss of steam petering to nothing. Even farm work stopped for the day. Nancy Hadleigh had refused for any work of any kind to go on at Manor Farm, bar the essential feeding and milking of animals, and the brewery and smaller farms had followed suit. Nobody could remember such a happening before, and nobody had ever heard such silence in Slaughterford. The quiet belonged to bygone years before any of them had been born. Voices were lowered outside the church, and though it might have been out of respect for the occasion, people kept turning to look down into the valley, to wonder at the gentle nudge of the breeze and the skylarks' constant song, and the incredible hush everywhere, as though they couldn't quite believe it. They searched the valley as though the view must have changed along with the sounds in their ears – the mill must have vanished, the brewery chimney toppled, the cottages swept away by some massive hand. When the breeze dropped they could even hear the river, parting sibilantly around the piers of the bridge. The stillness cast a magic spell that enthralled them all.

Alistair's body had come back from Chippenham that morning, in the undertaker's ebony carriage, its glass sides showing the glossy coffin and the multitude of white flowers inside. The horses were black, and wore black plumes; their harness had silver buckles, brightly polished, as did the carriage and the coffin. The whole sad parade was monochrome, and so wildly out of place against the greens, yellows and pinks of the flower-strewn churchyard that it might have dropped down from the sky. Or risen up from some underworld. Irene wore black from head to toe. She had a veil so thick she could hardly see out from under it, and, crucially, it was nearly impossible for anybody to see in through it – to see her face. Which didn't stop them trying, of course. Word had got about, as word will get about. Word of what Pudding had accused her of, and that the police superintendent had been up to Spring Cottage to interview her about it. Word that she hadn't loved Alistair, and that her grief was a sham. A rapid spread of incredulous words, passing through the villagers like an infection. She felt their looks, and felt them speculating. She felt, more than ever, her every move scrutinised; she felt that if she got one tiny thing wrong they would fall on her and devour her. She wondered if only Nancy were stopping them. As the coffin was carried, with excruciating slowness, from the lane to the side of the family grave, which gaped in readiness, Nancy took Irene's arm. It might only have been to keep herself standing, but it felt like unity. A show of support. Irene clasped her hand, never more grateful to Alistair's aunt, even if the gesture were not all it seemed.

Chairs were brought out for Irene and Nancy, and while Nancy sank carefully onto hers, Irene felt wound too tight to sit. When it seemed that things would not proceed until she did, she perched on the edge of the chair, her body thrumming with tension. The crowd of mourners seemed to cluster in and tower over her, like a wave that might break, and wash her into the grave along with her late husband. The black coffin was like a tear in the world. Looking at it gave Irene the same electric shock, deep in her bones, as the memory of Alistair's wounds; the same terrible lurch of dissociation from reality. She tried not to look at it because she couldn't help picturing him inside: pallid now, washed clean of blood but still broken and torn. She couldn't help picturing his sinking cheeks stuffed with cotton wadding, and his eyelids stitched shut and his lips entirely bloodless, and all the quietly violent things that would have been done to his insides in preparation for burial. As though what was left in the coffin were a doll of Alistair – a life-sized doll, put together from his remains in macabre imitation of the real man. It sent cold tingles over her scalp, and washed her cheeks with saliva, and she shut her eyes and longed for the moment when the thing in the coffin would be dropped into the ground and covered over forever. She didn't hear the sermon; she was concentrating too hard on surviving the horror of simply sitting there. When Gerry McKinley took her arm and helped her to her feet, she had no idea what he wanted. She panicked as he walked her closer to the grave, and tried to pull her arm away, until she saw that the coffin had been lowered in, and everyone was waiting for her to throw the first handful of earth over it. Then she had to fight the urge to fall to her knees and push great armfuls of it in, and shovel it in with her hands, and keep going until there was nothing left to shovel.

She and Nancy led the mourners up to Manor Farm, where there was to be a sedate wake for the higher-ups. The villagers and mill workers drifted away to their homes, or to the pubs – the White Hart in Ford and the White Horse in Biddestone – to raise a glass or several to their late master; a man they had loved, in a distant way, and respected. At the back of the crowd, their faces downturned, were Dr and Mrs Cartwright, and Pudding. No Donald, of course. The doctor looked pale and exhausted; his wife looked blank, but calm. Pudding's face was wet and ravaged, her normally bright eyes so puffy from crying that they looked piggish and ugly. Besides Irene, they were the most scrutinised of the gathered crowd. She glanced around and saw a variety of expressions directed at them, from bland curiosity to pity, anger and hatred. Pudding and her mother seemed oblivious to it all, which Irene supposed was a good thing. Only the doctor flinched from every face, every unspoken word. He looked like someone struggling to stay standing in a hurricane, and the three of them huddled together, subtly but completely cut off from their neighbours, as though such bad times might be contagious. Irene spotted Constable Dempsey, who, like most young people in Ford and Slaughterford, had known the Hadleighs all his life, and the sight of him set her heart thumping. But if he was there to watch her and report to his superiors, he was doing a poor job of it. He was watching the Cartwrights far more intently, and Pudding in particular.

They had the wake in the dining room, where the long table was laden with cold food, but people spilled into the sitting room and morning room, seeking the space to sit. Clara Gosling and Florence had extra help, on loan from the McKinleys at Biddestone Hall – two stony-faced girls who looked too smart for the farm in their crisp uniforms. They ferried out dirty glasses, ferried in clean ones, refreshed the trays of savoury pastries and petits fours and proffered them to the mourners, whose respectful silence grew less and less so as the first glasses of sherry went down. Irene stood where she was put and was commiserated with by many people, most of whom she didn't know. She neither ate nor drank, and hadn't all day, and soon began to feel the familiar lightness of being in need of nourishment. She let it carry her away from the crowd, into a vague place where she could do nothing about anything, and so expected little of herself. But then Cora McKinley appeared before her, and jarred her out of it. Cora's normally lively face was drawn, and set into hard lines that made her look older than her years.

'What will you do now?' she said, but Irene had no answer. 'I suppose you'll sell up – realise your assets, I should say. And move on to your next adventure.' Her voice cracked a little as she spoke, and she moved her glass of sherry from her left hand to her right, and back again.

'I don't know what I'll do,' said Irene, but the sound of her voice seemed to anger Cora.

'Well, you've all the time in the world to decide, I suppose.' She looked down at her feet for a moment. 'Father says it is just one of those terrible things that happen. But I can't help seeing everything that happens as part of a progression, from one thing to the next – the latter either caused by, or following on from, the former,' she said, her eyes beginning to gleam as her brother Charles appeared behind her. 'Alistair survives the war, marries you, and brings you here, and then is killed. I mean, it's one hell of a coincidence, isn't it? So I can't help wondering whether the latter might not have happened if the former hadn't either. If he would still be alive if you'd never come here. If he'd never met you.'

'Cora, that's enough!' said Charles, taking her arm. Cora wrenched herself free and stormed away, her face in her hands.

'Nobody thinks that, Irene,' said Charles, not quite able to meet her eye. 'Cora is just upset. We're all of us at the Hall so terribly sorry for your loss.'

'Everybody thinks it,' said Irene, quietly. Charles looked at her at last, his face sorrowful. 'She's only saying what everybody thinks. Isn't she? Everybody thinks I'm somehow to blame.'

'Irene . . . people just don't understand, that's all. They don't understand why it's happened, and grief makes people irrational.'

'I don't understand it either,' said Irene. 'I don't!'

'Dear girl, you must only try to think of getting through these dark days as best you may, and to remember how dearly Alistair loved you. I never saw him happier than when he came down to say you'd accepted him. It stripped years from him – he looked like a boy again, hooking the biggest fish out of my father's pond.' Charles looked down, his sadness tangible. 'It's a rum do, and no mistake,' he muttered, and gave her hand a squeeze before moving away. He hadn't invited her to visit them, or offered to return if she needed company. Without Alistair, Irene doubted she would see them again.

A tray of full claret glasses went by and Irene reached for one, taking a gulp and feeling the delicious heat as it reached her empty stomach. Then she left the room as discreetly as she could. She couldn't face going up to the bedroom – the room where Alistair had slept for so many years before she'd even come into his life. She had an oddly guilty feeling, as though she, too, had begun to blame herself for his death. She remembered the feelings of prescience that had beset her more than once since she'd been at Manor Farm. She racked her brains for some connection between them all, some sign or warning she had missed. She remembered Tanner's odd reaction to the old doll, and Ma's declaration that change was coming; she remembered the darkness that surrounded Hilarius, and the unflinching hardness of his eyes. Bewildered, she went through to the study, where the Hadleigh family portraits hung, and for a second felt the blessed relief of being alone. She shut the door behind her, letting out a long breath she hadn't known she was holding, and only then saw Nancy, standing silently in front of the portrait of her twin brother, Alistair's father. She was looking up at it with a broken-hearted intensity, as though she hoped the picture would come alive and offer her some comfort. At once, the weight of her circumstances settled back onto Irene, and she thought about slipping away again, unseen, just as Nancy turned and saw her.

'Irene,' she said, obviously unhappy at the interruption.

'Sorry, Nancy. I didn't know you were in here. I'll go.'

'Not on my account,' said the old woman, turning her gaze back to her brother. 'The atmosphere in there is awful, isn't it? All those people pretending to grieve as they shovel food into their mouths.' She shot Irene a wintry smile. 'Not that they weren't fond of Alistair. But fondness doesn't translate into true grief. Does it?'

'No,' said Irene, knowing that Nancy included her beneath that umbrella.

Irene stared up at the portrait of the first Alistair, and saw again how like his father her husband had been. Same height and build and demeanour; same light in the eyes, same arrangement of the face that made it seem permanently on the brink of a smile. 'Was he like his father?' she asked. Nancy sighed deeply.

'So very much like him, in appearance,' she said. 'Especially as he got older. Sometimes, in more recent years, it was so like having my brother back that I almost forgot they were two separate men. Almost.' She looked haunted. 'But my brother and I were in the womb together. I feel his absence wherever I go, and whatever I do.'

'How did he die? Alistair's father, I mean.'

'He had a reckless streak – my nephew had it too, but in a far gentler way, and I did my best to foster it out of him. But my brother had no fear – or rather, he *loved* fear. He loved the excitement of danger – foolish wagers, foolish business deals, foolish liaisons. When we were children, on one trip to the seaside, he jumped into the water from a high cliff that none of the others would even climb up to – just because they bet he wouldn't. Broke his ruddy ankle as he hit the water, the stupid boy, but he didn't care because he'd won the bet. Always racing, always climbing, always gambling with his money and his life – and his reputation ... He got better as he got older – his gentler side came more to the fore. But he simply couldn't resist a wager. He was racing a friend from Chippenham to Lacock when it happened – racing across country. Robert Houlgate's new hunter, which was a great black brute of a thing, strong as an ox, against Alistair's bay mare – she was lighter, built more like a thoroughbred, so not as strong in heavy going.'

Nancy stared off into the past for a while. 'It was madness. They didn't know the route or the fences overly well. The horses were green, the ground was waterlogged, and it was too long a distance – too tiring for the animals. They took a hedge side by side, as Robert described it afterwards, and didn't see the ditch on the far side until it was too late.

Both horses fell. Robert was thrown clear, and only broke his collarbone. Alistair fell underneath his mare as she rolled. And that was that. The horse had to be shot, and Alistair had been crushed to death before anyone could even try to help him.' Nancy turned away from the portrait as if telling the story had rekindled an old anger towards him.

'Perhaps that was even worse than what has happened to young Alistair now,' said Irene, with the wine in her blood loosening her tongue. 'In a way. That he could have chosen not to do it, I mean.'

'He could have chosen not to die? No, no – I know what you mean. Perhaps, in a way, you're right. I was angry with him for a long time. So angry I didn't know what to do with myself. And I made poor Robert suffer terribly – he'd suggested the race, you see. Dratted man. He knew my brother wouldn't refuse.' She shook her head, and picked up the framed photograph of young Alistair as a boy. 'Thank goodness I had my nephew to look after. I don't know what I would have done, otherwise. There'd have been little point to anything.' She held the photo close to her midriff, and slumped over it, slowly, like she'd been delivered a blow. 'And now he's gone too. And there *is* no point to any of it.' Her voice was muffled by misery. Irene tried to put a hand on her shoulder but she shrugged it off. 'No, please. I don't think I can bear to be touched just now.'

'I'm so sorry, Nancy,' said Irene, struggling to think what she could possibly add. 'I'll be gone soon. You won't have to have me around. And I . . . I won't be turning you out of Manor Farm, so please don't worry about that.'

'You're leaving?' Nancy's head came up fast, eyeing Irene intently. Irene swallowed.

'Well . . . yes. I thought you would be happy.'

'Happy?' Nancy echoed, as though the very concept were

alien to her. 'But you're the last Hadleigh, Irene. You belong here, at Manor Farm, where Alistair brought you. We're the last two. Unless...?' She kept up her scrutiny until Irene felt like running from it.

'Unless what?' she asked, uneasily.

'Unless there's any chance of a... a new beginning for the family?' Nancy waited, then tutted when Irene obviously didn't understand. 'Is there any chance – any chance at all – that you might be pregnant, Irene?' The hope in her face, and in her voice, was pitiful. Irene knew there wasn't – as did the servants at Manor Farm, since her period had come on suddenly in the night, three days earlier, and made a mess of her bedsheets. She could hardly bear to dash this last hope of Nancy's, and fail again, but she shook her head.

'I'm sorry, Nancy, but no. There's no chance.'

'Ah. A pity,' said Nancy, quietly.

'You might have had children of your own, mightn't you? Alistair told me you had suitors... you were even engaged.'

Nancy didn't reply at once. She gazed off into the dark corners – of the room, of her memory.

'I was,' she said, tightly.

'What happened?' Irene asked, made bold by the awful, alien day.

'I chose my brother. And his son.' Nancy shrugged. 'I moved away when he got married. I thought I'd give him and Tabitha some space here. And besides – I couldn't stomach the woman, with her American manners and her popish super-stitions. Such blind faith has always seemed half-witted to me. I went off on the grand tour; I met a boy in Rome. A man, I suppose. Frank Launceston. Nice enough; bright enough. Plenty of money.' She shrugged. 'But then Tabitha died giving birth to Alistair.'

'Your brother must have been broken-hearted.'

'Well,' said Nancy, still not looking at Irene, 'if nothing else, he was completely out of his depth. With a baby son, I mean, and with being here at Manor Farm on his own. It had never happened before, you see. He hired a nanny, of course, but Alistair needed people around him that loved him. He needed women. He needed me.'

'So you came back.'

'I came back.'

'And Frank?'

'Frank married some vapid girl who was willing to trail his coat-tails around the globe, without a care in the world. Happier for all concerned, I've always thought.' In the quiet the clock ticked, and the merry voices of the mourners came as a wordless babble through the wall.

'You've very dutiful, Nancy,' said Irene, thinking that if it had been her, and she had loved Frank, she would have married him, and been that vapid girl.

'I'm a Hadleigh, and I have always done what needs to be done at Manor Farm.'

Once all the mourners had gone, Irene kept drinking. She'd had three glasses of red wine, and was feeling much better – as though it had all happened to someone else and she might go home and forget about it, just like the people who'd been clogging up the house all afternoon. She might go home to Fin, somehow – when he saw her, he would realise how much he loved her, and find the courage to leave Serena. To her scrambled mind this seemed wholly plausible, though it didn't offer the comfort it once had. His awful letter, and the pain of reading it, had torn something irreparably; it had weakened the part of her that still cleaved to him. She sat on a window sill in the drawing room and watched the twilight gathering in the gnarled apple trees, and the bats come out to wheel and dive, and when she ran out of wine she went, unsteadily, to the back kitchen to look for more. Clara was at the table, listening to the wireless, drinking sherry and tucking into a huge plate of leftovers. She gave Irene a pinch-lipped look, half appraising and half guilty, then fetched her an open bottle of claret from the pantry.

'The master never liked to see women in their cups,' she said, flatly.

'The master isn't here to see it,' said Irene.

'No, he ain't,' said Clara, settling back into her plate as though seeking wisdom in it. Irene went out into the near-dark.

She left through the back gate in the low orchard wall and set off down the hill towards the village. The night was warm and still, the deep blue sky was freckled with stars, and a shining sliver of moon had risen. A pretty summer night, as oblivious to the events of the day as Irene wished to be. The mills were still silent, and the brewery never ran at night. The farm animals were asleep; the wild animals kept themselves to themselves. Without a torch, Irene felt quite invisible to the world. She'd meant to go down to the river. She wasn't sure why – she'd had a vague idea about bathing; river bathing, as Fin had told her he and his brothers had done as children, in the Tay, but as she passed the church she heard a noise that stopped her. Sounds of movement, and of breathing; sounds of a person, in the very spot they'd just buried Alistair. The hair stood up all over Irene's arms, and she was suddenly cold. But however strong the impulse, she couldn't run away. For a moment, the wild possibility that Alistair hadn't been dead when they buried him flitted into her mind, and the strength with which she wished him back surprised her. But she knew it couldn't be, and she pictured the Alistair-doll instead – empty of life, stuffed with other things; a grotesque mannequin, a mockery of life — somehow out of the grave and walking. It wasn't possible, but she had to see.

Shaking all over, the wine churning sourly in her stomach, Irene went through the churchyard gate and closer to the heap of flowers that marked the spot. There was a figure there, sitting on the sod alongside the grave; a figure that was clearly not Alistair. Irene's next wild thought was that the murderer had come back to revel in it, before she remembered that Donny Cartwright was in jail, and recognised his sister as the figure at the graveside, snivelling quietly. Again, she wished she could slip away, unnoticed, but at the sound of her footsteps Pudding turned with a gasp.

'Who is it?' she said, too loudly.

'It's . . . Mrs Hadleigh,' said Irene, not going any closer. She wondered if she should still call herself Hadleigh, since she felt no more of a Hadleigh now than the girl struggling to her feet in front of her.

'Have you come to gloat?' said Pudding. Her voice had a tremor of distress that belied the bold words.

'What could I possibly have to gloat about?' said Irene, and that seemed to stump the girl for a moment. In the darkness, the white flowers on Alistair's grave seemed to glow. Irene could suddenly taste her own mouth, dry and sour from the wine. She felt nauseated. 'You can't honestly think I had anything to do with . . . with this, can you?'

'Yes! Oh, I don't know. Perhaps not,' said Pudding, rubbing at her eyes like a child. 'All I know is it wasn't Donny, but nobody will listen to me.'

'But . . . he was there, Pudding. He was . . . holding the shovel,' said Irene, as kindly as she could.

'That doesn't mean he killed Alistair! It doesn't! I know you all think I'm just saying that because I don't want it to be true, but that's not it at all. I *know* it isn't true.'

'Is that why you accused me instead?' At this, Pudding hung her head miserably, then sat back down on the damp grass.

'I'm ... I'm sorry about that. I was so confused, and I ... I know you didn't love him.'

'That hardly makes me a murderess!'

'But how could you not love Alistair? And why on earth did you marry him, if you didn't?'

With a sigh, and her head beginning to ache, Irene sat down next to Pudding.

'People get married for all sorts of reasons,' she said quietly.

'Well, that's no kind of answer.' Pudding scrabbled in her sleeve for a handkerchief, and blew her nose. 'They're going to hang him, you know. Donny. If I can't get to the bottom of this, they're going to hang him.'

'Maybe not ... maybe, because of his injury ...'

'That just gives them an excuse.' Pudding shrugged helplessly. 'You heard that policeman, talking about him like he's a mad dog that wants putting down. That's not what he's like! Just because he's different now, because he's a bit slower about things than he was, and can't stand up for himself, they think they can paint him any which way they choose! And pin anything on him! Well, they can't. It's not fair.'

'No. It isn't,' said Irene. 'But, Pudding, there was nobody else around ...' She remembered again all the odd signs, and ill-defined feelings, and fought to keep the facts to mind.

'Nobody was *seen*.'

'Well, that's rather the point, isn't it?'

'I'll find out. I have to. This is Slaughterford – there are no real secrets here. *Somebody* will know. The person who did it knows, and the next person they saw after doing it – they know too. Somebody knows *everything*, here. I just have to find them.'

'How will you do that?'

'I . . . I don't know yet,' said Pudding, and started to cry again. Irene felt heat radiating off the girl, and smelt the salty damp where tears had got into the hair hanging around her face. Pudding exuded a kind of irrepressible vitality, even in her denuded state, which made Irene feel hollow, a husk, in comparison. She put her hand on the girl's shoulder and squeezed it for a moment.

'Come up to the house for a while. We'll have cocoa, and there's tons of food.'

In the kitchen, now empty of Clara Gosling, Irene peered helplessly at the stove, trying to work out how to make it hotter, and where to put a pan to heat milk, and what size or type of pan she should use. She opened the hatch into which she'd seen Clara pouring coal but there was nothing to see, just a small pool of darkness, stinking of smuts. Pudding watched her curiously for a while.

'You don't know how to do it, do you?' she said, eventually, incredulously. 'You don't know how to heat milk.' Irene folded her arms and stared at the stove. She was incredibly tired.

'No,' she said. 'I've never done it before.' She couldn't quite bring herself to look at Pudding, but the girl groom got up and set about it without another word.

'Can you fetch out the cocoa and sugar?' she said, returning from the pantry with a huge covered jug of milk. 'Back there, right-hand side, top shelf.' Soon, the childhood smell of warm milk was filling the kitchen, rising with the shreds of steam from the pan, and in the soft glow of the single lamp, Irene remembered being ushered out of the kitchen as a child, when she'd been drawn down to it by the warmth and the light and the voices because she was cold, lonely and sleepless. *Back upstairs where you belong, Miss Irene. If your mother catches you . . .* The servants had tried to be kind, but they knew her parents too well. Pudding and Irene sat opposite one another at the table, and in the corner of the room the tap dripped steadily into the stone sink, adding to the small stalactite of scale on its lip.

'You loved Alistair,' said Irene. 'Didn't you?'

'Everybody did. Well – almost everybody.' She glanced across at Irene. 'I've known him all my life. That is, I had known him all my life.' Having used the past tense, Pudding gulped. To ward off fresh tears, Irene spoke.

'The reason I didn't love him was not because I'm some . . . heartless thing,' she said, floundering. But the night was dark and she had no idea of the time, and the wine had left her lucid and uncaring. 'I know I haven't . . . got to know any of you. So, just like with Donny, people here have thought and said whatever they've liked about me. It's not that I don't have a heart, but rather that I have a . . . a broken heart.'

Pudding looked up at her in wonderment, as if this were a wildly exotic thing to have.

'Have you really?' she said. Irene nodded. The girl's eyes were like headlamps. Irene shifted in her seat. The joy and terror of having said it aloud were irresistible. She hadn't spoken a word about it since leaving London. 'Superintendent Blackman said you'd run away from a scandal. He said you were a woman of dubious character.'

'Well,' said Irene, her face heating up, 'perhaps I am. There was a scandal. And I was . . . I was a fool.'

'What happened?'

'I . . . I fell in love with a married man,' said Irene, and Pudding's eyes grew even wider.

'Who was he?'

'His name was . . . is . . . Finlay Campbell. And he was – is – married to a woman called Serena. Who was my friend.' She looked up to see if Pudding would judge her badly for this, but she didn't seem to.

'And she found out that you loved him?'

'It was worse than that. He was unhappy. He'd been unhappy for years, he told me. He told me he hadn't known what love was until . . .'

'Until he met you?' Pudding breathed, wistfully, and Irene nodded. 'How *romantic*.'

'Serena was a friend but not a real one. That hardly makes sense, does it? There was every semblance of affection between us, but it was only skin deep, and underneath it was a kind of competition, a kind of . . . envy and distaste. I had the money, I was the right class, the right . . . style. She had all the ease and charm I've never had. She bewitched people – virtually enslaved them. She enslaved Fin. I don't say any of that to excuse what happened.'

'What happened?'

'We . . . had an affair. I loved him so much, I agreed to an elopement. I agreed to run away with him, and live with him until he was free of his marriage, and then we would get married ourselves. He promised me, and I never doubted him for a second. And it didn't seem wrong, because it was true love.'

Irene shut her eyes for a moment and was back there again, on the concourse at King's Cross station, with her case in her hand and her coat buttoned up to her chin, on an unseasonably chilly day in early spring. She'd been shaking all over with pent-up nerves, excitement, love. All the mad terror of what she was doing, coupled with the certain knowledge that it was right – that she couldn't be without him, and could no longer keep her feelings a secret from Serena, her parents, their friends. It was love – the love people spoke about and read about but never seemed to feel. Not like she was feeling it. Women in furs, and felt coats and hats, and plain brown drab; men hurrying to work with bowler hats and leather cases; the stink and hiss of the hot trains waiting, breathing out plumes of soot and steam. Her ears had been full of echoes – voices and footsteps and engines – all bouncing about in the iron rafters far above her head. Pigeons had strutted everywhere; a small child was on his own, crying, and when his mother found him she gathered him up, her face white. The station clock was a ponderous presence, the minute-hand moving with a reluctant clunk every sixty seconds. Irene had watched that clock for a long time. She'd been too nervous to eat breakfast, and the smell coming from a handcart selling roasted peanuts had made her stomach rumble. She'd spent a long time wanting to buy two cones of them, one for her, one for Fin, but not daring to leave the agreed spot in case he missed her in the throng.

The minute-hand of the station clock, black and ornate against a white background. How many times did she see it go around, getting colder, getting hungrier, becoming more afraid? At least sixty times, before she realised that Fin wasn't coming to meet her. Their train – to Cambridge – pulled out of the station behind her, and she simply stood and let it. She stayed a long time after that as well, chilled to the bone, just in case he had simply been delayed. And in spite of the clock she had little idea what time it was when she finally left, and walked, dazedly, to the house where Fin and Serena had their apartment. She'd been sure something terrible must have happened to him, that he'd been injured in some horrible way; she could conceive of nothing else that might have detained him. Not until she saw the look of unabashed triumph on Serena's face at the door, and, as she smiled the coldest smile Irene had ever seen, heard her say: *What on earth do* you *want?*

'What did she say?' said Pudding, hanging on Irene's every word.

'Not much,' said Irene. 'She came down, took my case and threw it into the street. All my things went everywhere, and blew about. She said Fin didn't want to see me ever again. That my attempt to steal and disgrace him had failed.'

'But . . . *he* approached you first, you said?'

'Yes. Not that it matters, really. We were in it together.'

'You can't have believed what she said! Didn't he come out to talk to you?'

'He did.' Irene recoiled from the memory. Fin, entirely cowed, Fin crushed, Fin too ashamed to look her in the eye. She still had no idea what had gone wrong, how Serena had found out, how she'd made him change his mind, and give her up. Perhaps it had only been that strange power she had over him, the corral he didn't seem able to break free from. Perhaps it was something more cast iron than that – something she had over him. She swallowed painfully. 'He told me to go. He just . . . stood there, while Serena called me such things . . . words I'd never heard her use before.'

'And he didn't defend you?' Pudding was outraged. Irene shook her head. 'The . . . the *worm*!'

'Serena was just too strong for him. And she was his wife – is his wife. She told all our friends, my parents, everybody we knew – her version of events, of course. That I'd a passion for her husband and had seduced him into my bed, and tried to get him to elope with me, and had even thought he actually *would*.' She shook her head again. 'Not that there is a good version of the events, of course.'

Pudding thought about it for a while, and Irene finished the last of her cocoa.

'He can't have loved you. Not really,' Pudding concluded, crossly. 'To give you up like that, and let you take all the blame.' If the words were meant as a comfort, they had the opposite effect.

'No . . . no, he loved me,' said Irene. 'I'm sure of it. At least . . . at least, I *was* sure of it.'

'Perhaps he did, then,' said Pudding, retracting in the face of Irene's misery.

'What does it matter now, anyway? It couldn't matter less. He's made his choice, one way or another.' Her attempt to sound resigned to it was fake in her own ears. She thought of the mad, vain hope the wine had conjured only that evening – that she and Fin would somehow be reconciled. But she wondered then if that hope were still genuine, or merely a habit of the mind.

'So you married Alistair out of . . . revenge?'

'Revenge? No, not at all! I married him because he asked me, and he . . . he seemed a nice man. And he offered me a home away from London. And I . . . I couldn't think what else to do. My parents wanted nothing to do with me, they told me to marry Alistair or I'd be cut off completely; none of my friends . . .' She shook her head, and looked up at Pudding. 'Those probably don't seem like very good reasons to you, do they?' Pudding looked down, blushing a bit.

'It just doesn't sound very fair on Alistair,' she said quietly.

'It wasn't,' Irene agreed. 'But he knew it all, at least. He was right there, and saw it all happening, but he married me anyway. As much out of kindness as out of love, perhaps.'

'Yes.' Pudding sighed. 'That sounds like Alistair. No wonder Miss H hasn't warmed to you. Are there any sandwiches left? I'm ravenous.'

'Tons, in the pantry. Help yourself.'

Pudding came back to the table with a silver platter covered with a cloth, beneath which were a mixture of sandwiches – salmon, cucumber, cheese. She tucked in eagerly, then looked at Irene.

'Aren't you having any?' she said. Irene shrugged a shoulder, and took a cheese sandwich as much out of politeness as anything. It tasted heavenly, and her stomach squeezed in utter delight as she swallowed, so she picked up another.

'So you see,' she said, 'even though I didn't love my husband as he should have been loved, I had no reason to wish him dead. He rescued me. He was the only chance I had.' Pudding nodded.

'The policeman thinks you might have seduced Donny into doing it for you,' she said.

'*What?*'

'I don't think he *really* thinks it. But perhaps he does. I thought he almost believed me, you see, when I said it wasn't Donny. But it was just that he thought it might have not been Donny on his own.'

'You don't think that, do you? That it was me, I mean. Me and Donny.'

'No,' said Pudding, without hesitation. 'You could be Queen Titania and he still wouldn't have hurt Alistair for you. I'm ... I'm sorry I accused you. It seems stupid now. All I wanted was for them to know it wasn't Donny. But even that didn't work – even when Superintendent Blackman thought it might be you, he still thought it was Donny as well. So it was a waste of time.' They both reached for another sandwich, and ate in silence for a while, and it felt so good to have food inside her that Irene didn't know how she'd survived so long without it. The tap dripped, and their thoughts were a mystery to one another. Irene looked at the girl sitting opposite her, and tried to imagine how hard it all must have been for her.

'How old are you, Pudding?' she asked. Pudding gave a tiny smile.

'I was sixteen today, actually,' she said. Her face fell. 'My parents forgot. Not that I blame them. I almost forgot myself.'

'Oh. That's ...' Irene trailed off, not wanting to say *awful*, or *tragic*. 'Too bad,' she opted for, lamely.

'I don't think it's been a birthday I'll care to remember,'
Pudding said, quietly. Irene reached for another sandwich.
'Will you help me, then?' Pudding added then, her face light-
ing with sudden desperation.

'In what way?' said Irene, uneasily, feeling ill-equipped
to be this girl's ally. She still felt ill-equipped to be of use to
anybody.

'To find out who really killed Alistair, of course. To prove
my brother is innocent of it.'

'But I . . . I don't know how to,' she said, and Pudding sank
again.

'No,' she said. 'Neither do I.'

The two of them stayed at the table until all the sandwiches
were gone, and the petits fours as well, and fatigue was dragging heavily at both of them. Birds were starting to sing and
the sky was turning gauzy as Pudding fell into a guest bed,
still dressed, asleep before she was fully horizontal, and Irene
watched over her for a little while – noticing that she looked
even younger in her unconscious state, with her skin so smooth
and clear, and her bushy curls flung out around her, and her
mouth slightly open. She saw something angelic and something animal in Pudding then; an odd mixture of guts and
innocence. Then she went up to the room she'd shared briefly
with Alistair, where the beams still wriggled drunkenly across
the ceiling, and in the final moments before she slept realised
that she felt, in some intangible way, just a little better than
before.

7

The Roots of Things

The run of fair weather had gone on so long that people had begun to take it for granted – there was no need to look out for signs the night before to know how the morning would dawn. The thundery rain that had fallen on the day of Alistair's murder seemed to have been accepted as unnatural, just like his death; some people even said it had been nature's response to the killing. Now, again, the sunshine could be relied upon. Blue skies, high white clouds, the river getting a little shallower each day, the water slowing down as though tired. The whole By Brook valley seemed to be slowing down – the baby birds had all fledged and breeding was over, so the dawn chorus was a half-hearted affair; the marsh marigolds along the riverbanks had softened from their first vibrancy into a kind of leggy languor. Slaughterford basked; its residents basked; nothing was done in a hurry now that haysel was over and harvest not yet begun in earnest. In times past, mill production would have suffered with the lowering water, but Slaughterford Mill was immune to that now, with its boilers and steam generators, and production was back to normal just a handful of days after the hiatus for Alistair's funeral. George Turner was supervising the day-to-day running of things, as he had done before, and when he came up against a decision that Alistair would have made he consulted Nancy instead, who told him to do whatever he thought best.

Down by the privy at the back of Spring Cottage, the rhubarb was half as high as Pudding, with leaves two feet across in places. The stalks were a violent magenta, gone too thick and tough to be eaten, and in the dank shade underneath, slugs gorged on the soggy ruins of rotted leaves. The garden was criss-crossed with their silver trails – and those of snails as well. The hostas and carnations had been eaten into oblivion. Louise Cartwright no longer cared to keep up her war on the creatures – once, she had collected them in a bucket and walked them down into the valley to tip them into a hedge, ignoring Ruth's suggestion to apply a brick to them and have done. By the middle of the afternoon, when the sun was at its hottest, buzzards rode the thermals over the hills, so high up in the blue that their faint, triumphant cries could be heard when they were too distant for the eye to make out. It was glorious. It should have been glorious.

Pudding caught herself imagining the summer as though Alistair hadn't been killed – as though he were still alive, and Donny were at home, and life were going on as it had before. It hadn't been perfect, she reminded herself, but by God it had been better than it was now. The eleven days since his death had been like a bad dream in which familiar things looked wrong, and frightening. She kept waiting for a return to reality, only for the permanence of what had happened to reassert itself with sickening clarity. She hated to see Slaughterford returning to normal life; the shock of Alistair's murder being assimilated into its long history, like a rock thrown into the river – there were still ripples, but the surface had closed over, and the flow continued, unabated, as it ever had. People still talked of little else, but in doing so they had begun to make it commonplace. Donny's involvement was spoken of in tragic terms – a young man broken by the war. Shocking, terrible, but not shameful. Mrs Glover in the shop had even said as much to Pudding. *Nobody's blaming your family, Pudding.* As though Pudding ought to have been grateful to them for that, or reassured. She'd paid the shillings for the tea and sugar and left without a word. And she determined – increasingly, every day – to keep the water from smoothing over altogether. The mill might be running again, and the men back at work, and the crops ripening from green to palest gold; the main topic of conversation might have moved on to what Mrs Hadleigh might choose to do with the mill and land, and what that meant for the workers and tenants, but Pudding wasn't going to let it rest. She wasn't going to let the water close over Donny.

Her early incredulity at his arrest had hardened into steady dread when nobody else was caught – when nobody else was even questioned. When it became abundantly clear that the police believed they had their man. She wanted to shake them all. Their willingness to accept Donny's wrongful arrest and move on was excruciating. She didn't know how they could think it of him – Donny, who'd been captain of the boys' cricket team three years in a row; who'd once run straight into the carpenter's shed when it was on fire because the man's elderly terrier was sitting inside, stupefied by the danger; who'd once eaten an entire tray of lardy cake for a bet, and had such a bad stomach the next day he couldn't go to school. This was the Donald Cartwright they believed could pick up a shovel and batter to death a man he had known and liked all his life. Pudding remembered the white flash of Donny's smile in the gloaming, shot back over his shoulder as he'd sneaked out to meet Aoife one night just before the war; safe in the knowledge that Pudding wouldn't betray him. Safe in the knowledge that she loved him – adored him – and wouldn't let him down.

Pudding avoided talking to people as much as she could, worried that sooner or later something would burst out of her – something angry and desperate and harmful. She walked to work with her head down, watching her marching feet.

Not that avoiding people was difficult. In fact, her friends and neighbours seemed to welcome it, and paused as she passed, silencing themselves. If it hadn't been for Hilarius, Irene and Nancy, Pudding could have gone whole days without talking to anybody other than her parents. But on the morning a message came from the police station in Chippenham that Donny's hearing before the magistrate had been fixed for two weeks' time, Pudding found she *had* to talk to somebody. The magistrate would hear the facts of the case, and the evidence against Donny, and would decide what exactly he would be sent to trial for: manslaughter due to diminished responsibility, diminished understanding of the results of his actions, and the fact that he probably hadn't intended, and certainly hadn't *planned* to kill Alistair; or wilful murder, for which he would certainly hang if found guilty.

Two weeks. Pudding read the note with her heart walloping right up into the back of her throat as panic gripped her. She had just two weeks to find out who was really behind the attack, or to at least raise enough doubt about somebody else being involved that the police would keep looking, and Donny wouldn't be tried for wilful murder. And in spite of Irene Hadleigh's tentative support, she had no idea what to do next. Irene had asked, the day before, what she could do to help and what Pudding would do next, even though *she* was the adult, and eight years older than Pudding. And Pudding had no answers for her.

'Well, can't *you* think of something?' she'd cried, the last time, pushed beyond the bounds of good manners. Irene had flinched slightly, and gone away with a quiet apology, which had made Pudding feel awful. It was the twenty-eighth of July, a Friday; and on Friday, August eleventh, her brother's fate would be all but sealed.

*

Thomas Hancock turned his hat in his hands, looking profoundly ill at ease. He was a small man, bony at the shoulder, widening to a pot belly perched on skinny legs. Irene guessed his age at around sixty, but it was hard to tell with some of the villagers. Their lives were lived outdoors, in all weathers, so their faces were beaten and creased from an early age. Thomas came with a powerfully organic aroma, reminiscent of the sheep he farmed.

'Won't you sit down, Mr Hancock?' she said, and the old man cast a horrified look around at the floral furnishings of the sitting room. He was dressed for farm work in a smock from the previous century, over canvas trousers and caked boots, and Irene knew she'd brought him into the wrong room, but when Florence had announced him she hadn't had the first clue who he was or what he might want. She'd pictured some other acquaintance of Alistair's, come to commiserate.

'Beggin' pardon, ma'am, best I don't,' he said. Irene cleared her throat and tried to think of some way to put the man at his ease, difficult when she was so on edge herself. She attempted to smile, but that only made him fidget more.

'How may I help you?'

'Ar. 'Tis only this, ma'am. 'Tis this.' He paused and looked down at his hands, and Irene agonised for a moment over whether to instruct him to call her *Mrs Hadleigh*, instead of *ma'am*. 'What with our Brandon gathered to the Lord last winter, and I with the farmer's lung . . . what with all o' that, we'd fallen behind with the rent. On the cottage and land, see. Only your husband, God rest his soul, he told I 'tweren't a problem, and I could make it up through the year as best I could, see?' Thomas cast her a guilty, beseeching look, and flinched from Irene's frown, which in fact was only down to having to concentrate to penetrate his accent. 'I know we must pay up, 'twas ever my design to. Only I hadn't quite made it up when he . . . when he were taken. I suppose . . . I do suppose if the estate is sold up, such debts as mine will be called in.' He studied the hat in his hands again – a battered felt affair, dark with grease around the brim. 'Any new owner should want to begin afresh, I should think,' he mumbled.

The penny dropped, and Irene blinked. It appalled her that an elderly man should feel he had to come to her – quite literally cap in hand – to ask her for mercy. She felt, quite definitely, that she hadn't the right. She didn't belong in Alistair's place; it was a situation she had never contemplated. *There has been a terrible mistake.* She had to stop the words speaking themselves.

'Mr Hancock,' she said, shaking her head and dropping all attempts to sound authoritative. He looked up at her, and the fear in his eyes affronted her. 'You may continue to repay any arrears by whatever arrangement you had with my husband. I shan't be calling in any such debts, I assure you.' Thomas brightened.

'Then . . . you shan't be selling up, ma'am? There's to be no new squire?'

'I . . . I can assure you, you and your family will not be turned out of your home,' Irene hedged. 'I will see to it personally.'

'Well, now . . .' Thomas Hancock nodded. 'Thank you most kindly, ma'am. Thank you. You have taken such a weight from my shoulders . . . You're as good and as kind as your late husband, God rest his soul, and I shall see to it that folks start to know of it.'

'They think otherwise, then?' said Irene, and the old man looked sheepish.

'Beg pardon, ma'am.'

'No, you haven't offended me. No one could ever be as good or kind as Alistair was, in any case,' she said, quietly.

'Ar, that may be so,' said the old man. 'There never was a worse loss, round these parts.'

When the old man had gone, Irene stayed a while in the sitting room, lost in sombre thoughts that were beginning to feel like an inner blockade of some kind – one that she probed, uncomfortably, constantly, trying to dismantle. Nancy interrupted them, wrinkling her nose from the doorway.

'Here you are – what is that unholy stink?'

'Oh – one of the tenants came to see me. Thomas Hancock.'

'Woolly Tom? That explains it.' Nancy grunted, and crossed to open the window. 'I do wish the peasants would keep outdoors. They smell worse than the collies on a wet day – why on earth did you bring him in here?'

'I didn't know who he was,' said Irene, with a shrug.

'Asking for another extension on the missed rent, I'll wager.'

'It seemed kind to agree to it. He seemed most . . . anxious.'

'Of course he's anxious, he'll never be able to pay it back. Alistair knew as much, but he let them linger on. Soft as butter,' she muttered, without any real feeling.

'I intend to honour all such agreements my husband made with tenants and workers alike,' said Irene, with more heat than she'd intended. Nancy gave her a long look.

'You must do as you see fit,' she said, stonily, walking back towards the door.

'It's the right thing to do, wouldn't you say?' Irene called after her, not wanting to start a row. Nancy turned, and softened.

'I suppose it is,' she said, and left. Irene sat quietly for a while longer, and realised that her inner blockade was anger. She realised just how furious she was.

She was angry for Alistair, to have been robbed of his entirely blameless life. She was angry for all the people who relied on him for their livelihoods. She was angry with the world for letting it happen, and in some amorphous way with herself, for lying in bed while it did. She was angry that she was now alone, when for a heartbeat it had seemed as though she might actually start to live again. She was angry with whoever had killed him. Very, *very* angry. And it was at that moment she realised that she didn't believe it had been Donald Cartwright. Her anger was not directed at him but at some unknown, faceless other person; some figure on the edge of her vision; shifting, moving, always out of reach, and vanishing when she turned her head. It was maddening. She closed her eyes tightly and tried to see; tried to piece the fragments of thought and feeling and impulse into some kind of whole picture, but it wasn't long before she was forced to give up. Along with the anger came a small measure of Pudding Cartwright's desperation that her brother had been blamed, and the real killer was being allowed off scot-free. And yet, when Pudding had asked for Irene's help after the funeral two nights before, Irene had hedged, and stepped back, and been uncertain and afraid. As she had always been. She got up, and went out to the stables.

She found Pudding bent in half with one of Bally Girl's hooves between her thighs; she was smearing the inside with a sticky ointment of some kind. Pudding's eyes were red-rimmed, and her cheeks looked chapped.

'Hello,' said Irene, still keeping a safe distance from the horse. 'What's that you're doing?'

'Oh. She always gets cracked heels when the ground is this hard. See here, where the bulbs have gone all shrivelled?'

'Oh, yes,' Irene lied.

'The grease will help to soften it all.' Pudding put the hoof down and wiped her hands on a rag. 'Did you want to go riding?'

'No. Well, perhaps, later. I wanted to talk to you about...

about your brother.' At this, Pudding was immediately alert. 'I never really gave you an answer, when you asked for my help the other night. But the thing is . . . the thing is . . .' Irene paused, suddenly beset by doubt. Her feelings of unease and prescience might all be fiction; she simply couldn't tell. She might be encouraging Pudding into a false and damaging hope; engaging in a dangerous game of some kind. She might be about to interfere in serious matters that were no concern of hers, and make them worse. Irene checked herself. Alistair's murder was most certainly a concern of hers. 'The thing is, I'm really not at all sure of your brother's guilt.'

Pudding gasped, and took an involuntary step towards Irene. She simply stared for a while, as though lost for words.

'But . . . all those things you said about him being found with the shovel, and all that?' she said, in the end.

'I know. I might have been trying to convince myself, I think. Because, you see, I have a feeling about it. That sounds terribly feeble, I know. I shall try to explain.' So she told Pudding about her cousin Gilbert, and how he'd died; she told her about the other times she'd had odd feelings like that, down the years. 'It's always been quite rare – just a handful of times – but then, since I came here, there have been several. And somehow . . . I don't know how, but somehow I feel as though they're . . . connected. Connected to what's happened, I mean.' She paused, and tried to decipher Pudding's expression. It seemed entirely likely that the girl would think her mad. Irene was oddly breathless, her pulse too quick. 'It all sounds very . . . fishy, doesn't it?' she said. 'Quite fantastic. Perhaps I shouldn't have said anything.'

'Well, what feelings have you had since you got here? About what?' said Pudding, with a slight frown.

'The first one was when we found that old doll in the schoolroom chimney. That one was very strong. It was almost as though I recognised it – you know when you've seen a place or a person before, but you can't for the life of you remember where, or when? Then . . . then of course there was the very odd way Tanner reacted to it when he saw it, and Ma saying change was coming . . . That wasn't quite the same, but it must have been significant, don't you think? Change has certainly come, after all.'

'It has.' Pudding's voice sounded older than her years. Irene went on to describe the odd fire she'd found in the house on a hot day, which nobody would lay claim to having lit. 'Who could it have been, if it wasn't Nancy, or the servants?' said Pudding.

'Well,' said Irene. 'That's the thing. Who? And the other time I felt anything odd was . . .' She hesitated. 'Well, it was when I met Hilarius. The groom. And every time I have met him since.'

'Hilarius?' Pudding exclaimed. 'Well, *that* can't be right! Hilarius is fine . . . he's a friend. Of sorts.'

'I don't mean to speak ill of him, Pudding. I just . . . I felt some oddness. A darkness. That's the only way I can describe it. Like he cast more of a shadow than he ought to have done.' She stopped talking because Pudding was shaking her head.

'People have always taken against him because he's foreign, and not one of them,' she said.

'That's not the reason, and I'm not set against him. I was just trying to tell you everything. I mean . . . he could have lit the fire in the house; he is here all the time, after all.'

'Tending to the shires or sleeping, yes. I'd be willing to wager he's never once set foot inside the actual *house*—'

'He has,' said Irene, suddenly and inexplicably certain of it. 'Sorry.'

'Well,' said Pudding. She took a deep breath and let it out slowly. 'Cup of tea?'

Irene sat on a stool in the tack room while Pudding set a kettle of water to boil on the tiny stove. The small room smelled strongly of saddle soap, leather and neatsfoot oil, and Irene felt out of place in her skirt and blouse. She crossed her legs awkwardly, and clasped her hands over one knee as Pudding spooned tea leaves into a chipped brown pot. 'I didn't think you'd want to help, really,' said Pudding, not looking up. 'I only asked because of ... of everything being so desperate. But you're the first person to say they don't believe Donny's guilty.' She looked over at Irene with such a potent mixture of hope and fear that Irene said a silent prayer that they were right. 'Even old Jem, and Nancy ... They're all very sorry, but they all think it was him.'

'If nothing else, he had no reason to whatsoever, from what I gather,' said Irene. 'No reason to lose his temper, even.'

'Exactly!' said Pudding keenly. 'That's what the superintendent said – that he always likes to know *why*, to be sure he has his man. He's decided that Donny doesn't need a reason, but he does! He *does*! He would never have just ... attacked him! And I know that Alistair – I mean, Mr Hadleigh – wouldn't have said anything to Donny about the broken roses. He told me as much. Not that Donny would have been angry if he had, only sad, and—'

'Pudding,' Irene said, to halt her. 'Pudding, please. There's no need to try to convince me.'

'Sorry.' Pudding took a deep breath, and Irene saw how much sheer willpower alone was holding her together. She felt a flash of admiration for the girl, and then shame at the thought of how completely she herself had collapsed in the face of adversity. Collapsed and let it all march right over her.

'Don't be. I think the superintendent is right. If we can find out who wanted to kill him, and why, then . . . well, then we can't help but find the person who did it.'

'But how do we do that? There's nobody! Everybody loved Alistair.'

'Clearly, not everybody,' said Irene, quietly. There was an uneasy pause, then she went on. 'I can't help thinking about Mr Tanner. He certainly seemed . . . upset about something, when we saw him at his home that time. Very upset. And he is, by all accounts, the violent type.'

'Oh, terribly violent!' said Pudding, savagely mashing the tea leaves in the pot. 'But he has an alibi, remember?'

'Yes, I heard. But it's not so very far to Biddestone, is it? Couldn't he have come back in between being put to bed, so to speak, and being put out in the morning?'

'There'd have been plenty of time. But the landlord said he was there all night; he said he was unconscious with drink.'

'But he didn't actually *see* him there all night, did he? I mean, Tanner was alone in the shed. Nobody watched over him.'

'No. I suppose not.'

Irene accepted a steaming mug of tea, dark and bitter from its agitated brewing. She sipped it and thought back to the terrible morning of Alistair's death. The odd stillness in the house that had made her skin prickle; the grey veil of rain outside; the way she'd been disappointed, for the first time since she'd married him, not to have seen her husband before he'd left for the day. It brought a lump to her throat, and a renewed flare of anger.

'It rained very heavily the morning Alistair was killed,' she said.

'Yes. So what?' said Pudding.

'Well, if Tanner had perhaps only *feigned* his drunkenness, and had crept back to the mill in the early hours to attack

Alistair, and had then returned to the shed in order to give himself an alibi . . .'

'He'd have got soaking wet!'

'He would. His boots, at least, even if he'd had a raincoat that he got rid of somewhere.'

'So . . . if he was wet when Bob Walker kicked him out in the morning . . .'

'Then holes begin to appear in his alibi,' said Irene. Pudding chewed her lip for a moment, then put her mug down abruptly, slopping the contents.

'Let's go and ask him, then.' She stood, and hitched up her breeches.

'What, now?' said Irene, startled.

'Well, when, then?' said Pudding. Irene thought for a moment, then stifled her own fears and stood up as well.

Pudding had Dundee, the cob pony, hitched to the Stanhope in no time, and drove them to Biddestone with the nonchalance of long practice, trotting briskly along Ham Lane once they were up the steep hill out of Slaughterford. Irene had an uneasy sense of transgressing, of cheating in some way, but Pudding watched the lane between the pony's ears with a kind of fixed determination, clucking her tongue whenever they slowed. Irene peered along the driveway to Biddestone Hall as they passed it, but saw no sign of the McKinleys. They had possibly gone away after the funeral, to a place less dogged by sorrow. She remembered Cora's enthusiastic response to the tentative letter Irene had sent, on Alistair's suggestion; the trip to Cousin Amelia by the sea that had never happened. There hadn't been time before everything had fallen apart, but perhaps if they'd gone they might have been friends, in spite of what came next. But then, perhaps Cora was just one more person who'd loved Alistair better than Irene had; one more person whose grief was more visceral than her own.

The White Horse was an uneven whitewashed building set back from the green by the duck pond in the centre of Biddestone. It was nearing midday, and a few men from the wood mill were sitting outside, swigging from glasses of dark beer and brushing the sawdust from their hair. Pudding and Irene drew curious glances, and Irene wondered how they looked, the pair of them – herself so very overdressed and out of place, and Pudding scowling and grubby with her chest all but popping the buttons of her shirt. Irene did her best not to look awkward. They found Bob Walker, the landlord, in the yard behind the inn, carrying a stack of old news-sheets towards the outhouse. He was massive in both height and girth, with hands like paddles, stooped shoulders and blond hair that was thinning on top but spread down his cheeks in big, wiry sideburns.

'Ar? Help you ladies?' he said, when he saw them. Buck teeth gave him a way of leaving his bottom lip hanging that made him look simple, but he seemed friendly enough. Irene and Pudding exchanged a glance, and Irene realised that she was expected to speak first.

'Ah yes. How do you do? I'm Irene Hadleigh, and this is . . . Pudding Cartwright,' she said, realising that she still didn't know Pudding's real name.

'The doctor's lass.' Bob nodded, which set his chins wobbling. 'And 'ee can't be the new widow, can 'ee?' He shook his head. 'Fearful business.'

'Yes. Indeed.' Irene hated her own voice just then; hated how it turned all her words into empty things. She sounded, she realised, just like her mother. She hurried on. 'We were wondering if we might talk to you a little bit, Mr Walker, about Mr Tanner's . . . recent time with you. The night before the . . . incident at the mill.' At this Bob put down the papers and folded his arms, looking uneasy.

'Oh, ar?' he said.

'Yes. The thing is . . . The thing is, we wanted to ask whether you're quite, entirely certain that Mr Tanner was as drunk as he appeared to be.'

'That police 'un, the dark-haired fellow, he asked I the same thing. I'll tell 'ee like I told him – Tanner'd had enough drink to kill most men. In here all the afternoon long, he were. Sad about something, it seemed to me. Even saw him weep for a time, I did, though not a soul will believe a word o' that.'

'But he's a man well used to drink, is he not?'

'It's true he is. A most valued customer,' said Bob, with a grin.

'But doesn't he normally drink at the White Hart, in Ford?' said Pudding.

'Takes it in turns, we do, the Hart and I. He drinks here when he's barred from there; drinks there when they'll have him back.'

'Mr Walker, I wonder if you can remember, when you came to put him out in the morning . . . was he wet?' Irene asked. At this Bob pulled himself up straighter, and looked embarrassed.

'What possible cause can 'ee have to want to know that?' he asked, soberly. 'Whether a man soils himself or—'

'Oh, no! No – not in that way,' Irene said hastily.

'From the rain!' Pudding interjected.

'I cassn't follow 'ee.'

'Forgive me, Mr Walker,' said Irene, flustered. 'I know this must seem a very odd question. When you came to put Mr Tanner out in the morning, were his clothing, his boots – or perhaps his hair – wet at all, as though he had been out in the rain?'

'But he weren't out in it. He were in the shed, still sleeping like a babe, when I turfed him out.'

'Yes, I know. But can you remember specifically, at all? Whether he was wet or dry, I mean?'

'Well.' Bob squinted up at the roof of his own establishment, and appeared to think hard. 'Now 'ee mention it, I cassn't recall. He must have been dry, then, else I'd have found it amiss, and remembered, wouldn't I? Mind you, I was soaked right through from the short walk to the shed, and rain do wash in under the door of it, so perhaps if he were wet, I wouldn't have thought that amiss either.' He kept staring up at the roof, kept thinking, but nothing else appeared to be forthcoming.

'So . . . which was it?' said Pudding.

'I cassn't rightly say,' Bob confessed. Pudding deflated a bit. 'But if I had to call it, I'd say dry. I'd say he hadn't stirred an inch from when I dropped him there the night before. I s'pose that's why you're asking?' He looked at them shrewdly. 'If he slipped out and done some dark deed, and slipped back to have I give him an alibi?'

'Well . . . yes. Only please don't put it about that we were asking,' said Irene, her pulse quickening. She realised then how afraid of Tanner she was; afraid at some deep-down, gut level. Bob Walker nodded carefully.

'As far as I can tell it, Mrs Hadleigh, he was here all that time.'

The ride home had far less of an air of urgency. Pudding let Dundee dawdle so much that the pony paused now and then to snatch mouthfuls of the hedgerow. It was as though she didn't want to get back to the farm at all.

'Well, it struck me that Mr Walker was telling the truth,' said Irene, to break a long silence that was becoming strained. 'Not providing a false alibi.'

'Yes,' Pudding agreed, glumly. 'Tanner wouldn't have the

money to bribe him, anyway. And he could hardly threaten him. Bob's as big as a hayrick.'

'So . . . I suppose the next question is when did it start to rain?' Irene tried. 'I mean, if it didn't start until *after* Alistair was killed, then it doesn't matter whether Tanner was wet or dry.'

'But it also wouldn't prove one way or the other if he'd left the shed.'

'True. But if . . . but if it didn't start to rain until after he was killed, then the fact that Tanner stayed dry still means he *could* have sneaked out.'

'I suppose so,' said Pudding, and Irene gave up. It wasn't enough, as Pudding clearly knew. The white lane shimmered in front of them and clouded with dust behind; the sky was painfully bright; a few faint wisps of cloud seemed impossibly high above them. Squinting was giving Irene a headache, and she wished she knew of some way to encourage Pudding, or cheer her. What cheer there could be for her until, and unless, her brother were released, Irene couldn't think. Hers would be one more life blighted forever by whoever had stolen Alistair from them.

'Well, we still haven't got to the bottom of his motive, in any case,' she said, desperately. 'Why don't we go and talk to the foreman at the mill, about him being fired?' At this, Pudding straightened up a bit, and looked across at her.

'Good idea! Oh – but I need to get back and get Tufty in off the grass, before he explodes. I should have done it before we left, really. And Dundee will need a rub down, it's so blasted hot . . .'

'Well . . . I'll go, then,' said Irene. She could think of few things she wanted to do less than walk down to the mill alone, and return to the very place Alistair had been killed, but she refused to yield to herself. 'I'll go, and see what I can discover.'

'Right. I'll drop you at the mill, then,' said Pudding.

There was a terrible moment outside the mill offices. Irene halted at the door to the old farmhouse, caught between the prickling stares of the workers in the yard behind her and the remembered horror of the room in front of her. She stood for a long time, her eyes down and her heart thumping, entirely unable to go either onwards or back. The mill machines rumbled; the air smelled of smuts, metal and the river. They all had so many questions for her, she knew: whether she would sell their place of work, their homes and land; what she would do; what their lives would be from now on and how they would change. And, real or imagined, she felt them blame her for all of it. It felt like a huge wave about to break over her head, and it smothered the anger she needed for strength. She jumped when the farmhouse door opened. George Turner, the foreman, came out with his face full of concern.

'Mrs Hadleigh? Is everything all right?' he said.

'Yes. That is, no, not at all,' said Irene. George nodded kindly.

'Won't you come inside out of this sun? One of the girls just brought a jug of iced tea over from the canteen, and I have to say, it's not half bad. Plenty of cucumber.' He took her elbow and ushered her in.

'Thank you.'

Irene couldn't help but look at the place on the floor where, the last time she had seen it, Alistair had lain all bloody and dead. George said something else but it was drowned out by the thumping in her ears. As her eyes struggled to adapt, it looked, for a moment, as though a dark shadow remained; a patch of gloom that might have been his body, still, or the blackened crust of his blood. In a flash she was assailed by the thought of the Alistair-doll again, and the roots and creatures that would now be making their homes in what remained of him, buried in the ground. Her head swam.

'Do sit down, Mrs Hadleigh.' George touched her arm again, and Irene sank obediently into a chair, breathing deeply. 'We had the thought of closing this place up – perhaps even knocking it down. Knocking it down and building something new to house the offices. I wasn't sure . . .' He shook his head. 'I wasn't sure if Mr Hadleigh himself would have liked that. Such a dramatic gesture, and the destruction of such a trad- itional part of the mill. Miss Hadleigh has said she would prefer it razed to the ground.'

'Has she?' Irene had heard Nancy make no such request; she herself hadn't given the mill a second thought.

'Oh, yes. In no uncertain terms. But perhaps decisions like that aren't best made in the heat of the moment. A new building would be a considerable investment. For whoever had control of the mill.'

'Nothing's been decided yet,' said Irene, more sharply than she'd intended.

'Of course it hasn't,' said George, gently. 'Do have some of this tea, and tell me how I can help you.'

'Thank you. Sorry. I—' Irene gathered herself. 'You're very kind. I wanted to ask about Mr Tanner.'

'Tanner? What has the fellow been up to now?'

'Oh – nothing like that. Well. I wanted to ask you, was he fired from the mill? Recently, I mean. I know he has been let go before, and then rehired. Pudding said she saw him drunk on the job, just a short while ago.'

'Yes, that's right. He was indeed let go. It must be nearing three weeks ago now.'

'I see,' said Irene, trying to keep her voice neutral.

'It was a grave shame. He had kept off the drink for a goodly while, but then all of a sudden, something seemed to set him off. And he never does anything by halves, does Tanner. One drink leads to twenty or thirty, with him. Mr Hadleigh was sympathetic, but he had no choice but to let him go.'

'I imagine Mr Tanner was very angry about that.'

'Oh yes, all the usual bluster. But I know the man well enough to know that the person he's most angry with is himself. Not that he has the capacity to recognise that, of course. Mr Hadleigh told him he could have his job back again if he stayed sober a month long, and—'

'What?'

'He was told he could have his job back as long as he stayed sober a full month. It was an arrangement that had worked quite well before – the man needs a good reason to lay off it, you see.'

'So . . . it wasn't acrimonious?' she asked, sinking inside. George grunted.

'Oh, there's always acrimony, with Mr Tanner. He's the type to soundly reject any show of charity. But Mr Hadleigh had got onto his good side, over the years – as good a side as the man has, of course. He's a bad sort, and some men are just born that way. What other employer would have a man back, over and again, in similar circumstances? Precious few, I should think. I made the same point to the police super-intendent, when he asked about it. But when your husband saw a problem, or a person in trouble, he took it upon himself to alleviate the situation – or at least to try to – rather than to wash his hands of it.'

'Yes,' said Irene, thinking of herself. Their hasty marriage, the new life he'd tried to give her. Her eyes swam; the anger swelled in her chest.

'If you don't mind my saying, Mrs Hadleigh, why do you ask? Are you inclined to withdraw the offer?'

'What? I don't know, I—'

'Not that a decision is urgently required – Tanner shows no signs of regaining mastery of himself, as yet.'

'I fear I have taken up more than enough of your time, Mr Turner,' said Irene, tremulously. She was thinking about telling Pudding this news; about Tanner having not only a firm alibi, but no real reason to harm Alistair. She felt a failure.

'Nonsense. Your visit has brightened my day immeasurably,' said George.

He smiled but suddenly it slid away, and his face drooped. 'There is something weighing on my conscience, Mrs Hadleigh, and I beg your forbearance while I . . . disclose it,' he said, sombrely. Irene looked at him properly and noticed the shadows under his eyes, and that he had lost weight since she first met him. 'Your husband ought not to have been here so very early, on the day he died. He had given me time off because my wife . . . Since our little one came along, she has . . . struggled. With a lassitude, and a depressed mood she can't seem to conquer.' He looked down at the desk. 'Mr Hadleigh had been most understanding. I had been late to work several mornings, in remaining behind to help Elizabeth along. He said he would come in early in my stead, to oversee the change in shift.' He shook his head, and took a sudden deep breath, as though struggling to breathe freely. 'If I had been keeping to my regular hours, he would not have been here by himself at that hour of the day. And I know I shall never forgive myself for that.'

'Mr Turner,' said Irene, reaching out to take his hand, on impulse, and squeezing it. 'Please do not berate yourself. You are not in the slightest bit to blame.'

Back at Manor Farm, Irene saw Pudding out in the paddock

with one of the horses, and slipped indoors without going to talk to her. Her visit to the mill had only made it even more unlikely that Tanner was the culprit. If he'd been fired and rehired before, then it seemed highly unlikely he should suddenly react by attacking Alistair. More bad news, although Irene couldn't quite put her finger on why it was bad, was that the police had interviewed Mr Turner about it already. Just as they had been to talk to Bob Walker at the White Horse. Pudding and Irene were simply retracing the police's steps, and finding the same lack of evidence as they had, no doubt. She found Nancy in her sitting room cum study, writing out a list of some kind.

'Sorry to trouble you, Nancy,' she said, absently. 'I wonder if you can remember what time the rain started on the morning Alistair was killed?'

'What?' Nancy snapped, and Irene shrivelled inside at the tactlessness of her question. 'Why on earth would you ask me that?'

'I'm so sorry. I wasn't thinking.'

'But why do you want to know?'

'I was just . . . I was just thinking about that morning,' she said, knowing instinctively that Nancy would not be pleased about her trying to prove Donald Cartwright's innocence. Miraculously, her half-answer seemed to suffice.

'Yes. My mind plays those games with me, too,' said Nancy. 'What if this, what if that. I find it better not to indulge such thoughts.'

'You're quite right.' Irene turned to leave her.

'It started well after sunrise. It was a red dawn.' At this Nancy paused, her eyelids flickered and she swallowed. 'I wake with the birds, as you know. There was plenty of cloud, but the rain didn't start until about half past six.'

'So late?' Irene murmured.

'About when Alistair normally rose, which was why I assumed he would remain in bed. You remember what I told you about him being a terrible layabout on wet days.'

'I do. He went in early because George Turner's wife is sick, and he'd been having some time at home.'

'Yes. I know.'

'So he was there, at the mill, before the rain started,' said Irene, relinquishing all hope of using the weather to disprove Tanner's alibi.

'It won't help, you know,' said Nancy. 'Replaying it. Wondering if it could have been prevented. Which of course it could. But it wasn't, and never can be.'

At the end of the day the shires clopped back onto the yard, their massive legs dusty to the hips and elbows, the salt of dried sweat on their shoulders and flanks. Hilarius came out of the barn to take custody from the carters, dressed as always in his canvas overalls, no hat to cover his bald crown. He moved quickly, assuredly in spite of his great age, and the horses obeyed his every unspoken command, lining up at the rail by the barn to have their bridles unfastened, shaking their necks in relief as the heavy collars were lifted off. Irene watched him from a small window in the downstairs corridor. Pudding had been adamant that there was nothing sinister about the man, but Irene couldn't help the feeling she had, looking at him. Something hung about him, something grave; something cold and heavy and deadening. A shadow, as she'd described it to Pudding; a shadow darker than the one his wiry body cast on the cobbled yard. He would have been up even earlier than Nancy that morning, Irene didn't doubt. And she knew, she *knew* he had been inside the farmhouse. She didn't know when, or why, or why it was even significant, but she knew that he had. He could have lit the unexplained fire in Nancy's sitting room. Irene just didn't have the first clue why he would, or what it meant. Or whether it meant a damned thing.

She'd been thinking hard all afternoon, and had even spent a while in her writing room, jotting a few things down on paper, trying to draw connections between things that refused to be connected. She suddenly felt, quite keenly, that it would be hard to take Pudding the bad news without offering her some good along with it. Some idea to follow, some new thought. And it wasn't just for Pudding, she was prepared to admit. As she'd gone out to tell Pudding about her uneasy feelings that morning, she'd felt, for the first time in her life, that she was doing something useful. She'd felt that, having gone seamlessly from being her parents' charge to Fin's fool to Alistair's burden, she was now in charge of herself for the first time. It was a good feeling. And even better was the idea that she was, finally, doing a good and useful thing for Alistair, when he had done so many good things for her. It was too late, of course, far too late. But it wasn't too late for the Cartwrights. But in spite of her efforts, all she had come up with was that somebody might have paid Tanner to kill Alistair. Tanner was a poor man, a drunken sot and recently laid off; perhaps he might have been desperate enough to take such a job. There was certainly enough acrimony in the man, as George had said and she herself had witnessed. But all that did was return them to square one – searching for a reason somebody might have wanted Alistair dead. Irene hated to tell Pudding as much. She hated to disappoint her; she hated, having offered to help, to fail to do so.

On the hallway table, Irene was surprised to find a letter addressed to her in a familiar hand – the first since Fin's terrible letter, which seemed now to have arrived months, years, before. She opened it hurriedly, on the spot, absorbed the contents with a feeling that teetered between happiness and dread, and then went to tell Nancy.

*

As she worked, Pudding repeatedly calculated how much time remained until Donny's hearing – how many hours, minutes, seconds. The need to act was like a terrible itch, impossible to ignore, but however hard she tried, she couldn't think what to do next. As Irene had been forced to admit, hedgingly, the day after they'd been to Biddestone, until they could find out a motive, they were stuck. At lunchtime she banged on the front door of the house, ostensibly to ask for a glass of water but actually hoping to talk to Irene, but nobody answered. She went around the back to the kitchen and found Clara Gosling and Florence having their lunch, but since they, too, fell silent upon seeing her, Pudding retreated. In the great barn, asleep in a shaft of sunshine with his battered hat over his face, she found Hilarius. He slept there in the summer – carrying up his evening meal, which Clara gave him on a plate, every night – and if he had ever had concerns beyond the gates of Manor Farm then he'd long since left them behind him. Pudding thought about the darkness Irene said she sensed around him, but it seemed ridiculous. So ridiculous that it made her doubt all of Irene's odd instincts, though she didn't want to – just then, they were all she and Donny had. But Hilarius was a harmless old man; of few words perhaps, but he had only ever been kind to her, and the horses, and he never shirked in spite of his years.

Pudding felt awkward about waking him, but she couldn't help herself. She picked up a pitchfork and began to tidy the hay, noisily – letting the metal tines scrape against the cobbles.

'Thee'll start a fire, girl,' said Hilarius in his thick accent, not moving. 'Give up on't. I heard you coming from the house.'

'Oh, hello. Sorry to disturb you,' said Pudding, sitting down near him. He smelled comfortingly of horses, and the molasses he mixed into their feed.

'Doubt it,' he grumbled, but he tipped back his hat and looked at her without rancour. 'Still fretting on't, are you?'

'Yes.' She sat on her hands to keep them still, and hunched in on herself. A childhood habit, to make herself smaller. 'Even Superintendent Blackman said that he always sought out the why, in a case such as this. Though it didn't seem to bother him that Donny doesn't have a why at all – as though his ... as though the way he is is reason enough.'

'Are you good and sure it isn't?'

'Of course!' She flared up at once, but Hilarius had a way of watching, with such steadiness in the wrinkled slits of his eyes, that she actually stopped to think before she spoke again. She probed her own conviction, and found it watertight. 'I'm absolutely sure, Hilarius. He got into that fight last year, and he did lose his temper, and he did ... injure that other man. But there was a very good *why* – his Aoife marrying that chap, and about to have their first child. He might have got upset or lost his temper at other times, and it might have been ... alarming. But he never, *ever* directed it at anybody.'

There was a pause, then Hilarius nodded and put his hat back over his eyes, and Pudding wasn't sure he was going to answer her.

'Ar,' he said, in the end, which meant yes. 'I been thinking the same.'

'Really? You have? You don't believe it was Donny? Oh, Hilarius! Thank you.' For no good reason, Pudding's hope soared.

'Not a thanking matter. And nowt to be done about it.'

'But ... there *is*. I just have to find out who really did kill Alistair, do you see? I wanted to ask you if you could think of any reason – any reason at all – why somebody might have had a grudge against Mr Hadleigh. You've been here longer than anyone, haven't you?'

'Seventy years and mounting. Some days, I can feel each last one o' them.'

'Well, there you are then – longer than anybody. Is there anything you can think of, Hilarius? Anything at all? Irene still thinks it's Mr Tanner – that perhaps somebody hired him to do it, but we can't seem to come up with a reason why.'

'Easy for folk to lay blame on that family,' said Hilarius, disapprovingly. There was a pause. 'None of much as goes on here has owt to do with me,' he said. 'Nor ever has.' He lifted his head, and gave her a slow, shrewd look. 'I've no answers for you, girl, and it'd be best left alone, on that I be sure. But I'll say this. 'T'ain't no good holding a fruit in your hand an' looking up at the leaves and sky, puzzling where it came from, an' why it tastes the way it do.'

'A fruit? What do you mean? Where should I look, then?'

'Look down to the roots of it, girl. Look to the roots of the tree.' Pudding thought about this for a while, scratching her nose as the hay dust tickled in it. But before she'd formulated her next question, Hilarius was snoring softly, so she got up quietly and left him to his nap.

As Pudding walked home, she got lost in thoughts of her brother, and the day he'd come home from the army hospital. They'd all been delirious at the sight of him, but had tried so carefully not to overwhelm him, not to crowd him or fuss too much. The four of them – Ruth included – had followed him around the house as he'd rediscovered it, his face wearing a kind of wonder and puzzlement, as though a dream he'd once had was turning out to be real. Pointing out to him things that were new – a blue eiderdown on his bed; Pudding's height and size – and things that were just the same – everything else. Waiting for him to say or do something, to show he was still their Donny in spite of the horrors he'd seen and the violence he'd survived, and in spite of Dr Cartwright's warnings that he wasn't quite the same, that he didn't like to be hugged any more, that he needed time. Four tentative people, anxiously alert, holding their breath and hoping to feel happy soon. Returning to the kitchen, Donny had frowned a little and looked down at his toes. His right hand had strayed up, as it often did in the beginning, to brush nervously across the damage on his head, then he'd looked up and said, *Well, isn't there a cup of tea for a fellow, Ruth?* And Ruth had tutted about there being no rest for the wicked, and they had all exhaled, and the happiness had indeed begun.

Heavy footfalls scattered the memory, and the sight of Pete Dempsey jogging to catch her up gave Pudding a jolt, even though he wasn't in his uniform. Her throat immediately went dry. Since Donny's return she only seemed to encounter Pete when something bad had happened. She remembered him struggling to hold Donny while he fought, and refused to be led away after the fight in Ford the year before. She didn't doubt that Pete remembered it too, and had been thinking of it recently; she wondered if he thought Alistair would still be alive now had Donny been jailed back then, as he came to stand in front of her, red-faced from hurrying in the heat. Her heart thudded as she waited to hear what bad news he'd brought this time.

'Hello, Pudding,' he said, breathlessly.

'Hello, Constable. What is it?'

'I'm not Constable now, just Pete. I'm off duty.' He smiled as though this ought to have been funny, but it faded when Pudding didn't respond.

'Is there something new about the case? What can you tell me?' Pudding couldn't seem to do anything about the flat sound of her voice, not even for the sake of keeping a policeman on side. It seemed pointless to dissemble, anyway; she'd known Pete since they were children. He'd always been there, one of her crowd of peers, even though he was a few years older. She'd once seen him throw up all over his own boots when another boy had dared him to eat frogspawn from Worthy Pilton's pond, and he'd been daft enough to do it. He had always known Donny – deferring to him due to his size and age; slightly wary of him because he was so protective of Pudding. Now Pete represented the law, which was strange enough in itself; he had power over Donny and over them all, and Pudding didn't know how to square that away. She was oddly, and enormously, embarrassed.

Pete took off his cap and scrubbed his fingers through his sweaty hair, looking uncomfortable.

'No. I'm afraid there's nothing new,' he said.

'But are you still looking for the real killer?' she demanded, not able to look him in the eye.

'Are we what?' he said, with a puzzled frown. Then, as he understood, he looked away, awkwardly. They stood in silence for a while.

'Well, I'd better be getting home,' said Pudding.

'Pudding, wait.' Pete put out his hand to stop her. 'I've been wanting to say, since all this started . . . I've been wanting to say how sorry I am. I mean . . . I know you've enough on your plate with your mum being ill, and now this.' He cleared his throat, and Pudding's face flamed. 'I know what your Donny means to you, Pudding.' He spoke in a gentle tone she'd never heard him use before. 'I wish it hadn't turned out this way. I do wish it,' he said. Pudding still couldn't look at him. She stared down at his dusty boots instead; there was grit and chaff in the turn-ups of his trousers. She wanted to say that it *hadn't* turned out this way, and that she was going to bring Donny home with his name cleared, but she didn't think she ought to say that to the law. She doubted Pete would approve of the fact that she and Irene had been making enquiries of their own. And she knew he'd dismiss Irene's prescient feelings out of hand – Pudding wasn't even entirely convinced about them herself.

'Thanks,' she muttered instead, and this time Pete let her go.

Since Alistair's death, Dr Cartwright usually got home before Pudding finished work. He had fewer patients now, and once upon a time Pudding would have been happy about that – happy that he didn't have to rush about as much, and could spend more time with them at home. But he didn't belong in the garden – he never had, beyond sitting out in a lawn chair from time to time, to read the newspaper; it had always been Louise's domain – so he merely lingered about the house in idleness. And he was so listless, and looked so lost and tired, that in fact Pudding began to almost dread seeing him at the kitchen table when she got home. Quite often he wasn't even doing anything – not reading the paper or one of his medical journals, or writing out his bills or pharmaceutical orders; not listening to the wireless; not mending anything small and mechanical, replacing the wick in the stove or drinking tea, or oiling the chain of his bicycle with his sleeves rolled up and a rag tucked into his braces. Just sitting. Just as Donny had used to do. He seemed to deflate even further with every day that passed, and every new bit of bad news that came – like the date of Donny's hearing. Part of Pudding longed to throw herself into his embrace and sob all over him, but she couldn't let herself do that. He simply didn't look strong enough. Instead she made him tea, cut him a piece of one of Ruth's cakes, and patted his shoulder as she went about the house, doing whatever she could get done before supper time.

Ruth was stalwart. In spite of being a highly effective

conduit for gossip, and highly susceptible to it, she maintained her loyalty to the Cartwrights with puffed-up defiance like armour plate.

'Most folk don't know they're born,' she said, cryptically, when Pudding thanked her for staying on. Ruth opened the door to callers with folded arms, a gingham scarf knotted tight around her hair and a thunderous expression on her unlovely face that dared folk to peer inside, offer judgement, or hang about, eavesdropping. Not that many people came to call – they hadn't for a while, because of Louise Cartwright being unwell. If Ruth had abandoned them, Pudding knew, things would have been much worse. They'd all have gone hungry, for starters, since beyond toast and scrambled eggs, she herself was a dreadful cook. Not that any of them had much appetite – Pudding least of all. It had cheered her up before: great slabs of fruit loaf, covered in butter; bacon sandwiches on a cold morning before work; strawberries from the garden, drowning in cream. Now all she could think about, when food was put in front of her, was Donny in his cell in the New Bridewell in Devizes, eating prison stew and wishing he were home. Her parents didn't seem to notice her lack of appetite, and mealtimes were largely silent affairs. That evening, her father was even quieter than usual.

'What is it, Dad? Has something happened?' she asked, when Ruth had gone home and her mother upstairs. His forehead was all furrows and his lips looked pale. He shook his head. 'Please, tell me,' she said.

'I spoke to a fellow doctor today, Dr Whitley, in Devizes. He had ... been called out to the prison to see to Donny,' he said. Pudding gasped.

'Why? Is he all right? What happened? Is he ill?'

'*Shh* – your mother mustn't hear! He is all right now, but Dr Whitley had to give him a sedative to calm him, so that ... he could administer some stitches.' He had been looking down, fiddling with his spectacles, but now the doctor glanced up at Pudding. She stared back, aghast. 'The account he was given was that Donny had got into a fight with one of the other inmates. He . . . he wasn't able to tell me what the fight was about—'

'But that can't be right! Donny wouldn't have been fighting, and—'

'Pudding, please, just listen. The fight wasn't particularly serious. But Donny needed stitches to his hand where he . . . struck the other fellow, and he needed stitches to a head wound . . . a head wound that he . . . that he . . .'

'That he what?'

'That he gave to himself. Once he was back in his cell. He . . . he dashed his head against the wall. They were forced to restrain him.'

For a long time, Pudding couldn't find a single word to say. She swallowed, painfully.

'Poor, poor Donny,' she said, in the end, and the words came out wobbly, half-broken.

'Yes,' said her father.

'He must hate it in there. He must hate it so much! They won't understand him . . . they won't understand how he is! And that he needs to be allowed to . . . do things in his own time! And be shown how to do them. I bet this other man – whoever he is – I bet he picked on Donny, and drove him to fight!'

'Pudding—'

'Why would he hit his own head on the wall? Why would he? He must hate it there so much!' She started to cry, and tried to stifle it. 'They *must* let him come home!' she whispered.

'I wish they would. I wish it more than anything, my dear. He's clearly not able to . . . cope.' The doctor shook his head helplessly.

'Can't we apply to the judge to let him come home? A special order, or something – special circumstances! Donny isn't the same as other men . . .'

'Our best hope is to get a charge of manslaughter from the magistrate – then, perhaps, he could be allowed to leave on bail. If it's set at a level we can manage. But if he gets into any more trouble . . .'

'Oh, no, they'll use it against him, won't they?'

'I fear they might, Pudding. I fear they might.'

'But it's so *unfair*! He hasn't even done anything wrong!'

'Pudding.' The doctor put one hand over his eyes and shook his head slightly, as if he couldn't stand to hear her. Pudding took a few breaths to calm down. She was shocked by her father's visible distress; it was crushing him, making him smaller.

'You mustn't give up on it all, Dad,' she said. 'I'm going to think of a way to bring him home. Really, I am. I promise.'

'My dear,' he said, smiling sadly, 'you mustn't make promises you won't be able to keep. Especially not to yourself.'

'But I *will* keep it.' She felt something rising up inside, something quite like anger. The doctor shook his head again.

'I'm deeply sorry any of this has happened, Pudding, and that your young life will always carry the mark of this . . . dark time. It warms my heart to realise just how loyal you are to Donald – it warms it, and it breaks it.' Then he drifted away in silence, to help his wife get ready for bed.

Pudding lay caught in the shallows of an uneasy sleep all night, plagued by thoughts of Donny injuring himself, and the idea that, at any moment, he might be goaded into doing something that would keep him locked away forever. In the morning her head felt thick, and itchy. It was difficult to think clearly, but she decided on her next course of action – Ma Tanner. A wise woman of sorts, someone who knew Slaughterford and its people like the back of her hand, and had given Pudding and Irene a warning of change. Nobody was closer to Tanner himself, or more likely to know where he had been, and what he had done.

'Are you sure that's a good idea?' said Irene, when Pudding told her. 'I mean . . . given that our prime suspect is her son, and all that.'

'Well,' said Pudding, frowning, 'is he still our prime suspect? Anyway, we don't need to let on to her about that, do we? We'll just pretend we haven't a clue, and perhaps she'll let something slip.'

'We?' Irene shook her head. 'I'm sorry, but I can't go with you now, Pudding – I've to go into Corsham. My mother is coming to visit. Finally.' Irene's voice had a peculiar tone that Pudding couldn't decode. 'But she's never been an early riser – if you hang on until tomorrow, perhaps—'

'No!' Pudding took a breath, thinking of Donny hitting his head against the walls of his prison cell. She thought of telling Irene about it, but didn't want to make her think Donny was deranged. That he was violent. She could hardly bear to think of his pain and confusion. 'I mean, no, it's all right; I can go alone, and strike whilst the iron is hot.'

'Well. Do remember to be tactful, won't you?' said Irene, sounding uncertain. Pudding nodded but couldn't bring herself to speak. Tact was no use to Donny. She checked the horses over quickly, fed them and topped off the water trough, impatient to set off down the hill. When she was doing something – *anything* – towards bringing her brother home, Pudding could carry on; she felt she could breathe, in spite of all the fear and awfulness, and the yawning gap in the world where Alistair had once been. When she wasn't doing something, it felt like drowning.

There were hasty sounds inside Thatch Cottage when she knocked at the door – the creak of the wooden floor, footsteps on the stairs, muffled whispers – and when the door was opened by Trish Tanner, Tanner's wife, her face went through a rapid succession of expressions – from fearful, to crashing relief, to a shifting uncertainty that looked almost guilty.

'Pudding Cartwright,' she said, neutrally, not opening the door much wider.

'Hello, Mrs Tanner. I'm sorry to disturb you.' Pudding paused for Mrs Tanner to say it was fine, but she didn't. 'Er. I wonder if I might come in and have a quick word with your mother about something?'

'Mother-in-law. Now's not a good time.'

'Oh. Ah. Well, I suppose it is quite important,' said Pudding. 'May I? I won't take up much of her time.'

'That the doctor's girl?' came Ma Tanner's voice from within. 'Let her in, if she's something to say.' Pudding smiled hopefully, but again that fear flashed in Mrs Tanner's eyes, and there was a thump from upstairs that made her flinch. But she opened the door wider and stepped back.

'You'd best come in then.'

'Thank you.'

There was a hush inside, and Pudding felt even more watched than she had the time she'd come with Irene, even though there were fewer children around now, and the grandpa in the truckle bed was fast asleep, his jaw hanging open and his eyeballs flicking back and forth behind his lids. The windows were covered with thick felts and the unnatural darkness was stifling, worse than before. Pudding blinked, struggling to see as her eyes adjusted from the bright light outside; she breathed more deeply, feeling as though there wasn't quite enough air. Ma Tanner was out of her chair by the stove, adding various chopped roots to a stockpot, reaching to the high shelf for herbs. Her movements were quick and sure, and Pudding stared, realising that it was the first time she'd seen her on her feet, and that she'd always assumed Ma couldn't walk. Ma shot Pudding a mischievous smile.

'Life in these old bones yet,' she said.

'Yes,' said Pudding.

'Sit. I didn't think it'd be too long till you came knocking again. I fear you'll get no joy here, mind you.'

'Oh.'

'But ask away.' She put down her big chopping knife and wiped her wizened hands on her skirt as she sat down herself. 'Something to help you sleep, perhaps? Something to help the doctor relax?'

'No, no, nothing like that. Thank you.' Pudding tried to place Ma Tanner's odd tone. It seemed mocking, but only on the surface, not all the way through. As though she were hiding something else. 'I wanted to ask . . .' She paused, thinking hard. Saying anything without giving away her suspicions was going to be tricky. Somehow, she felt she only had this one chance to ask the right thing. From the table, Trish Tanner watched, listening unashamedly. Her face was empty of expression now, apart from its usual tension. 'When we came here before, with that doll Mrs Hadleigh found, and you said change was coming . . . was it Alistair's death you saw?'

In the pause, in the stuffy dark, Pudding knew she'd asked the right question. Ma Tanner eyed her for a long time. Her eyes gleamed in the low light.

'Not exactly,' she said, at last.

'But something to do with him?'

'Yes.'

'But why? How?'

'Can't tell you that, girl.' The old woman drew back but never broke off her stare.

'Did it tell you . . . did you find out anything about Donny from it? Did you know he would . . . he would be accused of something, and taken away?'

'No.' For a second there came a creeping disquiet into Ma Tanner's eyes, and then her face hardened off, quashing it. 'Not quite your brother since the war, is he? Not quite the full billing,' she said, crisply.

'Well, of course he's still my brother! He's a little . . . changed, perhaps. A little less able. But still Donny, through and through.'

'Easier to do without him now, perhaps.'

'No, not at all! How can you say that?' Pudding's eyes swam. She realised then that if life were a net in which to catch happiness, losing Donny would put too big a hole in hers. She had no hope of dealing with the rest of it – her mother, and Alistair – without him. 'We're desperate to have him home. And he's the gentlest soul really, whatever the war did to him. That he should have survived all of that only to hang for this . . . only to be known forever as a murderer, when he's nothing of the sort . . . It's unbearable.' She blew her nose on her shrivelled, overused handkerchief, and Ma Tanner held the silence. She locked eyes with her daughter-in-law, both of them stock-still, as though waiting for a sign, as though listening. 'Please,' said Pudding. 'If you know anything that might help him, please do tell me it now. Even if it's only a hunch . . . an idea. *Anything*. Hilarius told me to look for the roots of the thing, but I don't really know what he meant.'

'That old tinker is brighter than he looks,' said Ma Tanner. 'Is he? Why?'

'What he meant was that all the lives in this place – here in the valley, in Slaughterford – all the lives are tangled up. Have been for years. Years and years.'

'So . . . there is somebody with a . . . a grudge against

Alistair? Some grievance against him, for something that happened long before?'

'Could be. Or something them before him done, maybe. You're too young to see it yet, girl, but the roots of things go deep. I do suppose you think winter was a long time ago, don't you?' She smiled. 'I do suppose you think a lot's happened of late. Well, it's a drop in the ocean. There's plenty that's well out of your reach. Things you can't ever understand. But every last thing in life happens for a reason, especially those most foul.'

'That's enough,' Trish muttered, tersely. Pudding looked across at her, and saw fear in her eyes that was at odds with her angry tone of voice. Ma Tanner grunted.

'I daresay it is, yes.' She got up.

'But hold on – you haven't told me anything!' Pudding protested.

'I've told you all I can. If you can't let the lad go, then look further afield for the cause of all this. Now, on your way. You've a job of work to go to, and I've this stew to finish. Barley cutting's started, the boys'll be back with hollow guts come noon time.'

Feeling cross and useless, Pudding got up and followed Trish Tanner back to the door. There, the woman gripped her arm for a moment.

'Let it lie, girl,' she whispered. 'Please. Ma can't help you, and you'll only stir up more trouble.'

'But . . . my family couldn't *be* in any more trouble!'

'Believe me, you could.'

'They'll hang him – they'll hang Donny. I can't let that happen.'

'Try,' said Mrs Tanner, then tried to shut the door. Pudding put her boot in the way.

'Do you know who it was? Do you know who killed Mr Hadleigh?' she whispered.

'Course I bloody don't! What are you accusing us of? Same old story, is it – there's been a crime, so it must be a Tanner? Don't come around here asking that again, if you know what's good for you.' She kicked Pudding's foot away and slammed the door.

Feeling certain that the cottage had eyes, Pudding hurried across the barren yard, where the mud had dried and cracked, and the smell of the privy was stronger than ever, and the only things growing were dusty nettles and ivy. Thatch Cottage had always been a place to be wary of, a place of slightly menacing fascination. Now, for the first time, Pudding had the notion that it was the saddest place in the valley – apart from her own home, of course. She stood a while in the parched lane, with a fat, persistent bluebottle for company, looking across at the mill. She saw the towering brick wall of the new generator house, built on top of the original mill house; the old farm-house, its barns now used to keep machine spares rather than animals, its pigsties converted into privies for the workers. She saw the By Brook carved in two, the water split between its natural course and the mill race, and even into a third conduit on the downstream side – the open pipe of the waste water, siphoned off into dye beds to keep the river pure further south. Layers of life and work and industry; roots going back years and years. Pudding wished Irene had come with her after all. She missed her opinion and the careful way she listened, and thought; but it was good, she supposed, that Irene's mother was coming to visit. Nobody else had been to visit her. Pudding went through what she'd been told, and what it boiled down to was that both Hilarius and Ma Tanner thought that the *why* of Alistair's death lay further back in the past. What it was, and how far back, she still had no idea.

She was halfway back to Manor Farm when something Ma had said replayed itself in her ears, and rang a sudden bell. *Especially those most foul.* Most foul. The realisation hit Pudding like a cosh. She stopped in the middle of the street, by the bridge, and two lads driving the little wagon of half-stuff across from Rag Mill had to swerve around her when she ignored their shouts. Her next breath was full of oily smoke from the wagon's engine. Her heart had accelerated so radically, and was beating so hard, that she could feel it knocking against her ribs. For a moment Pudding was stuck there, on weak knees, as a shiver brushed over her skin. But when the moment of paralysis passed she turned on her heel, and ran for home as fast as she could.

All five women at Weavern Farm were waiting for the storm to break. As a precaution, Rose had made sure none of the girls were in sight before telling their father that Clemmie was expecting. None of them had any idea what his reaction would be, or who would be the main focus of his ire. For an entire day the farm work was done in near silence; all communication between the sisters and their mother was made by significant glance and covert gesture, as though William were omnipresent and might descend upon them at any second. As though, for that time only, they were as mute as Clemmie herself. The day was scorching. The cows stood limply in the shade, chewing the cud with their eyes closed; the hens lay stupefied beneath the coop; the river's rush had steadied, the water smoother and more sedate. Sweat beaded on their skin, and at least part of it was due to the unbearable tension. When, late in the after-noon, William came out of the house and banged the door behind him, they all froze. But he merely strode off along the steep path towards Weavern Lane, his hands in fists and his shoulders high, leaving his wife and daughters to glance at each other yet again, at a loss.

'Well, Mum, what's he said?' asked Mary, as they clustered in the relative cool of the dairy. Rose shrugged, beleaguered. She hadn't quite forgiven the girls for not telling her that Clemmie had a sweetheart, and, by extension, for letting her fall pregnant.

'He barely said owt at all. He just went quiet,' she said, curtly.

'Angry quiet? Or sad? Or what?' Josie pressed. Clemmie stood behind her, feeling odd at being the cause of so much consternation, and at it all going on with virtually no reference to herself. As though her pregnancy were a separate entity, to be dealt with by them and not by her. It didn't feel that way to Clemmie. It felt as though they were talking about her heart. Wondering what to do about her heart.

Down the years, plenty of babies had been baseborn in Ford and Slaughterford, and plenty of couples had been forced to get married in a hurry – it was usually seen as more of a misfortune than a disgrace. But it seemed to be different for Clemmie, because *Clemmie* was different. As though her getting into trouble could only have happened as the result of a misdemeanour. As though Clemmie herself were still a gormless child. Her mother and sisters tried every tone of voice they possessed to make her lead them to the baby's father, and Clemmie simply sat down in the dust when they tried to drag her. By the end of the second day, when it became clear that the explosion they were all expecting from William wasn't going to come, twin lines appeared between Rose's eyebrows. She ushered the girls out of the kitchen after supper, as the sky was turning from gold to grey outside, and they lingered on the stairs, trying to overhear the tense, hushed words that followed.

'Someone's had advantage of her – are you not going to do a damn thing about it, Will?' they heard her say, in the end, quite clearly. William's reply was too low to make out. Josie took Clemmie's hand and squeezed it, and even Liz looked troubled – disappointed, almost. Clemmie wished she could tell them that it was fine, that she wasn't worried or scared. Eli would make a plan – was already making a plan – and he meant to marry her, as soon as he could, and it would all be well. She already loved the baby almost as much as she loved Eli, and knew in her bones that nothing so loved could bring trouble.

'Mum'll set it right, Clem,' Mary told her, not sounding at all convinced. *But there's no wrong to right*, Clemmie didn't say. Later, when Clemmie set off to wander, Liz scowled.

'Shouldn't she be staying home?' she said, to anyone who'd listen.

'Let her be, if she's happy. She won't be for long. And not much worse can happen than already has, can it?' said Rose. Then she shook her head, dropped her chin to her chest, and clamped one hand tight over her mouth.

They tried to follow her, of course. They tried it more than once, but they had no practice at being quiet as they went, and no skill at it. Clemmie led them up the steepest slope to the quarry, on one occasion, and slipped into a hidden crevice to hide until they gave up. She smiled as she heard them fighting to get their breath back, Mary and Liz.

'She can't just bloody vanish,' said Liz, looking all around. 'Clemmie Matlock! You're a thorn in all our sides!' she shouted, crossly. Another time Rose tried to follow her, but her mother was even louder and more obvious than her sisters, and it was just as easy to give her the slip. Clemmie always made sure they were safely far away before she went on to meet Eli, and when she finally got him to understand about the baby, he was dumbstruck. His jaw dropped comically and his eyes emptied of thought so completely he looked confounded, and Clemmie laughed delightedly. She had no doubt that he'd be happy, once the idea had settled inside him and taken root. She was right: he held her fiercely, breathing like he'd been running, and a kind of wild triumph lit his eyes. Then he let her go abruptly.

'I shall have to handle you softly now, shan't I, my Clem?' he said. 'Though I don't know how I'll manage it.' He put his hands around her waist, which seemed, if anything, smaller now that her hips and chest had spread. Clemmie shook her head, smiling. She felt the opposite of fragile. She felt strong, alive, powerful. She felt like nothing could happen that she wouldn't be able to protect the baby from. It was still so tiny – she hadn't felt it move, and her belly was no rounder than before – but she knew it was the source of this feeling of life, this feeling of strength. It had appropriated her whole body, and was gearing her towards growing and shielding it, and she was perfectly content with that. Eli kissed her all over her face, and then cupped his hands around it and stared hard into her eyes. 'I won't be like my dad, Clemmie. I swear it, on my life. This child of ours won't ever feel the back of my hand; and I'll do right by the both of you. I'll find us a room, and I'll get work. It's going to be a good life for us – for us three. I swear it.' Clemmie wished she could say that she believed him, that she knew. Instead she nodded. 'Say nothing for now, for they'll all raise hell if they know it's us. If they know it's me,' he said, and Clemmie beamed, delighted that, such was the ease of things between them, he sometimes forgot that she couldn't say anything to anyone.

That ease of things was resoundingly missing from Weavern Farm, and most particularly with Rose, who chafed and fretted and made suggestion after suggestion as to the baby's father.

'Will you give it a bloody rest? There's clearly no point trying to make her tell us who it was, he's boggled her mind,' snapped William, finally, eyeing his daughter with an angry sadness that was almost disgust. And since that appeared to be his final word on the matter, it was left to Rose to do whatever she thought should be done next. The following morning she put on her best dress and a straw hat with a rumpled blue ribbon normally reserved for church, the harvest home and the like, and instructed her mute daughter to do the same.

'Come along, don't drag your heels,' she told Clemmie, whose silent questions about where they were going went unanswered. Clemmie didn't have any best shoes, and she generally went barefoot in the summer, but Rose forced her into her boots, ignoring her protests. Then they set off up to Weavern Lane and towards Slaughterford, and though Clemmie went meekly it was with a growing sense of unease. How people knew the things they knew was often mysterious to her – a lot of their interactions passed her by as she kept to herself. But Rose marched right past Thatch Cottage without a glance, and Clemmie relaxed just a little. Sweat soaked through the back of her mother's dress, making an oval shape in the small of her back, and Clemmie pulled on her hand to try to slow her down, only to be shaken off. 'No, Clem, this needs to be dealt with,' Rose muttered, her attention elsewhere.

They went to Manor Farm, and when she realised it, Clemmie tried again to refuse. Rose shot her a ferocious look that brought her to heel, and she fidgeted nervously as her mother banged at the door. The cob peered at them over his stable door, ears pricked; Hilarius, the horse groom, walked across towards the barn, raising one bony hand in salute as he went. Clemmie raised her hand in reply, but he'd already turned away. Then the door opened, and Rose clasped Clemmie's hand tightly, and the housekeeper showed them into a cool, stale parlour to the far end of the house. In the sudden stillness, Rose looked harried. Her face was red and wet from the walk, and she blotted at the sweat with her fingers to no effect. Frizzy hanks of her hair, as mad as Clemmie's, had escaped from beneath her bonnet, and when she caught sight of herself in the foxed mirror over the fireplace, she gaped in horror. They looked like a pair of scarecrows, and Rose coloured even more. Clemmie shrugged, to say that it didn't matter, but at that moment Nancy Hadleigh came into the room with her usual abruptness, and Clemmie slunk back slightly, looking down at the pattern of twisting vines and flowers of the rug, and her dirty boots, smudging it.

Nancy shut the door behind her and came across to sit on one of the chairs. She was wearing a plain black dress with no ornament, and no jewellery. Her hair was combed back and held, immaculately, in tortoiseshell combs, and her extreme composure created a severe contrast to her visitors. Clemmie could feel Nancy's antipathy for them – for her – sharpening her edges. She wanted more than anything to leave, and wondered what on earth her mother planned to say.

'Won't you sit down, the pair of you? Mrs Mattock, isn't it?' said Nancy.

'Matlock, your ladyship. Rose Matlock, and this is my girl, Clemmie.' Rose was clearly rattled; her wide eyes roved the room, and Nancy smiled faintly.

'No ladyships here,' she said. 'Miss Hadleigh will suffice. Yes, I know Clemmie. The one who'd been having lessons in speaking, down at the mill. Now, what brings you to see me?'

'Well,' said Rose. She nodded to Clemmie and they sat down, awkwardly, side by side on a sofa. 'I hate to disturb you, but I've been racking my brains over what to do. It's my girl here. She's ... been put into the family way.'

'Ah,' said Nancy. 'And yet I have heard no wedding bells of late?'

'No. No, there weren't no wedding, as yet.'

'She doesn't look . . . with child. Are you certain?'

'Oh, yes. That is, as certain as can be until she begins to round out in belly and breast. But certain enough.' There was a pause, and Nancy didn't blink.

'Do go on, Mrs Mattock.' This was delivered in a frosty tone.

'Yes. Well, Miss Hadleigh, my Clem here can't talk, as you know, in spite of Mr Hadleigh's kind efforts towards curing her of it. So she can't tell us who it was took advantage of her.'

'Yes, I can see how it would be difficult for her to do so.' Another pause, and Nancy's steely gaze fastened onto Clemmie. Rose swallowed, and Clemmie saw with sudden clarity what her mother's words, and what she was driving at, might seem to imply. Nancy Hadleigh had never liked her lessons, and had already sent Clemmie packing from the farm once before. She got up to go but Rose pulled her back down.

'Stay still, Clemmie! Well, your – Miss Hadleigh – what with Clemmie bringing the milk to the mill most days, I can't help wonder if that's where she met this fellow, whoever he might be. And I know this would have been better addressed to Mr Hadleigh, but with that not possible . . . My other girls tell me Clemmie has a sweetheart, you see, but she won't tell us who it is, so we've no other way to find him out . . . to make him marry her, see, and do right by her.'

'If he's free to marry, and willing to,' Nancy pointed out, coolly.

'Ar. That's so,' said Rose, miserably, as though she hadn't considered that possibility. 'I hope you understand only desperation has brought me here, to lay such a thing out in the open. But I hoped you might understand how such a thing could happen, and be willing to . . . keep it close. I've no doubt the whole world would know of it, quick as you like, if I were to go and ask around at the mill. But I wanted to ask if you could help us. If you had any idea who the villain might be. We've been so blind to it all, out at Weavern, but perhaps you've seen her walking out with a young man, or perhaps talking to one of your workers, down at the mill?'

The silence in the room rang. Clemmie didn't dare to look up. She hated to hear her life, her love, described in such terms. There had been nothing shameful in what she and Eli had done, nothing in the least bit demeaning. Or at least, there hadn't been until that moment. Nancy Hadleigh appeared unmoved, yet she radiated disgust. Bewildered, Rose ploughed on, though Clemmie tugged at her hand to make her stop. 'He'd have known, you see, that she couldn't tell on him. Do you see? Whoever he is, he'd have known that, and thought he could do just as he pleased with her, and ruin her, and not face the consequences.'

'Just what exactly are you implying?' said Nancy. Rose stared, and shook her head fractionally, and when she spoke her mouth sounded dry.

'I'm not implying, your— Miss Hadleigh . . . I only meant to ask if you'd seen her about the mill with anyone, or if any of the men working for you at the mill has spoken of it . . .' She trailed into silence in the cold glare of Nancy's suspicion.

'No,' said Nancy, at last. 'I've not seen her about with anybody, nor heard anything of it. Not that I tend to concern myself with the grubbier goings-on of the work force. All your sort have become far too used to Alistair being kind, and overly indulgent. I daresay he *would* have tried to help you, as you seem to think he would. But it wouldn't have been appropriate, and nor is your asking it. And I really don't see how we can help you. It seems to me to be a matter for your family to deal with, perhaps with greater discretion than you have shown here today. I imagine it would be best for your family's reputation that this did not become common knowledge.' She stood up, so Rose and Clemmie did the same.

'But what should I do, then? About bringing the fellow forward?' said Rose, hurriedly, in a last-ditch attempt as Nancy opened the door to dismiss them. Nancy watched Clemmie intently, and Clemmie shied away from her.

'We've more than enough to cope with here at the moment, Mrs Mattock,' Nancy said, tightly. 'I'll thank you not to lay your troubles at our door as well.'

They walked back down the hill in silence, Rose marching with just as much purpose as before, pulling Clemmie along by her hand when she dragged behind. Clemmie wanted to say, *Stop. It's all right, Mum, no need to fuss*. When they got to the bridge, Rose turned on her.

'Oh, do come *on*, Clem! Why must you lag like that?' She took a huge breath as if to go on, but then seemed to simply deflate. 'Can't you understand it, Clemmie – what a fix you're in?' she said. 'No one'll have you now, not with some rogue's bastard on your hip. You'll be on your own.' She shook her head, and Clemmie hated to see how careworn she looked, how tired and afraid. 'Perhaps your dad'll let you stay on with us, but I don't know. I just don't know. He's so strange since our Walter died, I don't know if he'll be stormy or fair. I never know.' Clemmie tried to take her hands to reassure her, but Rose pulled them away impatiently. 'You need to find a way to tell me, Clem. You *have* to find a way to, so we can get you wed, or get the man punished. It's the only way. Will he, do you think? Is he free to wed? Please tell me the bleeder's not already got a wife?' Clemmie shook her head at once, and Rose sagged slightly. 'Well, it's not much but it's something.' Rose heaved another sigh, pressing her fingertips deep into her cheeks. A soft breeze rustled the silver leaves of the riverbank willows, and it carried the scent of flowers. Clemmie breathed it deeply, and smiled. She couldn't understand how her mother wasn't feeling all the rightness she was feeling, in spite of Nancy Hadleigh's cold comfort. She pictured her wedding to Eli, and Rose jostling their child on her knee, and William thawing – his first grandchild starting to fill the hole that Walter's death had left. She pictured the time that was coming when all would be well, and wished she could pass her thoughts directly to her mother. With an exasperated sound, Rose marched on again, back towards Weavern, and this time she left her daughter to follow on at her own speed.

A quiet few days came next, and more hushed, terse conversations between Rose and William. Josie, Mary and Liz listened at doors, and underneath windows, and from the stairs, and Clemmie left them to it. She churned the butter and strained the curds and turned the cheeses, and walked here and there as she always had, waiting to hear from Eli. She waited to hear what his plan was, and when they would begin to live it, and in the meantime she saw babies everywhere. The sow had a litter of twelve, and at dawn the roe deer fawns tottered along at their mothers' heels on legs like stilts. A hopeless squawking woke them one night and they looked out to see a vixen carrying away one of the hens, three boisterous cubs bounding alongside her. Then, on the fourth morning, the atmosphere at the breakfast table was bleak.

'What is it?' asked Mary, but nobody answered her. Rose put her husband's plate down in front of him with a bang, and the eggs had black edges while the tomatoes were all but raw. He glowered at her, and she glared back, defiantly.

'Come along, Clemmie,' she said, undoing her apron. 'We've an appointment to keep.' Clemmie rose obediently, though she would far rather have known where they were going, and who they were to see. She noticed her sisters exchange a serious look, and Josie's eyes had gone very wide. Rose shut the door behind them far harder than was necessary.

Apparently, their everyday clothes were good enough for this visit, as were Clemmie's bare, dusty feet. Rose walked with her arms folded and her chin tucked in, as though, this time, she was as unwilling to go wherever they were going as her daughter. When they got to Thatch Cottage and Rose hurried up the path, her face still downturned, Clemmie panicked. She followed her mother with feet gone numb, on legs that shook, desperately trying to think how her secret had been discovered. Eli had told her his father still hadn't found work, and was around a good deal of the time, and he already had that crushed look his father gave him, along with a bruise on his jaw and bloodied knuckles from an argument with his brother. There hadn't been any visits to Mrs Tanner for a while, because of the risk of running into Isaac; no more cuddling the little ones or cups of nettle tea. Involuntarily, Clemmie made a noise in her throat – a whine of distress and fear. She had no idea what was about to happen, no idea what Rose would say. She only knew that it would not go well. If Eli were there, if Rose accused him outright, she didn't know what he would say, or do. She didn't like to think what would happen if Isaac were there as well. She shut her eyes and gulped for air, heart hammering, her mind in too much disarray to think or react, to do anything other than follow as her mother knocked, and the door opened, and they went inside.

Clemmie darted a look around the room, struggling to see in the darkness. Eli's grandmother was asleep in her chair, and his mother was sitting at the crooked table, and besides the two of them the room was empty, the house quiet. She breathed just a little bit easier. Mrs Tanner met Clemmie's eye with a look – questioning, and pleading for calm. Shaking, Clemmie tried not to give in to her panic, or let it show on her face. She was desperate to say out loud, there and then, that she hadn't asked for any of it, that she hadn't told anyone about Eli, and had no demands to make, other than to be left be. She sensed the stiffness in her mother's body; felt how she loathed to be there. But Rose wasn't angry. In fact, there was something almost apologetic about the way she stood, and clasped her hands, and waited to be spoken to. Mrs Tanner, without getting up, gestured for them to sit.

'Mrs Matlock,' she said, guardedly. She flicked her eyes at Clemmie, who felt sweat oozing down her spine and between her thighs. She was trembling so badly she was sure they would see. 'Something I can help you with?'

'This one's got a child inside,' said Rose, baldly. Mrs Tanner let her face register just a little surprise. Clemmie held her breath, certain that her mother's next words would be to name Eli, to demand marriage and retribution. The pause boomed in her ears, filling in the gaps between the thumping beats of her heart. She waited; she could only wait, with no idea of how it would end – of what Mrs Tanner or her mother would say next. 'It wants getting shot of,' said Rose. 'I've heard you know ways of doing that.'

It took a moment for the words to make sense to Clemmie. When they did, they hit her with such force that her body jerked out of the chair, knocking it onto its back, and she stumbled away until she hit the far wall, and stood staring, aghast. Rose gave her a quick, unhappy glance. 'Her father says as much, and there's no arguing with the man,' she said, turning back to Mrs Tanner. Clemmie began to shake her head, and tears made the room wobble and lurch. Mrs Tanner looked taken aback. She said nothing for a moment, then looked at Clemmie, meeting her eyes for a second. Clemmie saw sympathy there, and something like resignation. Mrs Tanner cleared her throat.

'How far along is she?' she said.

'Not long.' Rose shook her head. 'Won't be more than a worm, still.' *Not a worm*, thought Clemmie, *a piglet. A baby. Mine and Eli's.* She clasped her hands protectively across her middle, and stared at Mrs Tanner in terror. Mrs Tanner shook her head minutely.

'Is this what you want, girl?' she asked her, and Clemmie shook her head violently.

'She don't know what she wants!' said Rose, with a tremor in her voice. 'She can't know! What's she going to do with a baby? William won't have it – where's she going to go with it? How will she live?'

'Doesn't look to me like she wants shot of it,' said Mrs Tanner. 'I'll not do it against her will. It's not right, that.'

'Not right?' said Rose. 'None of this is right, by God!'

'Perhaps it might come so, given time,' said Mrs Tanner, carefully.

'Well, do go on and tell me how,' said Rose, shaking her head.

'Look at your daughter, Mrs Matlock,' said Mrs Tanner. Rose seemed reluctant to, but when she did, and when she saw Clemmie's distress, she slumped in her chair, defeated.

'But what'll she do? William will turn her out, he says. What then?' She sounded hopeless, and Clemmie wished with all her heart to be able to explain. Just then, she almost wished Mrs Tanner would speak on her behalf, and tell her mother about Eli, and ease her misery – if news that the baby was a Tanner had any hope of doing that.

Mrs Tanner got up and went to a cupboard on the wall. She fetched out a small paper packet and handed it to Rose.

'Perhaps you can find a way to change his mind on it,' she said. 'Take this. Give it to him in his tea or his beer.'

'What will it do?' Rose took it, a strange, suspicious kind of hope kindling on her face.

'It'll ... put lead in his pipe, shall we say. He'll need you then, right enough, and that kind of need, once tended to, makes a man grateful.' Mrs Tanner smiled slightly, and Rose fingered the packet speculatively.

'Been a goodly while since he needed that from me,' she said, then shook her head. 'He was so set though, so hard, I don't think he'll change his mind and keep her and the littl'un. I don't think she can keep it.'

'But look at your daughter – see how she holds her belly! See how rabbity she is! She loves that child already, loves it right through. You can't make her kill it, can you?' Rose turned to look at Clemmie, and Clemmie saw all her mother's resolve melt away.

'Do you love that baby you've got, my girl?' she asked, and Clemmie nodded at once, knees sagging in relief. Rose sighed heavily, like she was exhausted. She got up, still holding the paper packet in her hand. 'I pray God this works,' she said. 'How much is owed?'

'Nothing.' Mrs Tanner waved one hand to dismiss the suggestion. 'Take it with my good will, since you didn't get what you came for. Perhaps you got something better, mind you.'

The thought of leaving Weavern Farm had never occurred to Clemmie before. It occurred to her now, as they walked back home. Rose took her daughter's hand and held it tightly, and didn't speak. The Tanners might have her and Eli and the baby after they'd wed, and Clemmie tried to picture that – living there with all the listless children and frightened women, all the angry men and boys; in the unnatural darkness, surrounded by barren ground. The thought of it was like a weight, steadily crushing her. Shaking off her mother's hand, she darted into the trees, away down the hill towards the river.

'Clemmie! Come back!' she heard Rose shout after her, but she carried on. Nettles stung her ankles, brambles scratched her skin; the green smell of crushed leaves and the dusty tickle of pollen rose up all around her; flies and cobwebs and watchful, darting birds in the branches overhead. The ground was steep, and she careered from tree to tree to catch her momentum until she was at the riverbank, where she sat, putting her stinging feet into the water and letting the cold numb them. To live there, in the shadow of Isaac Tanner, would be to shut out the sun. To shut out air. Clemmie closed her eyes and tried to believe that it would be enough to be with Eli, to be his wife and have his child. But however much she told it to herself, she couldn't convince herself. She knew how Eli was when his father was around – so angry at the world that even the blood in his veins seemed to harden. She thought of the trampled mud around the cottage, the scarcity of food, the scarcity of joy. She thought of waking every morning and feeling, first of all, dread. And she knew she couldn't do it.

When she'd calmed down she told herself that living at Thatch Cottage would not be Eli's plan. It could not be. He despised his father more than anybody, and certainly wouldn't tolerate him laying a hand on Clemmie, as he was bound to sooner or later – nobody under his roof escaped his violence for long. It could end in murder; it could end in Eli swinging from a rope at Cornhill Prison, down in Shepton Mallet, where those other Tanners who'd killed had gone before him. That could not be his plan. She pictured them living out, as he had been, under hedges, in hollow trees; gone wild since they were both half wild already. But that would not do for the baby; not through the winter. Never before had she looked and seen, so clearly, that Weavern Farm was a place of safety and bounty. Constancy and warmth and food, especially in the winter months; even since Walter had died and part of her father had gone with him. Thinking of leaving was like thinking of cutting out some vital part of her, and doing without it. As she walked back to the farm at the end of the day, with sore feet and her throat aching from crying, Clemmie finally felt afraid.

Most of the household had already gone to bed, and only Mary was still up, sitting by the stove with her feet up on a stool, mending one of their father's shirts. The air smelt sweetly of hay from the chamomile flowers she liked to brew into tea. She looked up as Clemmie came in, but kept on with her work.

'They had one hell of a set-to,' she said, as Clemmie sat down opposite her. 'Josie went off in floods of tears to hear them. Soft as a kitten that one – even softer than you, I think.' *And will he let me stay? And my baby?* Clemmie asked, without a word. Mary sighed. 'I don't know, Clem. He went as red as a berry – I never saw the like of it. I thought he might go into a fit. I thought the blood might curdle in him. Mum said putting you out was just the same as killing you, and the littl'un too, and she laid it all on his head. That turned him quiet a while.' She stabbed her finger with the needle and tutted, sucking at the bead of red. 'That's it,' she said, putting the mending aside. 'That's the fifth prick I've given myself in half an hour. Time for bed. Come on, dawdler.' She stood, stretching her shoulders back, and picked up the lamp. Above their heads came a creaking, and muffled, rhythmic sounds, almost-words. Mary listened for a while, then flashed a quick, rude grin at her sister. 'She's working hard on your behalf, Clem,' she said, and Clemmie nodded that she knew. They went up the stone stairs as softly as they could, and Clemmie crossed her fingers tight.

*

William was already in the kitchen when Clemmie came down, early in the morning. She moved towards him cautiously. He looked tired but there was something softer about his face, some little sadness in his eyes that was sweet and sorry but not blank, not shut off as it had been for so long. Still, Clemmie didn't quite trust it, and when he came towards her and put up his hands, she flinched. William saw it, and she saw how it hurt him. How he accused himself. He put his hands on her shoulders and gripped them hard, gazing down at her for a while. She felt the warmth and weight of his hands through the thin cambric of her blouse, and smelled his familiar smells of grease and linen and cow. She saw how they had become all but strangers to each other, and how ill that sat with the love that remained, as fixed as the bones in their bodies. Then William cupped his hand around her cheek – rough, stained fingers; the skin gone leathery hard.

'Stay on here, then, girl,' he said. 'But I won't see hide nor hair of the louse that's done this and not come forward to marry you. Mark me, now. If he comes sniffing again I'll have his guts, and no mistake.' He turned from her then, and went out without another word. Clemmie watched the door after he'd gone, feeling her flash of joy curdle.

She worked in the sun all day, not leaving the farm's own fields, letting her head ache and the skin across her shoulders sting as it turned pink. She felt too tied to the farm to roam that day; too afraid to stray in case she wouldn't be allowed to return, or wasn't able to. She tried not to picture the future – where she would end up, and the baby, and Eli. She was tormented by the impossibility of ever reconciling her family to Eli when she hadn't the words to explain; by the unlikelihood of Eli ever being free of Isaac Tanner. He had such hold over his son – had made him what he was with the things he'd made him do. She had no answers, and the task of finding them was so huge that she hardly dared to look straight at it. She watched the cows graze, though they had no need of minding, listening to the tearing of the grass between their teeth, the wet curl of tongues and swish of thready tails. From where she was, in Weavern's highest field on the Biddestone side of the valley, the farmhouse and barns were hidden. The land rolled so steeply that it hid the buildings in its folds, and only the river was visible, looping away to the south. Her home was a nook in the green ground, as secret as a warren. Her home was a hidden place, separate from the rest. It was easy to imagine that nothing bad could ever come there. That Isaac Tanner would never find them, and couldn't touch them. She wished, passionately, that Isaac Tanner would quit Slaughterford for good.

In the afternoon, with the sun low and blinding in her eyes, Eli came and found Clemmie. She looked around hastily as he approached, but none of her family were about. There was a lightness in Eli's step, a new urgency, and he smelled of sweat and hot skin as he held her tight.

'I've got our plan, Clem!' he said, smiling, and she realised then that she had a plan of her own. She took his hands, meshed their fingers together, willed him to see it, and understand. But he was too excited, too defiant. 'If our families don't want us, then why should we linger here?' he said, keenly. 'I can wave a jolly fare-thee-well to my dad for good, God curse him! I've a cousin in Swindon that works in a foundry there, in the engine sheds – building *trains*, Clemmie! Imagine that. He reckons there's a job for me, just waiting. Low paid, but a job, and they'd 'prentice me up for it. We can lodge with him and his missus a while, for a few pennies, until we find our feet and get a room for ourselves. I've been to Swindon and it's nice, Clem. A good place, busy, you know? And plenty of fine folk there. Do you know it?' He took a breath then carried on describing it, because of course she couldn't say that she had never heard of it, that she didn't know where it was, that she didn't want to go, that her family *did* want them. Or at least, they wanted her, and she planned to make them take him too. At last, Eli noticed her unease, and he frowned. 'This is our chance, Clemmie. Our chance to be together and start a new life, and our very own family. A chance for me to start over, where my name ain't so well known, and I'm not suspected of something by every man I meet. A clean slate. This is the chance of it.' She looked away and he caught her chin, turning her to meet his eyes. The happiness in his face was dying, the spring in him waning. 'You do still want to come away with me, don't you, Clem?' he asked, intently. 'You do still want to be mine?'

❧ ❧

Hilarius and Irene didn't speak as he drove her, in the Stanhope, the handful of miles to Corsham station. Irene sat stiffly beside him, hoping Pudding hadn't told him what she'd said about him. The darkness about him remained; an overwrought phrase she'd read in a book kept coming to mind, however hard she tried to dismiss it: *the stain of death*. The old groom wore his battered long coat in spite of the season; it smelled of wax and animals, and there was mud and straw in the floor of the cart. Irene found herself glancing repeatedly at his gnarled hands on the reins, wondering if they still had the strength to inflict such injuries as Alistair had been given. Corsham was a small town of crooked, old stone buildings and cobbled streets, not much bigger than a village, but even so, the Manor Farm gig looked deeply bucolic in that setting. Irene shrank inwardly to think what her mother would make of having to ride in it, back through the narrow dusty lanes to Slaughterford. She'd tried to persuade Isadora Dalby to alight in Chippenham, since it wasn't such a one-horse town, but her mother had demurred, since Corsham was closer to Slaughterford and *you know how I hate to be in a carriage in the summer, with all the insects*, she'd written in her note.

Isadora's visit had come in response to Irene's hasty letter, sent soon after Alistair's death, asking to return to her parents in London as soon as possible. When an answer hadn't come directly she'd known that she would not get her wish, but that hadn't brought about a crushing disappointment – more of a neutral, disconnected kind of feeling that made her wonder if it was still her wish in any case. And now the thought of her mother being at Manor Farm was causing a steadily growing unease; the thought of her there, and of her meeting Nancy, was too odd, too unsettling. The two belonged in separate worlds, and it somehow seemed to Irene that their meeting couldn't help but bring about a cataclysm of some kind. And there was so much she would not be able to talk about – Alistair's murder, Donny, Tanner, her odd feelings, and how she was trying to help Pudding. It left her without much of an idea of what to say at all.

'I'll go down and collect her, if you'd like to wait here?' she suggested to Hilarius, as they arrived outside the small station with its cream-painted clapboard building and green picket fence. Hilarius nodded once and Irene climbed down. Deep within her, something shook at the thought of seeing her mother again. She couldn't tell if it were fear or excitement, hope or dread.

Isadora Marianne Dalby was taller than her daughter, without spare flesh but well-built. She had broader shoulders and hips than she'd ever liked, and a broader face across the jaw and forehead, so that she looked stately rather than elegant, and only ever wore shoes that she thought made her feet look smaller, even if they gave her corns. Still, she was handsome, and drew glances from the men on the stone wharf as they used winches, pulleys and sweat to load newly quarried Bath stone onto flat-bed wagons. She was wearing a calf-length fawn silk dress with a dropped waist, white kid shoes and a white sleeveless jacket with pearl buttons. Her hair was younger than she was – it was fair, not showing any grey, and she'd cut it short and set it in a permanent wave, after the fashion. Irene realised, seeing her from afar, that she herself hadn't seen a hairdresser since she'd arrived in Slaughterford the best part of three months before. Her hair grew slowly but she put up a hand and felt it resting on her collar. At least her mother couldn't criticise her outfit. Mourning was mourning, after all.

'Hello, Mother,' she said, holding out her hands. Isadora took them carefully, with her fingers only, and kissed her daughter on both cheeks. Irene caught her familiar scent – face powder, violets, the starchy smell of her clothing. London smells; smells from a previous time and place that sent Irene right back there, into echoes of her lonely childhood, her lonely adolescence, her lonely coming of age. She swallowed, and tried to smile. Isadora's expression was inscrutable, with something hard in the eyes. But then, that had always been there. 'Thank you for coming to see me.'

'Well,' said Isadora, with a minute shrug, and then hesitated. 'Perhaps it was about time,' she added, without conceding a thing.

'Hilarius has the Stanhope just up here. Where are your cases?'

'Oh, I'm not staying – did I not say? I'm sure I said.'

'You didn't say.'

'Well. Your father and I decided it would be best if I didn't impose on a household in mourning. And we've to go to the Duncan-Hoopers tomorrow, for their anniversary ball.'

'Perhaps the Duncan-Hoopers might have celebrated just as well with two fewer guests, and spared you,' Irene murmured, but her mother gave her a hard look.

'Their invitation was accepted a good while before yours arrived, Irene.'

'Well, I hadn't planned on my husband dying. Nor on you coming here – I'd planned to come home.'

'Let's not quarrel,' said Isadora, closing the subject and looking away with a tight smile as though to appease imaginary onlookers.

She took one look at the little cart, and at Hilarius, with dust bedded into the creases of his face, and suggested that they remain in Corsham instead. There was a pretty high street to walk along, and a park, though in the end Isadora declined to leave paved ground for grass, for fear of ruining her shoes. 'One forgets, living in London, that such tiny places carry on and thrive, all unobserved,' she said, looking vaguely dispirited.

'Well, they do,' said Irene, thinking that after so many weeks in Slaughterford, Corsham seemed quite lively, in fact, with its schoolchildren, butchers, and cobblers; unemployed men with tired eyes, smoking idly on corners; busy women running errands.

'What on earth do you do to entertain yourselves out here?'

'Mother, how can you ask such a thing, when I have written to you time and again of how unhappy I am here, and how much I would prefer to come back to town?'

'Well, pardon me, Irene. I was only attempting to be civil, when you've given us so much to talk about that is *un*civil. I daresay you *would* prefer to come back to us. But don't let's make believe that you are being unfairly kept away, or unfairly made unhappy – you brought this on yourself, after all.'

'I married Alistair, just as you said I should. I came all

the way down here, away from everything, just as you said I should.'

'You can hardly blame me for your current situation, dear. And I know that you continued to write to that man – oh yes, word of it got about. Serena has done her best to make sure your name raises a chuckle wherever it's mentioned – and ours, by extension.' Irene felt her face and neck grow hot, and her throat tightened at this latest betrayal – that Fin had not managed to keep her letters secret, that he had let her humiliation continue. 'Well might you blush, Irene,' said her mother. 'But your poor father's digestion torments him.'

'Father's digestion has always tormented him.'

'Well, he has always borne life's stresses and strains on our behalf, Irene. And you have always given him plenty,' Isadora snapped.

'Not always,' Irene demurred, but quietly.

They went for coffee and cake at the Methuen Arms, a large coaching inn, and Irene considered her mother's words about unhappiness, and fairness. She recalled something Pudding had said whilst they'd been out riding, two days before – just an observation; something Pudding had gathered from listening to Irene talk, but it had struck Irene. Once they'd let the subject of the identity of Alistair's murderer rest for a while, Pudding had asked a stream of breathless questions about Fin and London and love. It had been a relief, for both of them, to dwell for a while on far-off things. By now, Irene was relatively at ease hacking out on Robin, at a walk, with Pudding riding alongside on Bally Girl, one hand on her own reins and the other on Robin's lead rein. They'd gone at that sedate pace out of Slaughterford and up the valley towards Ford and Castle Combe, pursued by a cloud of dust and flies that couldn't spoil the late summer glory of the countryside.

When she had been Pudding's age, all of Irene's thoughts

had run to marriage. It had been the same for all her friends as well, though Irene's goal had been as much about getting away from her parents as it had been about getting close to anyone else. There was the agony, during the war, of fiancés being lost and killed, of hearts being broken; and for the unattached, the subtler distress, as news of the losses rolled in year after year, of realising that there would not be enough young men left for them to marry. Pudding Cartwright didn't dream of marriage, though. She dreamed of love. She dreamed of it as an abstract marvel, like a person might dream of flying; as though romantic love were something beyond the realms of her reality, and marriage therefore pointless to dream about.

'But when you fell in love with Fin, and you knew he loved you . . . did it make you *happy*?' she'd asked keenly, and not for the first time, as though the answer were of vital importance.

'Yes,' Irene had said, sensing that Pudding needed this answer. And the truth was that it had, for the brief times they were alone together. The brief times when she could pretend that other people, and the rest of the world, did not exist. It had been a feeling of safety and well-being. Otherwise, their love had brought a kind of hungry, desperate fear to everything she did. Pudding had frowned, perhaps sensing that Irene was holding back. She had, by then, extracted tales of night clubs and dinners and dances from Irene; the gossipy social whirl of London; the thrills and perils of fashion; mornings spent sleeping off the drink and despair of the night before; and she always asked for more details, more words to describe how that life had actually *felt*, and what it was actually *like*. Irene knew she needed an escape from herself, an escape from the situation, and she tried to provide it. But then, as they'd ridden back down the hill in Slaughterford, Pudding, sounding flat, had said: 'I always thought London would mean all the fun and excitement a person could wish for. But it doesn't sound as though you were very much happier there than you have been here. I hope you don't mind my saying?'

Which was true, of course, and what struck Irene was that she'd never realised it herself. It was simply all she had known. Her well-to-do upbringing, her passable education and finishing, and her parents, who had never shown anything more than a detached interest in their daughter – their only requirements ever having been that she comport herself as she ought, look the part and marry well. She'd had friends, of course, with the same goals and ideas as herself; she'd been to all the right places, and known the right people; and she'd fallen wildly in love with Fin, with all the terrified joy that had brought. But, during none of it, now she thought back, had she been particularly happy. With a jolt, she found herself at a loss to think why she was in such a hurry to return to that life – a life bound to be far worse, and far lonelier, since the end of the affair. Now, watching as her mother sat down stiffly, glancing around at the furnishings and the clientele as though she were on a different planet and keen to rise above the rusticity of the locals, Irene saw clearly how life would be, back beneath her parents' roof. The constant reminders of her disgrace, her flawed judgement, her failings. The search for a new husband with whom to pack her off into semi-respectability, which she knew would commence immediately upon her return. It was an exhausting thought. Their coffee arrived; Isadora took a sip and jerked up her eyebrows in response.

'What is it, Mother? Is something wrong with the coffee?' said Irene, sharply. Isadora trained her stony eyes on her daughter.

'It's perfectly delicious,' she said.

'Good. I'm glad to hear it. You've not once commiserated with me over Alistair's death, you know. You've not once said that you're sorry about it.'

'Well, I am sorry, of course, and I'm sure it must have been a dreadful shock. But it's not as though you loved the man. Let's not make-believe, Irene.'

'No. You never were keen on playing games, even when I was tiny. And I didn't love him, it's true. But I . . . liked him. And I miss him.'

'What are you driving at, dear?'

'Am I "dear"? I've never felt it. Perhaps I might have come to love Alistair – we were married for four months, after all. Did you ever think of that? That perhaps I might have come to love him?'

'The last time we spoke of love, you told me in no uncertain terms that you would love Finlay Campbell, and none but him, until the day you died,' Isadora pointed out, to which Irene had no answer, since it was true. It was the fact of not being asked that bothered her, the fact of her feelings not even being considered.

'But then,' she murmured, 'you and Father have always simply ignored what you didn't want to see.'

'What was that? Please don't mumble and mutter. I see your manners haven't improved, during your . . . time away, Irene. But then,' she cast her eyes around, 'I suppose this isn't exactly Paris.'

They sat in silence for a while, and Irene remembered all the times she had sat in silence with her parents before. At parties, at mealtimes, playing cards. Sitting up straight, minding her manners, saying next to nothing and not even really noticing as much, because she'd had nothing *to* say. She thought of Pudding's ready chatter, and guessed that mealtimes at Spring Cottage had been rather different. She wondered what it might have been like to have a big brother to play with, even one who teased, and parents who gave hugs and kisses, and baked cakes, and read to one another. She could hardly picture such a place, and how wonderful it might have been to grow up in. Before Donny had been injured in the war, of course; before Mrs Cartwright had begun to lose her faculties, and Donny had been arrested. Suddenly, she understood Pudding's need to talk, her need to act, even more clearly. She felt a flash of impatience to be wasting time, and not helping.

'A terrible thing has happened here, Mother,' she said, as she finished her lemon slice.

'Not terrible enough to curb your appetite, I see,' said Isadora, in an attempt at levity that fell entirely flat.

'I find that eating helps me to sleep, which helps me to cope,' said Irene, levelly.

'Well, finding a new husband will be harder work, if you let your figure thicken.'

'I've no wish to find a new husband.'

'Oh, don't talk nonsense, Irene. What else are you going to do with yourself?'

'I'm needed here, in fact.'

'Needed? By whom?'

'Those of us dealing with the terrible thing that has happened, Mother. Nancy Hadleigh, and the Cartwrights.'

'The aunt? And who are the Cartwrights – retainers? I thought you were desperate to be away from here – to come back to London, to us, and to society.' Her mother sounded wrong-footed, almost disappointed, as though she had a load of arguments marshalled against it that she wouldn't get the chance to use.

'I hadn't thought it through,' said Irene. 'But I see it clearly, now. I'm quite finished with London.'

'Well!' said Isadora, her eyes going wide and a breath staying high in her chest, ready to say more. But, as if she couldn't choose which to select, none of the words got spoken. 'Are you, indeed,' she said, in the end, somewhat weakly, and Irene saw that – for the first time in her life – she'd stolen the wind from her mother's sails.

'What time is your train back to London? I'm sure you have one in mind,' said Irene, and had the sad satisfaction of seeing her mother yet further taken aback.

Hilarius took her back to Manor Farm in silence, not seeming in the least bit curious about the change of plan. Only once they'd arrived back in the yard did he climb down, with remarkable nimbleness, and offer to hand her down. He'd never made such a gesture before.

'Thank you, Hilarius,' said Irene, taken aback. The touch of his hand caused a strange ache in her own. He nodded minutely.

'Ma'am,' he said, with a nod. Then all of his attention returned to the horse, as was more usual. Irene listened to the now-familiar rumble of the mill, and the reeling of swifts, the chipping of sparrows, the fussing of the hens and pigs. She stood in the yard and turned her hat in her hands, letting the sun dry her damp hairline, and felt curiously free, almost at ease. She asked Clara for a cold drink as she went through the house and out onto the rear terrace, to sit and think. The wooden slats of the seat were warm through her skirt. She saw Nancy down in the churchyard, sitting on the bench from which, Irene knew, she would be able to see the Hadleigh family plot; she saw Jem standing in the orchard, gently wrestling one of his ferrets free from a length of twine in which it had got tangled. The ferret twisted and kicked, objecting to the process. Then she saw Pudding Cartwright, struggling up the hill towards the back gate in a fast gait that was not quite a run, her face puce and her long legs and arms apparently at war with her.

Irene sat up and shaded her eyes to see better. The girl had a book in one hand, the pages flapping whitely. By the time Pudding made it to the orchard gate, Irene could hear her gasping for breath. She waved her free hand when she saw Irene, then waved the book as well, and tried to say something.

'Pudding! Sit down – get your breath. What is it?' said Irene, but Pudding, reaching the table, shook her head, bending over and dragging at the air.

'I've found it,' she said, eventually, still breathless. 'It came to me all in a flash – something Ma Tanner said, and Hilarius too.'

'Found what, Pudding? I can hardly understand you. What did Ma Tanner say?' asked Irene, and Pudding shook her head again. There was sweat running down her face and Irene forced her to sit and cool down and have a sip of lemonade before she said anything else. Pudding did as she was told, though impatience made her restless and jumpy. 'Now tell me,' said Irene, some minutes later. Pudding looked across at her with a wild expression, an electric mingling of hope and horror.

'Hilarius said to me to look at the roots of things – at the deeply buried *why* of Alistair being killed, but I couldn't think of a thing. Then I went to see Ma Tanner and she said more or less the same thing – that there would be a reason, and it'd be something in the past, or something like that. I went away and still couldn't think of a thing. But she said that even the *most foul* things – or *especially* the most foul things – happened for a reason, or something, and then I remembered!' She held out the book she'd been carrying, and Irene took it and read the title. *Murder Most Foul – true stories of dark deeds in Wiltshire.* A chill passed over her skin. She glanced up, thinking that the weather had changed, but it hadn't.

'Pudding, what can you mean?' she said.

'It's "The Maid of the Mill", all over again! Turn to page

ninety-six.' Irene did as she was told, and found a chapter with just that heading. Pudding couldn't wait for her to read it, though, and interrupted. 'I'd read it before – before any of this happened. I can't believe I didn't think of it sooner. I'm such a dunce! Years and years ago, last century, a young girl called Sarah something-or-other was murdered right here, in Slaughterford!'

'But . . . Pudding, what can that possibly have to do with anything?'

'You have to read it, but I'll tell you – she was murdered in just the same place as Alistair, in the same way as him – hit with a shovel – and . . .' Pudding paused to make sure Irene was listening, 'it happened fifty years *to the day* before Alistair was killed!'

'There was another murder at the mill?' said Irene, dimly, as a creeping dread breathed onto the back of her neck. Pudding nodded.

'A girl not much older than me, killed on the seventeenth of July, 1872. Exactly fifty years before Alistair! In the same place, and by the same means. It's not a coincidence. It *can't* be! It *has* to be the same killer – don't you see? It *has* to be! And Donny wasn't even born then!' Pudding finished triumphantly, and though Irene could see her mad relief and excitement, all she herself could feel was the same shift in things – the same point of before and after being reached – as she'd felt when she'd picked up the doll on the day it had fallen out of the chimney in her writing room. She closed her eyes, and tried to see.

8

Deeper Still

The police house in Ford was empty, so Pudding asked around and was told, in the shop, that Constable Dempsey was out in the fields, helping his father bind and stack the last of the oats. She was hot from the walk through the water meadows to Ford, but she carried on northwards, propelled by purpose, up a steep, wooded lane to the field where a row of men were all toiling together. Shirt collars open, sleeves rolled up, big boots up over their calves that must have been roasting. They were covered in sweat and chaff; their hands and arms were scratched, and when Pudding went across to Pete Dempsey, his colour deepened, caught off guard.

'What are you doing here, Pudding?' he said. Pudding had to squint up at him, and had the peculiar sense of there being two of him – the big, snub-nosed boy, three years her senior, who'd once eaten frogspawn and laughed at her when she'd got stuck in the manger at the Sunday School picnic, and this grown man with solid shoulders and a crop of brown hair on his chest peeping out at the neck of his shirt. He cast a surreptitious look at his workmates, some of whom grinned, and Pudding felt conspicuous, laughed at anew. She shook it off, although it made her notice how damp she was all over, and how strongly the smell of horse lingered on her clothes.

'I've new evidence in the case of the murder of Alistair Hadleigh,' she said, trying to sound serious and not like an overexcited child.

'You've what?' said Pete.

'I've new—'

'Yes, I heard you, I just . . .' He shook his head. 'The case against your brother is pretty well closed, Pudding. Superintendent Blackman's not even considering Mrs Hadleigh any more.'

'Well, of course not – she wasn't in the least bit involved. But what I've found out is completely different and it *proves* my brother is innocent!'

'But *you* were the one to accuse her!'

'I know that, but I was wrong, Will you just listen, Pete? I mean, Constable Demps—'

'You can call me Pete. As long as the boss isn't about.'

'Well. All right.' She wrestled the book of Wiltshire murders out of her satchel. 'I found it in this book – I'd read it before but I'd forgotten, but it's all here in black and white. Alistair Hadleigh's murder is an exact replication of a murder that happened fifty years ago. An *exact* replica. A local girl called Sarah Martock was killed – Donny couldn't possibly have done that one, could he? Just like he can't have murdered Alistair. This proves it!'

Pete Dempsey took the book from her and frowned down at the page, while Pudding looked on, impatiently. She was finding it hard to keep her hands still, so she clenched and unclenched them. Her thoughts danced about, as though her brain were too hot for them.

'Are we readin' psalms or fetching in the oats, lad?' called Pete's father, Cyril. He was on foot, leading the team of four that pulled the three-ton haywain onto which the men were pitching the oat sheaves. It was a massive, hoop-raved wagon, made for Cyril by the current wheelwright's father and as solid now as it had been then; it was painted blue with the wheels done in scarlet, and Pudding had been given rides in it when she was little. The team of gentle hairy shires pulling it were sweating into their collars, and she had the sudden memory of Donny riding one of them, barelegged in his shorts, and getting so covered in horsehair that he came running after Pudding and her friends pretending to be a werewolf – with much growling and gnashing of teeth – and sent them squealing off across the field.

'Coming, Dad,' Pete called. He passed the book back to Pudding with an apologetic look. 'I can't stop and read it now, Pudding. Miss Cartwright. Pudding.' He pressed his lips together. 'I'm all sweat and mess, anyway. Can you . . . do you want to meet me after? And tell me about it then?'

'Well yes, I suppose so. But isn't this an official police matter? I'd far rather—'

'Meet me after,' he insisted. 'Down at the pub, about six?'

'At the pub?' Pudding had never been before – not in the evening, when it was full of men. 'Er. That won't do – I've to get home for supper.'

'Well, we could always . . . We might . . . Well, all right. Eight, then,' he said, taking a breath as though the exchange had been strenuous. Pudding nodded and marched away, ignoring the half-formed comments from the others that followed her. The golden stubble whisked beneath her feet, and the ground was crumbly, studded with chunks of limestone. She walked with purpose even though, she realised, she had nowhere in particular to go.

She wondered about going back to talk to Irene again. She'd had one of her feelings when Pudding had told her about the story in the murder book – Pudding had actually seen it happen this time, since she'd been right there. Irene's face had turned almost fearful – the kind of fearful you got when you were out by yourself after dark, and thought you saw a figure moving beside you, hidden in the trees. A figure you couldn't quite see. She'd kept staring at the murder book with that look on her face, and had seemed relieved when Pudding had suggested she go at once and show it to Pete. And try as she had, Pudding hadn't been able to get Irene to say anything specific about what she felt, or what she thought; just that she agreed that the first murder was probably significant. So in the end, and with a good deal of willpower since she felt like she might burst if she didn't talk about it again soon, Pudding decided to give Irene time to digest, and went home instead.

When Pudding told her mother where she was going that evening, Louise smiled.

'What, with Cyril Dempsey's boy? There's a turn-up. But at least I know you're safe enough, I suppose, in the arms of the law,' she said. Still, Pudding wrote a note for her dad, in case her mum forgot before he got home from the call he'd answered. She had a bath and, having no idea what she ought to wear to a pub where she would stick out like a sore thumb in any case, she put on a plain skirt and a clean shirt, and did her best to coax her hair into a sensible shape. It didn't matter, anyway – she'd be flushed and clammy again by the time she got to Ford. There was no option but to walk since it was far too steep for her to bicycle. She put her satchel diagonally over her shoulder and set off. In the waning yellow light the river looked syrupy; a heron stood on its stilts on the far bank, idly preening its grey and white feathers, and a little brown and white dipper barely disturbed the surface as it fished. Towards Ford the sound of the mill died away, and Pudding heard the far-off fretting of sheep, and the whisper of the breeze in the long grasses; the swish of them as they tickled her calves. Along the final stretch of the meadow the knotweed was in flower, creating a swathe of waving pink tufts, impossibly pretty. Pudding could hardly believe such ugly things as had happened were possible, in this place of apparent innocence. She felt cheated.

The White Hart was housed in an ancient stone building that straddled the river. The By Brook ran through a leat beneath its rooms to the mill alongside, which had once turned grist and made paper before it went out of use. The pub was busy, with a hubbub of male voices inside, and warm light in the windows, and the door thumping as drinkers went in and out, releasing a belch of tobacco smoke each time they did. Women didn't usually go in in the evening – the odd one or two, of dubious reputation. Most bought a jug of whatever they fancied from a hatch in the wall, and took it home with them. There was absolutely no hard or fast rule saying Pudding shouldn't go in, she told herself. But there was convention and family law – and the throng of strange men – and her courage failed her. She perched on one of the benches outside, and waited for Pete Dempsey there. She was anxious, on edge; she'd expected her discovery to cause a wave of instant revelation, just like the one she'd experienced when she'd remembered the older murder. She'd expected Donny to be released – if not at once, then soon. But even though Irene had reacted appropriately it hadn't translated into any action, as yet; and Nancy Hadleigh hadn't reacted at all, other than to stare at Pudding from somewhere deep inside herself, without blinking. And then Pete Dempsey had just gone back to the harvest, and if she didn't manage to convince him, that evening, to take it seriously, then she'd have to take it directly to Superintendent Blackman in Chippenham. A frightening idea, but she would do it.

'Penny for your thoughts?' said Pete, sitting down beside her with a smile. He smelled of soap and his hair was still damp, combed back neatly. He'd caught the sun across his nose and cheeks, and the skin was shining and bronze. Pudding scrabbled in her satchel for the book, and handed it back to him.

'I was thinking that if you don't listen to me, I shall go and talk directly to Superintendent Blackman. But first you need to finish reading this,' she said.

'Shall I get us a couple of drinks first?' said Pete, looking crestfallen.

'Please, Pete – please just read it.'

'All right.' He frowned down at the book, and read the whole story – it was only two pages long, one of the shortest in the book, dealing mainly with the particulars of the girl's death. Pudding had all but memorised it by then, and there was little about who she'd been, or who might have killed her. Sarah was believed to have had a lover, though he never came forward, and it was thought that her murder was the result of a lovers' tryst, held in the warmth and privacy of the mill, that had gone badly wrong. *The case*, it said at the end, *remains unsolved, the murderer at large.*

'Well?' said Pudding, when Pete looked up at her. 'It *can't* be a coincidence, can it?'

'Well…' Pete shrugged slightly, but he was frowning, thinking. 'I think I remember my old nan talking about this, now you come to mention it – she worked at the little mill back then, sorting the rags. It's proper strange, I'll give you that,' he said.

'The murderer remains at large, it says.' Pudding flicked to the back of the book. 'This book was published nine years ago.' The year before the war began, she reflected, after which everyone lost their appetite for horror. 'Surely we'd have heard about it if it had been solved since then?'

'We would. It was most likely her fella, if he never came forward.'

'But the murderer is clearly *still* at large – the same man who killed Alistair Hadleigh. It *has* to be the same man!'

Pete was still frowning as he got up and went inside, then returned with two glasses of dark beer. Pudding chose not to mention that she'd never drunk beer before, and sipped cautiously. It tasted bitter, earthy, half good and half bad. She tried not to grimace as she swallowed. It turned warm and woolly in her stomach.

'You sure you won't come inside, Pud? Nobody'd mind,' said Pete.

'Well ... it's easier to talk out here, where it's quiet. And it's warm enough, after all.'

'That's true.' He smiled at her in a kind of soft, inconsequential way that made her chafe impatiently.

'Pete. Constable Dempsey! Will you *please* say something about what I've told you,' she burst out. 'I can't work out why nobody I've told is *doing* anything!'

'I was thinking on it all the while, Pudding – I was. The thing is,' he said, looking uncomfortable, 'there's two ways of looking at it. One is that Mr Hadleigh was killed by the same person as killed this girl fifty years ago – although that'd make the killer past seventy now, at least, you'd have to suppose.' Pudding paused. She hadn't considered that.

'Plenty of seventy-year-olds are still fit and strong enough to ... commit a crime,' she said.

'Plenty? I think that's a bit of a stretch, Pud.' He held up a placating hand as she drew breath to argue. 'But it's possible, I'll grant. The second way to look at it is that somebody who knew about the old murder committed this new one deliberately to make it *seem* as though the same person has done both.'

'But ... why would anybody do that?'

'Who knows? Who knows why anybody would kill Mr

Hadleigh – or this other girl – in the first place? I know it bothers Superintendent Blackman that we still haven't come up with a good reason why.' He took a long swig of his beer. 'I shouldn't be telling you any of this, really, Pudding.'

'You mean, he's still not convinced it was Donny?' said Pudding, keenly. Pete shook his head.

'No, no – that's not what I'm saying. He's convinced it was Donny – all the evidence points to it. But he'd prefer to know why he did it. And the thing is . . .' Pete paused, and looked at Pudding for a while. His eyes were wide in the failing light, and his face wore a kind sort of look that was almost pity, which made Pudding cringe inside. 'The thing is, if we go and tell him about this book of yours, and that's it's been lying around your house for a while . . . he's going to say that your Donny most likely picked it up and read about the first murder, and took his cues from it. He might even say that . . . it gave him the idea to kill Mr Hadleigh in the first place.'

Pudding stared into the near distance as the significance of this sank in. She felt like Cassandra, condemned to be disbelieved; she felt the awful weight of not being able to help her brother. Everything seemed hopeless, and just then despair felt like a welcoming place to lie down and rest. Pudding drank her beer down – more warmth, more woolliness.

'This is all like a nightmare,' she said, quietly. 'The book was only ever in my room, on the nightstand. Mum doesn't like me reading dreadful things, so I never leave it lying about the house. Donny never goes into my room. He never does,' she said, appealing to Pete, whose face still wore the sorrowful look. 'There's no way he would have read it.'

'I know you know that, Pudding – I understand, and I believe you. Trouble is, it can't be proved, can it?'

'You've known Donny since you were born, Pete. Do you believe he killed Alistair?'

'It doesn't make any difference what I believe,' he said, looking uneasy.

'It does to me,' said Pudding. 'I need to know who's on my side.'

'I'm on your side, Pudding – course I am. But I've a job to do as well, keeping the law. And I have to do it to the letter. I can't do anything else.' Pudding thought for a while, though the beer and bad news seemed to have turned her thoughts soupy. She bit the ends of her fingers to get her own attention.

'Well, you have to tell Blackman. Will you? If not, I'll tell him myself.'

'Even if it gives him the "why" he's after? He doesn't know Donny from Adam, don't forget.'

'Even so, it might make him think . . . you will tell him my idea, won't you – that it's the same killer?'

'I'll tell him, yes,' said Pete, sounding resigned.

'And . . . will you look into the first murder?'

'Look into it? How in hell shall I do that, Pudding? The case is fifty years old!'

'There must be records – notes on who she was, who was suspected, that kind of thing? Surely there'll be records of that, at the station?'

'Well . . . I suppose there might be, not that I'd have the first clue where to look. That's if I get permission, of course. I can't just go rummaging, willy-nilly.'

'But you could suggest it to your superiors, couldn't you? That it might be an idea to look into it?'

'I'll suggest it, yes.' Pete sat quietly, seeming to wait for whatever was coming next.

'Good,' said Pudding. 'Take the book and show him – but I want it back as soon as he's seen it.'

She got up abruptly, then had to wait while her head stopped spinning. Pete stood up to anchor her.

'Steady on, Pud . . . not got much of a head for the beer, have you?' He smiled.

'I don't know. That's the first time I've had any,' said Pudding, thinking that the sky was very far away, and that the ground sloped even though it looked flat. Pete cocked his head, still holding her arm.

'I forget you're still so young, Pudding,' he said. 'What with you so . . .' He broke off, gesturing vaguely at her figure before letting his hand and his eyes drop.

'What with me so what?'

'Never mind. Come on – I'd best get you home.'

'I came on foot, and I know the way,' said Pudding, grandly.

'Well, you're not going back on foot, I can tell you. Come on – up to the farm, and we'll take the pony and trap.'

'That'll take ages; walking'd be faster.'

'Well, Pudding Cartwright, if what you say about your Donny is right, then there's a murderer on the loose. Given that, if nothing else, what kind of police officer would I be if I let a young lady walk home all alone?'

The route to Spring Cottage that was navigable by pony and trap was long, and steep, climbing to the top of the hill out west of Ford and then dropping down again. The pony huffed and puffed, the trap swayed over stones and ruts, and Pudding fought to stay awake against a near irresistible drowsiness. Twice she jerked awake to find her head resting on Pete Dempsey's shoulder, with the warmth of him reaching her cheek through his shirt. She tried to move further away along the seat, but it was a very narrow seat. 'It's all right, Pudding, you can get your head down if you like,' said Pete, his voice half-hidden by the creak of wheels and clop of hooves. Pudding shook her head.

'You'll look into it then, and you'll talk to Blackman? You promise?' she said, as he set her down outside her home.

'I promise to talk to Blackman, and to do what I can,' Pete qualified. Pudding nodded sleepily, and turned to go. 'You'll be looking into it yourself, I bet,' Pete called after her, in a knowing tone.

'What do you mean?'

'Well . . . if it's the same killer and they're past seventy, and they've been in the area before and are back, or have always been here . . . then chances are some of the old-timers might have some thoughts on who that could be, don't you reckon?'

'Yes,' said Pudding, as neutrally as she could. 'Yes – I suppose so.'

'You be careful, Pudding Cartwright. I'd tell you to leave it to the law if I thought you'd take a blind bit of notice, but you be careful. Goodnight, then,' he said, turning the pony as Pudding waved him goodnight.

She didn't realise until the morning that she had forgotten to thank Pete for the drink, and for the ride home. But it didn't really matter – she had more important things to do. The beer had plunged her into a deep sleep, and she woke with a clear head, more convinced than ever that whoever had killed Sarah Martock in 1872 had also killed Alistair. And she knew exactly where she was going.

They walked a good way out of Slaughterford to catch the bus to Swindon from Castle Combe, so that the driver wouldn't recognise them. Clemmie had tied a shawl over her telltale hair, and was too hot, and her legs felt heavy all the way. Eli walked fast, with his face set, sometimes towing her by her hand just as her mother had done on the way to Manor Farm. But it wasn't just her legs that felt heavy; the heaviness seemed to be in all the muscles of her body and every bit of her head, a dragging unwillingness that she couldn't shake — the near irresistible urge to sit down and rest, and to then turn back. When she drifted to a halt, to stare at a skyline of hills that she didn't know and feel the horrible strangeness of that, Eli turned back impatiently.

'Come *on*, Clemmie!' he said, his desire to be away every bit as strong as her desire to stay. When she whimpered, he was gentler with her, and kissed her, and clamped her hands in his, like he was praying. 'Well, come on then,' he said. 'This is our new life we're running to. The three of us.' Murmuring and soothing until she carried on again. Cottages she didn't know; faces she didn't know; fields and gates and stiles she didn't know. Paths, green lanes, copses of trees; battered farmyards alive with geese and rats and children. She lost the edges of herself in the unfamiliarity of it; she felt herself blurring, getting lost. Once they were on the bus the changes only came more quickly, more alarmingly, and Clemmie had no way of saying that it felt as though the world itself had been swapped for one she had no hope of understanding. She gripped Eli's hand not out of love, but out of fear.

The bus was crowded, and spirits seemed high as they came out of the valley onto flatter ground, and the team of cobs trotted steadily along. Men with moustaches and bowler hats, some in waistcoats that had seen better days, carrying their jackets over their arms; strappers going between farms in just their shirtsleeves, stinking of sweat, work and the muck on their boots; two women so alike they had to be sisters, gossiping happily, going into town in straw bonnets and lawn frocks with old stains washed in at the hem, and offering a punnet of cherries around the other passengers. Eli scowled blackly at everybody, so nobody spoke to them. Clemmie cowered back in her shawl, too scared to look people in the eye, too scared not to look. The sun was high but she stretched her arms out from the shade of the hooped canvas roof while they changed horses in Great Somerford; reaching them into the sunshine, reaching for things she couldn't touch. Later, when Eli shook her shoulder to get her attention, Clemmie jumped. He pointed at buildings on the horizon, coming nearer – church spires, factory chimneys, tall townhouses. His face had come alive with triumph. 'We're all but there! And just think – your folks might not even have noticed you gone yet,' he said, jubilantly. Clemmie nodded, but couldn't bring herself to smile. 'Don't look so cowed, my Clem. I'm going to look after you, and it'll all work out well – I've said so. You believe me, don't you?' he said, and she made herself nod again.

Eli's cousin, Matthew, didn't look much like a Tanner. He was squat, pug-nosed and had brown eyes, not blue; his lips were too full, and had a damp, swollen look, and his hair was a greasy swathe of mouse-brown in need of a cut. But he had a wide smile, and the shiftiness in his eyes was more speculative than malicious. His wife Polly was so pregnant she looked like the moon rising. The weight of the bump had dragged her spine into an impossible-looking kink, and she kept her hands wedged there, bracing it, whenever she could. She might only have been twenty or so but her face sagged with exhaustion, and a toddler swung from her skirt as she let them in.

'Don't panic, missy,' she said to Clemmie, catching her staring in alarm at the size of the bump. 'This is due to drop any day now, and I've a feeling there's more than one in there – my ma was one of triplets, God help me. So chances are you won't come up half as big as this.' Matthew and Polly had been told that Clemmie was mute, but there was still that pause when she was expected to reply, and the slight awkwardness of moving on when she didn't. 'How far along are you?' Polly asked, before blushing, realising that Clemmie couldn't answer that, either.

'Only Clem knows,' said Eli, looking at her as though she'd worked a miracle. 'The rest of us must just wait to see.' Polly squinted at Clemmie, and, nodding for permission, grabbed her middle and gave her a prod.

'Early days,' she said. 'No more than a couple of months, I reckon.'

'Plenty of time for me to work, then, and find us rooms.'

'Ar, well,' said Matthew, not sounding too sure. 'You can stay as long as needs be. Family's family after all.'

'Well then,' said Polly. 'I'll show you where you'll be sleeping.'

Matthew and Polly had the ground floor of a cramped townhouse; two rooms, one at the front where they cooked and washed and ate, the other at the back where they slept with their first child, three-year-old Betsy. Outside the door to these rooms, narrow stairs ran to the upper rooms from a hallway with a grimed wooden floor. It was dark, and cramped, and most of the space was taken up with pots and boxes, brooms, pails and an old milk churn in a trolley that Polly used to fetch water from the pump at the end of the street. Cooking smells lingered, as did the damp and smuts aroma of neglected corners everywhere. Beneath the stairs, a thin mattress stuffed with rags had been laid, and draped with a blanket. It was just about wide enough for two people to lie side by side, shoulders tight together. Clemmie thought of the huge bed at Weavern Farm that she'd shared with Josie. It had been there long before her parents had taken over the farm, more a part of the building than a piece of furniture, and over the years the posts had been gnawed by beetles and wasps. But it had been soft and enveloping, and it had been at home. Safe. Here, people's feet would pass by in the street, not three yards from where her head would lie.

'I've had a word with old Mrs Shepherd upstairs and she don't mind. She hasn't managed the stairs in years anyway – only time she gets out is when we take her. Her daughter comes by every day to dress and feed her, and empty the pot, but you'll be up and about before she comes, I'm sure. Only thing we need to watch is the landlord. He comes by for the rent each month, usually on the first Tuesday, so he shouldn't spring us if we're careful – not that he'd put you out, only he'd be wanting more money for you staying here, is all.'

'Our thanks, Pol,' said Eli, dropping his canvas sack onto the mattress.

'Well, I'll be off on the evening shift,' said Matthew. 'I'll let the foreman know you're here. Hopefully he'll just say to bring you in with me in the morning, then he'll glance you over like he's weighing you up at market, but don't let it rile you – he's a tiny prick of a man, in all manner of ways.'

'Amen to that,' Polly muttered.

'So he likes to act big. Tug your forelock a bit, like he's cock o' the walk, and the job'll be yours, Eli.'

Clemmie couldn't sleep. It was stuffy and hot in the hallway, and there was no window to open. Betsy woke up yelling almost hourly, and upstairs Mrs Shepherd coughed, and coughed, and coughed. Eli fought in his sleep, twitching and muttering, and out in the street footsteps did pass, and Clemmie's skin crawled every time, wondering who it was and what business they could have, out in the black of night. She saw their shadows, in the gap beneath the door. She missed Mary's soft snoring, regular as a heartbeat, and the night birds outside the farm, and the quiet murmur of the river. Night after night, it got no easier. She still got sick in the mornings sometimes, and could no longer tell if it was the baby or the dizzy fatigue of sleeplessness. When Polly took her up to meet Mrs Shepherd, she and the old woman stared at one another with similar degrees of incomprehension. Mrs Shepherd was trapped in her iron-framed bed; trapped with her feeble body and her cough; trapped in her greasy lace nightcap until her daughter came to take it off. Her misty eyes, blinking rapidly, looked out at a world that she no longer understood, and Clemmie knew exactly how she felt.

Eli was gone at first light, with Matthew, to the early shift at the engine sheds. He came back tired, aching from shovelling coal and rubbing at eyes gone red and runny from airborne grit, but serene – the peace, Matthew said, of a man who'd done a day's work for fair pay. Matthew was an operator on one of the grinding machines, and paid slightly better than Eli, whose job it was to feed the furnaces, and to lift and move whatever needed to be lifted or moved. Polly spent her days moving, slowly and laboriously, between their rooms and the market place, the water pump, the draper's and her neighbours' rooms; stopping to grip her back, to wipe the sweat from her face, to catch her breath.

'Lord save me,' she said, again and again; a constant refrain, the voice of inner fear. Betsy tottered after her everywhere, sucking her thumb, clasping her wonky home-made doll to her ribs. Clemmie took it on herself to mind the child as much as she could – picking her up when she fell; taking foul things away from her before she could eat them; changing her drawers when she wet them – to give Polly a break. She also lifted, and poured, and fetched and carried, and helped fashion whatever meagre food Polly got from the market into a meal for the five of them come evening. Pies with greasy crusts made with lard or dripping; stews of peas and barley; nothing but bread and cheese, some nights. So far, all the money Eli had earned had gone to Matthew and Polly, for their food and lodging, but demand always seemed to outstrip supply. Midway through

Clemmie's ninth day in Swindon, Polly gripped her hand, suddenly, as they sat peeling potatoes, and smiled at her. 'I don't know how I got on before you came, Clem,' she said. 'I shan't ever want to let you go.'

Clemmie liked Polly, and she managed to smile, but she realised that she was merely waiting. Waiting to awaken from this disturbing dream she was caught in, in which she had to live there in the mêlée of a town, with the looming buildings and thronging humanity, the crush, the inescapable smells, and so little that was calm or green. When she shut her eyes she sent herself back to Slaughterford. To the sweep of the river and hills, the mill, and Weavern Farm. She even conjured the steady calm of Alistair Hadleigh's office – standing with her eyes shut and her back to the window, echoing his syllables as soon after him saying them as she could, a trick that sometimes seemed to help, at least with the easier sounds. She almost heard the race of the mill leat and the thud of the beaters, and smelt paper and the woollen rug from the Orient on the floor, and Alistair's hair oil and the expensive material of his suit cloth, and felt that easing of panic that had sometimes left her almost drowsy, when a lesson had gone well. She longed to feel it now, but fear clamped down on her when she opened her eyes, smearing away who she was and what she knew, and leaving no safe places. Nobody noticed her fleeing inside herself. They didn't know that even if she could have spoken, she would have been silent for days. She cuddled Betsy, and played games with her – giving her doll sips of tea, plaiting the few strands of wool it had for hair, and trying not to notice that it smelt of vomit. And she waited to be able to leave. She waited for Eli to say, *Let's go home*.

But he didn't say that. He worked, and he ate, and he went out to the pub in the evening with Matthew, and came back after Clemmie and Polly had put their heads down, smelling of beer and tobacco, burrowing his face into her neck and falling asleep in an instant. He no longer smelt of grass or earth or the hedgerows; he no longer smelt like a wild animal, but more like a machine. The town was putting its stamp on him. One night he saw Clemmie's downcast face as he and Matthew turned to leave, and took her along to the pub with him. She tried to be pleased, but it was all noise and smother, and men talking too loudly, and women with red paint on their teeth. The buildings along the street seemed to rear up too far and crowd in above, worse than they did in the daytime, and Clemmie felt crushed. She stayed for half an hour, hating it, then squeezed Eli's hand and slipped away to the bed beneath the stairs.

'Must seem strange to you, all this,' said Polly one day, when she caught Clemmie staring up at the narrow strip of sky above the street. 'What with you being raised up on a farm. And Swindon's not really a big city, you know – I went to Bristol once. By God, there's a place. All life is there; people like . . . ants in a nest, down on the docks. You wouldn't credit it till you saw it. But you can smell the sea from there – have you ever seen the sea?' Clemmie shook her head. 'Me neither,' said Polly, wistfully. 'I can't imagine it, 'cept that it must be beautiful.' She was silent for a while, and Clemmie struggled to picture a place more populous, more clamorous than Swindon. 'Clemmie is such a pretty name,' said Polly. 'Short for Clemence, is it? Or Clemency?' Clemmie shook her head. It wasn't short for either of those, but she'd no way to explain what it was short for. 'Well, it's pretty. Maybe I'll call one of this litter Clemency, if it comes out a girl.' She ran her hands as far over her bump as she could reach.

On Sunday they went along to the church at the end of their street, which had a pretty square of grass with iron railings around it to the front, and flowerbeds full of pansies and busy Lizzies. They had no Sunday best and went in what they wore most days, with the addition of hats for Clemmie and Polly. The sun beat down, and they sat with strangers in the shade of a horse chestnut tree laden with unripe conkers.

'This is the life, eh,' said Matthew, lying back and tipping his hat over his eyes. Eli smiled slightly, but Polly ignored him. Betsy was fractious and had an itchy rash that was tormenting her, and Clemmie merely wanted to say, *No. No, this is not what life should be.* 'Bet you're not missing old Isaac, now, are you, Eli?' Matthew went on, and Eli's face fell at once. He sat with his knees up, his arms resting across them, and squinted away into the distance.

'I hope never to set eyes on that man again,' he said, at length. 'And I might kill him if I do.'

'Can't say as I blame you,' said Matthew, grunting. 'I'll never forget the time I saw him—'

'Enough, Matt. I won't have him cast his shadow here,' said Eli, tersely, and Matthew shot him a startled glance before wisely dropping the subject. Isaac Tanner was what kept Eli out of Slaughterford, Clemmie realised. He may not have liked his own name, or the Tanner reputation, but he loved his mother, and grandmother, and several of his brothers and sisters; it was his father he couldn't stand to be near. If Isaac had been the one arrested for what happened at the mill – or for the robbery if the two things were separate – and if he hadn't come back, she and Eli might not have had to leave Slaughterford at all. And there was no chance of going back, she saw, whilst Isaac remained. And then, out of nowhere, she knew the answer to it. It came with a rush of nerves and hope, and at that exact moment Polly's face paled, and she gasped.

The labour lasted right through the afternoon, and right through the night. There was no doctor; the midwife was a neighbour who'd previously brought a hundred of Swindon's workers' children into the world, not counting those she'd delivered straight into little coffins. Polly held Clemmie's hand, and as the hours passed Clemmie felt her grip get weaker, her gouging fingers turning as soft and giving as fruit gone over. As she pushed, Polly was silent for so long Clemmie wondered if she'd ever breathe again. The room smelt of her sweat and urine, her dry throat and effort. By dawn there were two babies, a boy and a girl, long and skinny and crushed; the girl sucked in a breath and wailed, but the boy lay still and quiet, his skin an unearthly blue. He lived a half-hour or so then slipped away, and Polly was too spent to react. The midwife clamped Polly's new daughter to her breast, and the child drank as her mother lay unconscious.

Clemmie was never happier for a night to be over. All blood and darkness, pain and fear, life and death had been there in the room, hand in hand. The babies had fought to remain in the womb, not like animal babies that slithered out, eagerly enough. It was the city, she thought. It was all the buildings and the dirt and the crowding, the air not right, the horizon too close, the world too strange. It wasn't as it should be. When she came away from the bedside, exhausted, she carried on out of the front door and down the street, and might have carried on walking until she got home had Eli not run out after her, and fetched her back. *I want to go home*, she told him. She longed for him to hear her, and perhaps he did, a little. There was something in the way he scowled, something in the silence between them. In desperation, Clemmie took a piece of old newspaper from the privy they shared with four neighbours and drew a rudimentary map, and stick figures of herself and Eli, in between two places – a large sprawl of scribbled chaos behind them, and their faces turned towards a place with a curling river, a mill, an isolated farm.

'We can't go back,' said Eli, flatly, understanding at once. 'I can't. I won't be near him, Clem. You understand that, don't you? This is our life now. This is our home. I've got work, and we've a place to live, and family. I wish I could make you feel how I feel — to be out from under him for the first time in my life. To start over ... It's a marvel. And I won't go back to how it was. This is home now.'

But in the dark of night after the boy twin's funeral, who Matthew and Polly named Christopher, with baby Clemency crying and waking Betsy, and Polly wincing every time she moved, and smelling of milk and exhaustion, Clemmie made up her mind. Polly's need of help was like an extra set of ties, binding her, but if she stayed, she felt she would die. Not physically, perhaps, not straight away, but in some other, fundamental way. She thought of the soul that the vicar talked about; she thought about the spirit of things, the wants and needs and memories bred into each person by the generations that spawned them; and the land that fed them. People belonged in certain places, and not in others, and she and Eli — and the baby — belonged in Slaughterford. And if Eli would not return because of Isaac Tanner, then Clemmie knew a way to get rid of Isaac Tanner.

She knew what she had overheard; she knew the truth of it. Her mother often said that the simplest answer was usually the right one, and the simplest answer was that Isaac had planned to rob Alistair Hadleigh, and had taken his sons to the mill, and had done the deed. It would not be easy; she didn't want to implicate Eli in any way. She needed to find a way to say the words, or draw them, or write them. She would work it out with her mother's help — perhaps get her to ask the right questions. She might even see if she could go into Alistair's office, and recapture the calm of it to help her, even if he weren't there. She would find a way to say that Isaac Tanner was a guilty man, a criminal; the one who'd planned to rob the mill and the cause of all the violence. A man who had raised a generation of children too angry and terrorised to break away from him. Isaac Tanner was a shadow on the world, and she would give the police the chance they'd always looked for to take him away for good.

As if he could sense her intention, Eli lay close to Clemmie when he got home, and she could just see the glint of his eyes in the dark, and he spoke close to her ear.

'You won't leave me, Clem,' he said. His voice was tight, like the grip of his hands, and she couldn't tell if he was begging her, or commanding her. 'You'll not leave me.' But he fell asleep, couldn't help himself, and his hands slithered away from hers as his breathing deepened, and she edged away from him. At the last moment that their bodies touched, at the moment that they parted, Clemmie felt something tear inside, and her heart ached. He would not understand. He could not know her plan, and that she would make a home for them where they ought to be, at Weavern Farm. She hardened her heart as best she could, knowing that his might break when he found her gone. In the dark, and after the beer, Eli hadn't noticed that she was dressed. Eyes straining, Clemmie went into the front room as silently as she could. Eli slept deeply, but if he found her before she'd had a chance to vanish she knew she would never leave. And she was frightened. She knew how angry pain made him – pain of all kinds. She fetched the apple and slice of bread that she'd hidden earlier, wrapped in a cloth in the vegetable crock. In the front room the glow of the streetlight leached in through the thready curtains and outlined the furniture in lifeless grey. She didn't have any money for the bus or a train, and only a vague idea of the direction to go in – south, and west. She would walk for as long as it took, though, and try to hitch a ride. She could feel home pulling at her; she felt that this return journey would be all downhill, and easy.

Then there was movement behind her – a soft footstep, a

taken breath – and Clemmie whirled around, heart jumping. Words jammed in her throat, and behind her teeth. *I was only going on ahead, for you to follow. I have a plan too, Eli, you'll see.* But it was only little Betsy, glassy-eyed and half asleep in the doorway. Clemmie went quickly to kneel in front of her, to keep her quiet. Betsy yawned, and Clemmie smelt the sweetly awful smell of the child's tooth decay.

'Bye, Clem,' Betsy mumbled, then yawned again and rubbed at her eyes. Clemmie gathered her in, and held her tight. She had no idea how the little girl knew she was leaving; she didn't need to know, or to question it. She gave Betsy a kiss on her forehead, and put a finger to her lips. Betsy nodded sleepily, then turned to go. Before slipping into the darkness the child turned again, hesitated, then held out her doll to Clemmie. Clemmie couldn't say *you keep her*, so she just shook her head a little, but Betsy nodded, and thrust the doll out anew. So Clemmie took it, and dropped her head to one side to say thank you. Then she crept along the hallway and out into the street, and felt the tear in her heart get wider, deeper, as she shut the door on Eli's oblivious sleep. She knew what he would think when he woke, and it almost made her quail, and run back inside. She almost couldn't stand it. But she couldn't stand to stay either, and she had a plan.

❧ ☙

Nancy's daily visits to lay flowers on Alistair's grave had already taken on the feel of a ritual, just like her weekly ritual of visiting her brother Alistair's grave. The same grave, of course, beneath the same stone slab. Irene hated that thought – the newly dead lying alongside the desiccated, the eaten-away. She wondered how long it would be before the daily visit became a weekly one, and how Nancy would make that decision. Down she went after breakfast, with cut flowers from the garden to add to the still-fresh ones already on his grave, to spend time carefully clipping off any wilted leaves, any faded petals. The rose garden was running out of roses; already the only ones left were those that had begun to weep their petals onto the ground. Irene was beginning to regret having asked if she could go with Nancy one morning. She'd been pleased when Nancy said yes, but now she seemed committed to going every day, and she felt phoney, making gestures of a grief she didn't feel. But Nancy talked to her more on the walk there and the walk back, and if Irene was going to stay at Manor Farm, at least for the time being, then she needed the *entente* with Nancy to continue. A return to the spite and disdain of the early days would be excruciating.

'Did he ever tell you about the time he got lost on his own land?' said Nancy that morning. 'He was only about ten, but still – old enough to know the way home, you'd have thought. I went out as teatime came and went, and found him sitting in one of the hedgerows, crying his eyes out.' She gave a grunt, half affectionate, half incredulous. 'But do you know, the first thing he did was apologise for making me worry and come out looking for him. Dear, soft, silly boy. I'm afraid I gave him quite an ear-bashing. And now, of course, I regret every time I ever berated him.'

'I'm sure he knew it was well-meant,' said Irene. 'I hid from my parents once. It was Nanny's half day off. I tucked myself under the bed in a spare room upstairs – I can only have been about seven, I suppose. They didn't come to look for me. I fell asleep, and it was dark by the time I rushed downstairs, certain they'd have been worried about me.'

'I've a feeling you're going to say they hadn't noticed you gone,' said Nancy.

'Just so,' said Irene. 'So that taught me a lesson about my

own importance. I would far rather have been berated, I assure you.' She opened the little iron gate into the churchyard and held it for Nancy.

'I notice your mother never actually made it here, to the farm. Rather a short visit.'

'Yes. But I found it quite long enough, in the end,' said Irene.

'Good for you,' said Nancy. She sniffed. 'Let her taste her own medicine.' But then the silence that came over her at the graveside descended, and Irene went to sit on the bench, and had to resist the urge to tip her face to the sun, and let its warmth buoy her.

On the way back, when Nancy had turned sunken and grim, Irene sought to bring her out of herself again.

'Has Pudding told you about this other murder that happened, years and years ago?' As soon as she'd spoken she knew she'd said the wrong thing. Nancy's head came up but her eyes sparkled with anger.

'Yes, and I'm about ready to lose patience with the girl,' she said. 'Why on earth can't she just accept what's happened, as I have had to accept it, and let us all move on?'

'She loves her brother too much, I suppose,' said Irene, carefully, glad not to have let on about her own role in Pudding's covert investigation. Nancy sighed.

'She does. Of course she does.' She shook her head. 'Perhaps I would be just the same if my own brother had done such a terrible thing. But the fact is that *nobody* can really know a man as damaged as young Donald – or what he might be capable of. Who knows why he did it? Perhaps Alistair did speak to him about those ruined rose bushes. Perhaps he even talked to him about finding work elsewhere. But perhaps it was simply something inside his own head. We can't ever know what set him off.'

'But don't you think it's odd that the . . . killing so resembles this other one, all those years ago?'

'Everything about what has happened is odd; in the worst possible way.'

'Yes, but—'

'I simply do not wish to hear about it, Irene,' Nancy snapped, and Irene held her tongue. There was no way to make Nancy feel any of the injustice Irene was feeling on Alistair's behalf – as far as Nancy was concerned, her nephew's killer was in gaol, and would get his just deserts. Her grief was all-consuming, and didn't leave space for more considered emotions, like Irene's. She looked around at the endless sweeps of green, the endless daisies and buttercups and clover, and it felt as though it had been summer forever, and that the summer would last forever, just like when she was a child. She felt as though time had slowed there in Slaughterford – as though the extraordinary events had isolated them from the rest of the world. As if the place needed to be any more isolated, she thought.

Pudding knocked at the door after lunch, and to Irene's surprise, Nancy invited her to come and sit with them and have some of the ice cream she herself had hardly touched.

'Florence will sulk if it goes back to the kitchen, melted and unwanted.'

'Oh, thanks,' said Pudding, but Irene could see that food was the last thing on her mind. She ate a bit, dutifully, her eyes roaming the room, her body tense. Irene found herself dreading what the girl would say next, and wishing that whatever it was she'd button it until Nancy had left the room. Irene had the sense that she and Pudding were stirring a very deep, very old pond, and she was starting to feel uneasy about what they might bring to the surface. Things that might horrify them; things that might bite. She knew they couldn't stop yet, but she didn't want to be seen doing it.

'So, was there something about the horses you needed to discuss?' said Nancy.

'The horses? No – that is, not unless one of you wants to ride this afternoon?' said Pudding, but Nancy shook her head.

'I might,' said Irene, hoping to forestall Pudding, but failing.

'Oh. Good. Well, I spoke to P— Constable Dempsey about this other murder. He's going to talk to Superintendent Blackman, and hopefully he'll be looking into it.' There was silence at the table. Pudding put down her spoon and hurried on. '*He* – Pete Dempsey, that is – suggested that I look into it myself. You know, ask some of the older people in the village who were around then and now, and see if they have any idea at all who was responsible for the murders, and—'

'Oh, for heaven's sake, Pudding, you really do go too far,' said Nancy. She pushed back her chair and stood up. 'If anybody had had the first clue who was responsible for that girl's death back then, don't you think they'd have told the police?'

'Well, yes – and maybe they did.' Pudding's face reddened. 'I'm hoping that'll be in the police records, and I can go and ask them about it. If they're still around . . . But maybe there just wasn't enough *evidence* to support—'

'None of this will help your brother, child!' said Nancy. 'I hate to say it but it seems that somebody will have to. Donald attacked Alistair, and whether he meant to kill him or not, he did; and it is . . .' She paused, not able to look at Pudding. 'It is only right that he has been taken into custody.' Pudding stared at Nancy in horror.

'But how can you say that?' she asked, meekly. 'You *know* Donny!'

'I *knew* him. Before the war. Pudding, I know how hard this is for you – don't forget that I have also lost a brother I adored. Before you were even born. So if you're about to tell

me I don't understand, then believe me, I do. But one must . . .
face the facts, as they are, square on.'

'But I'm trying to *find out* the facts!' said Pudding, desperately. 'And then I'll face them. Donny told me it wasn't
him, and that he only found Mr Hadleigh lying there, and I
believe him. I need to talk to Hilarius again, and Ma Tanner.
And when did Jem start work here, do you remember? And I
wanted to ask you, Nancy – when did your family first come
to Slaughterford? Weren't the Hadleighs here at the time of
the first murder? Can you think of anybody you saw – perhaps
a stranger – who you think could have . . .' Pudding's words
broke against the cliff face of Nancy's silence.

'At a time like this, Pudding Cartwright, you're asking me
if I know who killed some peasant girl fifty years ago?' said
Nancy, quietly. 'Go back to the yard, and look after the horses,
and please stop creating more drama on top of the real crisis
we already have.'

Once Nancy had gone, Irene could breathe.

'Oh, Pudding,' she said. 'You have to tread more softly
around Nancy! I know you've known her a long time, but
she's under a terrible amount of strain. She might send you
away if you keep bothering her, and don't let her grieve in
peace.'

'I know,' said Pudding, her eyes welling. 'But I'm under
strain too . . . and my family. And poor Donny, locked away
in a cell.'

'I wish he wasn't. I wish none of this had happened! But it
has, and . . .' Irene wasn't sure what to add. 'I want whoever
really did this to Alistair to be caught. You know I do. I'll help
as much as I can, but—'

'Will you have a look through Alistair's things, and find
out if there's anything there that might . . . explain his death?'

'Would I do what?'

'Have a look ... through his papers and what have you. Perhaps there was something to do with the business that he hadn't told anybody. Trouble of some kind ...'

'But that would be spying. Spying on my husband.' It seemed an indecent thing to do.

'But ... Alistair's dead, Irene,' said Pudding. Irene blinked. Somehow this fact made the idea even less decent. 'He can't mind.'

'But I ... What exactly do you want me to look for? I'm sure there'll be nothing about the Tanners in there ...'

'Forget the Tanners! I mean ... perhaps it's not him, after all. I don't know. Or perhaps there'll be clues to who might have hired Tanner in there. Anything! Anything that ... might help explain *anything*.' Pudding spread her hands helplessly. Irene watched her, uneasily, sympathetically, and saw the girl take a deep breath. 'It's only a week now until Donny goes before the magistrate. I only have one week to find something that could help him, and maybe make them let him out on bail. He's ... he's not coping in gaol. He's suffering, and I ... I *can't* stand that.'

'All right,' said Irene. Pudding's fear and need were like a fog it was hard to see through, and they were contagious. 'All right. But I expect most of the business correspondence is down at the mill.'

'Well, you could look there, too.' Pudding nodded, like it was all settled. She gripped her chair as though to push it back but then hesitated. 'Irene, you looked ... frightened when I first told you about this other murder – the first murder.'

'Yes. Well,' said Irene. For some reason, the statement made her feel guilty.

'You looked as though you'd ... almost expected it. Or not quite that. Like you knew already, and me telling you only reminded you.'

'That's more or less how it feels.' Irene looked away, uncomfortably.

'Has there been anything else? Do you know... what it was you were afraid of?'

'Pudding, if I knew anything, I would tell you. The feelings I get are just that – feelings. Intuition, at best. I'd be worried if I thought you were relying on them, overly, and—'

'But what if they're right?' said Pudding.

'They might be, but they might not. I don't believe it's second sight or anything... supernatural...' Irene shook her head. 'It's just the notion that something important has been... hit upon, on each occasion. It's rather like... when you're looking at your own reflection in a window, and then you suddenly realise there's someone else on the other side of the glass. You have to change the way you're looking at it. But it's not that specific, you see.'

'Well. Please say, won't you, if you do think of anything,' said Pudding, as she got up. 'Or find anything. I'm sorry for upsetting Miss H. Would you tell her, when you see her? And do you really want to go for a ride?'

'If it'd help, yes.'

They rode for an hour, then Irene spent the rest of the afternoon in Alistair's study, feeling horribly intrusive as she opened the drawers of his desk one by one, lifted the contents onto the top and went through it all, one item at a time. Though she found nothing that could possibly have made anyone want to be rid of him, she soon found herself drawn in, fascinated, peering through a window into the life he'd lived before she'd known him. There was a box of letters from his relatives in America, stacked neatly in order, like library cards; the envelopes getting smaller and more yellowed the further back in time they went. She took out the first one, which was dated

April 1871, and had been written to Alistair's father from his mother, Tabitha, before they were married. Curious, she took it out and read it – a very chaste kind of love letter that spoke a good deal about respect, regard and beneficial union, and very little about love or passion. But that had been the spirit of the age, she supposed; and Alistair had told her that his mother had been a very devout Catholic. She remembered Nancy calling her a *papist delusionist*, but then, given how Nancy had loved her twin, Irene doubted whether any woman could have been good enough for him.

In another drawer, in a file labelled *Sundries*, was her own marriage certificate, and behind it Alistair's parents' one, issued in New York City on July 15th, 1872. Which answered the question of where the Hadleighs had been at the time of the murder of the girl down at the mill, Irene noted. Outside, the sky curdled to grey and thunder rumbled in the distance. Then it started to rain. The light in the study went flat and dim, and Irene found her interest waning, and all the letters and papers began to feel like what they were – remnants of past lives that she had no business looking at, which brought on a stifling, almost claustrophobic feeling. She flicked through more quickly, impatient to have done with the task.

One other thing caught her attention before she finished the search. In the cupboard containing Alistair's guns, binoculars, fishing tackle and the like, she found a box file of more papers, mostly old sports log books, postcards and maps, but in the bottom – deliberately hidden – a bundle of letters with Alistair's own writing on the front, tied up with string and with a covering note wrapped around them. *Dear Mr Hadleigh*, the note read, in an elegant, sweeping script. *I do regret any pain I have caused you, but must ask you to cease writing to me. It does no good, you see, for either of us. You were kind enough to release me from our engagement, for which I will always be indebted to you. Surely you understand that no amount of debate, and no set of circumstances, can possibly cause me to change my mind, having taken such steps as I have taken?* It was signed Miss Annabelle Cross, and dated July 12th, 1914.

Irene felt a thrill as she read it, a peculiar jolt, like she'd looked up, thinking she was alone, to find somebody else in the room. She'd quite forgotten that Alistair had been engaged elsewhere before proposing to her – and Nancy's claim to have extricated him. If it were true, then she'd done it by scaring the girl off somehow, not by talking her nephew out of it – just as Cora McKinley had said. She wondered what on earth Nancy could have said or done to cause the relationship to collapse so completely; she wondered if Miss Annabelle Cross had known that war would be declared so soon after she broke it off with Alistair, or that she would be sending him into battle with a broken heart. And his heart had been broken. Irene read only a few of his letters to Annabelle, first adoring and then frantic, but they were enough. She sat with the bundle in her lap, not wanting to spy on his heartbreak any longer, and feeling strange to find he'd loved another woman. Loved her enough to keep his own letters to her hidden away – because she had touched them, Irene supposed. Because they had traces of her skin, her scent; were relics of her.

So perhaps Alistair's quiet manner hadn't only been a result of the war, but of this heartbreak; and perhaps his sympathy for Irene's plight had been based as much on understanding how it felt to be publicly dropped by a person you adored as on his infatuation with her. She wondered if he'd ever known that his aunt Nancy had been the reason for Annabelle's flight. Somehow, she doubted it. She sat and tried to decide how she was feeling, and whether or not the needling resentment at the back of her mind was a touch of jealousy. Ridiculous, given that she'd made Alistair live with her continued love for Fin for weeks, and hadn't given herself the chance to fall in love with Alistair. There were no clues as to what had become of Annabelle, and Irene hoped that Pudding wouldn't think it was relevant, and want to track her down – she had no wish to trespass any further into her husband's humiliation.

She kept the bundle to give to Pudding and put everything else back as she'd found it, then went over to where her wedding photograph stood, on the mantelpiece. She picked it up and stared hard into Alistair's face, rendered in shades of grey. The happiness in his eyes was genuine. She felt she could see his whole soul right there in the picture – his kindness, his tolerance, his capacity for joy, coming off him like a soft, pale light. Her own face looked like that of a stranger. She looked like a shell, absent from herself. She hadn't even managed a smile, just a neutral expression like one painted on a doll. Shame washed through her. She didn't know how Alistair could have stood it, marrying her when she was in such a state. Alistair had deserved to be loved, of that she was wholly certain.

'If we'd had more time, I would have done,' Irene told him, surprising herself by speaking out loud. 'I know I would. I only needed a little time.' Suddenly, she desperately needed him to hear her, and believe her, but of course he never could. She kissed his image, on impulse, leaving a smudge from her lips on the glass. As she rubbed it away with her cuff she felt her anger on his behalf burn brighter, cleaner. She hadn't been much use to him while he was alive. Charles McKinley had said that marrying her had made Alistair happy, but Irene didn't feel as though that were at all good enough. She was going to make damned certain she was useful to him now. She put her wedding picture back carefully, slipped out of the study and closed the door as softly as she could, to make up for having invaded so completely.

As the light began to fail, and cooking smells seeped from the kitchen, Irene put on boots, a mackintosh and an oilskin hat, and went out for a walk in the rain. The claustrophobic feeling of the old papers had persisted, and after so many weeks of sunshine – the weather so settled it had come to seem as though she were waking up each morning cursed to live the same day, over and over again – she wanted to feel the rain hitting her head and hear it splashing under her feet. The low sky flickered yellow now and then, but the thunder stayed quiet and distant – more of a rumbling in her bones than a sound. She walked down into the centre of the village, near to where the mill steamed and thumped, and stood a while on the hump bridge across the river, watching the way the rain pocked the water. A pair of ducks made their way upstream, paddling laboriously. The banging of an engine got louder, and she watched a lanky lad, his hat pulled down low over his eyes and his face maudlin, drive a load of half-stuff across from Rag Mill in the little motorised wagon. Then, bracing up, Irene took the path that ran right through the mill. She passed the old farmhouse where Alistair – and where the girl, Sarah – had been killed, and had to force herself to look at it. The painted wooden door, closed now with the rain, a light on inside, and George Turner at his desk by a downstairs window, carefully inserting a sheet of paper into the micrometer. The sight of the place still turned her throat dry; she had a powerful urge to be somewhere – anywhere – else. She made herself walk slowly past, and then on through the yard with the towering brick generator house on her right and the beater house on her left, across the bridge and up to Germain's Lane. There she turned back towards the village, because she didn't want to go past the Tanner place. It was getting late, anyway; the thick clouds made it darker, and seem later still.

Past High Bank, the row of three cottages with the shop

at one end, Irene turned off the lane, went through the gate and into the paddock in which the church sat, walled off, all alone. This was the short cut to the farm that Pudding often used, though it was steep and you had to dodge the cowpats. The rain shone on the grass and the ground squelched, and Irene went slowly so as not to slip. She looked over the low wall of the graveyard and saw how the onslaught was ruining Alistair's flowers – stripping off the petals, battering the foliage. She hated to think how upset Nancy would be at the sight, so even though she was getting cold, and the rain had found a way through the seams of her mackintosh at the shoulders, she went in to see what tidying she could do. She had her face down, at the graveside, and was wondering where to start when she became aware of someone approaching, and looked up with a gasp. A tall, grey-headed man was coming towards her from around the church, and with a thrill of fear she recognised Tanner. He didn't seem steady on his feet, and she wondered if he'd seen her – or would see her before he barrelled into her. There was nowhere for her to hide from him, and she stood rooted to the spot until he was within two strides of her and still hadn't slowed. Then, inadvertently, she cried out in alarm.

At the sound of her voice Tanner threw up his hands and gripped her by the arms, peering through the rain. He had no hat and water slicked his grizzled hair to his head; she could smell alcohol on his breath, hot and sour. His eyes were red and swollen, so that it looked as though he'd been crying, but it was hard to tell with his face wet from the rain, and drunk as he was.

'You're his wife, ain't you? Came to the house with the doctor's girl before,' he said, roughly. Too alarmed to speak, Irene merely nodded. 'You found it. You found that doll up there.' He pointed up to the farm behind them, and Irene nodded again. Tanner's face creased peculiarly, and Irene was puzzled for a moment until she realised that he *was* crying, and that he was furious with himself for letting her see. 'It didn't ought to have happened,' he said. Swallowing, Irene found her voice.

'What didn't?' she said. Tanner gave her a shake.

'None of it!' he said. He shook his head like he was trying to clear it, his fingers still gouging into Irene's arms.

'Please let go of me,' she said, feebly. Her heart was hammering but at the same time she felt no specific threat to herself from Tanner – only that he was unravelled with drink and what appeared to be grief, and she had no idea what he might do next.

'I was glad of it, at first; now part of me wishes you'd never found it. For what good does it do? What good is any of it?' He shook her again, and the eyes that glared into hers were raw, and half mad.

'I . . . I don't know.' She gathered her wits. 'What . . . what did the doll mean to you?' she said, but Tanner ignored the question.

'What'll happen to the lad?' he demanded instead.

'Who? What lad?'

'The simpleton they've fingered. Will he swing for it?'

'Donald Cartwright? I . . . I don't know. If he's tried for murder then he'll most likely hang. That's what Pudding's afraid of.' Tanner stared at her for a moment then dropped his hands and pushed past her, stumbling towards the gate and leaving Irene with the hiss of the rain on the grass, and the soughing of her own breath in her ears.

She watched Tanner make his lurching way down the hill and vanish towards Thatch Cottage, and only then did she begin to relax. She had to tell Pudding. She clenched her fists because her fingers were tingling peculiarly. It seemed that her prescient feeling about the doll being important, and somehow the start of things, had been completely right. But there was absolutely nothing she could think of that the Tanners could have held against Alistair – nothing that Nancy knew of, or George Turner; nothing that she'd found in his paperwork; and they had checked Tanner's alibi themselves. She looked down at the smoking chimney of the mill, and knew she'd have to do as Pudding had asked, and look for clues in Alistair's papers there as well. Tanner himself hadn't been the only one employed there, after all – several members of his immediate family worked at the mill as well. Two of his sons, in their late teens or early twenties, had been with him the day she and Pudding had taken the doll to show Ma. Irene had been so fixated upon their father, she hadn't seen what the sons' reactions to it had been. Perhaps there was something else – some other feud or dispute, not related to Tanner's recent laying-off for drunkenness.

She turned away at last, and went around to the side of the church that Tanner had come from. There was usually only one reason a person might be found weeping in a churchyard. There were four gravestones in the narrow space between the wall and the church itself; the names on two of them meant nothing to Irene, and the names on the other two had been obliterated by weathering. Only the year was visible on one – a small stone, plain and leaning forwards towards the turf – and it caught Irene's eye: *1872*. And at the foot of this neglected headstone, a fresh bunch of wildflowers had been laid – blue forget-me-nots. Irene stared, and shivered in the rain, and felt a small, anonymous piece of the puzzle find its place in her mind.

9
Dead Ends

'But that can't be it,' said Pudding, tumbling down from another wave-crest of hope. Pete Dempsey shrugged apologetically. He'd come to the farm in his official capacity, sweating slightly in his tall helmet and fiddling now and then with the strap that cut into his chin.

'I was surprised he even let me look into it, Pud. So at least ... that's something,' he said, lamely. Pudding stared down at the sheet of paper on which Pete had written a scant summary of the 1872 case, and the hunt for the girl's killer, which concluded: *Though a member or members of the Tanner family were initially suspected and questioned, all had reliable alibis for the time of the murder. No other suspects were identified, and the case remains unsolved.*

'How can that be it, though?' Pudding demanded. 'I mean – there's a summary of her injuries here, and they were just as ... just as awful as Alistair's. Whoever killed her – and Alistair – is clearly dangerous. But they just ...' She waved a hand in frustration. 'Didn't even find anybody else to question?'

'Well, just like with Mr Hadleigh, nobody could think of a reason for the killing, and nobody saw anything. Her sweetheart, if he existed, never came forward to identify himself. The shovel that did for her was dropped by her body, and they weren't so good at collecting fingerprints back then. There was something in her ... in the blood on the floor that they supposed at first to be a footprint, but then decided that it wasn't.'

'Wasn't a footprint?'

'No. So they had nothing to go on, see?' Pete ran a finger under his chinstrap again, rubbing the red welt it left in his skin.

'Oh, just take it off, Pete,' said Pudding. 'I won't tell anybody.' Relieved, Pete took off the helmet and scuffed a hand through his damp hair.

'This heat,' he muttered. 'Makes it hard to think straight, doesn't it?'

'Why did they decide it wasn't a footprint?'

'I don't know, Pudding! It was too small, or something like that. Look, Blackman – I mean, the superintendent – listened to what I had to say, and he read the story in your book, and, well, it went as I thought it would. He let me fetch the old file out of the cellar – mouldy and half eaten-away it is too – and he read that as well. But as far as he's concerned, the only thing connecting the two killings is the description of the first in your book, which was most likely read by the perpetrator of the second.'

'It isn't at *all* likely that Donny read it! Well . . . could I see the actual file?'

'No, 'ee can't, Pudding. And it don't say a thing worth noting but what I 'as put down there,' said Pete, his accent thickening with agitation.

They were standing on the yard outside the cob house, beside a handcart of mucky straw that Pudding had just loaded. She leant on her pitchfork and took a deep breath, trying not to feel defeated.

'Well, then,' she said, but she didn't know well *what*. Every dead end was exhausting, and the effect of them seemed cumulative. 'I shall have to think of something else.'

'Have you spoken to any of the older folk?'

'Yes. None of them knows a thing. They all remember it

though – they remember the girl, Sarah, mostly because she was very pretty, by all accounts. And because they were all scared for a while, thinking there was a killer in their midst – people walked their children to school for a time, and that kind of thing. Old Hilarius was here then, but he just looked at me oddly when I asked him about it, and asked to borrow my murder book again; even though he read it before and didn't seem to like it.' She shrugged. 'But if he knew anything he'd tell me. I know he would.'

'He'd read it before, but he didn't say anything about the similarity between the two murders?' said Pete.

'No,' said Pudding. 'He didn't.' She frowned, thinking of Irene's odd reaction to the groom. She thought about the first time Hilarius had seen the murder book, when she'd left it lying around the tack room – his odd demeanour, and the way he warned her off reading it. She stifled an uneasy feeling about it. 'He probably just didn't think of it, like I didn't. He is ancient, after all.'

'How old is he, anyway?'

'I don't know. Eighty? Maybe even older. I'm not sure I'd have the guts to ask him, and what does it matter, anyway?' Pudding straightened up and handed the sheet of paper back to Pete.

'No, you keep it. I wrote it out for you,' he said.

'But it doesn't say anything remotely useful,' said Pudding. Pete sagged slightly.

'No, I suppose it doesn't. But keep it anyway.' They stood for a while in awkward silence. Behind them, the swallows' nests in the rafters were now empty and quiet; Nancy and the giant farm manager, Mr Lake, walked across to the rickyard, deep in conversation. Pete nodded in their direction.

'Miss Hadleigh's back up and running then?'

'I think she needs to keep busy,' said Pudding. 'To distract herself from how awful it all is.' As she spoke, Pudding was aware of Pete watching her with that infuriating, understanding, sympathetic expression, and she suddenly saw that everybody thought exactly the same of her as well — that she was simply keeping busy, to distract herself. She blushed. 'Well, I'd best get back to work. Thanks for trying, Constable,' she said.

'Righty-ho. Well. I wanted to ask as well, Pudding, whether you might like to . . .' He turned his helmet in his hands. 'Perhaps. Another drink, perhaps, one evening. To discuss . . . everything. Or a walk?' Pudding frowned at him, puzzled.

'Well, have you got anything else to tell me that you haven't told me now?' she said.

'No,' Pete confessed.

'Well then.' Pudding shrugged, laid the pitchfork across the handcart and began wheeling it towards the muck heap. She looked back when she reached it and began forking out the dreck. Pete was still standing where she'd left him, looking down at his feet. Then he put his helmet back on and walked away at the speed of a man with nowhere in particular to go.

❧ ❧

Pudding had already gone home when Irene got back from the rain-sodden churchyard, and dinner had been ready to serve. Nancy had given her a fishy look when she'd suggested going off to find the girl groom at that hour, and then, in the morning, asked Irene to go into Chippenham with her, to visit the pharmacist, the bank and the dressmaker. She made Irene drive the Stanhope along the quieter roads.

'It's no good you always having to be driven, Irene. You're a Hadleigh, and Hadleighs can manage. If you're staying on, you'll need to learn, and it's easy enough,' she said, in that way she had that made it impossible to argue. And it proved fairly easy, in fact, even though Irene had barely got used to being in charge of a horse she was sitting on, let alone one she was only connected to by two lengths of leather rein and a whip. 'Use your voice, like I told you,' Nancy coached. 'Look – see how his ears flick back like that? He's waiting for your next instruction.' The errands took well over an hour, and then they stopped to have coffee at the Bear Hotel before setting off back to Manor Farm, so Irene didn't get a chance to speak to Pudding about what she'd seen and heard before lunch. By then, she knew better than to say anything about it to Nancy.

When lunch was over Irene watched from a window until Nancy had gone out with Lake, and Constable Dempsey had wandered off, disconsolately, and Pudding was finally by herself, shovelling horse manure onto the heap and turning ruddy with the work.

'Pudding! Hello – did Constable Dempsey have anything new?' she called. Pudding stopped shovelling and leant on her fork with two hands, catching her breath.

'No.' She thought for a moment and frowned. 'Or maybe – something he's not saying, perhaps. He keeps suggesting we go for a walk, or a drink,' she said. Irene stared at Pudding for a moment, but her incomprehension was complete.

'Does he really? And ... you can't think of any other reason he might want to do that?'

'No. Why? What do you think he wants?'

'Well ... Never mind that for now, perhaps,' said Irene, smiling slightly. 'I have to tell you what happened yesterday.' Pudding came down from the heap to listen, and Irene told her about Tanner, and what he'd said about the doll, and the gravestone from 1872 with fresh flowers on it. 'And then he asked about Donny, and what would happen to him. But he said "the one they've fingered for it". That means he doesn't think Donny did it, don't you think? That the police have just arrested him to solve the case?'

'Does it? Yes, I think you're right!' Pudding gripped Irene's hand in excitement, and Irene tried not to mind how filthy it was. 'He *must* know more about it. The police will *have* to speak to him again – they didn't press him, or his boys, once they'd given their alibis, they just took Donny away and that was that! Well, they'll have to now, won't they? There are still a few days until Donny's hearing – it's not too late, if we hurry!'

'But if Mr Tanner's arrested he'll know it was me that reported on him,' said Irene, alarmed.

'I doubt it.' Pudding shrugged. 'He was blind drunk, you said.'

'Yes, but still. I should hate to get on the wrong side of him.'

'Irene, the truth is *far* more important. And in any case, Tanner might end up in jail himself! Then nobody needs to be scared of him any more.'

'Well, let's not get ahead of ourselves. But isn't it just the queerest thing about the doll? What do you think it could possibly mean?' said Irene.

'It's certainly queer – and just as queer is that you *knew* it was important. I mean, right back when you found it, somehow you knew,' said Pudding.

'But I still don't know *why*,' said Irene, cautiously.

'And the flowers on that grave – he must have put them there. Do you think it was this girl, Sarah, from the first murder?'

'Well, the year is certainly a coincidence, if it isn't. Do you think we could find out?'

'Yes, of course. It'll be in the church register – we'll have to see the vicar about having a look. Do you think Tanner killed her, and is racked with guilt? Do you think he feels guilty about killing Alistair now? And about Donny being arrested?' said Pudding, avidly. She paused, counting under her breath.

'He's old enough. He'd only have been a lad in 1872, but he could have done it!'

'Now — just hold on. No more accusations without good grounds,' said Irene, and Pudding looked chastened. Her need to act seemed to fizz around her like a static charge.

'All right, but we *have* to talk to the police again — you have to go and tell Superintendent Blackman, Irene,' she said.

'Me? Can't you?' said Irene. She'd found the policeman strange, and difficult, even before Pudding had accused her of colluding in Alistair's death.

'He'll need to hear it from you — first-hand, you see. And, anyway . . . I don't think he'd listen to anything else I had to say.' Pudding took a deep breath and hitched up her britches. 'He just thinks I'm a nuisance. And I have to go and talk to Tanner.'

'Pudding, no — leave it to the police!'

'But he might disappear before the police get to him — he's done that before, when something's happened around here that they might want to talk to him about. No — I need to go and catch him unawares.' Pudding swallowed, not sounding half as sure as her words, and Irene saw how nervous she was.

'I really don't think it's a good idea. Just . . . wait a bit. Wait until we find out something else . . . why don't you come with me to the mill, to look through Alistair's papers there?'

'Haven't you done that yet?'

'I haven't had the chance. And I don't want Nancy to know — she wouldn't approve one bit.'

'All right. But first let me run after Pete, and get him to take you in to see Blackman.'

Superintendent Blackman's eyes, behind his round glasses, were as dark and inscrutable as Irene remembered them. He sat her down in front of his desk with a few stiff words, offered her refreshment politely enough, then sat watching her with his hands loosely grasping the arms of his chair, all the while making her feel like a guilty schoolgirl. Perhaps it was the way he never smiled, and hardly blinked.

'I understand you have something you'd like to tell me,' he said, his eyes never leaving her face, and Irene wondered if he thought she'd come to confess to something. She cleared her throat.

'Yes. I think ... I think Miss Cartwright might be on to something, linking my husband's murder to the earlier murder she's uncovered, in 1872,' she said, as calmly as she could.

'The investigation into your husband's death is closed, Mrs Hadleigh.'

'Well, perhaps it oughtn't to be,' she said. Superintendent Blackman continued to stare, but Irene thought she detected a subtle interest kindling in him. He didn't speak, so she hurried on, and described everything in the graveyard, just as before. When she got to the end, and could think of nothing to add, Blackman still hadn't moved or said a word. Irene waited, uncomfortably. When Blackman suddenly reached forward and picked up his pen, she jumped.

'This would be Mr Tanner of Thatch Cottage, Germain's Lane, Slaughterford?' he said.

'Well, yes. You must know him? I thought the police—' Irene cut herself off.

'It never pays to make assumptions, Mrs Hadleigh. From what I've learned, a good deal of the Tanners' reputation is based upon rumour and ... grudge. A community needs villains – scapegoats, if you will.' He gave her that blankly piercing look again, and Irene's pulse picked up.

'I only came to relay a conversation I thought might be relevant. For no other reason than that ... well, it might be relevant,' she said, trying not to sound rattled.

'Indeed,' said the policeman, adding something to the notes

on his jotter. 'But perhaps Donald Cartwright being cleared of suspicion would also clear suspicion from other people of his acquaintance.'

'If he didn't do it, oughtn't he to be cleared?'

'Indeed. However, I see absolutely no reason to suppose that he didn't do it, Mrs Hadleigh,' said Blackman. 'Tell me more about this doll, if you would. Where exactly was it found, and how did Mr Tanner come to know of it?' So Irene told him in as much detail as she could, and when she finished Blackman fell still, pen poised, staring into space. After a while, he looked up as though a little surprised to find her still there. 'Was there anything else, Mrs Hadleigh?' he said.

'No,' said Irene. 'Well, no.' She got up, and Blackman rose as well, though he made no move to come out from behind his desk. 'So, will you look into it? Will you talk to Tanner – Mr Tanner?' she asked, knowing that she'd face the same questions from Pudding. Superintendent Blackman seemed surprised to be asked.

'If I deem it necessary, Mrs Hadleigh,' he said.

'Oh,' she said, defeated. 'Good day, then.' She let herself out.

Pudding was as let down by the superintendent's reaction as Irene, who was getting used to seeing the girl's shoulders drop and her chest deflate as all the fight went out of her, just for that moment.

'It's like he doesn't *want* it to be anyone but Donny,' she said, heavily.

'I know.' Pudding looked in need of contact – a hug, or a reassuring squeeze of her arm, at least. Other people did such things so easily, so naturally. Irene was still wondering the best way to go about it when Pudding picked herself up yet again.

'Well. Never mind. We've done all we can do with the police, and it looks like we'll have to carry on without their help.' It was lunchtime, and they were sitting at the table at Spring Cottage as Ruth cleared away the plates. Louise Cartwright was sitting with them, but in that peculiar way of hers she was simultaneously *not* with them. She turned to watch whoever was speaking with a look of benign incomprehension, as though Pudding and Irene were children, talking of a game she knew nothing about. She smiled whenever Irene looked across at her, and Irene smiled back, having all the while the gnawing feeling that she was being horribly rude. From the sink, Ruth tutted her tongue.

'First time in history the coppers *don't* want to think some rotten deed was done by a Tanner, and sure enough they couldn't have picked a worse time,' she said, grimly.

'The superintendent said he thinks their reputation is based mostly upon sour grapes,' said Irene.

'Don't you believe it, Mrs Hadleigh. That Blackman's new 'round here – down from Hereford, I heard; he don't *know*. Maybe they ain't each last one of them bad to the bone, but most of them are. And as for Tanner himself . . .' She shook her head. 'God knows, I shouldn't like to meet him in the lane on a dark night.'

'Well,' said Pudding, to Irene. 'Shall we go down to the mill?' They looked at one another, and Irene knew that the same nightmare images as were in her own mind were in Pudding's too. Alistair, lying dead with Nancy weeping at his side; his blood on the floor; his wounds so obscene, so darkly black and red and grey. The thought of going into the old farmhouse still filled her with dread.

'I suppose we must,' she said, and Pudding nodded.

The door to the offices was open, propped with a chunk of stone. Irene caught Pudding glancing across into the generator room, and remembered that her brother was wont to wander in there, to watch the machinery. When Pudding turned away, it was with the wince of someone being forcibly reminded of a loss. A look of such intense sorrow passed over her face that it brought a lump to Irene's throat.

'Ready?' said Irene, swallowing. Pudding looked up at her with haunted eyes; it was the first time she'd returned to the mill since the murder. The bustle and thump of the machines filled the silence between them. Inside, they heard George Turner at his desk, clearing his throat. Without another word Irene knocked lightly, stepped into the comparative darkness within, and into another moment of panic almost as bad as the time before. The spectre of the Alistair-doll reared up in front of her, and she stepped backwards directly onto Pudding's toe.

'Ow!' Pudding cried, staggering slightly to get out of the way. Irene turned, and the sight of Pudding's freckled face, her clear blue eyes and stubborn hair was so familiar, and so comforting, that her panic lost its grip at once.

'Sorry,' she said. 'I just . . . I thought for a moment . . .'

'It's all right,' said Pudding. 'Nothing's broken – you weigh almost nothing. You should hear me yell when Baron stands on my toe.'

'Ladies,' said George Turner, who'd got to his feet. 'How may I be of service?'

'Hello again, Mr Turner.' Irene's nerves thinned her voice. 'How do you do?'

'Passably well, thank you, and it's kind of you to ask, Mrs Hadleigh. All our thoughts here at the mill continue to be with you.'

'Yes,' said Irene. 'Thank you. And Mrs Turner?'

'I believe we have seen an improvement of late, thank you.' George smiled kindly and then stood, waiting, his hands behind his back. Pudding gave Irene a nudge.

'I was . . . we were . . . just going up to my husband's office.

To see . . . well,' she said, floundering, but George merely nodded.

'Of course, Mrs Hadleigh. You'll find the door unlocked. Is there anything I can fetch for you?'

'No, thank you.' With a shiver, Irene walked across the place where Alistair had died, and took the stairs with Pudding at her heels. The office junior watched, bored, from behind his cramped desk at the far end of the room.

Sunlight streamed benignly onto Alistair's leather-topped desk, where there wasn't a single speck of dust. Nor was there a speck on his bookshelves, which were full of files, ledgers and books about paper-making; nor on the elm floorboards that showed around the fancy crimson rug; nor on the brass fender around the fireplace, swept clean for summer.

'Somebody must still be coming in here and cleaning,' said Irene, and Pudding nodded.

'Ready for you to come in and . . . er . . . do business, I suppose,' said Pudding. Irene blinked. 'You own all this now, don't forget.' Pudding went to the window and pointed out at the array of buildings, the stores and workings, the busy employees. 'All of this is yours. Crumbs, that must feel strange. Does it?'

'Stranger than I can tell you,' said Irene. It didn't feel at all real to her.

'Look at it all,' Pudding breathed, running her eyes along the shelved files, all neatly labelled and in order. 'We've quite a task.'

'Surely . . . you can't mean for us to look through *everything*?' said Irene, incredulously.

'Well . . . why else are we here?' said Pudding. 'We don't know what we're looking for, that's the problem.' Irene took a deep breath and let it out slowly.

'We mustn't make a mess,' she said. 'We must leave it all

just as we find it.' She didn't know why that was important, just that it was. She sat down in the captain's chair and ran her hands along the edge of the desk, worn smooth by being leant against and polished, over and over again. The leather top had been warmed by the sun, and Irene spread her hands on it, seeing how pale and frail her fingers looked against the bottle green. She felt, again, that she didn't belong where she was, so could achieve nothing, but this time she fought back against it. She could get justice for Alistair, even if she didn't belong.

'Are you all right?' Pudding asked, and Irene nodded, pulling herself together.

'Yes. Well. Best to make a start, I suppose.'

She opened the top drawer of the desk, and found bottles of ink, pens, pencils, a sharpening knife, paperclips and a paperweight fashioned from a chunk of quartz. The drawer had a familiar, schoolroom smell but no papers at all, so she moved on to the next, and so the afternoon ticked by. Now and then they heard George Turner talking to his junior, or to somebody who'd come into the farmhouse; now and then the foreman went out on some errand elsewhere in the mill. Other voices, those of workers, echoed in the yard as the shift changed, but other than that, and the constant noise of the machines, the office was a peaceful, almost drowsy place. Even Pudding, devoted to the task, sighed each time she stood, returned a file to the shelf and fetched another. At five George Turner came up to them with a tray of tea, his face registering mild concern.

'If there's anything you'd like to learn, Mrs Hadleigh, I'd be more than happy to oblige you, if it's within my capacity to do so.'

'No, thank you, Mr Turner. That is, not unless . . .' Irene considered her next question. 'I'm sure the police have already spoken to you, Mr Turner, only I'd be most interested to know if there was anyone here at the mill, or anyone my husband had dealings with, who you think might have held a grievance towards him.' Irene held her nerve, and the manager's eye, as she waited for his reply. She saw his discomfort and confusion.

'Well, now,' he said, uneasily, flicking his eyes towards Pudding, who coloured. 'Surely . . . surely there's little question as to what happened to your husband, Mrs Hadleigh?'

'But I should like to know, all the same,' said Irene.

'As I told the authorities, everyone who'd ever had business with Mr Hadleigh knew him to be an honest man, fair and straight in all his dealings. No business acquaintance of his can have had a grudge against him. Not even Mr Tanner.'

'What about the other Tanner boys working at the mill?' said Irene. 'Have they . . . been in any trouble?'

'Trouble? No, not at all. Young Elijah is a firebrand – he takes after his father, and no mistake. He sent some black looks my way when Tanner was laid off again, and now it seems he's taken himself off somewhere else. But for the most part they need the work, and they work hard. And they would be more likely to be angry with me than with Mr Hadleigh.'

'Why's that?' said Pudding.

'I counselled that Mr Tanner ought to be let go for good this time, but your husband was always very tolerant towards the family. Too generous by half, I always thought. But Mr Hadleigh said if he didn't give them a chance, what chance would they have?'

'Yes,' said Irene. 'That sounds like Alistair.'

'But might Mr Hadleigh have had an argument with any of them, and not told you?' asked Pudding.

'No.' George shook his head. 'I'd have been informed.' Irene nodded as she took this in. She trusted her instinctive fear of Tanner; the memory of him coming at her in the churchyard made her shiver, as did thoughts of her visit to

Thatch Cottage. But if he'd had cause to hurt Alistair, then the reason for it was something far older, and far darker, than an argument over a job.

Irene was suddenly completely certain that they were wasting their time looking through invoices and receipts. She felt a flare of impatience, and the maddening sensation that she *knew* the answer, but couldn't see it, and was about to suggest that they called a halt when she was cut off by the sudden sound of quick, determined footsteps on the stairs. Nancy strode into the room, glaring as though they'd all been caught in her bedroom, going through her smalls.

'I heard your voices – what on earth is going on?' she demanded, and before anyone could answer, added: 'This is Alistair's office! *Nobody* should be in here.'

'Nancy, Pudding and I were just looking for some ... clue, I suppose. Something that might help to explain what's happened,' said Irene.

'If you'll excuse me, ladies,' said George Turner, uncomfortably. 'I've some matters to attend to.' Nancy didn't even look at the foreman. Her eyes were fixed on Irene and Pudding, and blazing.

'There is no question about what happened.' Her voice was low and trembling. 'I simply do *not* understand why you must keep on ... muckraking in this way! You're only making things worse.'

'They can't get worse,' said Pudding, meekly, but Nancy's glare silenced her.

'Shame on you, Irene,' said Nancy. 'I thought you were starting to show some sense, on the whole. But now I find you recklessly encouraging the dratted girl in her fantasies – you're only making it worse for her in the long run, you know. Pudding's a child and doesn't know any better, but you ought.'

'Pudding isn't a child,' said Irene, her pulse racing. As she said it, she realised how true it was. However naive Pudding was in some ways, the responsibilities she'd been forced to shoulder had pushed her beyond her years. 'And I don't think she's a fantasist either.'

'Really? And what about when she pointed the finger at *you* for Alistair's death?'

'Well, never mind that. I . . . I have had an encounter with Mr Tanner myself, which has made me think that perhaps—'

'No.' Nancy cut her off, stonily. 'I don't want to hear any more. I won't hear any more. Every time you bring it up it's like you're . . . you're disturbing Alistair's grave! It's obscene! I want you out of here, the pair of you. You've no business going through my brother's things like a . . . a pair of *thieves*. Go on – I insist that you leave.'

'Sorry, Miss H,' Pudding mumbled, making for the door with her eyes down, but Irene put out a hand to stop her.

'Wait, Pudding. Nancy . . . I'm sorry, but we're not finished yet. These are my husband's things, not your brother's – or your nephew's – any more. I know this is hard for you – that seeing anyone in here must be very hard for you. I promise we will leave everything just as we found it.' As she spoke, Irene began to feel calmer, more resolved.

'You will leave,' said Nancy, and she and Irene stared at one another for a long time.

'We will, when we've finished,' said Irene. The air between them seemed to freeze, and a second later Nancy turned on her heel and left them there, and Pudding exhaled massively.

'Heavens, Irene,' she said, 'I've never seen anyone face down Miss Hadleigh like that before!'

'I'm not surprised,' said Irene. She perched on the edge of the desk for a moment, pressing her fingers to her lips. 'I hope I don't live to regret it.'

*

Clemmie slunk back into Weavern Farm like an errant cat – silently, after dark. She curled up under the blankets next to Josie and went straight to sleep, feeling that while much was still wrong, much was also right again. In the morning, Josie gave a little gasp when she opened her eyes and found her sister there, but then she smiled.

'You're back,' she said. When Mary and Liz woke up they clustered around her, peering closely, pinching her and pulling detritus from her hair.

'Have you been living under a hedge? Smells like it.'

'You gave us quite the jolt. It wasn't the same without you, Clemmie,' said Mary. 'Where on earth have you been?' But Clemmie couldn't tell them about the long hours of walking, lost, through Swindon's confusing streets, and the feeling of starting to fly as she left the city behind her; or that she'd hitched two rides – the first with a farmer in his high-wheeled gig, who'd been travelling back from burying his brother. She'd had to run away when he'd turned in at a field gate and made a grab for her. The second was with an elderly couple who spoke no more than she did, and only nodded for her to climb into the back of their small wagon, which carried a load of old furniture – a carver chair, a commode, a washstand with a cracked top, all mildewed. Clemmie had slept for hours with her head on a rat-chewed prayer stool. They'd brought her as far as Marshfield, and she'd walked the last stretch, tired and afraid but driven forwards, pulled towards home. 'Oh, why can't you talk?' said Mary, but she didn't expect an answer. 'Ma! Clemmie's back!' she shouted down from the top of the stairs, and they all heard Rose's oath from below.

She was berated and hugged in equal measure by her mother; scowled at and ignored by her father; questioned and cajoled by her sisters. Clemmie paced and gestured and even tried some sounds – anything to prompt them to start asking the right questions, but they did not. Only Josie got close, as they were milking.

'Clemmie – did you go off with your sweetheart? With the baby's father?' she asked, and Clemmie nodded eagerly, and waited for her to ask more. 'But where is he now? You've left him?' Clemmie nodded and then shook her head. 'Yes *and* no, Clem?' Josie frowned. 'But how can that be?' She thought for a moment, chewing her lip. 'Is he coming here, Clem? Is that it? Will you be wed?' Josie's face lit up, but Clemmie only frowned. She couldn't say yes, not when she knew Eli would never return to live in Slaughterford while his father remained. She *had* to make her plan to get rid of Isaac Tanner work, and she couldn't let herself think about what Eli might be thinking, or feeling. Abandoned, discarded; cheated out of his new life, his new family, his fresh start. He would be in so much pain. Such thoughts made her weak with remorse, and something else, nearly unbearable – something close to terror. She sent out thoughts to him, and longed for him to hear them, and know the contents of her heart. At times, her projected thoughts made such a loud roar in her head that she was sure he must hear them; at others, she knew he could not and never would. She wondered if he would think she planned to turn him in for what happened at the mill. She wondered if he would come to find her, and gut instinct said that he would. She wondered if he was on his way, if he was getting closer, if he was almost at her heels. And one thing that was clear, once a few days had passed, was that however much she could show them that she needed to tell them something, her family were never, ever going to ask her the right questions. She would have to say out loud what she needed to say.

Her need to speak kept her awake all night, and in the daytime made her wayward and tearful. Her mother, Rose, came to check on her frequently, appearing wherever Clemmie was with a worried expression that eased when she saw her daughter, and coming out with some excuse.

'Oh, there you are. I was just wondering if you'd ... seen the filleting knife?' At which Clemmie would rise from whatever she was at and take her mother to where the filleting knife lay, in the drawer where it was always kept. Whenever she was alone, she began to practise. She needed as short a sentence as possible, with words as short as possible, and she needed to decide who to say them to. She thought she ought to say them directly to one of the policemen who'd been around the mill in the first days afterwards, but they'd all gone now and she didn't know how to find them. There was the police constable in Ford, and the one in Corsham, but they were both strangers, in any case, and that would only make it worse. She thought about Nancy Hadleigh, who was the kind of person who would get something done in Alistair's absence, but then she thought of Nancy's grief, and her anger, and her misunderstanding, and knew she couldn't approach her. There were her mother and father, of course, and there was Mrs Tanner, Eli's mother – but afterwards, when they went to the police, it might just seem like some scheme cooked up between them to point the finger at Isaac. Then there was the foreman at the mill with the foxy whiskers, who had always been kind and treated Clemmie as a whole person. He might be the one. But she needed the right words to say, and she needed to be able to say them.

If she could say *Isaac* then she wouldn't need to say *Tanner*, which was good, since the letter *t* was one of the worst with which to start a word; if she could say *rob* then she wouldn't have to say *attacked*; if she could say *guilty*, *revenge*, *money* and *I heard*, then she wouldn't have to say *Eli*, *innocent* or *threatened*. The phrase she came up with, though the thought of actually having to say it was exhausting before she'd even started, was: *I heard Isaac say he would rob Mr Hadleigh; he is the guilty one.* If she was believed then more questions would be asked, and she could answer yes or no; then surely the police would have to take Isaac away, and then perhaps the Tanner clan would have the courage to speak out against him, and keep him locked up for good. And word would get out, and Eli would come back, and when he knew what she had done he would understand her whole plan, and then they would wed, and she would bring him to Weavern Farm and they would not be turned away. Clemmie shut her eyes and thought through this chain of events so many times that it started to seem less unlikely, less fly-away, and began to seem like it could actually happen. Like it *would* happen – because it had to. Clemmie could think of no alternative, since she could not live where Eli was, and he could not live where she was. And there was the chance – just a slight chance, that she didn't dwell upon – that he would not let her live apart from him. She began to practise the words, and she started with *Isaac.*

❧ ❧

Superintendent Blackman was driven up to Spring Cottage in the black car by a young constable; the car's roof was folded back so that both men had a fair dusting from the lanes. Blackman was polishing the lenses of his spectacles when Pudding rushed out to find out what was new, and to invite him inside, but Blackman held up a hand to forestall her. He took off his hat and patted the dust from it as Dr Cartwright came out to stand beside his daughter.

'Thank you, Miss Cartwright, Dr Cartwright, but I'll not be stopping long enough for tea today,' he said. 'I only wanted to let you know that I have interviewed Mr Tanner again, and not only has he a firm alibi for the time of Mr Hadleigh's death, he has no reason at all to have harmed him.'

'But what about the doll, and the grave where he laid the flowers – the one with the year 1872 on it, the year of the first murder?'

'Mr Tanner denies being the one who laid those flowers; he claims not to know to whom that particular grave might belong, and he looked mystified when I mentioned the doll Mrs Hadleigh found at Manor Farm. And given that there is not a scrap of evidence—'

'He's lying!'

'And given that there is not a scrap of evidence that he was involved, please, let that be an end to it, Miss Cartwright. I understand you will be disappointed at the termination of this new line of enquiry, but I beg you not to seek a fresh one. Make no more accusations, Miss Cartwright.'

'Pudding?' said Dr Cartwright. 'What new line of enquiry is this?'

'But . . . what about all the things he said to Irene, in the churchyard?' said Pudding to Blackman, ignoring her father. 'He's lying about the grave – I just have to find out who's buried there. There has to be a connection – Tanner is old enough to have killed them both. It *has* to be him!' Pudding felt breathless with the need to be heard, to be believed. She felt it all slipping away from her – the chance that she could bring Donny home, and the strength that had come with that. Without it, she didn't know what she would do. How she would carry on. 'The Tanners are thieves and liars and killers! Everybody knows that!'

'Pudding, that's enough,' said the doctor firmly, putting his hand on her shoulder. Frustration filled her eyes with tears, but she was sick of crying.

'Casting a wide net of aspersions won't help your brother, Miss Cartwright,' said Blackman. 'I've already spent more time following up your theories than I ought to have.'

'Well, what *will* help Donny?' Pudding demanded. The superintendent looked at her gravely.

'Addressing himself to his conscience, as best he can, and remaining calm tomorrow, in front of the magistrates,' he said. 'I've come to talk to you in person, Miss Cartwright, to tell you that it's time to let things stand. The investigation is closed.' He put his hat back on and turned to climb back into the car.

'It's not closed,' Pudding murmured, staring at Blackman as his constable inched the car forwards and began, jerkily, to turn it around. At the last moment, Blackman opened his mouth as though he might say something else, but in the end he didn't. Pudding wondered if he looked as wholly convinced as his words sounded, but then, that might just have been wishful thinking, and wishful thinking had yet to get her anywhere.

The car chugged away and left a cloud of dust that the low sun turned golden. The first mad green of summer had passed, Pudding realised; it was the tenth of August and the land was drying out, ripening, going over. Pudding put up her hand to shield her eyes, squinting as the breeze swirled the dust around her and her father. They both stood where they were until the sound of the car's engine had completely disappeared, and only the tinkling of the spring into its trough remained. With no patients to see, Dr Cartwright didn't seem to know what to do with himself. And if she had no leads to chase, then Pudding didn't know what to do with *her*self, either. A black and white cat appeared from nowhere and wound around her shins, but when she reached down to stroke it, it dodged away. Laughter drifted up from the potato field behind the mill, where youngsters were picking the tubers from the turned dark furrows.

'Well,' said Dr Cartwright. 'Come along inside, Pudding, and let's think about some supper, shall we?'

'I'm not terribly hungry, Dad.'

'No. Well. Nevertheless, you must eat. We've a big day

tomorrow.' Pudding looked at her father and he gave her a sad smile. He didn't need to say it might be a terrible day; one of the worst. The day of Donny's hearing in Devizes.

'I really didn't think it would come to this, Dad,' she said. 'I really thought I'd find out who truly killed Alistair, and that tomorrow they'd let Donny come home.'

'They may yet; they may yet. I know you've done your best. We all know you've done your best.' He took his watch out of its pocket and buffed the surface against his waistcoat, peering down at it. 'Five o'clock,' he said, though Pudding hadn't asked. 'Some tea, at least,' he said, absently. 'I'm sure your mother would love a cup.' He patted her shoulder again before going inside, and Pudding realised that he had given up completely. Given up on the idea that Donny would ever be released. She stood a while in his absence, fighting against the similar death of her own hopes. Without them, the world was a bleak and empty place.

Louise Cartwright insisted on coming with them to Devizes the following day, and wouldn't be persuaded otherwise. Pudding and her father exchanged a long look. The thought of her confusion when they got to the New Bridewell and she saw Donny with his hands cuffed and his head stitched, in his prison clothes and as pale as he'd become, was awful. But in the end they couldn't refuse her.

'Tell me a good reason why I oughtn't to see my son?' she said, quite firmly, and neither of them could.

'I'll come too,' said Ruth, frowning. 'I needn't come inside, but I can wait in case you need . . . any help with anything.'

'Thank you, Ruth,' said Dr Cartwright. Pudding put on her smartest clothes, with the nagging feeling that it somehow might help Donny's case. She wore a sky-blue skirt that came to the middle of her calves, and a white voile blouse embroidered with dobby spots. Her mother usually watched her like a hawk when she wore it, just waiting for her to spill something down it, or lean against something grubby. But the triumph of arriving in Devizes still pristine, after a bus ride to Chippenham and two trains, was very much muted. Louise smiled politely at the prison guards as they were led through to the sad, cold room where visits were permitted, but none of the guards smiled back. They sat themselves down on one side of a long, unadorned table, and Donny was brought in to them, looking hollow, hunched and vacant.

'Oh,' said Louise, her eyes fearful. Pudding took her hand and squeezed it tight. Pudding had seen Donny every week of his month-long incarceration, and his steady decline had been obvious each time. To Louise, seeing him for the first time since his arrest, the change was clearly shocking. He was so much thinner, and his skin had a yellowish pallor; a sore on his lip was crusted and weeping; the bruising around his head wound had deepened to an alarming crimson; but worst of all was the look of lost exhaustion in his eyes. 'Oh, my boy,' she said. 'What's happened? What's happened to him?' she demanded of her husband.

'There, there, my dear. I am sure they're looking after him. He took a bit of a knock on the head, but he was seen by a doctor. It's really only the want of a bit of sunshine and a few home comforts that ails him.' The doctor didn't sound at all convincing.

'Hello, Mum, Dad. Hello, Puddy,' said Donny, looking at each of them in turn.

'Hello, Donny,' said Pudding, reaching for his hand and smiling.

'Oh!' said Louise, and started to cry.

'I should like to come home now,' said Donny, and Pudding did her level best not to start crying too.

They were only allowed to sit with him for twenty minutes, and in that time Dr Cartwright did his best to explain to Donny what was going to happen during the hearing, even though the lawyer had already done so. Donny just nodded now and then, when prompted, and didn't seem interested. He looked like half the person he had been before, and that person had been only half of the one who'd gone off to the war. Pudding didn't like to think how much more halving her brother could survive. She felt numb, and a kind of sickness crept up on her, which thickened her throat and made it hard to talk. It felt like her heart was struggling to beat, and when she followed her parents out of the prison and over to the courthouse to wait in the public gallery, she felt as though half of her had gone missing as well. Louise Cartwright turned glassy and faint, and Ruth went with her to catch an earlier train home.

'You go too, Pudding. You look done in, and there's no need for you to stay – Donny will see that I'm here, and he'll know you—'

'I'm staying, Dad,' she said. Dr Cartwright nodded wanly, and pushed his spectacles up his nose.

'We must prepare ourselves to be stalwart in the face of . . . of fear and distress, Pudding,' he said. Pudding didn't think she could, and didn't like to lie, but she nodded, for his sake. And then Donny's case was called, and they brought him in and he confirmed his name and address, with some prompting, and a thudding in Pudding's ears meant she could hardly hear him.

Donny pleaded not guilty to wilful murder, and not guilty to manslaughter on the grounds of diminished responsibility. The prosecution lawyer spoke, and none of their witness statements were contested by the defence. The defence lawyer spoke last, and asked Donny to describe what he had seen and done on the morning of Alistair's death, but since Donny was better at answering exactly what he was asked than he was at expanding or volunteering information, he didn't say a great deal, and seemed uncooperative. More uncontested statements, mostly about Donny's good character and his head injuries, were submitted, and the magistrate, who had a face like a rook's – all beak and bright eyes – sifted through them. And then he expressed a heavy heart, given Donny's service in the war, and sent him to stand trial before the crown at the next Wiltshire assizes, for the crime of wilful murder. Due to the nature of the crime, and to continued incidences of violence whilst he had been in custody, no bail was set. And Pudding was entirely powerless to do anything about it.

Afterwards, Pudding and the doctor stood on the platform in silence, waiting for their train back to Chippenham. The breeze rolled and rustled an old news-sheet along the tracks; pink and white fleabane crowded the rails, and sparrows hopped around, picking up crumbs from people's sandwiches. One of Pudding's earliest memories was of being on a train, when she was no more than four. She didn't remember where they'd been going – the destination wasn't half as exciting as the ride there. She remembered Donny, twelve or thirteen, leaning out of the window as they rounded each bend, trying to catch a glimpse of the engine in full steam, then turning back to them with smuts in his teeth, his hair on end and a grin from ear to ear. Pudding took a sharp breath and tried to banish the image, which only seemed to make it worse. Wherever she stood, she couldn't seem to get away from a cloud of pipe smoke wafting from an elderly man along the platform. It stung her eyes and made her throat itch, and was as distracting as a cloud of midges.

'Please stop fidgeting, Pudding,' her father snapped, shooting her a harried look before returning to staring at the ground.

'What should we do next, Dad?'

'Do?' The doctor looked at her as though she wasn't speaking sense. '*Do?* There's nothing more we can do, Pudding.'

'But oughtn't we to . . . appeal against there being no bail, at least? Donny should be at home until the trial, where we can look after him. The other men might pick on him . . . or goad him into doing something. I've got until the trial to find out a way to save him, so—'

'Enough, Pudding!' Her father's sudden shout stunned Pudding to silence. She couldn't remember when she had last heard him raise his voice. The man with the pipe, and several others, glanced in their direction. 'Just . . . stop it. Please. Stop talking about "finding something out to save Donny". Stop trying to think of ways to bring him home.'

'But . . . you mustn't give up, Dad!' Pudding's throat ached as she spoke, and her voice came out strangled. 'You mustn't. Donny's innocent, and I—'

'No, Pudding! No!' Dr Cartwright shook his head, and wouldn't look at her.

'You can't mean to say . . . that you think Donny did it? You can't mean that.'

'Donald is my son.' The doctor spoke so quietly that Pudding could hardly hear him. 'He's my son, and God knows that I love him. But he . . . the war changed him. And now he has done this thing. And it can't be undone, Pudding. However much we wish it.'

'No, Dad – Donny didn't do it. I *know* he didn't – Irene knows it too!'

'Who?'

'I'm not going to give up. I'm going to find a way to bring him home, Dad, I promise.'

'No, you *won't*, Pudding! You must stop this! It . . . it does no good. It does no good at all! We have . . . we have lost your brother. However hard it is, it is the truth. And we must strive to . . . We must endeavour to . . .' The doctor trailed into silence, shaking his head. He sounded faint, and far away.

The train squealed and hissed to a halt beside them. Dr Cartwright climbed aboard without ushering Pudding ahead of him, or waiting to see if she were following. As though he'd forgotten she was even there. For a second, Pudding imagined it was true. She imagined that Donny had killed Alistair, and would now be hanged for it. It turned her cold all over, and exhausted. It felt like being lost in the middle of the night, all alone, and knowing that she could never go home. She shuddered, and refused to think it, silently reiterating her belief in Donny's innocence. But the lost feeling wouldn't go, because they were going to hang him anyway.

❧ ☙

A letter from Fin. Irene stared at it on the breakfast table and couldn't decide what to feel. After so many weeks, after so much had happened, and after he had told her to stop writing, he had written to her. Nancy cleared her throat as Irene came into the room, dabbed the corners of her mouth with her napkin and got up to go without a word.

'Nancy, please,' said Irene. 'Can't we declare peace? I'm sorry if I . . . ran roughshod over you. But it was important.'

'Was it indeed.' Nancy's face was as immovable as ever, but there were shadows under her eyes and the whites were shot pink with blood.

'It was. Won't you forgive us for going in there?'

'It's yours now, of course. All of it's yours. You may go where you wish, and do just as you please, without my blessing.'

'But I don't plan to do just as I please at all. Really, I don't. It's only fair that Pudding be allowed to . . . to try all she can to reach a peace with what's happened. And to help her brother.

❧ 349 ☙

Don't you agree?' As she spoke, Nancy's spine softened just a fraction. It did every time Irene reminded her that whatever Pudding did, she did for her brother.

'I suppose so,' she said, with a sigh. 'You and Pudding are certainly thick these days. But a young friend is better than none, I suppose. Aren't you going to open that?'

'Yes,' said Irene. 'Though I can't for the life of me think what he might have to say.'

'Well, if you're still in one piece afterwards, come and find me in the top skillings, if you'd like. The new curly-coat pigs are arriving.' Nancy took a final sip of her coffee before leaving the room.

Irene drank some coffee and ate some toast and marmalade, still unsure how she was feeling. Then she took a deep breath and opened Fin's letter. It wasn't long – his spidery writing barely filled one side of the paper. He had only recently heard about Alistair, and sent his condolences. They had been out of the country. He was now back in London on business, though Serena had stayed away. He asked if she was in town. He asked if she wanted to meet with him, discreetly, of course, perhaps at a location between London and the west – at a hotel, for example. Irene read it twice more until she was quite sure he was suggesting what she thought he was suggesting. The hurt of it was there, and her love for him as well – still there, beneath the surface, like a bruise. But that was it, she realised – it was like a bruise now, deeper beneath the surface and far less like an open wound or a broken bone. The pain was no longer crippling. She remembered standing beneath the station clock at King's Cross; she remembered her clothes blowing down the street after Serena had thrown her case from the steps – Finlay in the house behind her, overhearing the scene, doing nothing. She thought about replying to his letter and using the word Pudding had used – *worm*. But in the end she simply tore it into two neat halves, tucked it into the bucket of kindling by the fire, and went out after Nancy.

❧ ❧

Clemmie risked a visit to Mrs Tanner. For two hours, she waited in the shade of the Friends' chapel halfway up the hill, sitting on a mossy gravestone, watching Thatch Cottage to be sure Isaac Tanner was not inside. Only when she was certain did she pick her way down to the yard. There were raised voices from within; both were female, but since Clemmie didn't recognise one of them, she lurked beneath a window and waited.

'Well, it's good and ruined now, isn't it? By my reckoning, you owe me a new 'un!' said the voice she didn't know.

'How's it ruined, then, Dot? It'll still keep the rain off you. Working fine, by my reckoning.'

'That'll be the last and final time I lend you a thing, Annie Tanner, make no mistake!'

'Well, then, it'll be the last time I let you pay me in favours,' said Mrs Tanner, calmly. There was some more grumbling, in lower tones, then a skinny woman with brown rats' tails for hair stomped out and marched away towards the lane, carrying a black and white umbrella. Cautiously, Clemmie slipped into the open doorway.

'Clemmie! What in hell are you doing here? Come in, come in,' said Mrs Tanner, looking surprised and confused to see her. 'There's tea just brewed. Dotty didn't stay in the end.' She gave a chuckle, and Clemmie tipped her head curiously. 'Silly mare. She lent me her umbrella and now she says I've spoilt it. We gave it to the old man upstairs to hold while we whitewashed his ceiling – he can't get up, see, and he don't like to be moved. Now it's got a pattern of spots on it and she's not happy.' She gave Clemmie a quick hug then sat her down at the table, her eyes searching. 'Never mind that. What are you *doing* here? Where's Eli?'

Clemmie heaved a wobbling sigh, and since she couldn't say, and the weight of it was so great, she started to cry. She pictured Eli there with her, as he had been the last time; fetching out the special doll for his little brother, and stroking the boy's hair. The thought of him supposing she didn't want to be with him was becoming intolerable. Mrs Tanner watched her carefully for a while. 'Eli's not back with you, then? Did something happen to him?' she said, and Clemmie shook her head. 'That's a mercy – that he's well and that he's away. Isaac's been going wild over him running off – he calls it disloyalty, and he never would stand for that.' For a moment Mrs Tanner's face was heavy, and careworn. 'Best Eli stays away a goodly while yet, and lets the dust settle. The baby – you've still got it?' Clemmie nodded again, and Mrs Tanner patted her hand, relieved. 'So, what then? You've left him?' At this Clemmie's face crumpled. But she had to nod. Mrs Tanner nodded too, and thought for a while. She leaned towards Clemmie and looked her deep in the eyes. 'You love my Eli, don't you?' she said, and Clemmie nodded urgently, grasping at Mrs Tanner's hands. 'Did he raise his hand to you?' she asked, flatly. Clemmie shook her head, and Mrs Tanner thought some more. 'Then... you missed your home too badly?' Sorrowfully, Clemmie nodded, and Mrs Tanner sighed. 'Ar, well. I don't know what he was thinking, trying to take you off to live in the city. What with you as natural as the day you was born.' She shook her head.

They sat for a while with their tea, listening to Eli's grandmother snoring by the stove. She stirred and muttered at a sudden flurry of noise as a knot of children ran in, dodged about, arguing, then ran out again. There was an angry thumping from upstairs, and Mrs Tanner rolled her eyes. 'I shan't bother to answer him; he'll nod off again soon enough,' she said, to nobody in particular. 'Well, Clem, my girl. What's to do?' she said. Clemmie wiped her streaming nose and wet chin on the backs of her hands. 'He'll know where you are, of course, even if you didn't tell him. I hope to God he doesn't come looking for you just yet. Did he have work? Good. That might hold him there a bit. Have you thought about what you'll do?' Clemmie thought for a moment, then nodded. Mrs Tanner studied her serious expression. 'Something's afoot with you, isn't it?' she said. 'By God, if I could feed you a herb that'd bring you to speak, then believe me, I would.' She sighed again and looked away, and Clemmie felt exhausted with everything she was carrying, and all the unspoken words that had been building up; she felt like a dam about to burst; a bridge about to crack. She shut her eyes and concentrated, and as her heart began to thud she gripped the edge of the table, gouging her fingernails into it.

'I,' she said. 'I . . . I . . .' She took another breath, and her tongue stuck to the roof of her dry mouth. 'I . . . Isaac,' she said. Eli's mother stared at her, dumbstruck.

❧ ☙

When Pudding got to the stables the following day, Irene came at once to ask what had happened at the hearing, and then clearly didn't know what else to say. There was nothing *to* say, Pudding supposed. Hilarius came across from the barn, hands in his pockets, when he saw her tying up Bally Girl out on the yard. He nodded as she set about the mare with a dandy brush.

'Good girl,' he said, shortly. ''Tis the only way.'

'Is it?' said Pudding, but she had no stomach for any kind of argument. She had no stomach for anything. Hilarius watched for a long time. When Pudding glanced at him she saw his eyes following her every move, until she couldn't stand it any more. 'What is it, Hilarius?' But the old man simply looked away and worked his jaw behind his closed lips, chewing on whatever he wasn't saying. In the end he took her copy of *Murder Most Foul* from his coat pocket, and handed it back to her.

'Plenty o' truths in there,' he said. 'And all of 'em bitter.'

'Yes, well,' said Pudding, putting the book on the cobwebby window sill of Bally Girl's stable. 'It's a book about violent crime. It would be bitter.'

'You're not looking deep enough, girl,' he muttered.

'I am!' Pudding snapped. 'I did! And I know that whoever killed that girl fifty years ago killed Alistair. But it doesn't do any good because I can't prove it and Donny has been sent to trial and won't be let home . . . and none of it does any *good!*' she cried. Bally Girl turned her head and blew softly at Pudding in consternation.

'It weren't the same person. No,' said Hilarius, with a shake of his head. 'I do doubt that.'

'Well, unless you can tell me more than who it *wasn't*, please . . .' She took a steadying breath. 'Please just leave me alone.'

At lunchtime she couldn't face going into the farmhouse, or going home. At home they were walking on eggshells around one another, waiting to see who would crack first. Her father, who had been turning inwards on himself ever since Donny's arrest, now seemed all but oblivious to the rest of them. Her mother was agitated, even when she couldn't quite remember what was upsetting her. She was clumsy and tearful and Pudding didn't have the wherewithal to soothe her just then. Ruth had been left to hold the household together, which she did by scowling, berating them for moping, and cajoling them through their daily routine. Pudding flip-flopped between resenting her and being grateful to have her there.

'Not all days'll be like these days,' she'd said to Pudding at breakfast that morning.

'No. Some'll be worse,' said Pudding, thinking of the long wait until Donny's trial; the trial and how it was likely to go; Donny being moved to Cornhill Prison in Shepton Mallet, where Thomas Pierrepoint was said to be able to hang a man with such precision that death was instant and painless. Pudding knew that was a good thing, of sorts, but it felt like nothing of the kind.

'Want to just lie down and die, then, do you?' Ruth had said, thrusting out her chin belligerently. 'Then chop-chop and get on with it. Or buck up, and pass me those plates. It ain't over till it's over.'

Swallowing past the ever-present ache in her throat, Pudding wandered away from Manor Farm towards the churchyard. She missed Alistair almost as much as she missed Donny, and knew that if he'd been there he would have got everything sorted out somehow, in his calm and gentle way. Which was ridiculous since, had he been there, Donny would have been too, and there'd be nothing to sort. It had been a long time since she'd been to his grave, and though it wasn't even nearly the same as seeing him, she couldn't think where else to go. She went around to the 1872 headstone that Irene had found, but the forget-me-nots were shrivelled and spread about, their colour quite gone, and they hadn't been renewed. She ran her fingers over the weathered stone, with its pattern of silver and orange lichen, but the inscription was no clearer to her than it had been to Irene. Wearily, she remembered that she hadn't got around to finding out whose grave it was. It didn't seem to matter much, anyway. It wouldn't help Donny, and she had no curiosity left for anything else. Alistair's grave was immaculate and only too fresh in comparison. The turves that had been lain over the mound were crisping at the edges in the sun, and needed watering. Did one water a grave? She could make almost no connection between the sight of it and the memory of the man she'd loved. Alistair seemed a million miles away, somewhere else altogether. She spent a while there, and thought about telling him out loud what was going on, but it seemed every bit as pointless as everything else. She left the churchyard and went down into the village, and only realised where she was going when she was almost there.

She paused for a moment at the gateway to Thatch Cottage. She knew she wasn't welcome there, but somehow she wasn't afraid any more. She couldn't care less, in fact. She wanted them to know that their deeds and their lies had put a noose around Donny's neck, and even if they weren't sorry she could at least hope that it would gnaw at them, somewhere deep inside. Either way, she wanted them to *know*. She regretted it as soon as she stepped into the yard, though. She saw movement behind the cottage, near the outhouse, and a woman's frightened face as she turned and hurried away, and then Tanner himself, glowering blackly at her. Pudding froze in shock. Tanner came striding towards her, his arms loose at his sides, hands curled into fists.

'You,' he said, jabbing a finger at her. Pudding took a step back and thought about running, but that wouldn't do. She was there for Donny, so she stood up straighter and met the man's eye. '*You* brought the police to my door! You and that chit of a thing from up the farm.' He stood close enough for her to feel the heat of his breath, and smell the animal scent of his skin and hair and unwashed clothes.

'Yes, we did. I did,' she said. Her mouth had gone dry but she felt oddly calm.

'We don't talk to the bloody police, here. You send 'em round again and I'll—'

'You'll what? Kill me like you killed Alistair Hadleigh? Like you killed Sarah Martock fifty years ago?' Quick as a flash, Tanner dealt her a slap to the side of her face with the back of his hand; it was light, it barely hurt, and she knew he could have hit her far harder, but the shock of it left her speechless and tears flooded her eyes.

'Watch your bloody tongue, or I'll have it out,' said Tanner, but there was no weight behind the words. They sounded like a habit, and his eyes had gone wide and he had paled, and he seemed startled by something she'd said. He was silent for a moment, his eyes searching the distant trees for something. 'Watch your bloody tongue,' he repeated, quietly this time, almost absently. Pudding wondered if he were drunk again, but for once alcohol wasn't part of his smell.

'Do what you like,' she said, tremulously. 'I know you lied – I know your alibi was a lie! I *know* you killed Alistair! Why – because he was going to sack you from the mill for good? It was no better than you deserved! I saw you asleep in the coal heap, hugging an empty bottle! I saw you! And for *that*, you killed him? Or did he find out something about Sarah Martock? And now you're three times a killer, because they're going to hang my brother for it – did you know that? They've sent him to be tried for wilful murder, and the case is closed, and they'll hang him for it! So I hope you're happy with yourself! I hope you can live with yourself. No – I hope you *can't*!' she cried, and turned on her heel. Tanner caught her arm; she looked back, alarmed, and though her vision was a blur his expression was not what she'd expected. His face was twisted up in some emotion, but it wasn't anger or cruelty; it looked more like pain, and it turned his wrinkled eyes to slits so that only a sliver of blue showed through. 'Let go!' Pudding shouted. 'Let go of me!'

Tanner kept up his grip on her arm and there was no hope of breaking it. In spite of his age he was all bone and sinew; his hands were long and strong.

'I never . . .' he said. He shook his head but didn't finish the sentence, and Pudding thought she saw a glimmer in his eyes. But that couldn't be right. Tanner didn't cry. Tanner was a monster and a drunk, who terrorised his family and everyone he met. And he was a killer. 'Is that true, girl? 'Bout your brother?' he said eventually.

'Of course it's true! Why would anyone make something like that up? I'm surprised you haven't heard – everyone's gossiping about it; everyone has their opinion about it, and none of them seem to care a damn for the fact that Donny didn't *do* it!' She wrenched her arm again and this time Tanner let her go. He was scowling and silent; eyes downcast. 'Get gone,' he said, gruffly. 'And don't come round here again.'

'Why would I want to?' Pudding shouted. 'Why would I want to be *anywhere* near *you*?' And with that she walked away, more slowly than she would have liked but it was hard to see, and she couldn't get her breath for the sobs hitching in her chest. Her arm throbbed where Tanner had held it, and her cheek stung where he'd hit it, and she knew, beyond a shadow of a doubt, that he was the guilty one. *He* was the one who deserved to be punished. The thought sent a tingle right through her. Her footsteps slowed, then stopped.

❧ ☙

Irene stood at the kitchen window and looked out at the woman with the pale, unruly hair, who was waiting by the back gate to the apple orchard. The woman walked slowly away down the hill at one point, but stopped halfway to the church, put her hands on her hips, twitched her head and turned back again, seeming to be in an agony of indecision. When she noticed Irene at the window their eyes locked, and Irene found she couldn't look away. She went out onto the terrace at the back of the house.

'Hello,' she called, and gave a small wave. The woman simply stared, frozen in place, as the warm breeze pushed locks of fluffy hair into her eyes. Irene wondered whether to invite her inside, but her clothes were a mess and she looked half-wild, so she thought better of it. She was just about to go across and try to speak to her when Nancy appeared beside her.

'She's here again, I see,' said Nancy. Irene turned to her.

'You know her? I've seen her outside here before, too.'

'She lives out on one of the farms.' Nancy raised a hand to shield her eyes, and beneath it her mouth was thin and lipless.

'It looks as though she has something she wants to say,' said Irene.

'Oh, she never says anything. She just lurks.'

'What do you think she wants?'

'Who knows?' Nancy dropped her hand and folded her arms, and Irene was wondering whether to call out again when Nancy stepped down from the terrace and walked towards the woman at the gate. She'd gone only three paces, however, when the stranger stiffened, gave Irene one last glance and set off across the field towards the church. Nancy stopped and watched for a while, then returned to the terrace with a grunt. 'See? Odd creature,' she said, and went back inside. Irene waited in case the woman turned back again, but she had soon disappeared behind St Nicholas'.

The day felt odd, to Irene. It had since the moment she'd woken from a frightening dream that had vanished in an instant; as though, again, the world were holding its breath for something – had cut itself and was waiting for the pain. She paced from room to room, seeing nothing amiss, and then retreated into the cool, clammy quiet of her writing room. She'd yet to write a thing in it apart from letters; there was a film of dust on each key of her typewriter, since Florence was too worried about damaging it to clean it. Tense, Irene sat down on the edge of her chair and stared at the fireplace with its brand new marble surround. Then she looked around the room slowly, remembering the way Alistair had wanted her to make it her home. Instead, she had recreated a corner of her parents' house. Nothing looked right – all the expensive things she'd chosen, close together in this one room, looked garish and smug. The opposite of comfortable. She would ask Nancy about swapping a few of her things with others from the house. Her eyes came back to rest on the fireplace, which leaked a steady draught of air that might have been warm when it had entered the chimney pot at the top, but was cool and reeked of smuts by the bottom. Just as Nancy had warned it would. She thought back to the day it was opened – the day Verney Blunt and the young Tanner boy had broken off the boards and let the slew of soot and mess carry a lost, bedraggled doll out into the room.

On a whim, Irene went to fetch the doll from where she'd stowed it, wanting to see it, and perhaps provoke again the feeling it had given her, in case it was any clearer this time. But it had gone from the drawer. She pulled open a few more drawers, in case she'd remembered wrong, though she knew she hadn't, but the doll was not in any of them. Irene went to ask the housekeeper.

'I don't make it my business to take things out o' drawers in the family rooms, Mrs Hadleigh,' Clara told her, stiffly.

'No, I'm not accusing you of anything, Mrs Gosling. I just wondered—'

'Nor Florence, neither. She's a good girl,' said the house-keeper, folding her arms.

'Right you are,' said Irene, retreating. She found Nancy looking through invoices for sheep drench and pig pellets in the corner of the back sitting room where she had her desk. 'I'm sorry to bother you, Nancy, only I've misplaced that old doll we found in the chimney of the schoolroom. I just wondered if you'd seen it anywhere?'

'You've what?' Nancy peered up over her reading glasses, and Irene marvelled that after so many weeks under the same roof, and with the tumult of the emotions they'd survived, she still couldn't read a thing from Nancy's face.

'That doll we found in the chimney. I put it in a drawer up in our room, and now I can't find it.'

'Well,' said Nancy, and blinked. 'I expect Clara put it out with the rubbish, where it belonged.'

'She says not – quite adamantly.'

'Well, gracious, Irene, I'm afraid I haven't a clue,' Nancy said with some asperity. 'Is it terribly important?'

'I suppose not. It's just . . . strange, that's all.'

'I don't know why you wanted to keep it anyway. It was hideous.' Nancy adjusted her glasses and returned to the invoices with such immaculate unconcern that Irene's nameless unease increased.

She was halfway across the yard to see Pudding when she stopped. Old Hilarius was sweeping out the cob house, which was one of Pudding's jobs, and she realised at once that the wrongness of the morning was that Pudding wasn't there. Not even the day of Alistair's death – the day of her brother's arrest – had she not turned up for work. Irene turned and searched the yard, then stared out at the paddocks; all the horses were there, grazing, swishing their tails, not being ridden by Pudding. Anxiously, she suppressed her reluctance and went over to Hilarius, who had stopped sweeping and was watching her with his far-off eyes. The summer had put a deep crimson shine across his hawk's beak of a nose, and turned every other scrap of exposed skin the colour of saddlery.

'Hilarius, has Pudding not come up today?' Irene asked. The old man shook his head but didn't speak. Irene looked around again. 'Well, it's odd, isn't it? I don't like it. There isn't a phone anywhere in the village, is there? I shall have to go up to them. Is Dundee in?' she said.

'Out. Trouble, you reckon? Quicker to walk,' said Hilarius. 'You know the footpath to Spring Cottage, far side of the river?'

'Yes,' said Irene. 'I'll go right away.'

'I'll come along.' Hilarius leant the broom against the wall. 'She wanted to be careful,' he muttered. 'I never said, when I should o' said. She wanted to be *careful*.'

'Pudding ought to have been careful? Careful of what? What's happened?' said Irene, suspiciously, as the old man led her out of the yard, but before he could answer, the creaking of a bicycle chain and the sound of laboured breathing stopped them, and Constable Pete Dempsey pedalled up the hill towards them.

'Mrs Hadleigh,' he gasped, swallowing, fighting for breath. 'I'm looking for Pudding. Is she here?'

'No – we were just going to try to find her. Is she all right? What's happened?'

'I don't know – I don't know where she is, but we have to find her! The most *unbelievable* thing has happened!'

❧ ☙

Clemmie was awake before dawn. She slid out from under the blankets, and tucked Betsy's doll under her arm. It reminded her of Eli, in a strange way – it was the one thing, besides herself, that had been in the place where she still pictured him.

In the quiet dark she ran one hand over her middle, where there was definitely a bump now – a tautening of the skin, the flesh beneath less giving. The baby was growing: safe, well, on its way. Betsy's doll would be its first birthday present, Clemmie decided, and when she thought of that day – the day she would finally hold the piglet – she pictured a roaring fire in Weavern farmhouse; it would be winter, and her mother would be red-faced and clammy from the heat, and she herself red-faced and serene; she imagined the baby's first cries softening towards sleep; her sisters hovering about, and Eli upstairs with her father, waiting, possibly drinking; or out at work on the land, if it came in the daytime. She willed this future into being, as she hurried up the path between the fields, and along Weavern to Germain's Lane.

She had managed to say *Isaac* in front of Mrs Tanner. It might have seemed a small thing to most people, but to Clemmie it was huge. But she worried that even that one word had been too much to give away – or rather that that one particular word had been the wrong one to say to Eli's mother, who loved her son but was married to Isaac, a man who would not tolerate disloyalty. Mrs Tanner had asked many more questions after Clemmie had managed to say it, but none of them had been the right ones, and Clemmie hadn't managed to say another word. She never could when she was upset or afraid – it took focus, and as much calm dissociation as she could muster, when instead she was hounded by the feeling that time was somehow running out. Rose still watched her daily, and her sisters pestered her with their theories and ideas and all their wrong questions, and she knew she needed a peaceful place. So she was going to the mill, to Alistair Hadleigh's empty office, to find it.

The mill was quiet; the first shift hadn't yet started and there was almost nobody about. Two men crossed the yard, their footsteps echoing in the early calm, but they were used to seeing Clemmie and paid her no mind. The air was as still and smooth as deep water; softly grey, neither cold nor warm. She waited outside the old farmhouse until she was sure that the foreman, with his red whiskers, was not inside. However kind he was, she was sure she wouldn't be allowed up to Alistair's office by herself. Satisfied, she crossed from the lee of a storehouse and slipped inside. Up in Mr Hadleigh's room she shut the door behind her, softly.

The office was cool, steady and still. Immediately, Clemmie felt steadier herself. She leant against the door and let the breath run out of her lungs. His desk, his books and papers, his heavy wooden chair, the brass instruments he used to check the paper – all were unchanged by his absence. It was subtly different without him – as though a piece of furniture had been moved out of its normal place and she couldn't put her finger on what had changed. Someone had brought up a bucket of coal for the scuttle, and had left it and a grubby shovel against the wall by the hearth, which would never have happened if Mr Hadleigh had been there. But it was still the room in which, under Alistair's tutelage, she had managed to say more words than anywhere else. At once, she began to remember some of the things he'd made her try – breaking a word into its separate parts and saying each part on its own – in the wrong order, even – rather than trying to run all the sounds together; starting with the second sound a word made rather than the first, if the first wouldn't come; using a rhythm, like in a clapping game, and almost turning the word into a song. She put her back to the window, closed her eyes, imagined Mr Hadleigh there, and got to work.

The sun slid higher, flooding the sky outside with colour, but Clemmie didn't notice. She hummed some sounds, and sang others, and spoke the ones she could. She went through the two phrases of her declaration in her head until she knew them back to front and inside out, and could come at them sideways, surprising her tongue with them. Some were easier than others. *Isaac*, she could say with relative ease, but *heard* refused to take any kind of shape. She could say *Mr Hadleigh* well enough, as long as she left off the H; and she could say *he is the one* almost fluently, as long as she left out *guilty*. Other parts of her statement dodged and darted out of her reach, or tied her up in long minutes of agonised silence, but she persevered, and tried not to let herself get angry, or impatient, or wound up. It was exhausting; she could feel the blood pounding hotly in her face. At one point she realised she had Betsy's doll in a chokehold, her fingers gouging holes in the fabric and disfiguring its face. When she felt despair creeping up on her, and felt it all slipping out of her grasp, she went back to the phrases she had mastered. *Mr Hadleigh. He is the one*. Over and over. Immersed in the sounds and the labour of it, she forgot where she was and didn't notice time pass. And then the office door was flung open without warning, and Clemmie gasped in fright.

10

Two Confessions

Pudding went through to the lock-ups at the back of Chippenham police station with a feeling she couldn't name. Her pulse was ticking in her fingertips, and it didn't feel as though her head were connected properly to her body. Just a few weeks ago – the longest weeks of her life – she'd been there to visit Donny; now she was there to visit Alistair Hadleigh's real killer. A tall man, almost elderly but not quite, was sitting hunched on the narrow bench, just as Donny had sat. He looked up as Pudding came to stand in front of the iron bars that ran from floor to ceiling, caging him, and he was at once familiar and unknowable to her. A strange expression worked across his face, like clouds crossing the sun; it was an expression his face looked ill-built for – like years without practice had left it unsuited to anything so tender. But it vanished again as he stood up, hidden by resentment and well-worn anger lines. Pudding took a step backwards as Eli Tanner came to the bars.

'Have you come to crow?' he said. His breath was stale, his grey hair dirty and his chin furred with whiskers. Pudding swallowed, and shook her head.

'To say thank you,' she said. Tanner was silent, waiting. 'They've . . . they've let my brother go,' she said, still hardly able to believe it. 'He's at home now – Superintendent Blackman brought him in the motor car. Donny thought it was the best fun ever; he had this huge grin on his face by the time they got home . . .' She trailed off, realising she was gabbling. 'Why did you do it?' she said.

'It weren't right, them hanging the lad when he never touched Hadleigh. Why'd he have to go and pick up that shovel, and carry it away? Why'd he have to go and do that, the gormless bugger? I had my alibi all sorted up at the pub... I had 'em convinced I was out of it, so I could slip away and back come morning, and not be seen. The coppers wouldn't 'ave known where to look, till he went in and picked up that bloody shovel. I thought I could let him swing for it, with him being dummel, and half shot-away. But I couldn't. She wouldn't have wanted me to. It was like the kit rabbit I let go for her, back when first we met – it would 'ave been a wrong thing. A wrong killing. I knew it then and I know it now.'

'No – I mean, I understand why you've confessed, and I'm... I'm glad you have. But I meant to ask why you killed Mr Hadleigh in the first place.' Tanner stared at her, hard and unreadable. Pudding waited a good while, but he didn't reply. 'Please, I... I have to know,' she continued, her throat tightening. 'I mean, he was... such a good man. Such a kind man. I'm sure he'd never hurt a soul in his whole life... Was it because you were fired from the mill? Were you... drunk when you did it?'

'That's what folk say, is it?' Eli grabbed the bars angrily, putting his face up close to them. 'That a Tanner'd kill for so small a slight? That *I* would – kill a man that showed me and my family more respect than anyone, because I'd had too much beer? And you believe it, do you?'

'But *why* then?'

'I'll tell you for why!' Tanner yanked at the bars but they didn't budge, so he jolted himself instead. 'He killed the one person I loved more than any other! He killed a girl as innocent as a newborn!'

'What? What girl?' Pudding shook her head. 'Alistair never killed anyone!'

'I did for him same as he did for her. In that old farmhouse, cut down with a shovel.'

'You can't mean...' Pudding's mind ran to catch up. 'You can't mean Sarah Martock, the "Maid of the Mill"?'

'Matlock. Her name was Matlock, not Martock. That weasel from the newspaper wrote it down wrong, then everyone copied his mistake. Sarah was her given name but she weren't ever called that,' said Eli, his voice thick with grief. 'She was called Clemmie.'

'But that was *fifty years* ago!' said Pudding. 'Alistair wasn't even born!'

'My Clemmie. We were to be wed.' Eli wasn't listening to Pudding; he was in the past, looking at a face she couldn't see. 'I only found out about her real name after she died; her mother told me it. To me she was Clemmie, for Clematis – nicknamed after that mad hair of hers; and it did look just like a winter hedgerow, snowy with the stuff. She were that lovely.' The old man shook his head. 'She were that lovely she stole your breath away. I should 'ave come straight after her from Swindon. But I wanted to keep that job, and find some way to fetch her back. If I'd come right after her, it wouldn't 'ave happened.'

Pudding touched his knuckles gingerly to get his attention. Eli's eyes jerked back to her and she flinched.

'Mr Tanner,' she said. 'She died fifty years ago – how can Alistair Hadleigh *possibly* have killed her? It's madness!'

'His father, then! The other Alistair Hadleigh! How else did Betsy's doll wind up hidden in the manor these fifty years? How else? I'd waited half a century for some clue... for something to prove who took her. She'd carried that doll about with her ever since Swindon, her folks said. She was even killed in his room at the mill, but that family were above suspicion. Above everything! She used to go to him to get lessons in speaking, since she was mute. She was in and out of there, all the time. I wish I'd known it then; I could have put a stop to it. But her family and me never spoke till after.' He curled his hands into fists around the bars, turning his knuckles white with the force of it.

'You . . . you killed Alistair to punish his *father*?'

'How else could I take anything from the man? When he took *everything* from me?' Eli shook himself against the bars again; his eyes sparkled, and there was rage and pain in the tears. 'She had our baby in her belly when he did it.'

'Oh, no,' Pudding breathed.

'Only the Hadleighs knew, outside of our families. Rose Matlock went and told 'em, like they'd have helped. But it weren't her fault – she never knew about me and Clem till after. We never told the police – they'd only have painted her a harlot. But it was my baby. My family.'

'Mr Tanner . . . that's so awful. It's so sad.' Tears prickled Pudding's nose, and turned her face hot, but they were for Alistair – her Alistair. 'But you shouldn't have. You shouldn't have! Our Alistair was the best of men. It wasn't his fault, if his father did . . . what you say he did.'

'He did it all right!' said Eli, vehemently. 'As soon as you and the new wife brought that doll down to the cottage, I knew it. All this time I waited . . . long years of strife, just waiting to find out who took that girl from me, then in you two walk, carrying Betsy's doll, I knew I finally had my answer. And I could finally punish the man that hurt her. When you love like that . . . when you're loved like that, it doesn't ever go.'

'But Alistair was innocent!' Pudding blew her nose and stepped back from the bars. She shook her head. 'It wasn't right. Whatever his father did, it wasn't right!' Tanner's face twisted in anger.

'Well, the law'll agree with you, I daresay, so don't you fret.

I'll swing for it soon enough. And I don't mind that so much. Not now I know I've done what I could for Clemmie.' He let go of the bars, shoulders sagging, face sagging. 'Best part of me died with her anyhow. Scant difference it'll make.'

❦ ❧

Irene knew something was wrong as soon as Pudding relayed to her everything Eli Tanner had said. The girl suffered a fresh storm of weeping when she finished speaking, but it was less bitter than it had been; less frightened, more sorrowful. They were sitting either side of a pot of tea at Manor Farm's kitchen table, and Pudding blew her nose wetly into the handkerchief Irene passed her.

'Why are you frowning like that?' she said. Irene shook her head.

'Look . . . something's not right. I think . . . I think Mr Tanner's got it wrong. Well – he must have,' said Irene. Pudding's eyes went wide.

'What? Why? He was adamant – the doll you found belonged to Sarah Martock. Matlock, I mean. Old Alistair used to try to teach her to speak in his office – she was mute, you see – and that's where she was killed . . .'

'Yes, but, Pudding – Alistair's father was in America when she was killed! He was getting married to Alistair's mother. I've seen the marriage certificate. There's no way whatsoever he could have travelled between here and there so quickly. It's impossible,' said Irene. Pudding stared ahead blankly as this sank in.

'Oh, hell and damnation,' she said. 'He *has* got it wrong, then. He's killed Alistair for no reason at all. Oh, *Irene*! It's just too bloody awful!' she cried. Irene nodded, and Pudding put her face in her hands for a moment. 'I know I should be happy because they know Donny didn't do it – and I am happy! And I know nothing could ever have brought Alistair back. But . . . but for it to have happened for *no reason* at all? How can that be fair?'

'It isn't fair,' Irene agreed. She got up and went around to Pudding's side of the table, put her arm around her and squeezed. 'Life isn't, as my mother likes to say. Sadly, it's true,' she said.

'And whoever *did* kill Sarah – Clemmie, Tanner says she was known as – has got off scot-free.'

'It seems so. But, you know, she was killed *fifty* years ago. To have found out the truth now would have been remarkable.'

'But then . . . how on earth did Clemmie's doll get into the chimney here at the farm?'

'I don't know . . .' Irene thought about it. 'Somebody who was working here, perhaps . . . or I suppose anybody could have sneaked in.' She thought of old Hilarius, and felt a thrill all along her spine. But she hunted around for positive things to say. 'At least Donny's home. Your parents must be so happy.'

'They can hardly believe it. Dad, that is,' said Pudding, blowing her nose again. 'Mum carries on as if he never went anywhere. Dad has this look of . . . astonishment on his face. He keeps checking on Donny wherever he is, as though he might just vanish again.'

'And they must all be so grateful to you,' said Irene, smiling at her. 'After all, if you hadn't kept digging at it, the truth might very well have stayed hidden forever.'

'I don't know,' Pudding demurred. 'Perhaps Mr Tanner would have confessed anyway.'

'I'm not so sure.'

'Gosh, what a turn-up,' said Nancy, when Irene told her the news. She wore a strange look, as she always did when discussing anything to do with her nephew's death – tense, distant, almost as though waiting for something. Irene wondered if some part of her were waiting to hear that it was all a mistake and he hadn't been killed at all. Nancy raised a hand to her lips for a moment then let it drop back into her lap, where her withered fingers grasped her other hand, claw-like.

'So . . . we'll have young Donny back at work, of course?' said Irene.

'What? Yes. Yes, of course,' said Nancy.

'Right. I'll let Pudding know,' said Irene. She thought about touching Nancy, since there was something abject in her posture, in the way she sat, so straight and hard that she looked as brittle as glass. But she still wasn't sure enough of herself, or of Nancy.

'Have we any idea *why* Tanner killed my boy?' Nancy asked, in a small voice, as Irene turned to go. Irene paused.

'He . . . it was revenge, it would seem. Served very cold. He's convinced that . . . your brother, Alistair's father, killed Sarah Matlock, who was his sweetheart. His betrothed, really, but it was all secret. They'd planned to wed, and she was carrying his child when she died.'

'*His* child?' said Nancy. She looked bewildered, her eyes searching for something in the corners of the room but not finding it. 'No,' she said, quietly.

'I know. It couldn't possibly have been him – you were all in New York, for the wedding,' said Irene. Nancy blinked, and nodded. She opened her mouth but didn't speak at first.

'Foolish,' she said, eventually.

'Well,' said Irene. 'Shall I get you some tea, Nancy?'

'Oh, no,' said Nancy, her eyes still so veiled that Irene couldn't tell if she was refusing the tea, or something else altogether.

She went into the kitchen to put the kettle on, more for something to do than out of any real desire for it. Something was still pestering the hindquarters of her brain, preventing her from feeling any satisfaction at all at the real killer being brought to light; at having got justice for her husband. It wasn't done yet, she knew. There were missing pieces. She was staring out of the window at the sun-drenched fields of daisies and dandelions when she saw a familiar figure at the orchard gate – the same woman she'd seen several times before, dressed like a peasant, surrounded by a long mass of frizzy hair gone white with age. Irene took the kettle off the stove and went straight out to her, and they met in the shade of an apple tree older than both of them put together.

'Hello, I'm Irene Hadleigh,' she said. The old woman nodded.

'I know that. I'm Rose Matlock,' she said, in a voice as thin as winter sun.

'Matlock?' Irene lit upon the name. Rose nodded.

'Clemmie's ma.'

'You've been trying to come and talk to me for a while, haven't you? Did you know that . . . that Eli Tanner had killed my husband?' she asked. Rose nodded. Through her hair, her scalp showed pinkly; as pink as the rims of her pouched eyes, and the gaps in her gums when she spoke.

'I don't blame Eli, mind, and I were willing to let it lie till they took that boy for it instead.'

'You'd have let Eli Tanner get away with it?' said Irene. Rose's face hardened.

''Bout time my girl had some justice. An eye for an eye.'

'But my husband didn't kill her!'

'Blood's blood,' said Rose, darkly.

'His father didn't, either. Mr Tanner got it wrong – Alistair senior was in America when it happened, getting married. All the Hadleighs were. He couldn't have killed your daughter.'

'We'll see,' said the old woman, and Irene wondered if her

wits were quite intact. 'What else was Eli supposed to do? Ever since you showed him that doll he's set about falling apart all over again.'

'It was her grave he was visiting when I saw him in the churchyard, wasn't it? I saw him crying, and he'd taken flowers.'

'He loved my Clem like breath, though I only found it out after she was killed.'

'Why was that?'

'Well, she couldn't tell us – she might not've even if she could. Thought we'd never accept him, they did – especially Clemmie's dad – what with him being a Tanner.' She shook her head sadly. 'Maybe they was right about that, but if he'd only got around to wedding her, we'd have taken them in, and the baby, all three. William would have come around in the end. But there was other trouble with the Tanners that summer – a robbery at the mill, and the office boy bludgeoned near to death when he stumbled upon it. He lay in a stupor for weeks afterwards, and the police arrested some pedlar who happened to be passing. Had to let him go again, o' course, since he weren't to blame. Isaac had bought himself an alibi but folk knew who to blame – near as good as evading the law as they are at breaking it, that family. Old Isaac was the devil himself, and he'd just been laid off from the mill again. And I suspect he'd made Eli go along with him. Eli tried taking Clem off to Swindon to start over, but she had her roots in this land and came back without him.' Rose fell silent for a moment. 'People pointed their fingers at the Tanners for murdering her, but seventeen strappers saw Isaac sleeping it off in Obby Hancock's hay barn at the time, and Eli was in Swindon. Not that he'd have harmed a hair on her head. We never did know who done it, till you found that doll Betsy gave her. She was never without it after she was back from Swindon. We guessed she'd had it with her when she died, but we never found it. Till now.'

Irene caught the old woman's scent, hanging around her. Milk and cow manure, unwashed clothes and carbolic soap. Her hands, though gnarled, were spotlessly clean.

'You live out on one of the farms, Nancy told me?' she said. Rose nodded.

'Weavern. My eldest, Mary, has it now, with her husband, Norman. My William's long dead – a seizure took him not long after Clemmie went. Her death broke what was left of his heart after our little Walter. He was killed when Rag Mill's boiler blew up,' she said. 'So many have gone on before me, but I weather on. Not many folks my age can still climb these hills, and I can still help with the milking,' she said, with a touch of grim pride. 'I've been on that farm since I was a girl of seventeen, and I'll leave it in my coffin, whenever that day may come. They left it a sad place for me, though, my Walter, and my Clemmie, and Will.'

'Why did you want to talk to me, then, if you weren't going to give Tanner away?' said Irene. Rose thought before she answered. The breeze fluttered her worn-out blouse against her ribs, and Irene saw how thin she was, how frail. 'Would you like to come inside, and sit down?' she said, but Rose shook her head at once.

'I'll not set foot in that house again,' she said. 'I mean no offence, I'm sure, ma'am. Thing was, folk used to say my Clemmie was touched. They thought she was slow, because she was silent, and some folk treated her like she was worth less because of it. And she only half belonged to us, it's true – half to us, half to the birds and bees. But she was right as rain, truly, just different to the rest – just like the doctor's boy. They were quick enough to believe he'd done it, because he's different to the rest of them. People can be as vicious as rats in a nest, eating their weakest.' She shook her head. 'My Clemmie would have burned with the injustice of it. I came up here because I wanted to say it weren't him. But I couldn't say who it weren't without sayin' who it *were*, see. So.' She shrugged. 'Eli came to see me when you found that doll. Told me what it meant, and what he would do. Since they took the doctor's boy off, I've been working on his conscience to come clean.'

'You . . . you *knew* Tanner planned to kill Alistair? And you told nobody?' Irene went cold.

'Ar. Tell that to the police and you'll find my wits quite scattered by my very great age,' said Rose, curtly. 'Blood for blood. A lot of things got broken the day she died, Eli Tanner's heart not the least of them. He'd waited long enough to make a body pay for that.'

'But the *wrong* body. The *wrong* man. A good and blameless man!' Irene cried. She found her eyes stinging with tears of outrage, and wiped them away with her fingers. 'Why come now and tell me any of this? It changes nothing, after all,' she said. Rose Matlock nodded slowly.

'I wanted you to understand. I'm sorry for your loss. It's all of it a pity, and a black stain on each of us. In some folk, grief is like a slow poison; I hope it won't be so for you. But I wanted you to see, Eli had no choice. Somebody had to pay.'

'Yes! But it ought to have been the *right* person.' Irene was suddenly angry at the skin and bones woman in front of her, with her flawed logic and her defensive stare. Alistair's death had been as entirely futile as Pudding had declared it, and the unfairness of that was staggering.

'I'm sorry for your loss,' Rose said again, nodding as if Irene had agreed with everything she'd been told. 'But the real crime happened before you were even born, ma'am. In time, you might come to see it.'

❧ ❧

Ma Tanner sat in her carver chair and flexed her hands around the armrests. Her eyes were on the old man, asleep in his truckle bed against the far wall. Pudding sat awkwardly, her hands clasped around a cup of tea she was loath to drink. It smelled of mouldy hay, and the cup had a crust of grime around its rim.

'Isaac Tanner, you're the fount of so much grief,' said Ma, at last. Pudding followed her gaze to the old man, whose face was so slack and grey in sleep he looked like a corpse. 'That man there. Do you know why I married him?' she asked. Pudding shook her head. 'Because I was *frightened* of him. What a way to start out a life together. What a way to bring a clutch of babies into the world! He fancied the looks of me, and I was too scared of him to turn him down.' She shook her head. 'We wed when I fell pregnant. I figured he might change. Ha! What a fool. Figured having littl'uns about would soften him, I did.'

'Oh,' said Pudding, uncomfortably.

'He only ever got worse. Not his fault, you understand?' Ma switched her stern eyes back to Pudding. 'His own father brutalised him, and sent him out into the world thinking that was the only way to be. Why I should be surprised that he then brutalised his own, I don't know. Why I should be surprised that Eli . . .' She paused, shutting her eyes for a moment. 'Why I should be surprised that my soft Eli should end up swinging for murder, I don't know.' She opened her eyes with a snap. 'He had a *chance*, he did! He *loved* that girl from Weavern! He'd got away from Isaac . . . They had a chance, the two of them.'

Pudding took a sip of the tea for something to do, and, sure enough, wished she hadn't. She tried to think of Eli Tanner as *soft*, but couldn't. He was a figure of evil legend, and she'd been afraid of him all her life. She wasn't sure why she'd come back to Thatch Cottage, other than because of a vague sense that she had somehow contributed to the chain of events that had led Ma Tanner to lose her son, and the agonising thought that it had been for nothing.

'Eli's ... been very brave, in turning himself in,' she said, then cursed herself silently for reminding Ma what would soon happen to her son. The old woman sighed, and looked pained.

'Loyalty,' she muttered. 'In a family like this, if you can't count on that from each other, what can you count on? I would never have uttered a word against my boy, no matter what I knew.'

'I understand,' said Pudding, biting down her anger on Donny's behalf. But Ma Tanner saw it.

'The way you feel about your brother, child, is how I feel about my Eli,' she said, pointedly. Pudding refrained from saying that Donny hadn't killed anybody. She didn't count the war; she refused to think about the war.

'You know he's wrong about Alistair's father being the one to kill Clemmie, though, don't you?' she said, cautiously. Ma Tanner was staring at Isaac's denuded figure again.

'He done the robbery at the mill that summer, and was never fingered for it. Not long before Clem was killed. Made Eli and John go with him; made them guilty too.'

'There was a robbery?'

'He'd been fired from the mill — been on the bottle again, he had. We were that hard-up, that year ... I thought we'd starve come winter, I did, and the bairns along with us. He took the boys and went down to rob the wages from the mill — and rob it they did — but one of the office boys was there, working late. Isaac gave him such a blow on the head he damn near killed the kid. He lay in a stupor for such a long while, and I held my breath the whole time, waiting for him to die. Waiting for Isaac to have made murderers of my boys.' Ma sighed again. 'He came to, eventually, thank God, but it was the last straw for Eli, I think. The violence of it; the shadow of the noose. That finally gave him the strength to get away from his father. That, and the chance Clemmie gave him. A chance of something better.'

'Why didn't they just get married? And move away?' said Pudding. Ma shrugged one shoulder.

'I suppose they couldn't without telling her folks. They hadn't a coin between them. And Clemmie wasn't like the rest – she needed to be here. She needed her farm, and her family. Besides, you don't know the . . . the *hold* a person can have on you, if you're scared o' them. Once you're proper scared o' them, they've a hold on you it's fiendish hard to break. But Eli was doing it . . . he might have done it for good, if Clemmie hadn't been killed. After it, he got more and more like Isaac with every day that passed. After it, he was in ruins.'

They sat in silence for a while, and Pudding raised her cup to her lips, remembering just in time not to drink. The injustice, and the pointlessness, of Alistair's death was like a dreadful ache that she couldn't ignore. She knew she shouldn't say anything else about it, but she also couldn't quite bring herself to leave until she had.

'Still,' she said. 'Poor Mr Hadleigh—'

'Poor Mr Hadleigh indeed,' Ma Tanner interrupted her. 'Lord knows, he were a good sort. But he got caught up in something bigger and older than himself.'

'But he wasn't caught up at all! It was nothing to do with him – not if his father wasn't the original killer!'

'Is that so,' said Ma, cryptically. Eli's wife, Trish, came in, carrying a heavy sack that she let thump to the floor inside the door. She straightened to stretch her back. At the noise, Isaac Tanner opened his rheumy blue eyes and glared at her. Pinch-faced, she glared right back.

'All right, Annie,' she greeted Ma, wearily. 'I got a good price on 'em.' When her eyes adjusted and she saw Pudding,

Trish Tanner stopped, and stared. Her expression was openly hostile, and Pudding shrank from it.

'Well done. Go on out and see that the sow hasn't rolled on any more of the littl'uns, will you?' Ma said. Trish folded her arms and puckered her mouth, but obeyed without a word. 'She don't like any mention of Clemmie,' Ma explained, when she'd gone. 'God help the woman, but she only went and fell in love with Eli. He married her just for the sake of it, though, and she knows it. He never stopped loving Clem, and she knows that too.'

'Ma, what did you mean by "is that so"? There's no question as to where Alistair's father was at the time.'

'No, there ain't,' Ma agreed.

'What then?' she pressed. Ma studied her calmly, as though weighing up what to say, and what not to say. Just as she always had before.

'Spoken to that old tinker, Hilarius, have you?' she said, in the end.

'Yes. Well, no – I don't know. What about?'

'He owes the Hadleighs his whole life, you know. They took him in when he was a tiddler, and his folks had died – they were tinkers, travelling folk, and they froze out in the snow one night when no one round here would take 'em in. That was a fierce winter, and no mistake. Not that the Hadleighs raised him as one of their own, but they fed him and kept him warm, and gave him work. He was about five when he came here, I think, and he never left.'

'You can't mean...' Pudding was astonished. 'You can't mean that he's "the snow child", from my murder book?' She felt as though she'd just seen a paper bird flap its wings, and take flight. Ma Tanner shrugged. 'In my book, *Murder Most Foul*, in the story of "The Snow Child" ... It says the family went from door to door asking for shelter, and that everyone who turned them away was partly guilty of murder. His mother and father died on either side of him and his sister. They died trying to keep the children warm.'

'As foul a thing as any these parts have known, and the whole village has carried the guilt of it ever since. Folks has never warmed to him, have they? Expecting him to hate them, you see. Expecting him to take revenge on 'em somehow. Feeling that they deserve as much.' Ma shook her head. 'I was six, the year it happened, but I remember it. They came here, see. We turned them away, same as everyone. We had no space, no food, no wood to burn. My grandmother died that same winter, for want of hot food. We heard them knocking and we didn't even open the door – didn't want to let the cold air in. So we're as guilty as all the rest.'

'But they must have tried at Manor Farm as well. And been turned away. Did the Hadleighs feel guilty – is that why they took the boy in afterwards?'

'Who knows? But he's loyal to that family, make no mistake on it. He owes them what life he's had, and he'd not speak out willingly. Not unless you ask him the right questions. But he'll not lie – have you noticed that? He says little enough, but what he does say, he means, and it's always the truth.'

'What questions? What should I ask?' said Pudding, still befuddled by the incredible thing she'd been told. Annie Tanner settled back into her chair, staring resentfully at her bedridden husband, and Pudding thought it through. 'Irene has never warmed to him, you know. To Hilarius,' she said, in the end. 'She says she can see a darkness around him, or something like that. A shadow – something unnatural.' At this, Annie's eyes came sharply into focus. 'He read about Clemmie's death in my murder book, when I left it up in the tack room, and he asked to read it a second time, and yet he never said a word about the two murders being the same. He must have realised it though, surely? He was here in Slaughterford for both of them, after all,' she said.

'Sounds to me as that city girl has a touch o' the sight,' said Ma, and then wouldn't say another word about it.

❧ ❦

They found Hilarius applying a poultice to the hoof of one of the shires. It had pierced the sole of its foot on a sharp stone; a stinking puddle of black pus, which Hilarius had drained from the abscess, was on the cobbles, and the horse had a shiver to its skin and sweat on its shoulders. Irene blenched at the smell, and held her nose. She drew breath to speak but Pudding took her arm, and shook her head. They waited until the sticky dressing – kaolin clay, ash, certain herbs – was bandaged tight to the hoof, and Hilarius had let go of the horse's leg and straightened up. The shire rested its toe gingerly on the ground, and looked miserable.

'Will she be all right?' said Pudding, as Hilarius wiped his hands on a rag and kicked straw over the pus, on which flies were attempting to land. He shrugged with his eyebrows.

'If the fever is less by tomorrow, we'll know.'

'Could we perhaps go outside?' said Irene, still struggling with the stench. Once they were in sunshine and relative fresh air, Irene looked at Pudding, and Pudding looked at Irene, and the old man looked at both of them.

'Out with it,' he said, gruffly.

'Hilarius,' Pudding began, 'I went to see Ma Tanner.'

'Ar. And how is the hag?' he said, without rancour.

'Well enough. Upset about her son, of course,' said Pudding. 'Angry with her husband.' Hilarius nodded.

'Isaac Tanner were a scourge, back when he had the strength to be.'

'Yes. Well. She told me . . . she told me how you came to be here at Manor Farm, Hilarius. Your story is in my murder book, isn't it? Is that what you meant when you said there were plenty of truths in it?'

Hilarius fiddled with some clay on his fingers, frowning down at them, and Irene realised that the darkness she had always sensed around him had indeed been the shadow of death – the deaths of his parents and his sister, who died with their arms clamped tight around him, bodies pressing in, hardening as they froze. How could such a thing not leave a stain? And he had been inside Manor Farm – the morning afterwards, when he was found and brought into the warm. 'Do you . . . do you remember your parents?' Pudding asked, her fascination for the story getting the better of her.

'Pudding,' Irene checked her. She felt strongly that the old man's grief ought not to be touched.

'Not a lot,' said Hilarius, still not looking at them. 'My sister's name was Ilsa, and she had hair the colour of a copper pan. I remember the night they all died. The wind was a shriek, and full o' knives, but I felt warm.' He fell silent, though Pudding's face was rapt, and she would clearly have loved to hear more.

'It must be terrible to think about,' said Irene, to head Pudding off. 'Ma Tanner said something else, in fact,' she said, and Pudding nodded.

'Yes. She told me . . . how loyal to the Hadleighs you are,' she said, at which Hilarius's head came up, and unease filled his narrow eyes. 'She told me how they took you in, and that you owed them an awful lot, and wouldn't betray them willingly.' In the pause chickens hectored one another, and the mill rumbled. When it became clear that Hilarius wasn't going to elucidate, Irene took a breath.

'There's still a mystery, you see, about how the girl's doll came to be hidden here at the farm – Sarah Matlock's doll. Her family are sure she had it with her when she was killed, and Eli Tanner recognised it at once, when he saw it. *Somebody* put it up the chimney in the schoolroom, but it can't have been Alistair senior, whatever Eli thinks. The Hadleighs were all away at his wedding when it happened.' Irene waited, and Pudding fidgeted, but Hilarius still said nothing.

'Hilarius, do you know?' Pudding burst out. 'Ma said I'd have to ask you the right questions . . . Do you know who hid it in the chimney?'

'No. I don't *know*,' said the old man, and Pudding deflated.

'But you suspect?' said Irene, and got no reply. 'Was it you?' she pressed, to more silence. Pudding chewed her lip, and Irene felt the nagging threads of something, just out of her grasp.

'The day Alistair died, you said to me that he had gone a long way towards lighting the darkness here, or something like that,' said Pudding. She glanced apologetically at Irene. 'I only just remembered,' she said. 'What did you mean, Hilarius?' There was a long pause.

'You got to be certain o' what you think is fact,' said the old man, at last. He shook his head, and turned to go.

'What does that mean?' said Pudding.

'Which part have we got wrong?' said Irene, catching on. Hilarius glanced back, and gave her a shrewd nod.

'Think along them lines.'

Pudding heaved a frustrated sigh, but Irene held up a hand to forestall her. She raked back through everything they had just said, looking for a fact that might be wrong. And then she thought of the unseasonal fire she'd found, smouldering in the grate in the back sitting room, weeks ago, before Alistair had died – the overheated fug in the room, and the tantalising scraps of blue in the ashes. Blue, like the dress Clemmie's doll had worn. The empty drawer where she knew she'd stowed it. She gave Pudding a startled look, and turned at once for the house.

'What is it, Irene?' Pudding called, hurrying after her. Irene went straight to Alistair's study, where his parents' wedding photo hung on the wall, framed in ebony, overshadowed by the vast family portraits. She stared at it, then took it off its nail and over to the window for more light. 'What is it?' Pudding repeated, but Irene didn't answer her until she was sure. She handed the photograph to Pudding.

'Look. It's Alistair's parents' wedding party. Alistair and Tabitha's wedding party. The whole wedding party, in New York, in July 1872.' Pudding stared at it for a moment – the old-fashioned bouffant hairstyles, the tailcoats and hooped skirts and corsets.

'So what? What should I see?' she said.

'Where's Nancy?' said Irene. Pudding frowned and looked again. She tipped the photo to the light. The moment stretched, the air seemed to grow heavy. Then she looked up at Irene, bewildered.

'She's not there.'

'She's not there,' Irene echoed. 'Come on.'

They went back out to the yard and found Hilarius simply standing in the barn, as if he'd been waiting for them to return. His arms were loose at his sides, his face hung sadly, and he seemed awkward, as though he didn't know what to do or how to behave. He nodded as they approached.

'Hilarius ... did Nancy go to her brother's wedding, back in 1872?' asked Irene. Hilarius took a deep, slow breath and let it go, and Irene thought she saw relief in his eyes.

'Couldn't stand to,' he replied, shortly. 'Said somebody needed to stop here and oversee, but the truth of it were, she couldn't bear to watch.' Irene remembered the hints Cora

McKinley had dropped, about Nancy being all *too* close to her twin brother.

'Do you remember when the fireplace in the old schoolroom was blocked up? Was it that summer?' she asked. Hilarius gave a single nod, his unhappiness and reluctance all too plain. Pudding had gone silent and still, and Irene had to remind herself that the girl had known – and respected – Nancy Hadleigh all her life. She steeled herself, dry-mouthed and recoiling already from what she knew was coming. 'Hilarius, did Nancy ask for the fireplace to be blocked up?' she said.

'Who else?' he said.

'Did you . . . see her, the day Clemmie Matlock was killed? Did you see anything . . . untoward?' Hilarius stared at Irene for a long time, until she understood how long he had known, and how heavy the knowledge had been, and yet how loath he was to give it up now. Then he nodded.

❧ ❦

Alistair Hadleigh's office door banged against the wood panelling as it opened, and Clemmie jumped around in fright. Nancy Hadleigh's face was ashy white, and the red patches on her cheeks looked too bright in comparison; her dark hair shone in its elaborate braids. She slammed the door behind her, walked three smart paces into the room, kicking up her hem, then stopped in front of Clemmie with her fists at her sides. Clemmie stayed still, rooted by shock.

'You . . . you *thief*!' Nancy hissed at her. Clemmie shook her head, confused by the accusation. 'I heard you – I *heard* what you're trying to say! All this time he's been teaching you to talk, out of goodness, and yet you'll use your first words to defame him, will you? Is that gratitude, you wretch?' She swept her eyes over Clemmie, curling her lip in disgust as she took in the curve of her midriff, and the doll clasped in her hands. 'How dare you?' she ground out, through her teeth. 'You little trollop, how *dare* you?' Clemmie didn't understand what she was being accused of; she didn't have the words to defend herself. She tried to dodge around Nancy and get away, but Alistair's sister stepped in front of her. She was slight, but her body was hard with anger. She put her face too close to Clemmie's as she spoke. 'He's been ... he's lain with you, I know. You aren't the only one – don't go fooling yourself that he loves you!' Clemmie shook her head. 'You won't get a thing from us for that bastard you're carrying – I won't let you ruin this for him. For us. I won't *let* you, do you understand? I demand your word you won't name him. I want your word!' she snapped.

Horrified by Nancy's inexplicable rage, Clemmie whimpered, twisting on the spot. Then she took flight, barging past Nancy and sending her reeling back, making for the door. Nancy made an incoherent sound of fury. Clemmie had the door knob in her grasp. Her hands were shaking so badly that she couldn't turn it far enough; she yanked at it but the door wouldn't open. Then a fire blazed through her head, and the world turned itself upside down; she had the taste of the woollen rug on her lips, the smell of iron in her nose, and a stabbing pain inside her that made her more afraid than she had ever been. *Eli, come to get me!* she thought, wildly, desperately. Then she sank down into darkness.

❧ ☙

Irene requested a tea tray from Clara and took Pudding into her writing room – the old schoolroom – to think before they acted. She spoke a great deal, but Pudding took in very little of it. Paper birds were taking flight again – stories from books were coming to life; the ground was made of clouds and the sky of stone. She didn't know what to do, or say, or think; she didn't trust her own memories any more, or any of the things she thought she knew. It felt as though someone had picked up her brain and shaken it until nothing was in its right place. She was profoundly grateful to have Irene there, who seemed to have gone very calm – though it might have been shock. Pudding hoped she would eventually tell her what they should do, because she herself had no clue.

'Well, what do you think?' said Irene, looking right at her with those smudged, dark eyes.

'What?' said Pudding, helplessly. Irene blinked.

'Right. Pudding, I think you should go home. Go home, and I'll ... I'll talk to Nancy myself,' she said. 'There's really no need for you to be ... involved.'

'No,' said Pudding, stirring herself. Part of her wanted nothing more than to go home and be hugged by her father, to see her mother's vague smile, and Donny waiting patiently at the table for his tea. But in spite of that she knew she couldn't go until things were finished. 'I'll stay,' she said, after thinking for a time. 'You might ... you might need me.'

Irene nodded.

'The footprint they found in the blood, in 1872 – the footprint in Clemmie's blood,' said Pudding, muzzily.

'What about it?'

'They discounted it as a clue. Pete said they decided it couldn't be a footprint because it was too small,' said Pudding. They both went silent for a while, picturing Nancy's tiny feet.

Nancy wasn't anywhere in the house, and without needing to think Irene led Pudding out of the farm, and down across the field to the churchyard. There they found her, sitting on the bench all dressed in black, staring at the grave plot that contained her parents, her brother and her nephew. She didn't look up as they approached, and they stood awkwardly in front of her, blocking her view. Nancy's face was closed off; her mouth was a straight line, cheeks hollow, hands clasped in her lap.

'There's really nothing you can tell me that I don't already know,' she said, stiffly. Pudding stared at her and tried to believe what she was having to – that Nancy had killed Clemmie Matlock, fifty years before. It was unreal. It was berserk.

'Berserk,' she said, then bit her tongue to keep quiet.

'Yes,' said Nancy. 'I suppose I was a bit, that summer.' Now she looked up at Pudding, her eyes crystalline. 'You of all people ought to understand, Pudding,' she said.

'Me?' said Pudding, shocked. 'Why me?'

'You'd do anything for that brother of yours. Well, so would I have.' She looked away. 'So I did,' she said, more quietly.

'But why, Nancy? Why on earth did you do such a thing?' said Irene. For a long time, Nancy didn't reply. Her eyes, her face, were blank.

'She was going to ruin everything. Tabitha was devout. Everything depended on the marriage – our whole life here depended on it. Everything!'

'You thought Clemmie's baby was your brother's? And that would jeopardise his marriage?' said Irene.

'But it wasn't!' Pudding cried. 'It was Eli Tanner's baby! They were going to get married.' Again, Nancy said nothing. Irene shook her head.

'I don't understand,' she said. 'The wedding was already going ahead – it had already gone ahead, two days before. There was no way Tabitha could have found out about any . . . indiscretion . . . beforehand, and called it off.'

'It would have made things difficult,' said Nancy, tonelessly. 'I did what I had to do to keep my family together. To keep our good name. As I have always done.'

'You can't be talking about the bloody Hadleigh standard, surely?' Irene shook her head again, thinking hard. 'No. It wasn't that, was it? What could possibly have made you angry enough with her to kill her?'

A soft breeze tugged at them, and made the flowers on Alistair's grave bob their heads prettily. Nancy gritted her teeth, working the muscles beneath the skin at the corners of her jaw. Otherwise, she didn't react. Pudding felt at a complete loss.

'No,' said Irene again, her eyes locked on Nancy, her face tense as she thought it through, and worked it out. 'It was Alistair you were angry with, wasn't it? It was *him*, not her. You were angry with your brother for getting married, and leaving you.'

'He had no choice,' said Nancy, stonily. 'Her money was the only thing that could keep us here.'

'Because *he* had gambled it all away!' said Irene. 'It was all his fault. But you couldn't take it out on him. You loved him too much. You had to move away when Tabitha came here, didn't you? Was that one of her conditions, or could you just not stand to be around them – around her?' Nancy showed no sign of having heard. Irene fell silent for a while, a frown of concentration putting a crease between her eyebrows. 'Were you . . . were you *jealous* of Clemmie? When you thought she and your brother had . . .' At this, Nancy's head turned sharply.

'Don't be *disgusting*!' she said

'Is that why you took the doll? I can't work out why you'd do that – take something so incriminating from her. But perhaps it was a symbol of . . . of . . . I don't know.' Irene thought again. 'A symbol of the child she carried? Or rather, the one you thought she was carrying? A symbol of your brother's child?' Irene was relentless, and Pudding began to feel exhausted. So tired she might be sick, or just lie down there, on the grass. But no – she didn't want to be near Nancy. She wanted to be nowhere near her.

'Let's just go, Irene,' she mumbled, but Irene didn't seem to hear her.

'That dumb wretch,' said Nancy, quietly. 'Why should she have had anything of his?' And then she shuddered, as if the warm breeze had turned suddenly chill. After it she seemed somehow smaller than before, and less alive.

Pudding took Irene's arm, and tried to tug her away.

'Let's just go,' she said again. Irene looked round at her, and nodded. They turned to leave, but Nancy's voice called them back.

'Well,' she said, her glass edges beginning to fracture, giving them a glimpse of the fear inside her. 'What will you do?'

'Hilarius saw you come back from the mill, carrying the doll and with your clothes all bloodied. He heard you telling the laundress the dogs had killed a sheep. He remembers you asking that the schoolroom chimney be boarded up, with the doll inside it,' Irene told her.

'What doll?'

'I saw it, before you burned it. Several Tanners did too; Verney Blunt, and Pudding here. And I saw the remains of it in the grate.'

'Hilarius won't testify against me. It'd be cruel of you to ask him,' said Nancy, and her voice sounded different, not like her at all. Pudding had never heard her sound uncertain before – not once. 'And nobody would believe anything a Tanner had to say.'

'I'm not so sure about that. Superintendent Blackman isn't as ready as everybody else to denounce the Tanners.'

'You can't be serious, Irene?' said Nancy. She'd tried to sound scathing, Pudding guessed, but merely sounded panicked. 'After fifty years? Don't be *absurd.*'

'You don't think you ought to be punished, Nancy? For killing an innocent girl?' said Irene. Nancy seamed her lips tight together and turned away, back to her silent study of Alistair's grave. 'But then . . .' Irene went on. 'What you did back then has led *directly* to your nephew being killed now. I hope you realise that. Blood is blood, as Rose Matlock said to me. I think perhaps she guessed the truth; and Ma Tanner as well. So perhaps Eli Tanner has got his vengeance for Clemmie after all – in making you responsible for the death of the one person you loved most in all the world.' Before they turned to go, Pudding saw the realisation of this truth hit Nancy Hadleigh. She slumped bonelessly, her rigid posture failing her; her chin dropped onto her chest and her hands came up to cover her face. She looked so unlike herself that with little effort, Pudding could imagine her to be a different person altogether to the one she'd known.

II

Beginnings

In the cool of early morning, Pudding put the kettle on to boil. It *was* cool – the night air had dropped several degrees in the past few days. It was nearly September, and the long summer was finally running out of steam. The kitchen tiles beneath her bare feet were on the verge of being chilly. Pudding went to the back door of Spring Cottage and looked out across the valley, to where Manor Farm was visible through a slight mist on the opposite hill. The fields were golden now – even the pasture. Thistles had turned brown and frizzled; the dandelions were all clocks; the lambs were almost the same size as their parents, and too busy eating to gambol any more. There were crisp brown edges on the horse chestnut leaves. The kettle hissed; Dr Cartwright came out of the privy at the bottom of the garden and looked at his watch; upstairs, Pudding could hear her mother moving about, getting dressed. And Donny was weeding the vegetable patch, where the last of the beans were turning thick and stringy and the lettuces had bolted. He'd been helping Louise with it more, since coming back from the New Bridewell. He didn't like going to the mill any more, and spent more time at home.

'Pudding – how did you sleep?' said her father, putting a kiss on her cheek.

'Well, thank you,' she said. 'Cup of tea?'

'No time, I fear. I said I'd call on Mr Long first thing, and he's a very early riser.' Since Donny had been cleared and sent home, the doctor had more patients again. As though some taint had been removed from him, and people felt sheepish for having believed in Donny's guilt. He picked up his bag from its spot by the door, patted a pocket for his spectacles and gave her a smile. 'Cheerio; I'll be back for lunch.'

By the time Louise came downstairs, anxiously fingering the buttons of her cardigan, Pudding had got breakfast on the table, and she and Donny were tucking in.

'I'm awfully sorry I'm late,' said Louise.

'It doesn't matter at all, Mum,' said Pudding. Donny had muddy fingernails, and was licking marmalade off them; the dent in his head was as hideous as ever and he was having nightmares again, but he was home. Louise had more days when she was confused, to some degree, than days when she was not. The horrible notion that she was slipping further and further inside herself, out of their reach, was ever-present. But the four of them were together again, and were going to remain together. Knowing that, Pudding found, made the rest of it seem surmountable. As she set off down the hill to work, with Donny walking calmly at her side, Pudding wondered how many more times she would make the journey. Irene Hadleigh had put Nancy and Alistair's horses, Bally Girl and Baron, up for sale, and ancient Tufty was unlikely to last out another winter, which only left Dundee and Robin – hardly enough work for a full-time girl groom.

'What'll you be doing today, Donny?' she asked. Her brother frowned, trying to remember.

'Cutting the grass in the orchard,' he said at last, and Pudding smiled.

'Your favourite,' she said. Donny nodded. He liked the visible results, the neat lines he created, pushing the mower up and down in stripes. Donny had a job for life at the farm, Irene had said, but if she didn't stay on there herself, what then? And if Pudding didn't stay on either, where would she go instead? Things were very different to before. The mill looked the same; Manor Farm looked the same, as did the village and the yard and Spring Cottage. But they weren't the same. Everything had changed, and Pudding didn't know if she could carry on there, confronted at every turn by memories, and the echoes of her previous, more innocent life. She put her shoulders back and her chin up. She certainly wouldn't be going off to any secretarial college, or leaving her family, so whatever came next, she would just have to get on with it.

When the horses were done and the stables clean, Pudding hitched Dundee to the Stanhope and Irene came across from the house, pulling on leather gloves, still looking too smart in a diaphanous shirt and block-heeled shoes.

'Ready?' she said, looking decidedly uneasy.

'Yes, if you are.' Pudding nodded. They climbed aboard and Irene took up the reins, clucking her tongue at Dundee. 'That's it,' said Pudding. 'And if he's feeling lazy and doesn't budge, just say "*up*", in a sharper tone.' Painstakingly, Irene steered the cob – who knew exactly where he should go anyway – out of the yard, and down the hill. They went sedately through Slaughterford; past the tiny shop, the bridge and the mill; past Thatch Cottage, at which neither of them looked too closely. They didn't know quite how to feel about the Tanners, after all that had happened. There was no rancour, but there could be no forgiveness either, and certainly no forgetting. The leather collar creaked as Dundee leant into it up the steep hill of Germain's Lane. Where the track curved towards Biddestone they turned right, onto Weavern Lane. They were going to see Rose Matlock and Mary Black, Clemmie's mother and sister. It had been Irene's idea, and she'd asked Pudding to go with her, as much for courage and support as she drove, Pudding suspected, as for the visit itself. But Pudding had been happy to go. She'd been to Honeybrook Farm once before, when her whole family had been invited to supper after Dr Cartwright had nursed their littlest, Daniel, through whooping cough, but she'd never been to Weavern. To Pudding, Clemmie Matlock was one more paper bird who'd taken flight; the thought of seeing her home, and meeting her mother, had the compulsive allure of a pilgrimage.

The track wove down into the wooded valley, steep and stony.

'How on earth do they manage in winter, when it's muddy?' said Irene, as the little gig squeaked and rocked along the ruts, and Dundee's hooves rattled with a hollow sound against chunks of limestone.

'On foot, I think,' said Pudding. 'Or out the other way, perhaps – I think there's a better lane southwards, up to the Bath Road.' On the far side of a small stream the track rose steeply again, through woods, and then finally crested a rise to reveal Weavern Farm, huddled at the feet of the fat green hills. The By Brook curled past it in a series of wide loops, golden in the sun, and a small dairy herd was grazing the paddock between the yard and the water; mellow farm buildings sat neatly around three sides of a square yard.

'Gosh, isn't it pretty?' said Pudding.

'It looks like a Victorian painting of the English country-side,' said Irene, and Pudding wasn't sure if that was supposed to be a good thing or not. As they approached they saw that there were tiles missing from the roof; the window frames were peeling, and some had lost their glass. The yard was cracked earth, dotted with nettles, dock and poultry mess; a butterfly bush was growing in the gutter, and another up by the chimney; dry grass whispered along the farmhouse's foundations; toadflax and pennywort had invaded the wall around the well. A solitary pig gazed at them from behind the bars of its door, but the rest of a long run of open skillings sat empty. Weavern Farm was in its declining years. The yard gate hung skewed from its hinges, and was tied shut with string. Pudding jumped down to open it, and Irene manoeuvred the Stanhope through with the frowning concentration of someone walking a tightrope.

'Where shall I park?' she called down to Pudding, who tried not to smile.

'Park? Oh, er ... over by the barn there. Look – there's a post we can hitch Dundee to.'

A tall woman opened the door to them. Her face was ruddy and hard, drawn tight over her cheekbones and jaw; her hair was iron grey, and she stood with the stoop of a body tired out by decades of work. Pudding was slightly taken aback. She knew, of course, that Clemmie's sister would be more or less the same age as Eli Tanner – seventy or so – but somehow, since Clemmie was frozen in time, she'd pictured her sister Mary the same way. Still young, still a girl. A fresh-faced milkmaid. Mary led them into a large kitchen and sat them at the table, sweeping a chicken aside with one arm as she did so. The hen clucked in outraged tones as it made its way outside, and then Rose Matlock came through from a room at the back of the house, her thistledown hair tucked away beneath an old-fashioned cotton sun bonnet, her figure swamped by a shapeless pinafore. She sat down at the table with them and a strange silence prevailed, neither awkward nor comfortable, whilst Mary made tea and came to join them.

'First time in all the long years we've had a visitor from Manor Farm,' said Rose. 'Even when the first Alistair Hadleigh asked to try and teach our Clemmie to speak, he did it by a note.' She cleared her throat, coughed, then grunted. 'He never did manage to get her to talk, mind you. I wondered ... I did wonder for a while, after it happened, if he was the one as had got her into trouble.' She shook her head. 'Never thought for a second he would hurt her though. Not till Eli came along last month, and told me you'd found Betsy's doll. And even then, I had doubts. Doubts I couldn't put my finger on.' She gave Irene a steady look.

'You've worked it out, haven't you?' said Irene. 'That's what you meant when you said "blood's blood" to me. Eli blamed the wrong Hadleigh.'

'Blamed the wrong one, but punished the right one.' The old woman nodded.

'If it hadn't been Alistair Hadleigh that took the doll and hid it, it had to be his sister,' said Mary. 'And Nancy always was a half-mad bitch.' Her language made Pudding flinch, and then feel oddly as though she might cry. Nancy had been one of the foundation stones of her whole life. Not as lovable as Alistair, not as easy to like, but constant; Pudding was having a hard time relinquishing the affection she still felt for her.

'I wanted to come and tell you. I wanted to make sure you knew who had really killed Clemmie, because I . . . thought you ought to. Nancy thought it was Alistair's baby too, you see,' said Irene.

'I remembered. Too late for your husband, Mrs Hadleigh . . . But I remembered that his dad was off at his wedding when it happened. Eli's pickled his brain in beer and gin over the years – I'm surprised he can fetch up his own name, some days – but I remembered in the end. Alistair was off getting wed, and his sister stayed behind. I'd tried talking to her about the baby, see. That's how she knew about it, though everyone would have seen it before much longer. That's what I say to myself, when I get to blaming myself for it.' Rose shook her head sadly, and Mary gave her a hard glare.

'Ain't no one to blame but that shrew at Manor Farm, Mum,' she said.

'She's not there any more,' said Irene, firmly. 'Nancy's gone, and she won't be coming back.'

The silence returned, and Pudding looked around at the cluttered shelves looped with cobwebs; the ancient, grimed stove, black with smuts and baked-on grease; the skin-and-bones cat asleep on the window sill. The wind nudged in through the open door and set the peeling labels on ranks of dusty jars and tins to flapping. There was something spectral and ineffably sad about the place. She knew, from things Rose had told Irene and from things they had found out from Ma Tanner, that Clemmie had had three sisters, and all had still been at home at the time of her death. She knew that their little brother, Walter, had been killed while he was still a child, in the accident at Rag Mill when the boiler had blown up. She knew that the sisters had married and moved away one by one, and that Mary and her husband Bert Black had moved back when her father, William, had died. Josie had died at the age of forty, of the flu; Liz in her late twenties, giving birth to her third child. It was no wonder the farm felt as though its heart had stopped beating.

'Have you a picture of Clemmie?' Pudding asked. 'I should love to see it. I first read about her ages ago, in a book of mine, you see. I never dreamed of her being a real person, if you see what I mean. I never dreamed I should ever sit at the table where she grew up . . . and ate her suppers . . .' Pudding stopped, wondering if she was being horribly tactless. But their pain was old, not fresh, and Mary simply shook her head.

'We never had a picture of her, nor of Walter. You didn't take photographs just like that, back then. It cost money to go into town and have one done, and that money was far better spent elsewhere. I can still see her face like I saw it yesterday, though. She was the prettiest of all of us, and we had our fair share of admirers. Who can describe that, though? She had blue eyes and mad hair the colour of cream, like Mum; cheeks, forehead, chin, same as any of us 'as got, but on her they came together that much better, somehow. And a faraway look in her eyes – like she knew more than everyone else, but nothing at all at the same time.' Mary shook her head again. 'Used to drive us potty sometimes, she did. Mooning about, not pulling her weight and getting away with it, even with Dad. None of us knew what she meant to us till she was dead. The world didn't seem right after that. Blameless as a babe, she were. I saw the world different after what happened to her.'

Rose nodded heavily, but said nothing for a while. Pudding watched Irene sip her tea and stifle a wince. It managed to be weak and stewed at the same time.

'I'd have had Eli Tanner as my son, I would,' said Rose, eventually. 'He weren't like the others. At least, not then. Now,' she gave a shrug, 'now he's a tosspot, and a killer. But what made him a killer? Not being a Tanner. Not something he was born with. *Nancy Hadleigh* made him a killer.'

'But you didn't know him before Clemmie died, did you?' said Irene.

'We got to know him after. We got to hear of his plans for them, and how he loved her. How he despised old Isaac and wanted nothing to do with the villain. All of that died with her. He stayed in the village – trying to find out who'd killed her, at first, but then simply treading in his father's footsteps. He was eaten up with anger over it, and took to the drink, and turned so black inside people came to fear him just as they feared Isaac. The lad I caught a glimpse of just after she died . . . the lad with all the plans and the desire to make a better life . . . that lad was murdered as sure as Clemmie was.' At this, Irene looked down into her cup, and said nothing. Pudding guessed she was thinking of the Eli Tanner who had killed their Alistair in such a horribly violent way. Trying to imagine him as a lad, madly in love and planning a new life with a young wife and child, was difficult. 'He'll not mind being hanged,' Rose said, flatly. 'He'll not mind it at all.'

'No,' said Pudding. 'He said as much to me when I went to see him.'

They didn't stay long. There was nothing much to say, and Pudding was sure she could see the same claustrophobic sadness creeping over Irene as was creeping over herself. She was relieved when Irene stood and thanked the two elderly women for the tea. They had no words of comfort for one another; the two wrongs that had been done would never add up to a right. Pudding felt sorry for them, and sorry for the farm, in a peculiar way. She was sure it had been a happy place, once; vibrant with life and the laughter of its youthful inhabitants. Now it felt forgotten; it was neglected, unloved by the handful of inhabitants that were left to it, and dogged by the hopeless air of all abandoned things. Pudding's grief for Alistair waited for her every morning at Manor Farm, and she knew she would keep missing him, and always think of him, but at least the *place* was still alive, and had a chance of moving on, thanks to Irene and the servants and the inexorable sense of life going on. Weavern Farm was more like the corpse of a place, steadily decaying. Pudding and Irene didn't speak as Dundee towed them back up the hill, through the trees and onto Germain's Lane. Each lost in their own thoughts, they stared straight ahead until, at the shop, Irene pulled the pony to a halt.

'Let's get some biscuits for tea from Mrs Glover,' she said, impulsively.

'*Bought* biscuits? But . . . Mrs Gosling will be outraged,' said Pudding.

'I know,' said Irene, smiling. 'Isn't it terrible?'

*

Pudding performed a self-conscious twirl in front of the mirror. They were up in Irene's dressing room, with early evening light gilding the furniture and their faces.

'Well?' said Irene. 'What do you think?' She'd let out a dress she'd found at a frock exchange in Chippenham for Pudding; the girl's height – and bust – made it hang shorter on her; it was just below the knee, which was becoming the fashion in London but would definitely raise eyebrows in Wiltshire. The dress was made of a teal-coloured fabric that draped nicely, was flattering over Pudding's more exuberant curves, and brought out the blue of her eyes.

'Are you *sure* I don't look like a ship in sail?' Pudding fretted, smoothing the fabric over her hips.

'I think you look wonderful,' Irene assured her. 'Very sophisticated. And I am *completely* sure that Constable Dempsey will agree with me.' At the mention of his name, Pudding blushed. She was still having trouble dealing with Pete Dempsey's blatant regard for her, even though the reflection in the mirror was of a tall, handsome young woman with one hell of a bosom, not a chubby little girl. Her hair was still a bushy thatch, but Irene had trimmed it, and pinned it as close to her head as it could be induced to go. Pete was taking her to see *Dick Turpin's Ride to York* at the pictures – their first official excursion together. 'Really – you look thoroughly dashing. And nobody ought to be calling you Pudding any more,' said Irene. 'What's your real name? I asked Alistair, once, but he never told me.'

'Laetitia,' said Pudding, looking dismayed. 'Laetitia Marie Cartwright. Oh dear,' she added, and Irene smiled.

'Laetitia? That's ... so grown-up. It's a lovely name,' she said, but couldn't keep her smile from widening when Pudding met her eye. 'I fear it might be difficult to make it stick, after all this time,' she said.

'Won't it just,' Pudding said, ruefully.

'How about Tish? I think I could get used to Tish. Perhaps Pete might, too.'

'Pete? Oh, there's no chance of that. He's known me since we were knee-high — I'm sure I'll always be Pudding to him.'

'Ah, well.'

Irene picked a thread off her skirt and got up, hooking a thumb under her waistband to reposition it. She might have to let out a few of her own clothes soon, if she kept on eating the way she had been. The thought caused a residual tweak of anxiety, until she remembered that she wasn't in London now, or anywhere near her mother, and didn't need to care about being so thin she hardly had the energy to stand. 'I was thinking, Pudding, about you having enough to do once we're down to two horses and Tufty,' she said, and saw from Pudding's worried expression that she had been thinking about it too. 'I have a number of ideas,' she said. 'But, obviously, it'll be entirely up to you. Could we rent out some of the stables and grazing to people who need extra, do you think?'

'Oh, yes! Livery service, that's called — it's quite common.'

'I've no idea if there's any demand for it, around here,' said Irene. 'Since there's so very much grass everywhere. But we could try. And, you know, Hilarius would probably like a little more help with the shires, come the winter. He's not getting any younger, after all.'

'Do you mean to stay on, then?' said Pudding, looking hopeful.

'I . . . I haven't completely decided. But I shan't simply sell up and leave you all in the lurch, I promise.' Irene hurried on to forestall Pudding's crestfallen expression. 'You might even get your own horse, Pudding, and keep it here if you wished.'

'Really? Oh! That would be stupendous!' Pudding cried. Then she sagged. 'I should never afford the livery and keep.'

'I dare say we could hash something out,' said Irene, smiling.

The house was very quiet after Pudding had gone – off up the lane with Pete in his dad's pony and gig. His face had blazed appropriately when Pudding had emerged in the teal dress, and he'd stumbled through the debonair *good evening* he'd clearly been rehearsing. Irene wondered about hiring more servants to fill the space, but there was hardly enough for Clara and Florence to do as it was, with only Irene in residence. She took a book and went out onto the terrace. The house felt slightly off kilter somehow, and Irene suspected it was because Nancy had gone, and none of them had yet adjusted to her absence. For the first time since the hiatus between Alistair's father marrying and then becoming a widower, Nancy Hadleigh was not in residence. And would not be, ever again.

Irene had thought it all through at least twenty times before concluding that there was nothing to be gained by reporting Nancy to the police. The doll was flimsy enough evidence, and they didn't even have it any more. Whatever Hilarius had seen, it had been fifty years ago, and his testimony alone wouldn't be proof enough if Nancy denied it all. And she was being well punished by Alistair's death, and her role in bringing it about – Irene was certain of that. She would carry the grief and the blame around with her the rest of her days. A slow poison, as Rose Matlock had termed it. As the mistress of Manor Farm, Irene had told her to go, and never to come back. Nancy had given her a steely look that hadn't quite concealed the fear and anger it was meant to, and Irene had gone along with her to Chippenham station to make sure she got on the London train. The Hadleighs still had their Mayfair apartment, but as far as Irene knew – thanks to a letter from Cora McKinley – Nancy had gone to Italy on a one-way ticket. It had been a tentative olive branch of a letter from Cora, full of apologies for absence and curiosity about the events at Manor Farm.

Irene sat a while in the sinking sun, absorbing the last of its warmth. St Nicholas' sat in the middle of the field below, doing just the same. There were fewer flowers on the Hadleigh plot since Nancy's departure, but Irene had resolved to visit once a week, and to refresh a small arrangement there whilst there were still flowers to be had from the garden. The mill steamed, down in the valley, and the brewery leaked its hoppy smell, and she noticed that the stone tile roofs of the cottages had moss in the crevices of their northern slopes. The tall trees on the valley sides were a darkening green, and dusty. She couldn't stay on at Manor Farm. She simply didn't belong there, though she had no idea where else she might belong. She would be too lonely, for starters. She had a friend in Pudding, but that was all. Somehow, she would have to find a way to make more. There was still an emptiness where Alistair should have been; it was still his house, *his* home, not hers. He had wanted her to make it hers too, but without him she didn't know if it could ever feel right. She had to admit to herself, though, that the view of the valley had come to look beautiful to her, and the smells of the farmyard were familiar rather than offensive now, and she liked the walk down the hill to the bridge across the By Brook. She even liked riding out with Pudding, though she still wasn't ready for the lead rein to be taken off, and objected to the way the smell of horse lingered for hours, even after she'd scrubbed her arms to the elbow. She took a slow breath, and tried to hear Alistair's footsteps on the terrace behind her, coming from the house with a smile and a gin and tonic. She wished she would hear it; wished to see his smile one more time, and fall into the safety net he'd offered.

Hand in hand with the loneliness she knew was coming was

the certainty of boredom, since clearly she didn't have anything to write about, just yet – unless it were some chronicle of her new life – a humorous, fish-out-of-water type of thing. The idea caused barely a flicker of interest. Or, of course, the story of Clemmie Matlock's short life – how it ended, and how that had led to the death of Alistair Hadleigh. A story of lies, secret grief and secret jealousy; a story of ruined lives and lost chances. A sudden conviction took hold of her, a sudden surety. She would write it, and it would be her final act of gratitude towards Alistair: the truth of his death. And in a way it would be an act of justice towards Eli Tanner, since his life had been ruined too, many years before. However gravely he had transgressed now, he had been gravely wronged himself. A little justice for Clemmie and Eli and Alistair. A little justice, of a different kind, for Nancy. She would wait until Eli's trial was over. The truth was bound to cause a stir; it might even cause the police to question Nancy – if they could find her. Any money the book made could go to the Tanners and the Matlocks, and however unhappy some people might be about what she would write, it would be the truth. So that was that. Not too long before, she would have shied away from causing any kind of trouble, and drawing any kind of attention to herself. But it didn't scare her as it once had. Some things were simply more important.

She would have to find a way to involve herself in the farm, and the mill, and the village – which might be even harder now, since she was sure she'd be blamed for Nancy's sudden departure. She wouldn't be able to tell people the true reason, at first, and just had to hope that Clara or Florence had been listening at doors as usual, and that word would get about. Ruth, the Cartwrights' daily, might be quite useful in that regard as well. The church fête, and dinner parties; the hunt meet and Sunday school outings. She couldn't possibly take it all on. The thought of knocking on doors and introducing herself, of sending out invitations and holding parties for people she barely knew – these things did still fill Irene with dread. But she would have to start, if she stayed. Perhaps she could begin on a small scale – making peace with Cora McKinley, for example. She might even invite some of her old school friends down from London, in due course. There were a few who might have got bored enough of the London scandal, and be curious enough about the Slaughterford scandal, to accept. She went into the pantry for a glass of lemonade, fetched paper and a pencil, then returned to the terrace and continued to make her plans. Because that was what she was doing, she realised, as the sun slunk lower towards the western hills. She was making plans to stay.

Author's Note and Acknowledgements

Whilst Slaughterford and its mills, geography and prominent buildings do exist, and have been recreated with some historical accuracy in this novel, all the people and events I describe are entirely fictitious – with the exception of the boiler explosion at Rag Mill, an accident in which three people, including ten year old Vincent Watt, were killed. This tragic event took place in November 1867.

My thanks to Michael Woodman, for talking to me about his life and work at Chapps Mill, and for lending me his books; to Angus Thompson and Karin Crawford, the present owners of Chapps Mill in Slaughterford, for showing me around; and to Janet and John Jones at Manor Farm, for sharing their memories and letting me look around their home.

A huge thank you to my brilliant editor, Laura Gerrard; to my wonderful agent, Nicola Barr; and to all the talented people at Orion Books, working so hard behind the scenes.